Former Editors
Clifford Leech 1958–71
F. David Hoeniger 1970–1985

General Editors
E. A. J. Honigmann, J. R. Mulryne,
David Bevington and Eugene M. Waith

THE ROARING GIRL

THE REVELS PLAYS

THE REVELS PLAYS

THE
ROARING GIRL

THOMAS MIDDLETON
and THOMAS DEKKER

Edited by

Paul A. Mulholland

MANCHESTER
UNIVERSITY PRESS

© Paul A. Mulholland 1987
All rights reserved
Published by
Manchester University Press
Oxford Road, Manchester M13 9PL, UK
and St. Martin's Press Inc, 175 Fifth Avenue,
New York, NY 10010, USA

Reprinted in paperback 1992, 1994

ISBN 0 7190 1630 4 *paperback*

British Library cataloguing in publication data
Middleton, Thomas
  The roaring girl.—(The revels plays)
  I. Title   II. Dekker, Thomas   III. Mulholland, Paul A.   IV. Series
  822'.3   PR2741.R6

Library of Congress cataloging in publication data
Middleton, Thomas, d. 1627.
  The roaring girl.
  (The Revels plays)
  Includes index.
  1. Cutpurse, Moll, 1584?–1659—Drama.   I. Dekker, Thomas, ca.
  1572–1632.   II. Mulholland, Paul.   III. Series.
  PR2714.R6   1986   822'.3   86–21666
  ISBN 0–7190–1629–0

FOR MARY

Printed in Great Britain
by Bell & Bain Ltd, Glasgow

Contents

Illustrations

General Editors' Preface

The series known as the Revels Plays was conceived by Clifford Leech. The idea for the series emerged in his mind, as he explained in his preface to the first of the Revels Plays in 1958, from the success of the New Arden Shakespeare. The aim of the new group of texts was 'to apply to Shakespeare's predecessors, contemporaries and successors the methods that are now used in Shakespeare editing'. The plays chosen were to include well known works from the early Tudor period to about 1700, as well as others less familiar but of literary and theatrical merit: 'the plays included,' Leech wrote, 'should be such as to deserve and indeed demand performance.' We owe it to Clifford Leech that the idea became reality. He set the high standards of the series, ensuring that editors of individual volumes produced work of lasting merit, equally useful for teachers and students, theatre directors and actors. Clifford Leech remained General Editor until 1971, and was succeeded by F. David Hoeniger, who retired in 1985. David Hoeniger has been General Editor for the present volume.

The Revels Plays are now under the direction of four General Editors, E. A. J. Honigmann, J. R. Mulryne, David Bevington and Eugene M. Waith. The publishers, originally Methuen, are now Manchester University Press. Despite these changes, the format and essential character of the series will continue, and it is hoped that its editorial standards will be maintained. Except for some work in progress, the General Editors intend, in expanding the series, to concentrate for the immediate future on plays from the period 1558–1642, and may include a small number of non-dramatic works of interest to students of drama. Some slight changes have been forced by considerations of cost. For example, in editions from 1978, notes to the introduction are placed together at the end, not at the foot of the page. Collation and commentary notes will continue, however, to appear on the relevant pages.

The text of each Revels play, in accordance with established practice in the series, is edited afresh from the original text of best authority (in a few instances, texts), but spelling and punctuation are modernised and speech headings are silently made consistent. Elisions in the original are also silently regularised, except where metre would be affected by the change; since 1968 the '-ed' form is used for non-syllabic terminations in past tenses and past participles ('-'d' earlier), and '-èd' for syllabic ('-ed' earlier). The editor emends, as distinct from modernises, his original only in instances where error is patent, or at least very probable, and correction persuasive. Act divisions are given only if they appear in the original or if the structure of the play clearly points to them. Those act and scene divisions not found in the original are provided unobtrusively in small type and in square brackets. Square brackets are also used for any other additions to or changes in the stage directions of the original.

Revels Plays do not provide a variorum collation, but only those variants which require the critical attention of serious textual students. All departures of substance from 'copy-text' are listed, including any relineation and those changes in punctuation which involve to any degree a decision between alternative interpretations; but not such accidentals as turned letters, nor necessarily additions to stage directions whose editorial nature is already made clear by the use of brackets. Press corrections in the 'copy-text' are likewise included. Of later emendations of the text, only those are given which as alternative readings still deserve attention.

One of the hallmarks of the Revels Plays is the thoroughness of their annotations. Besides explaining the meaning of difficult words and passages, the editor provides comments on customs or usage, text or stage-business – indeed, on anything he judges pertinent and helpful. Each volume contains a Glossarial Index to the Commentary, in which particular attention is drawn to meanings for words not listed in *O.E.D.*

The Introduction to a Revels play assesses the authority of the 'copy-text' on which it is based, and discusses the editorial methods employed in dealing with it; the editor also considers his play's date and (where relevant) sources, together with its place in the work of the author and in the theatre of its time. Stage history is offered, and in the case of a play by an author not previously represented in the series a brief biography is given.

It is our hope that plays edited in this fashion will promote further scholarly and theatrical investigation of one of the richest periods in theatrical history.

E. A. J. HONIGMANN

J. R. MULRYNE

DAVID BEVINGTON

EUGENE M. WAITH

Preface

In preparing this edition I have been assisted by the kindness and generosity of many. I am grateful to librarians of numerous institutions and collections who have made available to me copies of the 1611 quarto of *The Roaring Girl*, microfilms, photocopies and other research materials, and who have been helpful in many other ways. My thanks are due also to several directors of the play for answering questions about their stage productions and for providing me with related documents. I am especially grateful to Mr Barry Kyle and Miss Helen Mirren for taking time to discuss the Royal Shakespeare Company production. Students of Middleton and Dekker owe particular debts to previous editors and scholars. In the case of the present play special mention must be made of Professor Fredson Bowers and Professor Cyrus Hoy; acknowledgements throughout this edition to them and to a host of other investigators give the measure of my own debt.

I wish also to thank Professor Brian Parker and Professor Anne Lancashire who very kindly read drafts of the introduction and gave me the benefit of their judicious and incisive criticisms, and Professor Richard Hosley whose valuable comments broadened the scope of my discussion of the play's original staging.

My greatest debts however are to those who have been most closely involved with my work on *The Roaring Girl*. I am deeply grateful to Dr Stanley Wells for advice, guidance and encouragement as supervisor of my doctoral dissertation edition of the play and for many kindnesses and courtesies besides. The edition has since undergone considerable change and revision in growing up to become a Revels Play. Apart from introducing routine alterations I have had occasion to rethink numerous readings, make fresh discoveries in dating, textual and other matters, and to explore second and third thoughts on particular passages and on the play as a whole. Throughout this process I have greatly appreciated the patience, helpfulness and good humour of my general editor, Professor David Hoeniger. His suggestions have saved me from infelicities of various kinds and have improved all parts of the edition. I am grateful to the University of Guelph Research Advisory Board and to the Social Sciences and Humanities Research Council of Canada for grants which assisted further research and aided completion of my work.

Throughout my involvement with another Moll my wife has endured at least as much as Mary Fitzallard (though her trials have been of a different sort), yet she has borne all with no less patience and has been equally understanding and supportive.

PAUL A. MULHOLLAND

Guelph, 1986

Abbreviations

Abbreviations for individual copies of the 1611 quarto and for previous editions are given in the Introduction, pp. 1–3.

(A) WORKS OF REFERENCE, ETC.

Abbott	E. A. Abbott, *A Shakespearian Grammar* (new ed., 1879).
Bentley, *J. & C.S.*	G. E. Bentley, *The Jacobean and Caroline Stage*, 7 vols. (Oxford, 1941–68).
Bowers, *Dekker*	F. Bowers (ed.), *The Dramatic Works of Thomas Dekker*, 4 vols. (Cambridge, 1953–61, and rev. edd. 1964–70).
Brooke	C. F. T. Brooke, *The Shakespeare Apocrypha* (Oxford, 1908).
Bullen	A. H. Bullen (ed.), *The Works of Thomas Middleton*, 8 vols. (1885–7).
Chambers, *E.S.*	E. K. Chambers, *The Elizabethan Stage*, 4 vols. (Oxford, 1923).
E. in C.	*Essays in Criticism.*
E. & S.	*Essays and Studies.*
Herford and Simpson	C. H. Herford and Percy and Evelyn Simpson (edd.), *Ben Jonson*, 11 vols. (Oxford, 1925–52).
H.L.Q.	*Huntington Library Quarterly.*
Hoy	Cyrus Hoy, *Introductions, Notes, and Commentaries to texts in 'The Dramatic Works of Thomas Dekker'*, 4 vols. (Cambridge, 1980).
J.E.G.P.	*Journal of English and Germanic Philology.*

Linthicum	M. C. Linthicum, *Costume in the Drama of Shakespeare and his Contemporaries* (Oxford, 1936).
M.S.C.	*Malone Society Collections.*
M.S.R.	Malone Society Reprint.
M.L.N.	*Modern Language Notes.*
M.L.R.	*Modern Language Review.*
M.P.	*Modern Philology.*
N. & Q.	*Notes and Queries.*
O.D.E.P.	*Oxford Dictionary of English Proverbs*, comp. W. G. Smith, 3rd ed., rev. by F. P. Wilson (1970).
O.E.D.	*Oxford English Dictionary.*
Partridge	Eric Partridge, *Shakespeare's Bawdy*, rev. ed. (1968).
Pendry	E. D. Pendry (ed.), *Thomas Dekker, Selected Prose Writings* (1967).
P.M.L.A.	*Publications of the Modern Language Association of America.*
P.Q.	*Philological Quarterly.*
R.E.S.	*Review of English Studies.*
S.B.	*Studies in Bibliography.*
s.d.	stage direction.
s.h.	speech heading
Shakespeare's England	*Shakespeare's England*, 2 vols. (1916).
S.P.	*Studies in Philology.*
Sh.S.	*Shakespeare Survey.*
Stow, *Survey*	John Stow, *A Survey of London*, ed. C. L. Kingsford, 2 vols. (Oxford, 1908).
Sugden	E. H. Sugden, *A Topographical Dictionary to the Works of Shakespeare and his Fellow Dramatists* (Manchester, 1925).
Tilley	M. P. Tilley, *A Dictionary of the Proverbs in England in the Sixteenth and Seventeenth Centuries* (Ann Arbor, 1950).

(B) TEXTS

1. *Middleton*

Where abbreviations for Middleton's works, including some at times attributed to him, have been used, they follow those given in R. B. Parker's Revels edition of *A Chaste Maid in Cheapside*. As Bullen's is the only edition of Middleton with line-numbering, it has been used for reference; other individual editions which have been used are noted below.

A.F.Q.L.	*Anything for a Quiet Life.*
B.B.	*The Black Book.*
B.M.C.	*Blurt, Master Constable.*
	The Changeling, ed. N. W. Bawcutt (repr. 1970).

C.M. in C.	*A Chaste Maid in Cheapside*, ed. R. B. Parker (1969).
F.Q.	*A Fair Quarrel.*
F. of L.	*The Family of Love.*
F.H.T.	*The Ant and the Nightingale; or Father Hubburd's Tales.*
G. of L.	*The Ghost of Lucrece*, ed. J. Q. Adams (1937).
H.K.K.	*Hengist, King of Kent; or the Mayor of Queenborough. Honorable Entertainments*, ed. R. C. Bald, M.S.R. (1953).
M.W.M.M.	*A Mad World, My Masters.*
M.T.	*Michaelmas Term.*
M.D.B.W.	*More Dissemblers Besides Women.*
N.W.N.H.	*No Wit, No Help like a Woman's.*
	The Puritan; or The Widow of Watling Street, ed. C. F. T. Brooke, *The Shakespeare Apocrypha* (Oxford, 1908).
	The Revenger's Tragedy, ed. R. A. Foakes (1966).
R.G.	*The Roaring Girl.*
S.M.T.	*The Second Maiden's Tragedy*, ed. A. Lancashire (Manchester, 1978).
S.G.	*The Spanish Gipsy.*
T.C.O.O.	*A Trick to Catch the Old One.*
W.B.W.	*Women Beware Women*, ed. J. R. Mulryne (1975).
Y.F.G.	*Your Five Gallants.*

2. Dekker

Where abbreviations for Dekker's works, including collaborations and works on occasion attributed to him, have been used, they conform to those given in Cyrus Hoy, *Introductions, Notes, and Commentaries*. Except where noted, references are to F. Bowers's edition of Dekker's *Dramatic Works*, and to the original texts for the non-dramatic works.

Dramatic Works

1 H.W.	*The Honest Whore, Part I.*
2 H.W.	*The Honest Whore, Part II.*
I.T.B.N.	*If This Be Not a Good Play, the Devil Is In It.*
N.H.	*Northward Ho.*
N.S.S.	*The Noble Spanish Soldier.*
P.G.	*Patient Grissil.*
Sat.	*Satiromastix.*
S.H.	*The Shoemaker's Holiday*, ed. R. L. Smallwood and Stanley Wells (Manchester, 1979).
V.M.	*The Virgin Martyr.*
W.B.	*The Whore of Babylon.*
W. of E.	*The Witch of Edmonton.*
W.H.	*Westward Ho.*

Non-Dramatic Works

	The Belman of London (1608, 'The third impression, • with new additions').
F.B.N.A.	*Foure Birds of Noahs Arke* (1609), ed. F. P. Wilson (Oxford, 1924).
G.H.	*The Gull's Horn-Book*, in *Thomas Dekker, Selected Prose Writings*, ed. E. D. Pendry (1967).
L.C.	*English Villainies Discovered by Lantern and Candlelight* (1608–32), ed. Pendry.
O.P.	*O Per Se – O* (1612), ed. Pendry.
P.W.	*Penny-Wise, Pound-Foolish* (1631), ed. Pendry.
	The Raven's Almanac (1609), ed. Pendry.
R.R.	*A Rod for Run-awayes* (1625), in *The Plague Pamphlets of Thomas Dekker*, ed. F. P. Wilson (Oxford, 1925).
S.D.S.	*The Seven deadly Sinnes* (1606).
	The Wonderful Year (1603), ed. Pendry.

In addition to those cited above, the following Revels editions of works by other dramatists have been used:

Francis Beaumont and John Fletcher, *Philaster*, ed. Andrew Gurr (1969).
Thomas Heywood, *A Woman Killed with Kindness*, ed. R. W. Van Fossen (1961).
Ben Jonson, *The Alchemist*, ed. F. H. Mares (1967).
——, *Bartholomew Fair*, ed. E. A. Horsman (1960).
——, *Volpone*, ed. R. B. Parker (1983).
Thomas Kyd, *The Spanish Tragedy*, ed. Philip Edwards (1959)
Christopher Marlowe, *Poems*, ed. Millar Maclure (1968).
John Marston, *The Malcontent*, ed. G. K. Hunter (1975).
John Webster, *The Duchess of Malfi*, ed. J. R. Brown (1964).
——, *The White Devil*, ed. J. R. Brown (1960).
William Wycherley, *The Country Wife*, ed. David Cook and John Swannell (1975).

The titles of Shakespeare's plays are abbreviated as in C. T. Onions, *A Shakespeare Glossary* (ed. 1953), p. x; line references are from Peter Alexander's edition (1951). Except for the Revels editions listed above, Jonson's works, including *Eastward Ho*, are cited from the Herford and Simpson edition (Oxford, 1925–52). Unless otherwise noted, information given about the dates and auspices of plays cited is based on Alfred Harbage, *Annals of English Drama, 975–1700*, rev. S. Schoenbaum (1964).

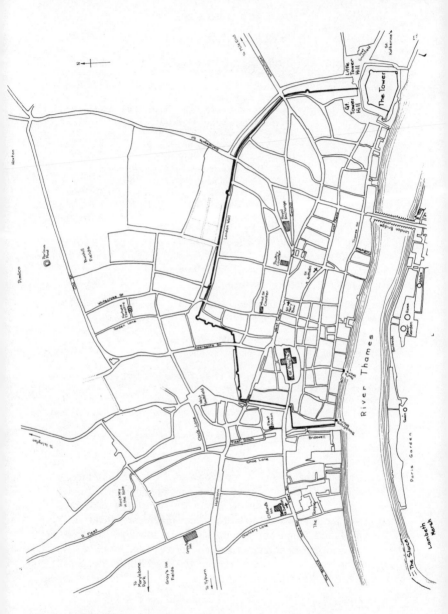

Map of London *c.* 1610

Introduction

Editions

The only known early edition of *The Roaring Girl* is the quarto of 1611 printed by Nicholas Okes. Its collation is: A–M (A1 and M4 blank), 12 sheets. The title-page reads:

> The Roaring Girle./OR/*Moll Cut-Purse./As it hath lately beene Acted* on the Fortune-stage by/*the Prince his Players.*/Written by *T. Middleton* and *T. Dekkar.*/ [woodcut of Moll 100 mm × 70 mm., down the inner margin of which is printed: My case is alter'd, I must worke for my liuing.]/Printed at *London* for *Thomas Archer*, and are to be sold at his/shop in Popes head-pallace, neere the Royall/Exchange. 1611.[1]

The first entry of the play in the Stationers' Register was most probably 18 February 1612:

> Ambr: Garbrand   Rd of him for thentrance of a booke concerninge Mall Cutpurse } vjd.

This entry is matched by a fine of the same date in *Records of the Court of the Stationers' Company 1602–1640*, ed. W. A. Jackson (1957), p. 449:

> Ambr: Garbrand   received of him for a fyne for printinge the booke of Moll Cutpurse without entringe it } vijd

Nine days separate these entries from the occasion of the penance of the real Moll Cutpurse at Paul's Cross on 9 February 1612: this circumstance would appear to explain Garbrand's connection with the book, since he was very likely a friend of Thomas Archer, the publisher, and had a stall conveniently located near the site of the penance in St Paul's Churchyard. The fine importantly reveals that the book cited in the S.R. was already in print on the date of entry and so removes the main obstacle preventing acceptance of the entry as *The Roaring Girl*. The Register also records a transfer of copyright in February 1631 from Thomas Archer to Hugh Perry, formerly thought to be the original entry.

The following twelve copies have been collated at first hand or on microfilm for the present edition (abbreviations for reference are given at the left; the state of the copy and provenance, where known, follow in parentheses):

BL 1   British Library, *162.d.35* (cropped: many running-titles affected; lacks A1, M4).

BL 2	British Library, *Ashley 1159* (slightly cropped; some running-titles restored in ink; lacks A1, M4; T. J. Wise's copy).
V & A	Victoria and Albert Museum, *D. 26, Box 33/4*, Dyce Collection (lacks A1, M4).
Bod	Bodleian, Oxford, *Malone 246 (1)* (lacks A1, M4).
NLS	National Library of Scotland, *Bute.368* (lacks A1, M4).
CCC	Corpus Christi College, Oxford, *φB.1.3 (5)* (some inked-in alterations; Brian Twyne's copy).
Bost	Boston Public Library, Massachusetts (lacks A1, M4).
Folg	Folger Shakespeare Library, Washington, D.C. (badly inked; A4 bound before A3; lacks A1, H2, M4; ?Isaak Reed's copy).[2]
Hunt	Henry E. Huntington Library, San Marino, California (lacks A1, M4; leaves disbound and remounted; John Philip Kemble's copy).
Yale	Beinecke Rare Book and Manuscript Library, Yale University, *1977/2724* (lacks sheet A, M4; Norman Holmes Pearson's copy).
Pforz	Carl H. Pforzheimer Library, New York.
Taylor	Robert H. Taylor Collection, Princeton University Library.

The following later editions have also been collated (abbreviations for reference are given at the left):

Reed	R. Dodsley, *A Select Collection of Old Plays*, ed. Isaak Reed (1780), vol. VI.
Scott	*The Ancient British Drama*, supposed ed. Sir Walter Scott (1810), vol. II.
Collier	R. Dodsley, *A Select Collection of Old Plays*, ed. J. P. Collier (1825), vol. VI.
Dyce	Alexander Dyce, *The Works of Thomas Middleton* (1840), vol. II.
Bullen	A. H. Bullen, *The Works of Thomas Middleton* (1885–6), vol. IV.
Ellis	Havelock Ellis, *The Best Plays of Thomas Middleton*, The Mermaid Series (1890), vol. II.

Bowers   F. Bowers, *The Dramatic Works of Thomas
                          Dekker* (Cambridge, 1953–61), vol. III (rev.
                          1966).

M. Thesis   P. Mulholland, *A Critical, Modern-Spelling
                          Edition of 'The Roaring Girl', by Thomas Mid-
                          dleton and Thomas Dekker*, University of
                          Birmingham Doctoral Dissertation (1975).

Gomme   Thomas Middleton and Thomas Dekker, *The
                          Roaring Girl*, ed. Andor Gomme, The New
                          Mermaids (1976).

To avoid possible confusions, 'M. Thesis' is used to denote a reading which originated in my thesis edition. 'This ed.' indicates a reading or line arrangement which first appears in the present Revels
edition. When a reading is cited which was first used, but independently, in my thesis edition and in Gomme, both are given.

Reed provided a rudimentary modernization with a number of
obvious corrections and a modest commentary. Scott and Collier
made minor changes but substantially reproduce Reed's edition.
Most alterations adopted by later editors derive from Dyce's edition.
Bullen's is based firmly on Dyce's, with only a few improvements.
The Mermaid text draws on Dyce and Bullen, with changes mainly
in presentation. Bowers introduced a number of interesting new
readings and relineations, some persuasive, others doubtful. Cyrus
Hoy's *Introductions, Notes, and Commentaries* considerably enhances
the usefulness of Bowers's edition. Andor Gomme's New Mermaid
edition, which presents some new emendations, has helpfully broadened the play's readership. Also consulted were the Pearson reprint,
The Dramatic Works of Thomas Dekker (1873), vol. III, an old-
spelling text with only the most obvious misprints removed, and the
at times unreliable edition in Russell A. Fraser and Norman Rabkin,
Drama of the English Renaissance II: The Stuart Period (New York,
1976). A photographic facsimile of the BL 1 copy of Q was issued by
J. S. Farmer for Tudor Facsimile Texts (1914), and reissued by
A.M.S. Publishing (New York, 1973). A manuscript translation and
a printed translation of extracts into French are recorded in M.
Horn-Monval, *Répertoire bibliographique des traductions et adapta-
tions françaises du théâtre étranger* (Paris, 1963), v, 26.

The 1611 Quarto and the Printer's Copy[3]
Although the 1611 quarto lacks his imprint, ornaments show that
Nicholas Okes was the printer.[4] General freedom from gross errors

reflects care in the printing and a fairly clear manuscript. A single skeleton was used and setting was by formes. Proof correction is preserved in nine of the text's twenty-four formes; only sheet H shows evidence of correction in both formes. The invariant formes are for the most part clear of major errors, so they may have been proofed for literals at an early stage of printing.[5] Extensive resetting occurred in inner I, apparently the result of some accident at press which caused the type to pie – possibly in the course of proof correction as Bowers has suggested. The reset substantive variants have no authority, however, and the original setting is almost certainly closer to the manuscript copy (Bowers, *Dekker*, p. 4). This condition does not apply to a set of recently discovered variants on inner D, however, the most important to come to light. These involve altered speech prefixes and consequent redistribution to different characters of several speeches at the conclusion of II.i. I have argued from both textual and literary positions that in this instance the reset state gives the authoritative reading.[6]

Which of the dramatists (if either) provided the printer's copy is uncertain. Price and Bowers though for different reasons favour Dekker, but the evidence adduced is inconclusive. D. J. Lake, who subscribes to Bowers's position, proposes that the forms ''t has' and ''t had' are Dekker's versions of Middleton's ''tas' and ''tad'; but these occur also in Middleton's unassisted plays, as his chart indicates,[7] and could well reflect compositorial intervention. Other evidence, such as unusually light punctuation to terminate speeches (comma and semicolon in particular) and peculiarly Middletonian forms in Dekker scenes (e.g. 'i' the'), suggests Middleton's orthography.

The manuscript in whatever form is unlikely to have been theatrical. Stage directions are in the main accurately positioned and reasonably complete. No entry is placed significantly early. While all entrances are given, possibly as many as eight exits are missing, which would be unlikely in theatrically derived copy. An apparent inconsistency in imperative and indicative stage directions is noted by Price (p. 181) in support of prompt-copy. But Bowers discounts such discrepancies as normal in the work of experienced dramatists; in any case, the position of the directions (if in reference to the speaker, imperative; if not, indicative) explains all but a handful of oddities. Numerous literary and permissive directions are not consonant with theatrical practice; e.g. '*Enter* ... NEATFOOT ... *with a napkin on his shoulder and a trencher in his hand, as from table*' (I.i.0.2–3),

'*Enter three or four* Servingmen *and* NEATFOOT' (I.ii.42.1). In addition, several omissions, relating for example to the letter which Mistress Gallipot produces in III.ii or the provision of a court-cupboard and viol in IV.i, would probably have been supplied by a bookholder. To account for 'a general consistency in forms between scenes that may reasonably be attributed to Middleton and scenes that are unquestionably by Dekker', Bowers proposes that the printer may have worked from a scribal transcript made from authorial fair copy prior to preparation of prompt-copy.[8] The possibility has some appeal, though Bowers does not support his statement with examples of word forms by the two dramatists or an allocation of respective shares. Evidence bearing on the hand of the printer's copy, the dramatists' shares, and the compositors' stints is at times either so tightly meshed as to defy disentanglement or simply inadequate. A cloudy condition which varies in degree accordingly confuses attempts to deal with any one matter in isolation and prevents confident conclusions.

Two or three compositors appear to have set the play. If compositors A and B are separate workmen, they alternated irregular stints from sheets B to E inclusive; in sheet F they were apparently joined by a third, compositor D,[9] who seems to have taken over from them, completing the remaining formes, including most of sheet A. Type recurrences more or less throughout suggest that a single case was used in setting most of the play. Speech prefixes transferred whole or in part from one forme to another along with type shortages reveal halting progress in setting and printing *The Roaring Girl*. Continuity in the running-titles and transferred prefixes suggests, however, that work proceeded fairly steadily – possibly even with sporadic haste. This text was apparently set under conditions of concurrent printing.[10] Okes may have wanted to make good progress on several books at once; he had enough type to do so, and no other rationale adequately explains recourse to a single skeleton and some type-shortage peculiarities. Running-title analysis and speech-prefix transfers demonstrate that the inner forme preceded the outer through the press.

Bowers has dismissed the only speech-heading discrepancy of note (*S. Dap.* and variants, I.ii; *Sir Dauy.* and variants, III.iii) as inconsequential on the grounds that both scenes are by Dekker. Middleton's presence in the later scene cannot be entirely ruled out, however, and the variant form may be his, even if he is not the main author.

The list of characters would seem to be Dekker's on the basis of the heading 'Dramatis Personae'[11] and the use of the term 'Ministri' for servants, which occurs also in *The Whore of Babylon* and not in Middleton. The spelling 'Sergiant', unique to the list, appears also in Dekker and Wilkins's *Jests to make you Merie* (1607). Omission from the dramatis personae of Sir Thomas Long and Tearcat, two characters who appear only in V.i, along with such other curiosities as the apparently nascent forms 'Wentgraue' for Wengrave and 'Yong *Wentgraue*' for Sebastian, suggests that the list is from an early stage of composition, possibly before the content of the canting scene had been fully worked out and set down.

This Edition

The present text is based on the 1611 quarto (referred to as Q).[12] I have been generally conservative over substantive alterations; a number of emendations made by previous editors have accordingly been rejected. In most instances I have emended where compositorial error appears to be responsible for a suspect reading. Emendations are recorded in the Collation along with feasible alternative readings from other editions. Several problematic cases are also discussed in the Commentary. Conjectures, as distinct from emendations, are denoted by *conj.*; and *subst.* indicates an arrangement of text substantially that of a previous edition.

Square brackets have been used only for editorial additions to stage directions and scene divisions; additions within the text are noted in the collation. Stage directions are not collated unless changes have been made, and only significant additions or alternatives by later editors are collated. All of Q's directions have been preserved; others have been provided in cases of manifest omission (e.g. a required *Exeunt*, as at II.i.418), or generally to clarify the action. Speech headings have been silently normalised and are recorded in the Collation only if they incorporate substantive changes. Turned letters and other obvious mistakes where there is no doubt of the required reading have not been collated. All inverted commas are editorial additions. Ampersands have been expanded; and italics, except where they conform to Revels practice, have not been preserved.

Spelling and punctuation have been silently modernised except where meaning or metre is affected; such cases are recorded in the Collation. In the process of modernising I have in the main been guided by proposals set out by Stanley Wells in *Modernizing Shakespeare's Spelling* (Oxford, 1979) and *Re-editing Shakespeare for the Modern Reader* (Oxford, 1984). With regard to the punctuation, my primary concern has been for clarity. Q's punctuation is generally light, often using commas and semicolons, for example, to separate clauses, occasionally in place of full stops within clause sequences, and even at the ends of speeches. In many cases the pointing appears to be rhetorical. Some passages have called for delicate decisions of the kind that Stanley Wells describes; several of these are discussed in the Commentary. Where seventeenth-century punctuation may admit more than one reading, modern pointing tends to be more controlling. I have tried to strike a balance between straightforward intelligibility and retaining the flow of the original. The dash, which appears with some frequency in Q, has proved serviceable in this regard. In general it is used as in John Russell Brown's Revels edition of Webster's *The White Devil* (1960), to indicate a change of sense but not necessarily a pause in delivery. Often an attempt to render spontaneous thought which is not strictly grammatical or which does not follow in logical sequence is involved. Q's parentheses have been abandoned. They are not used with discernible consistency, and are often indistinguishable in function from commas. Where parenthetical expression is called for I have used dashes.

In line with Wells's proposals, I have normalised most of Q's elisions. Various forms of 'you're' and 'thou'rt', for example, appear, but in many instances they approach or reproduce the modern rendering which I have adopted. Such forms as 'cam'st' and 'fantasticalst' have been expanded in prose; the precise form and pronunciation of these elisions may be left to the actor. Such elisions have been retained in verse, with some exceptions (usually for metre), and preterite endings have been printed in full, with voiced endings where unusual indicated by a grave accent. In accordance with the dominant Q usage, the weakened form 'a'' has been regularised to 'o''. Some contractions in prose have been retained (e.g. 'o'th'', 'i'th'') in an attempt to preserve colloquial fluidity and rhythm. The early spelling, 'Hogsden', has been retained for the sake of a possible word-play (II.i.406); and for the sake of its intended associations with 'maribone' or 'marrowbone' (see Commentary), the form 'Marybone Park' (III.i.4 and 6) has been preserved. Place names not governed by such considerations have been modernised.

Lineation in this play as in many Middleton plays presents special difficulties. Departures from Q are given in Appendix A. A number of problems may stem from Middleton's peculiar manuscript habit of beginning a verse line with a lower-case letter. But the play's verse is in any case irregular, and its prose, which often has a metrical pulse, further complicates the matter. I have relined some of Q's prose as verse and vice versa, but have tried to resist the temptation to wrest verse lines from intractable prose simply for the sake of a uniform texture. The result is sometimes an apparently arbitrary alternation between verse and prose which may represent a deliberate contrast of, say, artificiality or formality and colloquial suppleness, but may equally signify no more than an unpolished state.[13]

Occasional snatches of foreign languages, including Tearcat's garbled speech at V.i.100–4, have been left substantially as they appear in Q, because they probably reflect phonetic pronunciation, and any errors or mis-spellings may well be intentional. The canting of Moll, Trapdoor and Tearcat has been regularised as far as possible in accordance with *O.E.D.* and spellings established by recent modernised editions of Dekker's underworld pamphlets.

2. COLLABORATION

Recent studies in linguistic analysis have helpfully set out numerous features of Dekker's and Middleton's writing. Both D. J. Lake and MacD. P. Jackson arrive at much the same conclusion about the division of shares in *The Roaring Girl*.[14] My investigations temper rather than overturn their findings. Despite disclaimers, as in Jackson's preface and Lake's introduction, p. 3, a scene-by-scene division tends to give the impression that shares can be sharply defined. While this may be the case in some plays, it seems less valid for *The Roaring Girl* since most scenes reveal evidence of both dramatists. Further, the procedure of subtracting trait totals of one dramatist from those of the other in individual scenes flies in the face of the more reasonable conclusion that both made significant contributions to them. Moreover, statistical tabulations are in some cases misleading: where evidence is meagre, for example, Lake and Jackson accord to slight traces undue weight. The role of chance in the preservation or occurrence of only a few traits has probably been underestimated. Assignment of a scene on the basis of a single trait (as Lake does I.i and III.iii, for instance) appears rash, especially in the light of ignored balancing evidence. In this regard, both Lake and Jackson choose to overlook traits which they themselves list in comprehensive tables for the study of other plays. Nevertheless, their studies have valuably extended the range of features distinctive of each dramatist and thereby rendered the ground for hypothesis somewhat firmer. As *The Roaring Girl* was apparently the last joint venture of the two writers,[15] a less formal, freer division of responsibilities may well have evolved. At all events, caution is called for, especially since certain obstacles to a thoroughly confident division cannot be removed. Irresolvable questions relating to the nature of the printer's copy, for example, cloud the matter of discernment of traits.

The caveats and strictures set forth in S. Schoenbaum's *Internal Evidence and Elizabethan Dramatic Authorship* (Evanston, 1966) notwithstanding, certain general points relating to style deserve mention. Middleton's gift for terse, wittily cynical dialogue, especially that carrying secondary sexual meanings, though conspicuous in II.i, declares itself also in II.ii, III.i, IV.i and possibly parts of III.ii. Dekker's work contains much overt moralising of the kind found in Openwork's statements at IV.ii.211ff. The genial tone at the conclusion of this episode seems also to bear Dekker's stamp. The final moments of the Gallipot action, on the other hand, are more in keeping with Middleton's preference for ironic revelation. Middletonian irony, subtler and denser than Dekker's, is likely in evidence elsewhere too, but distinguishing clearly and convincingly one from the other eludes objective analysis. Middleton seldom writes very musical verse. Dekker's rather loose and more lyrical style appears to show through in certain passages, as for example at I.ii.79–89. But since his writing verges at times on self-parody, this stylistic aspect is highly susceptible to imitation. Parallel passages from both dramatists' other work are cited in the Commentary and referred to more generally below. The following discussion draws on the findings of various studies.[16]

I.i contains contradictory evidence. Both Lake and Jackson cite 'Vmh', a characteristic Dekker form. But the Q spelling, 'sleightly', may signify Middleton, and the soliloquy in which it occurs reveals a compression of thought and feeling unusual in Dekker. In addition, a trait (Lake, Band 1 (i)) peculiar to Middleton ('-ly welcome') occurs at l. 21. Chorus speeches, nautical imagery and the form 'God a mercy' (l. 249) betray Dekker's presence in I.ii; but a Middleton form not found in Dekker ('Spoke like') occurs in the latter part of the scene involving Trapdoor (l. 234). Terms such as 'backfriend' and 'mess of friends' also signal Dekker.[17] One or two word-plays (e.g. l. 106ff.) suggest Middleton. G. R. Price has noted a relatively high percentage of feminine endings – a Middleton trait – in the scene's verse ('Shares', p. 614).

Abundant linguistic forms in II.i point to Middleton ('puh' × 6, 'push' × 3, ''has' × 2, 'mass' × 4, 'life' × 5, 'pox' × 2, 'you'r',[18] 'sh'has', "t has', 'I protest', 'by my faith', 'heart', 'by this light' × 2, '*All*', 'misticall').[19] The racy dialogue with a persistent undertow of sexual innuendo is a characteristic feature of his writing. A few parallels suggest that Dekker may not be entirely absent, however. Middleton's forms predominate also in II.ii ('I've', 'life', 'sh'has', 'while', 'we're'). Lake has remarked on Middleton's exceptional fondness for the word 'comfort' (pp. 13–14): 'comfortablest' occurs at l. 46. Although linguistic evidence offers little support, Cyrus Hoy (*Introductions*, III, 12–13) feels that Dekker is prominent in this scene.

III.i contains numerous Middleton features ('you'r' × 3, 'life' × 2, 'I've', 'mass', 'i'faith' × 2, 'a pox' × 2, 'spoke like', 'Innes a Courtmen', 'toward'). In another connection Cyrus Hoy has remarked on 'frampold' ('phrampell' in *The Roaring Girl*) as a Middleton usage.[20] Dekker's predilection for fishing images possibly hints at his involvement in Moll's speech (ll. 96ff.), though this imagery ties in with the thematic scheme of the play as a whole.[21] Both Lake and Jackson assign III.ii to Dekker, disregarding evidence of Middleton ('i'faith', 'pox' × 2, 'beshrew your heart', '-ly welcome', 'comfort', 'hold my life' × 2, 'Be Lady', 'hoyda', 'vp and ride', 'sh'has' × 2). Dekker forms run through the scene also ('Vmh' × 4, 'vp and down', 'zounds', 'Vds', 'Gods', 'tush' × 2). Traits of both are mingled throughout; none of the scene's three distinct parts contains features exclusive to either. III.ii has the play's highest proportion of rhyme (69.6%) – generally seen as a mark of Dekker – but the sixty-six lines of verse comprise only a fraction of the scene. The precontract device closely resembles that in *A Trick to Catch the Old One* and may indicate Middleton's as the shaping hand. On fairly slight grounds Lake and Jackson assign the following scene (III.iii) to Dekker. But Middleton features appear here also ('you'r', 'i'faith', 'pox', 'spoke like',[22] 'vppo'th''). The comparison of counters to universities (ll. 85ff.) is the fullest expression of an idea presented in earlier Middleton plays. The image of 'conjuring in circuits and circles' (l. 130), common in Dekker, occurs also at V.i.330–2. A Dekker form ('hump') and his 'men-midwives bringing ... to bed' construction appear in the scene.

Linguistic and other traits of Middleton are scattered throughout IV.i ('I've' × 3, 'you'r' × 2, 'we're', 'i'faith', 'faith', 'troth', 'life', 'push', 'pish', 'pox'), while evidence of Dekker is negligible. 'Mysteries' is possibly a Middleton usage;[23] and the prose/verse/prose form of Moll's speech, ll. 130–46, may reflect

Middleton's manuscript habits. Either author could have written the bawdy songs.[24] The evidence of IV.ii favours Dekker ('zounds', 'tush' × 2, 'Vds', 'God' × 2, *Omnes* × 4, "las' × 4, "sdeath', "s heart', 'lord', 'puss-cat'). In addition, a number of close parallels, nautical images and, as Price has observed, play allusions, point to him.[25] "Sfoot' × 2, 'i' the' × 3, 'toward', 'push', and *'aloof off'* are associated with Middleton, however, and suggest that he contributed, if only in a minor way. Laxton's plot with Greenwit disguised as an apparitor echoes Gerardine's in IV.iv of *The Family of Love*.

V.i has been confidently attributed to Dekker; his presence is signalled by numerous traits throughout ('zounds' × 4, 'Vds', *'Omnes'* × 14, 'boone voyage') and extensive borrowing from the underworld pamphlets *The Belman of London* and *Lantern and Candlelight*. But exclusive attribution must account for a number of Middleton traits ('faith', 'i'faith' × 3, 'by my troth', 'mass', 'pox', 'heart', 'you'r'), most concentrated in the latter part of the scene after Trapdoor and Tearcat have departed and the canting is over. Further, six occurrences of 'i' the' – a trait not found in Dekker[26] (Lake, Band 1 (f)) – also hint at Middleton's involvement in the scene if only as reviser or transcriber (elsewhere 'i' the' and 'i'th'' cut across apparent compositors' stints). V.ii reveals only slight evidence of Dekker. Linguistic forms ('i'faith' × 3, 'you'r'' × 2, 'vppo' th'', 'hoyda', 'with a vengeance', 'heart', 'I've', 'life', 'comfort' × 5, 'comfortable', 'while') and the spelling, 'revenewes', point to Middleton. Since the scene is almost entirely in verse, Price's calculation of feminine endings (the highest percentage of any scene with a high proportion of verse to prose) is perhaps more valid than in others – a condition which also favours Middleton. Moll's cryptic rhyming speech near the close, however, resembles a rhyming prophecy in Dekker's *Whore of Babylon*, I.ii.230–51, and 'whiles', l. 105 (Lake, Band 1 (d)), not found in Middleton, occurs in this scene. The Epilogue with its probable reply to Martin Markall is very likely Dekker's, and the Prologue may well be his also. Jackson notes the abundance of parentheses in both and assigns them on this basis to Dekker; but a scene-by-scene distribution of shares on this plan greatly oversimplifies the problem. In sum, the question of relative shares is a slippery one. Few scenes point conclusively to either dramatist as the main writer. As Cyrus Hoy has remarked, 'the designation "Middleton and Dekker" is the only one appropriate for much of the play'.[27]

Whether Middleton or Dekker revised the play to bring it to its final form remains a matter for speculation. None of the evidence so far adduced persuasively tips the balance in either direction. Too little is known about how dramatists worked in collaboration. Division by acts, such as Bentley has proposed as common for Henslowe plays, appears not to have been the system here.[28] Each writer may conceivably have revised the other's work, and that perhaps more than once – a circumstance which could account for the apparent presence of both dramatists in most scenes. The play's freedom from glaring inconsistencies and loose ends which commonly result from poor joint authorship suggests along with other evidence that the writing overlapped in scenes, characterisation and plots. Where plotting threads appear to have antecedents, most derive from Middleton's work – a fair indication that he exercised considerable influence over the structure and shape. The collaborative creation of Moll equals or outstretches either dramatist's other attempts to breathe life into a character. Many of her qualities reverberate with those found in other of their characters, but nowhere else are they lodged together under one roof and in so singular an arrangement. She and the play benefit from the contributions of both dramatists, surely the most important element of a collaboration.

3. DATE[29]

Apart from the evidence of the title-page, the primary document for dating *The Roaring Girl* is an entry in *The Consistory of London Correction Book* from 27 January 1612 (see Appendix E) which gives details of Mary Frith's appearance on the Fortune stage about nine months previously.[30] Whatever the actual nature of this incident, its connection with the Epilogue's promise of further recompense from the real Roaring Girl a few days hence seems highly probable. Several topical allusions converge also on the spring of 1611. In V.i, Moll tries to recover a purse 'stolen at the last new play i' the Swan'. From 1599 to 1611 the Swan was used as a sporting arena rather than a playhouse. Theatrical performances resumed in April 1611, so the reference is presumably to an early one of these.

A remark by Gull at III.iii.207–9, concerning a butcher who cudgelled a 'great fellow' with a 'sword and buckler', very likely refers to a documented incident involving two butchers tried 'for abusing certen gentlemen at the Play House called The Fortune'. The butchers were released on bail on 26 February 1611 until trial at the next Middlesex Session of the Peace. Moll's apology for her way of life before Lord Noland and others in V.i closely resembles a part of the celebrated passage in Thomas Coryat's *Crudities* (1611) which treats of the author's experiences with the renowned courtesans of Venice. Behind Prince Henry's patronage of both Coryat and the company at The Fortune may well lie an explanation for the allusion in Moll's speech.[31]

The re-dating of the *Correction Book* entry removes solid evidence of Mary Frith's celebrity prior to the immediate time of the play, and thus argues against a significantly earlier date of composition. Epigram 90 of Thomas Freeman's *Rubbe and a great Cast* (1614) may have been composed at an earlier date as some have supposed, but how much earlier is open to speculation. John Day's lost *Madde Pranckes of Mery Mall of the Banckside*, entered in the Stationer's Register 7 August 1610, may be the earliest dependable reference to the real Moll, if she is indeed the title figure. The older Moll Frith is allowed to be – possibly twenty-five or twenty-six in 1611 – the more plausible is the mature stage figure. Although it does not pinpoint the year in 1611, Greenwit's citation calling the Gallipots to appear 'this Easter Term' (IV.ii.246–7) accords at least with the season. Internal and external evidence thus suggest early 1611 as the period of composition, and late April/early May as the date of performance.

4. SOURCES

Apart from fragmentary elements nothing has yet been identified which qualifies as an indisputable source. Several likely candidates may, however, be considered. The realism of Middleton's city comedies, as R. C. Bald has observed, derives largely from the adaptation of local experience to dramatic purposes.[32] The choice of Moll Frith for the play's centrepiece along with a palpable London setting provided a particularly rich opportunity for the exercise of such interests. Elements dependent on such ephemeral material are, however, difficult or impossible to pin down. Apparent printed sources may be no more than records of events or circumstances similar to others encountered through personal experience.

Mary Frith must have cut a striking and colourful figure in Jacobean London – one which clearly appealed to Middleton and Dekker but very likely threatened and disquieted many other of their contemporaries. Most commentators on the play have stressed her misdeeds and made much of the dramatists' 'slackness of truth' in their handling of her. With the available evidence, however, we really cannot fully judge how literally to take the statement about Moll's liability to slander. Reports of her pranks and misdemeanours are subject to the values and disposition of the writer; John Chamberlain, for example, is less than sympathetic in his account of her penance at Paul's Cross.[33] How might Falstaff appear to later times if we depended on similar records and litigation for knowledge of him? Moll plainly had underworld associations,[34] but they were used at least occasionally in the service of justice. In a Star Chamber suit of 1621 in which she claims to have had a royal commission to examine thieves for the retrieval of stolen property, she remarks that by her means 'many that had had theire pursses Cutt or goodes stollen had beene helped to theire goodes againe and diuers of the offendors taken or discouered'.[35] These particulars accord closely with the incident at V.i.303–5 of the play in which Moll acts similarly on behalf of one of her friends. Moll Frith lived to the age of seventy-four[36] – years unusual for the time and remarkable for one of her alleged profession.[37] If nothing else, her long life argues that she was exceptionally clever, astute and cautious in her 'trade'. The glimpse of her afforded by the Consistory Court record (see Appendix E) reveals a confidently irreverent spirit not entirely out of keeping with the stage character.[38]

Passages for which possible sources exist are mainly confined to the subsidiary actions. Rogue literature clearly lies behind V.i. Dekker had ransacked the writings of Awdeley, Harman and Greene for his own underworld pamphlets, generally conflating and expanding them. But the canting scene depends more directly on his own work than on his sources, and abundant verbal and other resemblances attest to the intimacy of the relationship; Moll's speech at ll. 131–8, for example, is matched by a passage in *The Belman*.[39] Awdeley and Harman make no mention of 'fights at sea', present here and in the pamphlet. Trapdoor's speech at ll. 161–6 closely resembles a description given by Dekker in the same work under the character of a 'kinchin co'; and the list of farm animals at ll. 165–6 matches one in *Lantern and Candlelight*. The canting song (ll. 214–27) shares many of the same terms, word order and rhymes with that at the end of *Lantern*, chapter 1. Moll's description of the cutpurses (ll. 281–92) likewise closely echoes a passage in *The Belman*. With a few exceptions, the canting phrases are to be found in the earlier rogue literature, but order, word combinations and rhymes (when they occur) bear Dekker's stamp.

A cony-catching device from Greene's *A Notable Discovery of Cosenage*,[40] noticed by Bald in connection with *The Family of Love*, aligns also with an episode in *The Roaring Girl*. Laxton acts on his knowledge of Gallipot's mistrust of lawyers and courts by staging a formal legal process for extortionary purposes. Greenwit plays the summoner's role and delivers a citation ordering the Gallipots to appear before the Court of Arches. As in Greene, the cosener has apparently played husband off against wife, for Gallipot claims to have given him money behind the scenes. The plan, however, hangs on Mistress Gallipot's complicity: once she sides with her husband, it collapses and the rogues are unmasked. Details of the earlier phase of the Gallipot action correspond to an episode in Middleton's *Father Hubburd's Tales* (Bullen, VIII, 91–2). An unwitting tradesman, his cunning wife, and requests for money by secret letters from her gentleman lover link up with this citizen plot.

The Batchelars Banquet (1603) has been noted as a source for *Blurt, Master Constable* (1601–2) and *A Chaste Maid in Cheapside* (1613), and a few situational fragments in *The Roaring Girl* may derive from it. This pamphlet deals mostly with wives who wear the breeches – a circumstance with general resonances in the play. A wife in chapter 3 exploits her pregnant condition to excuse capricious moods and desires (sig. B4r). *The Roaring Girl*'s situation may be by way of *Blurt*, which provides a significant development: there a feigned pregnancy is purported to be equally efficacious (III.iii.115ff.). In a similar vein Gallipot delightedly deduces from his wife's prickly scorn that she breeds (III.ii.35–9), and she in turn berates his solicitude.

R. C. Bald noted another possible borrowing from *The Batchelars Banquet* – the ruse of passing off lovers as relatives – in *The Phoenix* (II.iii.11ff.) and in this play (IV.ii.63–4).[41] Class tension as a source of marital discord is the subject of chapter 5, 'The humor of a woman that marries her inferior by birth' (sigs. D3v–4r). In II.i Mistress Openwork loftily rebukes her husband's presumption to serve nobility (ll. 169–70), and later parades her own gentility to attract Goshawk's notice (ll. 329ff.). Bald overlooked the self-parodying reiteration at IV.ii.151–3, however.

Henslowe first records the play *Long Meg* in 1594/5; and a mention in Nathan Field's *Amends for Ladies* (II.i.153)[42] suggests that it may yet have been in the repertory about the time of *The Roaring Girl*. Though the play is lost, various editions of its possible source, the anonymous jest-biography *Long Meg of Westminster*, survive.[43] This brief patchwork of anecdotes, feats and exploits contains several episodes with an inherent, if crude, dramatic quality. In such broad strokes of character as adoption of male dress and a virtuous disposition Moll has a natural affinity with the earlier sword-wielding virago. Several points of contact suggest that the dramatists may have been acquainted with some rendering of Long Meg's life which in the main agreed with the extant narrative. Resemblances are interesting also for points of departure which possibly betray adaptation for different effect or for specifically dramatic ends.

In the tradition of Robin Hood, honest Meg helps the poor and oppressed against the rich. Her occasional dressing as a man is always for a specific purpose. Moll's altruism is possibly drawn from life as noted above, but its dramatic forms have apparent literary antecedents in episodes of *Long Meg*. Beyond a weak verbal echo[44] at II.i.190–2 (see Commentary), the strongest resonance in *The Roaring Girl* is with Meg's encounter with Sir James of Castile in St George's Fields. Taking the champion's part in defending her mistress's honour, Meg, apparelled as a gentleman, engages Sir James in a duel. After administering light wounds and gaining the upper hand, she submits to his urgent pleas for mercy on condition that he serve her at her mistress's inn. He is there made the butt of general merriment when Meg reveals her identity. The incident accords at several points with Moll's skirmish with Laxton in III.i set in Gray's Inn Fields. Initial appearances (II.i and ii) in safeguard and jerkin foil Moll's first entrance in man's dress as the gallant's mistaken expectations make clear (ll. 34–5). Since the suitor in this case is the heroine's and the honour at stake hers also, no subsequent occasion for public disgrace is needed. Moll instead drives home Laxton's humiliation on the spot. She identifies herself almost immediately so that her would-be seducer knows full well that he is thrashed by a woman. Like Sir George, Laxton receives a light wound and soon finds himself at his opponent's mercy. Laxton, too, ignominiously begs for his life. The theatre audience may be thought to perform the function of the two witnesses to the knight's defeat and are to this end made party to her vindication. The stage representation is thus played off against real-life notoriety. Moll's victory over Laxton both wins approval at his expense and allows her to challenge, if only verbally, any in the audience who have not yet been won over (III.i.92ff.).

Other small correspondences may be drawn, but none so compelling as to outweigh claims for the dramatists' own invention. An incident in chapter 5 in which Meg takes pity on a destitute soldier may connect with Moll and Trapdoor. Disguised as a servingman, she meets her man in Tuttle Fields and, after an opening quarrel, they fall to blows. Strenuously opposed and wishing to do no injury, she reveals her identity and, as promised, gives the soldier his pay, new clothing and the advice to enter service. Moll shares Meg's regard for soldiers. At her appointed meeting in III.i with Trapdoor, who professes to be a discharged soldier, she uses her male dress as a disguise and sets out to test his loyalty and spirit. Trapdoor clownishly evades Moll's advances, although his feeble but persistent wit gives some satisfaction; in the end she retains him on probation. Like Meg, she offers a new suit (one of her own) and supplies a livery cloak. In chapter 6 Meg rescues a friend in danger of arrest, a situation echoed in Moll's frustration of the catchpoles' plans for Jack Dapper.[45] The fortunate gallant may well ask of Moll, 'was it your Meg of Westminster's courage that rescued me from the Poultry puttocks?' (V.i.2–3). In chapter 13 Long Meg marries, and in pointed deference to contemporary mores submits to her husband. The difference between the two women is perhaps nowhere clearer. Mary Frith's celibacy was an irrefutable fact, but its association with aggressive maidenhood and a sense of mission more fully accords with the stage character than a promise to submit to some future husband which the dramatists, bowing to convention, might have provided.

Many elements in *The Roaring Girl* appear in other of the dramatists' plays. Middleton made regular use of the precontract device;[46] *A Trick* (1604–7) provides the closest parallel to the false precontract in the Gallipot action. The supposed elopement of Moll and Sebastian may also be prefigured in *A Trick* by that of Witgood and the Courtesan. Mistress Gallipot's relationship with Laxton bears strong resemblance to others similarly based in *The Phoenix* and *The Family of Love*.[47] A Patient Grissil situation with the sexes reversed, as in *1 Honest Whore*, may underlie the Openwork plot. The female page, so disguised to gain access to her lover (possibly derived from Shakespeare), is seen in *1 Honest Whore*[48] and re-emerges with slight variations in a string of Middleton's later plays: *No Wit, No Help Like a Woman's* (c. 1613–27), *More Dissemblers Besides Women* (c. 1615), *The Widow* (c. 1615–17), *Anything for a Quiet Life* (c. 1620–1), and *The Spanish Gipsy* (1623).

5. CRITICAL APPRECIATION

Structure

The Roaring Girl contains structural features traceable to both dramatists' earlier work. The central romantic action is a variation on the New-Comedy formula, with the emphasis shifted away from the traditional conflict of generations – though not to its exclusion – to a scheme aimed at resolution. This takes the form of an action derived from a species of city comedy: the prodigal play.[49]

The motif of a licentious youth doting on a fallen woman – usually a whore – in preference to his virtuous and patient wife or betrothed underlies Sebastian's prodigal role. By pretending affection for the allegedly contemptible Moll Cutpurse, he aims to secure his father's approval of his true love, Mary Fitzallard. Sir Alexander responds according to plan as the father of a genuine stage prodigal might. In mounting a counteraction, he assumes a posture which aligns him with Moll's sanctimonious detractors who automatically style her a thief and a whore.

Although Sir Alexander stops short of disguising himself to spy on his son like Flowerdale Senior in *The London Prodigal*, for example, he twice enters secretly to eavesdrop. And his employment of Trapdoor as an infiltrator serves a similar dramatic function to disguise. True to tradition, the father's attempts at controlling his son fail. In the process, Trapdoor finds himself the servant of two masters and correspondingly vacillates between the pull of mercenary instincts and the urgings of a moral sensibility. In both his role and his internal conflict he recalls the Plautine type of managing servant.

Parallel patterning informs much of the play's structural organisation. Correspondences involving characters, incidents and situations link elements in several spheres of action and help to produce a measure of balance. The loosely connected tangent episodes involving Jack Dapper act as a foil to the mock-prodigal main plot. So as not to tarnish Sebastian's personal qualities in *The Roaring Girl*, it is Jack who has been endowed with the traditional prodigal's improvidence. His profligacy stands in much the same fitting relation to his usurer father, Sir Davy (III.iii.157), as Witgood's to his Uncle Lucre in *A Trick*. Jack takes no part in a love intrigue although the dramatic framework would have allowed an affair with Mistress Tiltyard. He is an innocuous simpleton, endearing enough to merit a rescue by Moll and Trapdoor. A. H. Gomme sees him as a precursor to the dim-witted Ward in *Women Beware Women*.[50] He spreads no pernicious influence over the play, and although his father reports his misdeeds (III.iii.6off.), we witness none.

Structural aspects of the prodigal motif are also present in the episodes of the shopkeepers and their wives, though in them the traditional role of the sexes is reversed: the wives who turn their households upside-down and abandon their husbands for the excitement of courtly lovers are the prodigals here. The husbands perform the passive role typically played by the prodigal's wife. The wayward parties in the end return to their faithful spouses; but contrary to tradition, they decide to do so of their own accord. Disaffection with their wanton escapades comes about in the absence of external agency. The characters and movements of the two intrigues are individualised so that each comments on the other. Unlike Gallipot, Openwork suffers no humiliation in the course of his wife's pursuit of Goshawk, and this is in part the measure of the husbands' different approaches as well as of their different natures. Brentford, the place of assignation also in *Westward Ho*, is reached by neither Laxton with Moll nor Goshawk with Mistress Openwork; in contrast to the earlier play, it remains elusively remote, emblematic of thwarted intentions.

Parallels and mirror-image contrasts extend also to scenic patterns. Incidents are frequently juxtaposed in a montage arrangement, as in Moll's successive encounters with Laxton and Trapdoor in III.i, for example. Laxton's openly sexual advances to Moll in II.i are similarly balanced against Sebastian's more earnest wooing in the following scene. The contrast continues as Laxton's approach proves disastrously abortive and Sebastian's, within the terms of his strategy at least, successful. In IV.ii Laxton's ill-fated playlet follows hard upon the Openworks' staged lesson for Goshawk; both anticipate the theatrical resolution of the main action. In the canting scene the good-natured frauds, Trapdoor and Tearcat, are matched against the slick professionals; and in the final scene, the mock marriage is counterpointed by the genuine one. Although the play does not schematise London in the manner of *Eastward Ho* or *A Chaste Maid*, for example, it presupposes an intimate knowledge of the city in its audience. Abundant local references and numerous topical allusions act accordingly as a minor cohesive force.

The single most important unifying agent is the figure of Moll about whom the intrigues and various interests revolve. She appears in seven of the play's eleven scenes and her spirit extends over the others. Sebastian's stratagem to outwit his father turns on her complicity, and Laxton's venture with her complements the two citizen plots. And so, although she falls from view as the shopkeepers' intrigues develop, Moll's influence continues into the later scenes. The Laxton episode is short, reaching its climax and conclusion in III.i. But, as its position makes clear, the gallant's defeat by Moll is a central event and presages his own, Goshawk's and Greenwit's handling by the citizens. Further, Laxton's muffled face serves as an effective reminder of the bout with Moll at subsequent appearances.

Moll binds the various actions together not merely by her engagement in them, but also by the combined galvanic force of her personal magnetism and a radiant, vigorous spirit which pervades the play at large and centripetally draws together its interests. One of the triumphs of the character is her rough-hewn but irresistible charm. Through interaction with her fellows, through her attitudes and beliefs, and through her formulation of moral decisions, we see her develop as a living individual. In terms of the dramatic mechanism, she recalls earlier Middleton figures. Like Phoenix and Fitsgrave she is the play's moral spokesman, but unlike them she is refreshingly free of the moral stiffness which is a corollary of their noble status. To dominate as well as to win favour and respect, the Roaring Girl relies not on the official exercise of power but on uncompromised and merry pursuit of virtue.

Themes, Imagery, Characterisation

But as literature, as a dispassionate picture of human nature, Middleton's comedy deserves to be remembered chiefly by its real – perpetually real – and human figure of Moll the Roaring Girl.[51]

Few critics have endorsed T. S. Eliot's praise of *The Roaring Girl*, although even he dismissed all but Moll as conventional. But Eliot's response is in another respect typical: Moll *is* the play's centrepiece, but criticism has focused on her at the expense of an understanding of the overall design and her part in it. Traditional attitudes and assumed conventions have remained buried and have been denied their place in the play's pattern and the dramatists' intentions. When taken in conjunction with such considerations, Moll becomes all the more attractive and the play rather more interesting and better crafted than has been granted.

In its featured characterisation of a living person of contemporary notoriety the play is unique, not merely in the work of the joint authors, but also in the drama of the age. Its uniqueness and shared authorship possibly go some way towards explaining why many critics, not sure (or caring) to whom it belongs, have either ignored it altogether or treated it as an orphan, the occasion of reference only when convenient. R. H. Barker, for example, in *Thomas Middleton* (1958) side-stepped *The Roaring Girl*, claiming it to be mainly Dekker's.[52] D. M. Holmes, on the other hand, dealt with the play unenlighteningly in the context of what he considered Middleton's didactic purpose.[53]

In recent years *The Roaring Girl* has received more attention, especially since A. H. Gomme's New Mermaid edition (1976). In a
stimulating and suggestive study[54] Simon Shepherd considers the
play and its heroine in relation to a tradition of women warriors, but
he tends to adopt an over-modern perspective and to overlook other
traditions both literary and historical. While the discussion sheds
interesting light on several aspects, it misrepresents some character
relationships and renders the play's ending unsatisfactorily open-
ended and ironic. To present Moll's stance as the model for all
women in the play is to ignore contemporary traditions to which
Moll herself refers as standards.[55] In approaching the play by way of
a hermaphroditic tradition the roots of which he finds in Plato's
Symposium, Patrick Cheney finds Moll 'a figure of love representing
the union of contraries, or the pagan mystery of *concordia discors*'.[56]
Cheney's observations usefully illuminate the significance of the hermaphrodite element, but presume a neatness in the resolution of the
subsidiary actions unsupported by the text. Larry S. Champion
similarly ignores problematic elements in the subplots, and disre-
gards balancing evidence in stressing what he sees as feminist aspects
of the title figure.[57] Some of *The Roaring Girl*'s many centres of interest are timely in speaking to modern concerns and issues; others are
less accessibly bound to the play's period. The modern cause of
feminism and the re-evaluation of women's place in society have
undoubtedly spurred the modest renewal of interest, but to interpret
the play by these lights alone is to risk serious distortion. Themes,
characterisation and imagery reveal qualities of intrinsic merit and
interest as well as elements which link with both Middleton's and
Dekker's other work. Not the least of its appealing features is a
dramatic vitality, however flawed, which shames its slight stage
history.

In addition to the structural elements discussed above, several
thematic concerns exert cohesive force. The illusion/reality theme
and changes rung on it constitute the central controlling interest.
Most conspicuous is the straightforward demonstration that appearances are deceiving, the arch exemplar being Moll herself. The
theme develops in several complementary ways which have a clear
moral orientation and connect with matters closely associated with
the health of society: the administration of justice and the exercise of
authority. In the wider sphere, it probes hypocrisy's double standard
of public posture and private interest, typically witnessed in a dis-
junction between word and deed. It also exposes various related

forms of deception and trickery, especially as corrupt instruments of prejudice, intolerance and slander. Several characters practise self-deception, foremost among them Sir Alexander who additionally exhibits the destructive force of immoderate passion.

As in so many other plays of the period, the depicted society is one in transition. Traditional values have slipped from their wonted places, rendering pretence indistinguishable from truth. A kind of blurred vision results according to which form can masquerade as content, outline as substance. Dekker emblematises the condition in a dumb-show of *The Whore of Babylon*: 'Falshood, (*attir'd as* Truth *is*)' (IV.i). Office and rank become mere masks for self-interest and corruption while the judicial system serves the very interests it should condemn. Reputation's power to foster rumour, groundless opinion and prejudice, and the immunity of office to suspicion likewise contribute to the confusion. Although the tone is on the whole buoyant – largely through Moll's dominating influence – the world depicted is under the threat of iron-age vices.[58] Corruption cuts across class and other boundaries, but its primary focus is on a figure of justice, Sir Alexander. The prevailing slippery conditions call for tests to distinguish appearance from reality. In this respect the play's crises and dilemmas essentially constitute a series of trial situations in which individual responses expose inner motives and define natures. Moll's declaration, ''tis impossible to know what woman is throughly honest, because she's ne'er thoroughly tried' (II.i.318–19), accordingly has wide reference, and her advocacy of a trial to determine true honesty establishes a moral and thematic paradigm. The Roaring Girl thereby sets the standards by which others are measured. Her authority is moreover shown to be supreme among those thought lawless, and she becomes a justice figure in her own right.

Further, the dramatic method serves the play's thematic scheme. The convention which projects the audience in the privileged position of judge of the play is invoked in both Prologue and Epilogue. *The Roaring Girl* offers nothing so elaborate as Jonson's contractual Induction to *Bartholomew Fair*, but it engages with similar interests. In its judicial position, the audience takes an active role in working through the play's issues and problems. Whatever preconceptions may prevail outside the theatre, within the play world characters define themselves and are judged by their speech and actions. Moll thus gains the privilege of equal footing with her adversaries. In addition, *The Roaring Girl* invokes expectations associated with the real Mary Frith's notoriety to balance them against the stage incarnation. Interplay between the fictional and the real co-ordinates with wider thematic interests. The levelling effect of the dramatic mode strips forms and exponents of coercion and tyranny – rank, office, reputation, slander and the like – of their power, and by exposing secret motives and hypocrisies, assists in the re-establishment of even-handed justice, the essential condition for repairing the network of natural bonds in such a society. At the close, the confused vision is realigned and corrected: falsehood wears the guise of truth no longer. The play thus partakes of the idealising spirit of the authors' civic pageants and such plays as *The Phoenix* and *The Whore of Babylon*.

Other forms of decay are probed in the exploration of shifting values. In his Revels edition of *A Chaste Maid in Cheapside*, R. B. Parker points to the sickness of Jacobean life manifest in various perversions of natural eroticism. Among these are the connection of sexuality with competitive materialism, class conflict and internal corruption insidiously undermining society's very foundation in the family. Though in *The Roaring Girl* the bleak vision is in the end effectively eclipsed, the same elements in muted form are present; and again the implied moral slanting which attends such imagery integrates with the play's interest in justice.[59]

Two patterns of imagery predominate in the undercurrent of sexual reference: animal and commercial. In plots distinctly reminiscent of cony-catching frauds, gallants prey for sexual or financial gain upon social inferiors. Venery's dual significations of game-hunting and pursuit of sexual pleasure – as ambivalently set out in Middleton's Epistle – are.effectively mingled throughout the intrigues. The hunt provides an abundance of sexually associated expressions (Goshawk's name is especially apt), and playful terms of affection (duck, pigsney, mouse, turtle) extend the double reference still further. Fishing imagery too is prominent. In this regard, Curtalax's 'All that live in the world are but great fish and little fish, and feed upon one another' (III.iii.140–2), stands as a stark icon figuring the depredations of one element of society on another, whether the terms be age, class, wealth, law, sex, office or some such combination. The many references to commerce expose a general preoccupation with affluence and materialism. Commodities are invested with lubricious innuendo, and wayward sexual transactions couched in business terminology. The main action is likewise shot through with sexual reference, much of it in perverse allusion to Moll. By contrast, her own speech, while racy and irreverent, is free and natural, in the healthy service of chastity and virtue.[60] When moved to answer depravity, she wittily deflects its scurrilous accents against itself. Such humour lightens the overall dramatic tone.

The outlines of the other characters are set and defined by their function in the play. Some are interesting variations on stock figures, but none can lay any real claim to depth. Moll, however, roams free of such constraints. She gives instead the impression of having a full existence outside the immediate dramatic context, able to conjure for herself, like other three-dimensional literary figures, an existence independent of the work in which she appears. Her flesh and blood sets off the conventional comic machinery with which she engages, and throws into relief associated levels of illusion.

Clothed in features distinctive of their London milieu, the characters who people the play provide a compatible array of individuals with whom Moll can plausibly interact. In other respects also the play goes to considerable lengths to depict the stuff of City life. Topographical references, topical allusions, street scenes involving typical London figures, and a lively shop scene establish onstage the ambience, manners and by-ways familiar to the audience. At points the stage illusion becomes self-conscious, calling attention to the double edge of the play/life metaphor:[61] Sir Alexander's description of his 'galleries' (I.ii.14ff.) offers an impressionistic view of the interior of the Fortune Theatre, incidentally warning of the presence of cutpurses, a real peril;[62] in addition, reference to well-known plays (IV.ii.137 and 284) and theatrical conventions such as the raising of flags (IV.ii.136) and images from playing and performance are embedded in the dialogue.

The opening scenes establish dramatically the same thematic terms. Sebastian's pretended interest in Moll develops into an active, genuine concern for her, and the supposed fictional narrative (I.ii.6off.) which his father offers as an amusing diversion evolves into an account of his own desperate predicament. Similarly, the asides and soliloquies in which Moll steps outside the action and addresses the audience convey the impression less of a stage character than of a spectator commenting on events and circumstances, as Mary Frith may well have done.[63] The effect recalls Will Summers's interplay in Nashe's *Summer's Last Will and Testament*. References to the real Moll in the Prologue and Epilogue bracket the play proper. Thus, while her stage representation bridges the internally explored worlds of illusion and reality, the character's mirrored contact with her original links the play with the real world outside. Moll not only

stands at the centre of the play's several actions, she is also the meeting point of its manifold thematic interests.

On the evidence of the thinly disguised account of himself in I.ii, Sir
Alexander is a self-made man; and, in accord with early seventeenth-
century trends, his prosperity presumably has a mercantile base.
Thus commercial allusions pervade his speech. His wealth, his
knighthood and his office of Justice of the Peace place him among the
Jacobean class of rising gentry.[64] A pattern of images introduced
early on effectively characterises his outlook:

> He reckoned up what gold
> This marriage would draw from him – at which he swore,
> To lose so much blood could not grieve him more.
> He then dissuades me from thee, called thee not fair,
> And asked, 'What is she but a beggar's heir?'
> He scorned thy dowry of five thousand marks.
> If such a sum of money could be found,
> And I would match with that, he'd not undo it,
> Provided his bags might add nothing to it.   (I.i.83–91)

The equation of gold with blood graphically figures his obsession.
Commercial imagery charges his language and defines a habit of
thought: affections, joys and cares speak through the medium of
finance (e.g. I.ii.37–9 and 40–1). His objection to Mary Fitzallard is
purely financial, and his opposition is in kind: threatened disin-
heritance. Love, suitability and virtue do not enter into such bartering; and without the smile revenue imparts, even beauty becomes
tainted. The handsomeness of Mary's marriage portion (5,000
marks), moreover, gives the measure of Sir Alexander's avarice and
ambition.[65] Though not developed through the introduction of a preferred match,[66] his opposition amounts to insistence on an arranged
marriage more agreeable to his financial, and presumably social, ambitions.[67] Avowed concern for his son offers a convenient pretext for
the imposition of his own will. His opposition to Moll has a similar
base: the scandal of association with her poses a threat to his sense of
place and position – as Sebastian has well calculated. In response, he
abuses the power vested in him as Justice by employing it to pursue
private interests. Conventional comic form would develop the tension between Sebastian and his father as the main conflict of the play,
but in *The Roaring Girl*, although Sebastian is prominent, the main
conflict becomes that between Sir Alexander and Moll, and essentially one of opposed schemes of values. Strife between father and

son, while keeping in sight related New-Comedy interests, provides
the dramatic vehicle and structure.

The withholding of Moll's first appearance until well into II.i pro-
motes the kindling of expectations, for her presence is strongly felt
from the start. Sebastian's suggestive sketch (I.i.98–101) is developed at I.ii.125–37 and 172, where Sir Alexander probably gives a
contemporary popular view of her as an androgynous monster, a
thief and a whore.[68] Unable to see beyond reputation to the individual it shrouds, his dire aim is 'To ensnare her very life' (I.ii.231);
and his strategy (echoed later by Laxton) betrays a cynical presumption that his values are universal:

> Cast out a line hung full of silver hooks
> To catch her to thy company: deep spendings
> May draw her that's most chaste to a man's bosom.   (I.ii.218–20)

Chastity and honour he likewise treats as vendible merchandise.
Material preoccupation, selfishness and hypocrisy are, however,
merely expressions of the more general malady of moral blindness.
As the sea image at I.ii.8off. and his later actions make clear, Sir
Alexander is in the grip of his passions, and, in accord with contemporary psychology, has lost his moral bearings and the capacity
for balanced judgement.[69] Grief and shame touched off by choler
(gall) are regularly discharged as taut salvoes of embittered frustration. The thorn of Sebastian's pursuit of Moll inflames what would
appear to be an entrenched condition, the implications of which
extend beyond the immediate romantic problem. But vestiges
of a reasonable outlook remain (II.ii.46–7, 65), though regularly
swamped by passion, and reveal that he is not thoroughly corrupt – a
point of some importance for the final stages of the action. At the root
of his discomfiture lie twisted values which feature a perverse concern with appearances and respectability. Although the play begins
on a personal, private level, its reference soon expands to embrace
society at large. Sebastian's trick to bring his father round to the
marriage with Mary evolves into a full assault on falsehood and deception in various forms and guises. Direct acquaintance with Moll
teaches young Wengrave the speciousness of reputation. In defending her, he discourses on the unreliability of popular opinion and the
injustice of prejudice, not simply to goad his father as before, but in
genuine response to her many qualities (II.ii.162–80).

Sir Alexander is the only main character to speak consistently in
verse, and in this, also, he is set against Moll. Extravagant at times,

his speech is typically stilted and authoritarian, never attaining the suppleness or fluid spontaneity of prose. With professional ease he slips readily into rhetoric,[70] the appropriate medium for his self-delusion and a dangerously powerful instrument in the service of half-truths and rationalisations. His image of prisoners urged to learn the arts of deception to ingratiate themselves with their keepers (III.iii.85ff.) comments broadly on a society in which falsehood prospers over honesty and justice. As Sebastian remarks, 'Plain dealing in this world takes no effect' (II.ii.195).

Moll's introduction by report is challenged by the lusty, appealing figure who swiftly turns all expectations on their heads. Disparity between advance description and our own witness gives the lie to the 'respectable' Sir Alexander. Surprisingly, she enters in female dress, and her irreverent wit and good humour project an irrepressible liveliness and a compelling spirit. Contagious vitality banishes the monstrous portrait of Act I: word and deed throughout the play consistently reinforce the authority of direct experience. At a polar remove from Sir Alexander's stiffness, Moll's discursive vernacular possesses exuberance and allure. She presses into figurative service elements of common experience and charges her turns of phrase with a disarmingly earthy – occasionally brusque – freshness and candour. Though more sinewy at the pitch of heightened expression, as in her diatribe against Laxton (III.i.72ff.), her imagery and style even in full career retain the stamp of colloquial idiom. Moll is far from the traditional ideal of the silent woman, and her male dress, like Rosalind's in *As You Like It*, affords her masculine licence. Rebutted and traded on by the dramatic persona, the real-life reputation becomes an exhibit in the attack on judgements based on report or any other prejudicial consideration. The stage Moll shows herself unimpeachably virtuous and thoroughly self-reliant – qualities which set her apart; and her dominion in the underworld and associated colourful language vitalise the conventionally dull image of virtue. The grave countenance of the morality tradition's allegorical figure here acquires a sparkling, at times puckish, appeal; and because all her energies are bent to the service of virtue, we are spared any concomitant teasing moral dilemma.[71]

Moll's conviction that many women are honest rather by chance than by choice has both general and particular implications:

> I am of that certain belief there are more queans in this town of their own making than of any man's provoking: where lies the slackness then? Many a poor soul would down, and there's nobody will push 'em!

Women are courted but ne'er soundly tried,
As many walk in spurs that never ride.   (II.i.319–25)

The casual, offhand advocacy of a test to determine true chastity pulls into sharp focus actions so framed. Having just turned Moll from her shop in a fit of jealousy, Mistress Openwork hypocritically consorts with Goshawk; and her neighbour courts infidelity in a clandestine affair. Nor is Moll herself excepted: in succumbing to Laxton's importunities, she too is on trial. The Gray's Inn Fields assignation weighs her in the same balance with the wives; and her subsequent drubbing of the gallant serves as an object lesson in morality.

But before that, Sebastian's awkward, tentative approach in II.ii contrasts strikingly with Laxton's brazen temerity. With his father behind, the pressure is on him in this first face-to-face encounter to be convincing and effective. Moll, moved by his earnestness, dissuades him with a reply of engaging ingenuousness, redolent of self-knowledge and an independent spirit:

> I have no humour to marry. I love to lie o' both sides o'th' bed myself; and again, o'th' other side, a wife, you know, ought to be obedient, but I fear me I am too headstrong to obey, therefore I'll ne'er go about it. I love you so well, sir, for your good will, I'd be loath you should repent your bargain after, and therefore we'll ne'er come together at first. I have the head now of myself, and am man enough for a woman; marriage is but a chopping and changing, where a maiden loses one head, and has a worse i'th' place!
>
> (II.ii.36–45)

Moll's high valuation of personal freedom renders it irreconcilable with marriage, so she chooses rather to live outside convention. While honouring the doctrine enshrined in religion, law and other thought, official and unofficial,[72] which regarded women as by nature the weaker sex, she astutely recognises that she could never dwindle into a wife on such terms. In rejecting marriage for herself, however, she does not adopt the stance of a rebel or reformer. Her poise embraces a capacity for self-mockery: she knows that she cuts an eccentric figure and playfully jokes about it. By contrast, convention reverberates throughout the citizen actions and in the match between Sebastian and Mary, as an important constituent of the social hierarchy.[73]

At Gray's Inn Fields Moll enters dressed as a man for the first time – not as a disguise, but as an emblem of her equality with men.[74] In assuming male dress, she takes on the manly, chivalric ideal of fortitude. The duel also enforces equal terms. By adding ten angels to

Laxton's she presses the point still further and demonstrates her incorruptibility. In setting out to 'teach his base thoughts manners', she plays bawdily on traditional associations of knives and phallic penetration, redirecting the gallant's crude wit back on himself with a trenchant glance at his original design. Under full steam she defies the calumny of report and corruption bred of irresponsible appetite. But behind this castigation burns a more general criticism of a society which fosters depraved values and sustains such parasites: her tirade leaves no doubt of the scope of her attack as it condemns through him all who by their vain impudence expect to win any woman and, successful or not, command her reputation. Immune to their venom, she strikes at slander and deception, and, proudly abjuring the charge of whore, spurns the censure of Laxton and 'the baser world':

> In thee I defy all men, their worst hates
> And their best flatteries, all their golden witchcrafts
> With which they entangle the poor spirits of fools:
> Distressèd needlewomen and trade-fallen wives –
> Fish that must needs bite, or themselves be bitten –
> Such hungry things as these may soon be took
> With a worm fastened on a golden hook:
> Those are the lecher's food, his prey. He watches
> For quarrelling wedlocks and poor shifting sisters:
> 'Tis the best fish he takes.   (III.i.92–101)

In repulsing him, Moll adumbrates the wives' later change of heart. The gallants' trial of their affections instils a measure of self-knowledge, so that although not directly related, their victories over themselves are of a piece with the moral climate she has brought about.

On crossing swords, Moll's battle-cry soars with the insuperable spirit and assurance born of a just cause:

> Would the spirits
> Of all my slanderers were clasped in thine,
> That I might vex an army at one time!   *They fight.* (III.i.113–15)

Triumphantly proof against his base intentions, hers is a strikingly moral as well as physical victory. Laxton's ignominy and humiliation are the greater for defeat at a woman's hands. Yielding purse and body and snivelling for mercy, the cowardly lecher ignobly prostitutes himself to her. Not merely the woman's champion, as an anonymous seventeenth-century pamphlet styled her,[75] Moll is the champion of justice in the context of seventeenth-century mores.

After Laxton has slunk away, she enunciates the code by which she
lives:

> she that has wit and spirit
> May scorn to live beholding to her body for meat,
> Or for apparel, like your common dame
> That makes shame get her clothes to cover shame.
> Base is that mind that kneels unto her body
> As if a husband stood in awe on's wife;
> My spirit shall be mistress of this house
> As long as I have time in't.   (III.i.133–40)

As Alexander Leggatt has observed, 'She refuses submission not
only to men, but to her own physical nature.'[76] Disdain for the
whoredom which follows from inversion of the natural relation of
mind and body co-ordinates with her resolve to defend against baser
needs and impulses those qualities – wit and spirit – which ensure
independence. Again, an image from marriage which relates to familial hierarchy has conspicuous significance elsewhere. Though its
accents are mild and not blazoned forth with fiery rhetoric, her stance
is heroic (perhaps the more so for that), and its image stands over all
of the other characters, for capitulation to venality is ultimately a
matter of individual responsibility and integrity. With the exception
of those aligned with her, the main figures are ruled by their own
passions and drives. As a coda to these events, Moll's bout with
Trapdoor gives her an opportunity to practise her own doctrine:
'Faith, he seems / A man without; I'll try what he is within' (ll.
147–8).

Sebastian's pretended interest in Moll leaves little room for development of his romance with Mary. The lovers' conventionality
accordingly answers the need for convenient shorthand. Their unim-
peachable earnestness and chastity set off duplicity in other relationships. Moreover, they are prerequisites to Moll's aid:

> *Sebastian.* Thou has done me a kind office, without touch
>   Either of sin or shame: our loves are honest.
> *Moll.* I'd scorn to make such shift to bring you together else.

> (IV.i.39–41)

Her charity wins sympathy, as D. M. Holmes has remarked,[77] but
beyond that, as with the rescue of Jack Dapper, it advances her for-
midable active generosity against a tide of self-interest. Sebastian
and Mary, like Jack, are victims of mercenary and uncompassionate
values. Moll, fired by a natural sense of justice, takes it upon herself
to redress the odds.

Far from indicating that the dramatists worked independently,[78] the doubling of names in Moll and Mary evokes suggestive links between the two characters. Several allusions to Moll as a common name of whores occur (e.g. II.ii.153–5 and 180). Moll herself at IV.i.66–8 plays on the intended connection with Mary. The proper form of the name conveys the contrasting biblical associations of purity, chastity and suffering – qualities immediately visible in Mary Fitzallard[79] and illuminated by reflection in Moll. This elusive inner dimension stands in striking contrast to the ebullient, sharp-witted free spirit that has provoked notoriety. In describing her as 'a type of the sort of woman who has renounced all happiness for herself and who lives only for a principle',[80] T. S. Eliot shows his insensitivity to the repeated demonstrations of her effulgent vitality and mirth. Yet independence and the stern discipline of chastity may exact a toll. Her two bawdy songs presented as 'dreams' (IV.i.102ff.), which distantly echo the citizens' actions,[81] possibly offer a glimpse of a more personal contempt for falsehood. Sebastian's early declaration 'to court another Moll' has particularly strong resonances in IV.i, where both are in male dress. The strange attractiveness of Mary in doublet and breeches connects with Moll's uncommon appeal, and helps to demystify the element of androgynous monstrosity by linking it to Mary, and beyond her to the convention of boy actors playing women's parts, frequently toyed with in contemporary drama. Similar points are raised when the two appear as brides in V.ii.

Balancing the earlier test of her reputation as a whore, Moll is in IV.i on trial as a thief. The glistering bait occasions only an apt meditation, however, which concludes with an attitude of tolerance reiterated elsewhere (IV.i.140–6, V.i.346–7 and 353–7). In backfiring, the trap demonstrates instead her virtue; and, as in II.ii, the stage picture of Moll and the lovers, with Sir Alexander in the background, images thematic and moral interests. When he comes forward, preoccupation with Moll and the pretence of a music lesson successfully deflect his attention from Mary. Determined not to let Moll slip through his fingers, he abandons indirection for manifest dishonesty. He remains blind to Moll's clear display of virtue. Possessed by passion and appetite, his mind kneels unto his body. In wider terms, the four false angels with which he pays her supposed musician's fees emblematise perverse values and corrupt justice. The inverted condition is reminiscent of that considered by Angelo in *Measure for Measure*: 'Thieves for their robbery have authority / When judges steal themselves' (II.ii.176–7). Moll's musical reproof of hypocrisy finds an early mark.

The canting scene, V.i, has not fared well in criticism mainly, I would suggest, because its place and function have been misunderstood. D. M. Holmes, for example, dismisses it as entirely extraneous.[82] Though it has dramatic weaknesses, the scene integrates with the play's imaginative scheme and makes an essential contribution to its design. Nor should its probable popular appeal be discounted: abundant pamphlet literature attests to the contemporary fascination with underworld exoticism. Indeed, the scene's undue length suggests that ministering to this itch got somewhat out of hand. The vision presented partakes of the same spirit seen in other dramatic representations, from Shakespeare's Autolycus to Brome's *A Jovial Crew* (1641),[83] but with a decidedly City rather than pastoral slant. Moll is at last shown in her element: a hierarchical organism of 'orders, offices, / Circuits, and circles' (V.i.330–1), subject to internally respected laws,[84] presented as a mirror image of the world at large. Within the commonwealth of rogues Moll improvises as a dispassionate arbiter who exercises fairness, resolution and mercy in the trial situations she encounters. Trapdoor's and Tearcat's disguises do not fool her, and she expeditiously sizes up the professional cutpurses and brings them to heel. In each instance her unchallenged handling demonstrates her authority – a reminder that she is not merely a fit instrument ''twixt lovers' hearts'.[85] At her insistence, the First Cutpurse promises to help recover Sir Thomas's stolen purse and plans to call a 'synagogue' – some sort of underworld tribunal – to bring this about.

As others have observed, the enlargement of the circle of Moll's acquaintance to include gentry and nobility reflects favourably on her; but it also lays the ground for developments in the following scene. The name, Sir Beauteous Ganymede, may additionally hint at an allegorical, mythic motif which prompts an understanding of Lord Noland, the play's highest authority, as a Jovian justice figure. Sir Thomas's and Lord Noland's questioning draws her into their sphere. Moll thus becomes linked to her upper-order counterpart in a hierarchical congruence of upper and lower worlds. Her companions' eager interest serves the transparent dramatic purpose of prompting Moll through her glossary of pedlars' cant; but her decoding of the underworld's baffling language aims also to dispel associated fear and distrust. At his re-introduction, Trapdoor performs in a minor way a choric function in decisively shifting allegiance from Sir Alexander to his mistress. If long-winded, the scene makes some reparation in robust, unsophisticated good humour.

In response to the informal cross-examination, Moll persuasively justifies the boldly individual and idiosyncratic ways which have already won sympathy and approval in action. The essential idea in her apology is familiar from Middleton's earlier work. It is not far, for example, from Prince Phoenix's disguised pursuit of crime,[86] or the Courtesan's laconic self-justification at the close of *A Trick to Catch the Old One*: 'She that knows sin, knows best how to hate sin.' Perhaps the most apposite articulation occurs in Middleton's dedication to *The Black Book* (1604):

> To all those that are truly virtuous, and can touch pitch and yet never defile themselves; read the mischievous lives and pernicious practices of villains, and yet be never the worse at the end of the book, but rather confirmed the more in their honest estates and the uprightness of their virtues.
>
> (Bullen, VIII, 5)

Moll has the courage of her convictions. Her position, moreover, is thoroughly unprejudiced. Free of vested interests and unconstrained by convention, she shows no reflex respect for rank, class or office. Nor has she any regard for popular opinion:

> Perhaps for my mad going, some reprove me;
> I please myself, and care not else who loves me.   (V.i.348–9)

Such freedom grants her awareness of elusive forms of falsehood and injustice which resonate throughout the play's actions and characters:

> How many are whores in small ruffs and still looks?
> How many chaste whose names fill slander's books?   (V.i.344–5)

Sir Alexander's continued absorption with those externals which Moll has just repudiated smartly jolts us back to his perverse world where other values reign:

> My son marry a thief! – That impudent girl
> Whom all the world stick their worst eyes upon!   (V.ii.1–2)

Given Sir Alexander's development not merely as the obtructor of marriage but chiefly as Moll's principal adversary and the representative of contrary values, the play steers away from a conventional dénouement: no revelation of suppressed nobility or of a previously undisclosed larger dowry eases Mary's acceptability as a daughter-in-law.[87] Sir Alexander must be reconciled to the marriage and its terms, not the reverse. To this end and to enable his inclusion in the final social order, a radical change must be effected. It is accomplished in a series of elliptical stages. Sir Alexander suffers a breakdown which has moral, emotional and mental dimensions. From the resulting condition of disarray, his vision is reframed to accord with the positive values of those around him. Thus the play offers a comic counterpart to the close of *Women Beware Women*,[88] while the strong theatrical element recalls similar resolutions in other Middleton plays; the masques, for example, in *Your Five Gallants* (which also features the administration of a moral purge), *No Wit, No Help Like a Woman's*, as well as *Women Beware Women*, and the concluding play-within-the-play in *A Mad World, My Masters*.[89] Each similarly side-steps probability in the form of a psychologically consistent conclusion in favour of a telescoped theatrical one. Forms of deception witnessed elsewhere in abstraction are here crowded together and made concrete as the contrived action approaches a surrealist anti-masque in which vicious torments serve to drive out fire with fire. For once, Sir Alexander is the unwitting principal actor in a drama of another's devising; the manipulator becomes the manipulated. Significantly different from that of the play's opening, the attendant group represents a more enlightened order. All take part in the scheme which precipitates the father's blessing and reconstructs his moral vision. Like him, the audience is not party to the plan which features Sir Guy Fitzallard as its guiding presence.[90] Neither Moll nor Sebastian, though prominent, are on stage long enough to perform this function; Goshawk and Greenwit, the reformed gallants, act as assistants, marshalling the stage traffic and at times the slant of the dialogue. Their asides (ll. 49 and 92) signal the element of contrivance[91] and give assurance that matters are under control.

The scene begins in turmoil. In desperate pursuit of Sebastian and Moll, Sir Alexander is impossibly drawn in opposite directions. The geographical division reflects inner torment: 'I'm drawn in pieces / Betwixt deceit and shame' (ll. 17–18). Stubborn adherence to false attitudes and values reduces his capacity for action to frustrated inertia, and he must as a preliminary stage stew in his own juices. Sir Guy's taunts and offer to stake his whole estate lure him into a wager which clearly sets out the issue: financial benefit against care for his son and acknowledgement of his son's independence. Disorientation is the initial strategy; Sir Guy bitterly chides him one moment, and makes a magnanimous offer the next. Indecision and loss of direction give way to complete confusion: 'How am I lost / In these distractions!' (V.ii.53–4). Moll aptly sounds the note of madness on her first entry (ll. 100–2). Early signs that a change is under way emerge in a moment of relative calm after the wager has been taken up. Sir Alex-

ander owns to wilfulness and shows an incipient appreciation of
Mary's worth:

> Cursed be the time I laid his first love barren,
> Wilfully barren, that before this hour
> Had sprung forth fruits of comfort and of honour;
> He loved a virtuous gentlewoman.   (V.ii.93–6)

Under the heady delusion that the marriage to Moll has been
thwarted, his thoughts range from their accustomed bearings and
veer toward their opposites, possessed of humanity and compassion:

> *Sir Alexander.* Whate'er she be, she has my blessing with her:
>   May they be rich and fruitful, and receive
>   Like comfort to their issue as I take
>   In them. 'Has pleased me now, marrying not this,
>   Through a whole world he could not choose amiss.
> *Greenwit.* Glad you're so penitent for your former sin, sir.
> *Goshawk.* Say he should take a wench with her smock-dowry:
>   No portion with her but her lips and arms?
> *Sir Alexander.* Why, who thrive better, sir? They have most blessing,
>   Though other have more wealth, and least repent:
>   Many that want most know the most content.
> *Greenwit.* Say he should marry a kind youthful sinner?
> *Sir Alexander.* Age will quench that; any offence but theft
>   And drunkenness, nothing but death can wipe away;
>   Their sins are green even when their heads are grey.   (V.ii.108–22)

Throughout this phase Sir Alexander vacillates between the conventional opposites, joy and grief, passions liable to overwhelm reason.[92]

The mock marriage intensifies his distraction and chastens him
still further. Before the unmasking, in a suggestive remark of un-
guarded candour, he even likens the bride to his first wife,
Sebastian's mother. But the shocking discovery of Moll makes plain
the gulf between the apparent and the real. No exultation in the
acquisition of Sir Guy's estate accompanies his winning of the wager,
so shaken is he by the collapse of his hopes. Bilked by appearances,
the old passions flare up again as he recoils for the last time into his
habitual refuge:

> O my reviving shame! – Is't I must live
> To be struck blind? Be it the work of sorrow
> Before age take't in hand!   (V.ii.142–4)

A final stage in the ordeal remains. Disallowed the false comfort of his
old haunts, Moll tents to the quick one of his greatest fears:

> You had no note before: an unmarked knight;
> Now all the town will take regard on you,

> And all your enemies fear you for my sake:
> You may pass where you list, through crowds most thick,
> And come off bravely with your purse unpicked!
> You do not know the benefits I bring with me:
> No cheat dares work upon you with thumb or knife,
> While you've a roaring girl to your son's wife!   (V.ii.154–61)

The brag incidentally gives a measure of Moll's authority: her power extends to corners unreached by his as a J.P.[93] On the practical level, in pretending to seek release from his 'rash bargain' (ll. 162–4), Sir Guy tests the wager's strength and forestalls any later attempt to renege on it.

Sight and blindness images are concentrated in the play's latter scenes and chart the progress of Sir Alexander's changing outlook. These too are keyed to the appearance/reality theme and the general concern with justice. In IV.i he stated in aside:

>   This were well, now,
> Were't to a man whose sorrows had blind eyes;
> But mine behold his follies and untruths
> With two clear glasses.   (IV.i.164–7)

There, though unknown to him, self-interest and distorted values had clouded judgement.[94] But late in the final scene, in reference first to Mary, and then to Moll, the image recurs, coupled with a humble plea for forgiveness. Sir Alexander acknowledges not only their worths but his own faults also:

> – [To Mary] Forgive me, worthy gentlewoman, 'twas my blindness:
> When I rejected thee, I saw thee not;
> Sorrow and wilful rashness grew like films
> Over the eyes of judgement, now so clear
> I see the brightness of thy worth appear.   (V.ii.191–5)

In granting Moll's exemplary honesty, he renounces the forces and forms of falsehood. Those passions which had formerly ruled him now seek pardon:

> To all which, shame and grief in me cry guilty.
> – [To Moll] Forgive me; now I cast the world's eyes from me,
> And look upon thee freely with mine own.   (V.ii.242–4)

The marriage provides the traditional celebration and emblem of new social harmony and reaffirms the importance of familial integrity: Sir Alexander's heart has been reached through the bond of kinship. Consolidated first at the private level, his change of outlook then receives a test at the public. Trapdoor takes as his cue to enter Sir Alexander's humble confession of wrong to Moll. Still under

Moll's influence, he fulfils his promise to 'maintain ... the old justice's plot to his face' (V.i.246–7). In widening the reference to the exercise of justice, his account concludes the pattern established in the foregoing action, and reintroduces an unresolved motif which has perhaps faded from view: the four hollow-hearted angels (the pun now sharply focused) from IV.i. Trapdoor reasserts his loyalty in asking Moll's pardon. The trial paradigm is once again invoked, this time with the tables turned. Publicly shamed, a repentant Sir Alexander sues for forgiveness from his intended victim. Trapdoor's disclosures before the assembled company do not stir him up to roughness. The lesson is one of humility, and the method comic inversion.[95] While acknowledging Sir Alexander's official position as J.P., Moll's reply – her final speech – phrased in her inimitable fashion, crystallises the values and attitudes for which she and her companions have been striving: generosity, justice and mercy. She eschews judgement, vengefulness and reprisal in a way which calls to mind the scriptural precept, 'Judge not that ye be not judged' (1 Cor. xi.31). Sir Alexander's offer in turn to 'thrice double' the value of the false angels by way of reparation, partakes of the new attitude of magnanimity.[96] The age of gold is transmuted to the golden age.

Other, more general features of the iconography of justice may lie behind the scene. Both dramatists reveal especially in their pageant and commemorative writing a familiarity with the conventional emblems and images. Envy is commonly opposed to justice in such representations – especially in Middleton[97] – and seems to inform a reference in Sir Alexander's apology to Moll: 'I see the most of many wrongs before thee / Cast from the jaws of Envy and her people' (V.ii.245–6). The etymological sense of the Latin word for envy, invidia (seeing with an evil eye), links with the blindness images. In a very broad perspective, the play may be seen as a vindication of truth against slander – the subject of *The Calumny* of Apelles in Lucian's account.[98] The name 'Alexander', which means 'guardian of man', may likewise figure in the pattern.[99] References to doomsday, the model of all judgements, at III.i.70 (in her rebuke of Laxton) and at V.ii.225 (after Moll has declared that her chastity and sense of mission are incompatible with marriage) have a special appropriateness also.

Among the play's puzzling features are the curious figures Lord Noland and Sir Beauteous Ganymede who appear only in V.i and ii. They may simply serve to demonstrate that Moll has noble friends, but if so, the element of self-mockery in the names seems out of place.[100] Nothing the two characters speak invites our critical laughter, so that if some mockery is intended, it is very light. A different interpretation, however conjectural, therefore deserves consideration. Method generally governs characters' names in both dramatists' work; Ganymede's mythic relation to Jove is possibly a significant clue in this instance. So understood, the two noble figures tie in with the masque-like elements of V.ii observed above and dimly adumbrate a rudimentary allegorical pattern underlying the circumstances especially of the last scene. The lord would thus give Olympian sanction to the marriage and, as a mortal 'Just-judging Jove',[101] oversee the final events of V.ii. – events which enlarge the reference to a kind of mirror for magistrates through the reassertion of positive values and the rehabilitation of an officer of justice.

Within the scheme of twin worlds proposed above, Moll's counterpart in the upper order would naturally be the highest figure of justice, the king. But the play's setting in contemporary London made fulfilment of such an ideal plan impossible because the representation on stage of a living monarch was forbidden. Subtle suggestions capable of being played up and rendered unmistakeable in performance may nevertheless be designed to associate Lord Noland with James I. Moll's odd greeting to Lord Noland, 'No tobacco, my lord?' (V.i.54), possibly intended as an allusion to *A Counterblaste to Tobacco* (1604),[102] is particularly suggestive. 'Noland' considered as a conflation of 'noll' (head) and 'land',[103] or possibly even 'know' and 'land',[104] would in this regard make better sense. Much of the detail I have sketched in is highly speculative, of course.[105] Seen in a different light, the significance of the two characters, Lord Noland and Sir Beauteous, may extend no further than the concluding pervasive lightness of tone.

At the end the forces represented by Sir Davy, Sir Adam and Laxton have been pushed from view by positive elements. But Sir Alexander's final speech does not conclude the play; the Epilogue takes up again the question of the audience's judgement and completes a modulation to the real world begun in Moll's deference to Sir Alexander's judicial authority, in the promise that Moll Frith, the real Roaring Girl, will appear a few days hence. The various levels of illusion – theatrical and figurative – are thus intertwined with the realities of life outside the theatre.

The Subplots

The subplots develop the thematic interests of the main plot in a complementary manner. Deception, pretence and hypocrisy figure prominently and co-ordinate with other aspects of the illusion/reality theme. Laxton, Goshawk and Greenwit, for example, give false initial impressions.[106] Laxton's smug disdain for all women (I.ii.155–6) may prefigure the phlegmatic dissimulation with which he panders to Mistress Gallipot's vanity while secretly despising her and holding her class in contempt (II.i.89–90 and III.i.13–15), but it jars with his attempted seduction of Moll. A variation on the Knight in *The Phoenix* who preys on the Jeweller's Wife,[107] Laxton dangles the promise of sexual pleasure before his benefactress but refuses to deliver the goods. He even derives perverse delight from her frustration (II.i.132–45). Word-plays on his name (lack-stone) reveal his double nature. He has squandered his patrimony (II.i.70–1, III.i.50–1) and, lacking testicles (I.ii.55–7), he is impotent. His deficiency resonates ironically with much animal imagery, as in the sparring with Moll over stallions and jades (II.i.268ff.) and, later, in their confrontation at III.i.64–6. By IV.ii his erstwhile victim, Mistress Gallipot, significantly terms him a 'lame gelding'. The collapse of all his ventures co-ordinates materially with his sexual inadequacy.

More conventionally sparked by straightforward lust, Goshawk takes perverse pride in a special talent for falsehood: 'a gift of treachery ... to betray my friend when he puts most trust in me' (II.i.29–30). But the gallant does not fool Openwork, who engineers a counterplot to test Goshawk's friendship and to dispel his wife's jealous fits. As in *Measure for Measure*, 'the doubleness of the benefit defends the deceit from reproof'. Masks provided by Goshawk in IV.ii sharpen the focus on deception; and Openwork's lecture on them at ll. 116–31 signals imminent figurative and literal expansions. Another form of illusion brings about Goshawk's own unmasking. The Openworks stage a scene of domestic friction which humbles the unwitting gallant to repentance. Mistress Openwork, purged of jealousy, voices a new appreciation of her spouse (l. 220). For his part, first-hand experience of what he terms the 'blemish [which] grows in nature' prompts Openwork to momentary despair:

> What's this whole world but a gilt rotten pill?
> For at the heart lies the old core still.
> I'll tell you, Master Goshawk, ay, in your eye
> I have seen wanton fire; and then to try
> The soundness of my judgement, I told you
> I kept a whore, made you believe 'twas true,
> Only to feel how your pulse beat, but find
> The world can hardly yield a perfect friend. (IV.ii.221–8)

But despite the brush with human frailty, he maintains a forgiving attitude and generously insists on re-laying the foundations of friendship. His test turns the threat to his own household to its benefit.

As in other parts of the play, patterns of imagery betray unhealthy attitudes and ailing relationships. Sexual reference is regularly tied to animal or business imagery and vice versa. Bawdy puns and word-plays run thick and fast through the gallants' shop-scene repartee to set a general tone. In the second citizen scene, III.ii, especially from the entrance of the Gallipots' guests and later Laxton, sexual in-nuendo with an animal bias abounds. In IV.ii, however, the wives push the gallants uncomfortably on the defensive. Hunting and fish-ing terms with the regular sexual loading stud the dialogue (ll. 82ff.); but now that the wives are no longer predisposed to romantic liaisons, the predators shrink to 'idle, simple things' – conies, about to be 'cony-catched' in the women's purse-nets. Imagery formerly at the gallants' command is thus turned against them.[108]

Mistress Openwork's initial street cries of II.i coin the bartering idiom current in the citizen intrigues. An association between sexu-ality and commerce characterises various transactions. Mistress Gallipot's improvised precontract tale prompts her husband to a business solution (III.ii.141)[109] in which personal worth and money are confused. Gallipot stretches the equation further by unflatter-ingly reifying his wife (ll. 246, 247, 250–1). Finally, as if to seal a satisfactory bargain, he insists that Laxton join him in a toast. The jaded gallant cynically congratulates himself on his serpent's role in inciting Mistress Gallipot to deception.

'Ne'er soundly tried', Prudence Gallipot and Rosamond Open-work are among those who, on the face of it, 'would down, and there's nobody will push 'em'. As elsewhere, a trial construction which has implications for all participants underlies their exploits. Citizen comedy virtually guaranteed the preservation of wifely chastity,[110] and vestiges of the convention possibly inform the particular circum-stances which stand in the way of actual infidelity and so exonerate the women of associated consequences. But the wives' self-motivated change of heart denoting a victory of mind over baser impulses marks a distinct departure. That change of heart is chiefly brought about, moreover, by their condemnation of the gallants' double-dealing. Early disenchantment with the lovers displaces the emphasis of the final citizen scene from a contrivance designed to bring the women back into the fold, to a moral lesson keyed to the dominant thematic interests.

While the conclusion of the Openwork/Goshawk action is clear, that of the Gallipot/Laxton plot is less so. Difficulties centre on the Laxton of the final moments of IV.ii. His speeches after the collapse of his extortionary ruse (ll. 303ff.), if taken at face value, cannot readily be reconciled with the character of the previous action. The problem can be dismissed as untidiness or confusion in the writing, but the play and the character are perhaps better served by a reading which sees Laxton as a wily escape artist when cornered by the citizens.

Like the Openworks' staged lesson, Laxton's little drama resonates with wider thematic concerns, and his abuse of a legal process instances yet another form of contempt for the operation of justice. In pursuit of more cash Laxton develops Mistress Gallipot's precontract invention, but overreaches himself and, like the other schemers, is finally hoist with his own petard. Greenwit's disguise disintegrates exposing the imposture, and Mistress Gallipot, who has more to answer for than her neighbour, strives to follow suit and make a clean breast of it. When she fails to dispel her husband's suspicion, however, Laxton seizes the opportunity to get himself off the hook. His account neatly leaves his own honour untarnished while allaying Gallipot's shame. It bears little relation to the circumstances as we know them, but offers just what the injured husband wants to hear. References to men's slanders and to one woman braving all men recall the reprobate's bout with Moll and suggest an undercurrent of cowardly reprisal – an impulse not beneath him. Both stories omit awkward details liable to misunderstanding or damaging to the speaker.[111] Laxton's prevarication wins the day, however; he thus escapes by way of his own fiction. Gallipot's credit of his cool rhetoric transforms his wife to the traditional model of silence.[112] If she draws a moral from her experience, she may recognise that she has strayed and appreciate now the perils of deception. Modern attitudes may question the justice of this conclusion and argue that she is hard done by, but they are wide of the seventeenth-century perspective. While liable to censure for high-handedness and blinkered vision, Gallipot is not, after all, the culpable party and has inflicted no hurt. And although we have no reason to expect a miracle which entirely reforms his character, he asserts himself in his last speeches as he has not before. Like Openwork, he adopts a forgiving and generous disposition in hosting a celebratory feast. A festive frame of mind does not resolve all issues, but it does hint at an improved vision. He possibly better understands 'how to handle a woman in her kind', and may have learned the danger of judging exclusively by his entrepreneurial lights. The family has been preserved and household hierarchy restored. Game imagery and a general mood of levity take the edge off the situation and reinstate a comic tone. In its final moments, the play aims to depict an integrated, healthy society. An inappropriate and jarring element of irony intrudes if the shopkeepers' mute presence is seen as merely perfunctory. Laxton's conspicuous absence from the concluding festivities to which the reformed gallants contribute marks his continued occupation of morally irresponsible territory.[113] He gives no sign of reclamation and will continue to prey on society. Thus his selfish and self-reliant wit and independence are set against Moll's justice and generosity. Although his cynicism is banished from the final act, he remains the play's most disturbing character.

6. PRODUCTIONS

The Original Staging

Recent discussions of the First Fortune Theatre (1600–21) have focused on the building contract, interpreting it cautiously to define dimensions and features,[114] but indications of stage practice drawn from Fortune plays are also helpful. The fire which destroyed the theatre in 1621[115] possibly explains the survival of only a handful of plays known to have been performed there: *The Honest Whore* (certainly Part I[116] (1604), and probably Part II (1604–5)), *The Whore of Babylon*[117] (1606–7), *The Roaring Girl* – all of which Dekker was involved in – and Samuel Rowley's *When You See Me, You Know Me* (1603–5).[118]

Although the manuscript behind the printed text of *The Roaring Girl* shows little sign of playhouse origin, Sir Alexander's impressionistic description of the interior of the theatre (I.ii.14–32) suggests that the dramatists had the Fortune specifically in mind in writing the play.[119] Moll Cutpurse's documented connection with the theatre and a probable topical reference (III.iii.207–9) lend additional support. Though for the most part undemanding in staging, the play has a number of points of dramaturgical interest. Chief among them is II.i, which, unique in the group of Fortune plays, calls for three shops. Jonson's *Bartholomew Fair* incorporates a multiple-booth setting for which canvas-covered wooden frames were probably used. R. B. Parker speculates that Ursula's pig booth and Leatherhead's puppet theatre were placed free-standing, forward of the two main stage entrances of the Hope Theatre to allow entrances from behind.[120] Although such properties cannot be ruled out in *The*

Roaring Girl, practical difficulties render them an unlikely solution. The booths of *Bartholomew Fair* remain on stage throughout, but the three shops of the present play are required for one scene only, and unless they were rather more simply represented, their setting up and dismantling would disrupt the action.[121]

Although the Fortune contract does not specify the number of tiring-house doors or openings, evidence from plays acted there suggests that three openings were a feature of the stage.[122] Accordingly, two main possibilities may be considered: use of the three doors to represent the shops individually, and use of a central discovery-space for all three. Three shops opening in a 'rank', as specified in the initial stage direction, suggests a close grouping. A discovery-space would probably be too narrow, however, for even if it exceeded dimensions proposed for the Globe or Blackfriars,[123] a width of less than three feet for each shop would be too cramped for two or more actors to manoeuvre in, as the scene requires.

The absence of interaction or dialogue between one shop and another – a condition not likely to prevail if squeezed close together – is also significant. Further, though the dialogue may not have a precise relation to the stage action, Moll's eight lines to take her from the tobacco shop to the middle shop, where Jack Dapper samples feathers, before passing over to the Openworks implies some space between them. Mistress Openwork's admonition at II.i.235–6 ('I warn ye my house and shop.') suggests the common arrangement of house with shop-front and counter at street level, as described by J. A. Gotch:[124]

> From the front wall of the house there often projected on the level of the first floor a sloping tiled ledge, called a penthouse; on the ground beneath there stood a stall, which served as a shop-counter when the householder was engaged in retail trade. . . . the buildings were contiguous.

The effect could have been conveyed by the tiring-house façade with each of the three openings used for a shop.[125] Such an arrangement has additional advantages: the scene changes could be managed quickly and each shop could provide sufficient space for movement as well as satisfy the other requirements of the scene.

The main difficulty arises from the approaches of other characters within the scene since the normal entrances would be unavailable. An appealing solution to the problem which involves use of the yard may perhaps be entertained, though in view of controversy over interpretation of the evidence, very tentatively. Allardyce Nicoll has argued that entrances were occasionally made from the side of the tiring-

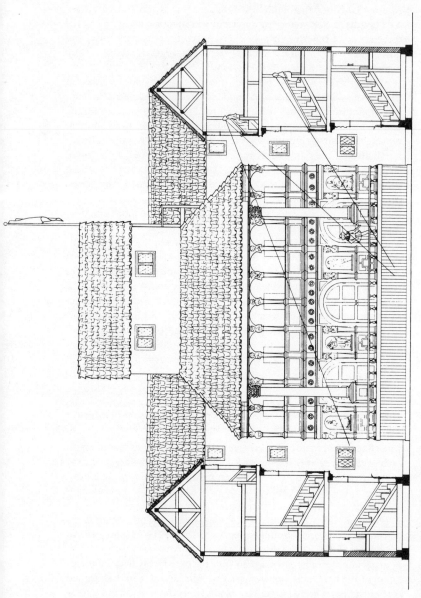

Reconstructions of the Fortune Theatre

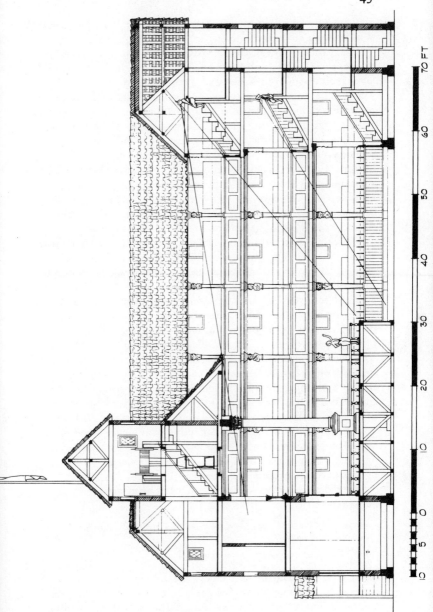

house through the yard by way of the 'ingressus' pictured in the De Witt drawing of the Swan, citing in support III.i (a shop scene) of *The Fair Maid of the Exchange*.[126] According to Nicoll's reading, the two gallants Gardiner and Bennet make their entry 'at yard level' and 'after their first few lines they walk across, enter the square and see Phillis in her shop'. Some aspects of *The Fair Maid* scene appear to resonate with the shop scene of *The Roaring Girl* and may indicate a similar approach on the part of Laxton, Goshawk and Greenwit. Laxton's 'Yonder's the shop' (l. 5), repeated by Goshawk at ll. 30–1, suggests distance, and the gallants' first exchange of about eighteen lines is clearly intended to be out of earshot of the shopkeepers. Left alone and not yet associated with any shop, Goshawk wishes to remain unseen by Openwork (ll. 39–40), perhaps making use of one of the stage pillars. Mistress Openwork's initial street cry establishes the locale, and may be general or directed at the gallants.

While the shops localise the action upstage, the downstage area remains neutral. The gallants' initial dialogue and the extended asides in which several characters treat the audience as confidant, could be delivered from here, away from the shops. Moll could likewise confront the Fellow with a long rapier in this area, and the duologues between her and Laxton, and later Trapdoor, if played in the neutral zone would be suitably remote from the upstage action.

Entrances and exits from the yard by Jack and Gull, the Fellow and Trapdoor would extend the play's realism and co-ordinate also with thematic interests. Movement through the audience would help to reinforce the implied mirror image. The 1612 Consistory Court record [127] documents Moll's resort to 'play howses there to see plaies & pryses', so her appearance at the Fortune is unlikely to have been an isolated instance. The real Moll may frequently have stood or sat among the audience or on the stage, and an entry from the yard by her dramatic counterpart would carry special significance in literally bridging everyday reality and theatrical illusion.

Other details which assist the play's realism appear in stage directions:

> *Enter ... NEATFOOT ... with a napkin on his shoulder and a trencher in his hand, as from table.*   (I.i.0.1–3)

> *Enter MISTRESS GALLIPOT as from supper ...*   (III.ii.0.1)

The characters do not merely come to life the moment they reach the stage, but create the impression of an ongoing, behind-the-scenes existence. The tolling of the bell towards the close of II.i signals an end to trade, and Master Tiltyard calls the citizens to shut up their shops: this neatly integrates the clearing of the stage with the scene's concluding action. Two further urgings to the women (ll. 404 and 410), if in reference to the dismantling of the shops and removal of properties, suggest that the business takes some time. Off for a meal or for sport, the movement of those on stage might again blur reality and illusion if the exit in some way involves a brush with the spectators.

Though movements to and from the stage via the yard have great appeal in the present instance, incontestable evidence that the yard was used for such purposes, apart from such specialised cases as Beaumont's *The Knight of the Burning Pestle*, has yet to be advanced. The proposed staging presumes that the doors localised early in the scene by the three shops remain so throughout, and is in this regard possibly influenced by modern practice and experience. In an alternative plan not bound by such a convention, the shops as they were being set up at the outset may have been associated with specific doors, but once this action was completed, the doors would again be available for entrances and exits by others. The shops, like the *Bartholomew Fair* booths mentioned above, would be placed far enough forward of the doors to allow entrances from behind, and might consist of no more than a table with various appropriate and necessary hand properties. Soon after entering through a stage door, the gallants would probably move to a downstage position and then continue as in the version considered above. Later exits and entrances could make use of the doors as required since they would be relieved of any particular association with the shops until the end of the scene.[128]

The location of I.ii is established chiefly by Sir Alexander's speech describing the interior of the Fortune Theatre as if it were his parlour. The impression is later followed up by the appearance of servants who bring on stage (and presumably remove at the end) chairs, stools and cushions for his guests. IV.i is likewise an interior scene which employs stage properties to assist the effect, although no stage directions indicate how or when they are brought on stage. Moll's exit with Trapdoor in the preceding scene and Trapdoor's entry three lines later provides a clue, however. The close proximity of exit and entrance may denote an interval between Acts III and IV, during which properties could have been set: a court-cupboard and a viol, presumably hung from the tiring-house façade (a conventional manner of indicating an interior), are required in the scene.[129]

The ambush of III.iii presents problems akin to those of II.i. One of the stage doors presumably represents the tavern out of which Jack sallies (the centre door is the most likely since the two others are required earlier). Curtalax and Hanger's whistlings and other signals suggest that they station themselves at a distance from each other on either side of the 'tavern' door, or possibly on opposite sides of the stage, making use of the pillars. The main difficulty concerns the entrance of Moll and Trapdoor and their subsequent restraining of the catchpoles. Entry from the same tavern as Jack seems unlikely, and the two other doors have been connected with Sir Alexander's faction. A solution which involves use of the yard would give special point to their jokes about lawyers since Inns-of-Court men are known to have been in regular attendance at the theatres.[130] But, as in the foregoing discussion, the presumption that doors retain their specific localisations through a scene such as this may be challenged. In an arrangement guided by looser staging conventions Moll and Trapdoor might enter by a door associated earlier with Sir Alexander and Sir Adam, or Sir Davy.

In any case, the two rescuers would probably spy the ambush from the downstage neutral area and proceed to steal behind the sergeant and his yeoman. Curtalax and Hanger apparently withhold springing their trap until Jack and Gull are well clear of refuge in the tavern – arrests were traditionally made from the rear; 'Honest sergeant', sung out by Moll (l. 210), would then take Curtalax by surprise just as he is about to strike. Though not entirely dependent on this staging, such an explanation of the action obviates the need to emend at l. 210.

Revivals[131]

Unless a reference to *The Roaring Girl, or The Catchpole* in Thomas Jordan's *The Walks of Islington and Hogsdon* (1641) is an allusion to a recent performance of the play,[132] no production is on record between 1611 and April 1951, when it was mounted by the Brattle Theatre Company in Cambridge, Mass. Character omissions in the cast list give clues to the nature of the adaptation.[133] Several small roles were cut: Sir Adam Appleton, Master Tiltyard, Gull and the Tailor; and, with Goshawk deleted, the citizen action apparently focused almost exclusively on the Gallipots. The final act seems to have been much reworked: Sir Guy Fitzallard, Sir Thomas Long, Sir Beauteous Ganymede, Lord Noland and the Cutpurses were omitted. Settings and costumes were Restoration or eighteenth-century – a circumstance which significantly affected Laxton at least, who is described as a 'foppish lover' and an 'amorous dandy' in criticisms.[134] This treatment suggests also that the play was presented mainly as a kind of period piece. The action was compressed into two locations: 'a room in Sir Alexander Wengrave's House' and 'The New Exchange'. In line with the Brattle Company policy, the leading role was played by a performer of established status, in this case an actress with a reputation as a musical-comedy comedienne, Nancy Walker.[135] Several critics commented on her small stature as a handicap in the role, but responded favourably to her broad comic style, 'her over-all droll comic manner' and 'swaggering bravado'.[136] The effect was described by the *Boston Traveler* reviewer as 'a sort of combination of Groucho Marx and Mae West'. Several songs were added, presumably to give rein to Miss Walker's musical-comedy expertise. The performance of Trapdoor by Jerome Kilty won commendations from all critics, suggesting that the role achieved a special prominence; the cast was otherwise criticised by some for 'pushing too hard'. Jack Dapper's rescue in III.iii occasioned a 'Keystone Kops' chase sequence, a production highlight. Most reviewers referred to the play as a farce, suggesting that the approach taken stressed action and broad physical comedy.

A version of the play adapted for radio was broadcast in the B.B.C. Third Programme on 15 and 17 January and 9 June 1956.[137] The project was directed by R. D. Smith. Several contemporary songs were added to those in the play, all with music composed and arranged by Edward Williams. A playing time of just over ninety minutes points to considerable condensation; but despite surgery, the adaptation aimed to preserve the play's structure and retain all of its actions; all named speaking characters are represented except Greenwit. An interesting change was the replacement of the Fellow of II.i by Neatfoot. A chorus introduced the play with a passage from Middleton's Epistle. J. C. Trewin in *The Listener* (19 January 1956) praised Fay Compton's 'ebullient Mad Moll' and pronounced the Roaring Girl 'a flashing centre for a lively Jacobean farce'. *The Times*'s critic, very appreciative of the play and the 'vigorous production', remarked that Miss Compton 'roared, if not as gently as any sucking dove, with a very likeable lustiness' (16 January 1956).

In 1970 the Dundee Repertory Company staged the play under the direction of Keith Darvill, 18 June to 4 July. Again character omissions hint at the nature of the adaptation: Sir Adam and the Tiltyards were removed from the early action (one reviewer refers to a feather-seller, however, which suggests a conflation of roles), and Sir Thomas, Sir Beauteous, Lord Noland and the Cutpurses were cut from Act V. Settings and costumes were Jacobean. *The Journal*'s critic commented, 'In a scene-changing marathon, down from the ceiling in rapid succession came trees, archways, shops, bedrooms, pubs and market crosses' (20 June 1970). A playing time of over three hours including a fifteen-minute interval suggests that the pruning was not severe (several reviewers wished for a shorter evening). Moll appears to have been treated as a colourful historical curiosity; programme notes included brief diverting passages from *The Life and Death of Mrs. Mary Frith* (1662) and an excerpt from John Chamberlain's account of Moll's penance at Paul's Cross in 1612, presumably to suggest a perspective from which to view the character. The director introduced some dialogue of his own into the text; and the final note struck was of Moll's voice, as though from the grave, intoning a couplet from the close of *The Life and Death*, 'This life I lived in man's disguise; / He best laments me that in laughter cries.'[138] Alan Dunsmore in *The Journal* complained that this production and the play had little to say to a modern audience. Other critics were more favourably disposed towards both play and performance.[139] Laura Graham brought an 'amazonian figure and stentorian tones' to the role of Moll; but her performance was not regarded unanimously as successful. Several actors won plaudits from different reviewers: Barrie Rutter as Sebastian, Martin Matthews as Laxton, and David Hargreaves as Trapdoor.

Three productions associated with universities followed these professional treatments. Their tone marks a watershed in attitudes towards the play and its heroine. The least conventional of productions was an all-women adaptation performed at the Durham Studio Theatre, University of California, Berkeley Campus, 24–6 May 1979.[140] Its subtitle, 'A Feminist Infiltration', proclaims the approach; the play was freely adapted to the interests of the director, Sue-Ellen Case. The female cast aimed to reverse the ironies and suggestion of the Jacobean all-male convention. Other aspects were also affected: Mary Fitzallard was played by a black actress wearing a blonde wig. Issues touched off by the play during the rehearsal period found voice in a counter-play written by the director set in a theatre dressing-room which in production shared the stage with *The Roaring Girl*, at times competing with it for attention. Pressures generated in the dressing-room caused the main play to fall apart as revolutionary and/or feminist sentiments from behind the scenes prevailed. After the release of tensions in this upheaval, a decision was taken to resume the play, and the final scene of *The Roaring Girl* was performed 'straight', to use the director's word. A host of cuts and omissions gave Moll special prominence; most of the subsidiary action was removed.[141]

In late August 1980 a version of the play was presented at the Edinburgh Festival by a university group, The Cambridge Mummers, directed by Brigid Larmour.[142] The play was heavily cut and sought to make Moll its clear centre: the second and third citizen scenes were excised and much of the dialogue relating to subsequent action, except where it related to her, deleted from II.i. This production did, however, retain Lord Noland and Sir Beauteous (Sir Thomas was cut and his remaining lines divided between these two characters). No reconciliation was permitted between Sir Alexander and Sebastian, and the action concluded on a sombre note, though followed by Moll's delivery of the Epilogue. Response to both the production and the play was enthusiastic, reserving special warmth for Annabel Arden's Moll.[143] John Barber remarked, 'what delights capacity audiences ... is a casual, a thoroughly-relaxed vitality combined with an inborn sense of mischief' (*Daily Telegraph*, 26 August 1980). Several critics commented on a feminist slant in this production – a slant assisted by the cutting.[144]

Royal Holloway College, University of London, staged the play in March 1982. To highlight feminist matters, this production, directed by Andy Piasecki, took an ironic approach calculated to undercut practically all character relationships through emphasis on mercenary interests of various kinds.[145] Even Sebastian's 'use' of Moll to assist his designs fell within this scheme. Sir Beauteous, Sir Thomas and Lord Noland were cut: Jack Dapper took over most of Lord Noland's lines in what remained of a pared-down V.i (most of the canting was deleted); and Sir Davy Dapper was brought back to perform the duties of Lord Noland in V.ii, so that the social group at the end differed little from that at the beginning. The women generally fared poorly in the depicted man's world.

The most important revival to date was that by the Royal Shakespeare Company in 1983; it was undoubtedly the most lavish. *The Roaring Girl* was paired in a pattern of alternation with *The Taming of the Shrew* to make contrasting points about women in society. The pairing suggests some of the production's emphases. Several actors were cast in both plays in an attempt to underline specific elements.[146] The text was considerably reworked. Some scenes were juggled around in addition to cutting, rewriting and other adaptation. The setting, a massive collection of edifices, with platforms and interiors visible through windows, pressed together at random angles, featured the heads of Elizabeth I (surmounting the central structure), and James I (on top of the stage-right roof). Elizabeth's was in the early stages of decay, while James's was still under construction. The setting thus sought to place the play in the historical context of a period experiencing great change. On stage left was a large clockwork mechanism with large gears and races which aimed to represent the interests and workings of commerce. Although costuming and setting were Jacobean, crucial parts of the play were interpreted according to a specifically modern perspective. The handling of the final scene, for example, attempted to deal with Sir Alexander in accordance with modern psychology: Trapdoor's final revelations produced a hushed atmosphere of shame, such that Sebastian on his exit with Mary shunned his father's extended hand. Reconciliation which had begun was shattered at this point. Among other interests which director Barry Kyle wished to stress was the disruption within the class system caused by Jacobean 'profiteering and self-interest'.[147] Moll accordingly had a thick Cockney twang and in this as in other ways stood apart from most of the other characters. She was presented as a woman ahead of her time: her tightly fitted costume, for example, strayed widely from the Jacobean style adopted for the production as a whole, and the frizzy wig (a change from the Stratford trial run in January 1983) gave a distinctly modern cast to the character, vaguely reminiscent of the current trend of 'punk' styles. The most important textual changes involved reversing the order of III.i and III.ii, which significantly altered the nature of Laxton's involvement with the Gallipots and how Laxton's approach to Moll is understood,[148] and the splitting up of IV.ii and V.i to produce a dove-tailed arrangement of four scenes. The resulting shift in rhythm and texture was apparently the guiding spirit of the changes. Critical response was mixed and divided essentially along lines of those sympathetic to the play and the value of a revival, and those left cold by both play and production. Helen Mirren's spirited, tough-minded Moll caught the imagination of most reviewers and was widely, if not universally, praised. Jonathan Hyde's Laxton projected a cool sinister quality which effectively complemented the character's cynicism. David Troughton was cast against type as Sebastian, apparently to down-play conventional romantic appeal. As a corollary, the scenes with Mary were played with considerable reserve. David Waller contrived to make Sir Alexander come to life as a believable human being, introducing a range of idiosyncratic, often amusing, elements into his performance to give the role dimension. The production aimed to capture the sprawl of Jacobean London and in this prompted inevitable comparisons (usually disappointed) with Dickensian London as seen in the recent, hugely successful R.S.C. production of *Nicholas Nickleby*. Interest for feminists was highlighted, occasionally by cutting ('As if a husband stood in awe on's wife', III.i.138, was deleted, for example), at other times through emphasis in performance. This spilled over into the Gallipot action which concluded on a sour note for Mistress Gallipot.

In the most recent stagings the tide of issues related to the role and position of women in society has importantly influenced treatment. The play has been shaped by a combination of cutting and some form of adaptation to reflect, in varying degrees, current concerns. As a vehicle for such concerns the play has undoubtedly been given new life; but, although the authors might sympathise with the new perspective, they would probably not recognise the play in its modern trappings as their own. Be that as it may, future productions are likely to pursue similar interests. Whatever our minds on the matter, we may be thankful that *The Roaring Girl* has at last found 'gallery-room at the playhouse'.

---

1 A facsimile of the title-page appears on p. 71.

2 This copy, marked up with spelling and punctuation alterations, footnote numbers, and casting-off signals was clearly the copy-text for Reed's edition, but it is listed in neither the auction catalogue of his library, *Bibliotheca Reediana* (1807), nor that of George Steevens's, *Bibliotheca Steevensiana* (1800). See R. C. Bald, 'Sir William Berkeley's *The Lost Lady*', *The Library*, 4th ser., XVII (1937), 423. Prior to Folger's acquisition, the copy was in the possession of Edwin Thomas Truman.

3 The present account is based on the work of a number of investigators, as follows; I have tried to summarize the findings of these studies rather than set out the fine points of evidence and conflicting arguments in detail: F. T. Bowers, 'Thomas Dekker: Two Textual Notes', *The Library*, 4th ser., XVIII (1937), 338–40; J. G. McManaway, 'Thomas Dekker: Further Textual Notes', *The Library*, 4th ser., XIX (1938), 176–9; F. T. Bowers, 'Notes on Running-titles as Bibliographical Evidence', *The Library*, 4th ser., XIX (1938), 315–38; G. R. Price, 'The Manuscript and the Quarto of *The Roaring Girl*', *The Library*, 5th ser., XI (1956), 180–6; Textual Introduction in *The Dramatic Works of Thomas Dekker*, ed. F. Bowers, (Cambridge, 1953–61), III (rev. 1966), 3–9; three

studies by the present editor, 'The Date of *The Roaring Girl*', *R.E.S.*, new ser., XXVIII (1977), 18–31; 'Some Textual Notes on *The Roaring Girl*', *The Library*, 5th ser., XXXII (1977), 333–43; and '*The Roaring Girl*: New Readings and Further Notes', *S.B.*, XXXVII (1984), 159–70.

4 Price, loc. cit., p. 180.

5 Cf. Peter W. M. Blayney, *The Texts of* King Lear *and their Origins*, I (Cambridge, 1982), 216.

6 '*The Roaring Girl:* New Readings and Further Notes'.

7 D. J. Lake, *The Canon of Thomas Middleton's Plays* (Cambridge, 1975), p. 54; see also Band 2 (e).

8 *Dekker*, pp. 5–7.

9 Compositor designations are taken from Price ('The Manuscript and the Quarto'); see also this editor's '*The Roaring Girl:* New Readings and Further Notes'.

10 Blayney (*The Texts of* King Lear, I, 77) has observed a similar phenomenon in other Okes books, but refrained from concluding that concurrent work necessarily accompanied single-skeleton printing.

11 Lake, p. 101, n. 1.

12 Where the corrected state of Q needs to be distinguished from the uncorrected, the two are designated respectively, Qc and Qu.

13 See, for example, IV.i.130–46.

14 *The Canon of Thomas Middleton's Plays*, pp. 52–6, and *Studies in Attribution: Middleton and Shakespeare* (Salzburg, 1979), pp. 95–101, respectively. Jackson also cites the approach and main statistics of Matthew Baird's Oxford B.Litt. thesis (1928).

15 Known joint works include *Magnificent Entertainment* (1604), *1 Honest Whore* (1604); *Blurt, Master Constable*, *Family of Love*, as well as other plays and prose works, have also been proposed.

16 For consistency I have normalised Q forms in citations. In addition to those noted, I have drawn on the following investigations: G. R. Price, 'The Shares of Middleton and Dekker in a Collaborated Play', *Papers of the Michigan Academy of Science, Arts, and Letters*, XXX (1944), 601–15, R. H. Barker, *Thomas Middleton* (1958), pp. 170–6, G. R. Price, 'The Authorship and Bibliography of *The Revenger's Tragedy*', *The Library*, 5th ser., XV (1960), 262–77, P. B. Murray, *A Study of Cyril Tourneur* (Philadelphia, 1964), E. D. Pendry (ed.), *Thomas Dekker: Selected Prose Writings* (1967), p. 20.

17 Jackson, p. 99.

18 Lake (Band 1 (f)) lists only one occurrence in Dekker; the form varies in *R.G.*: 'you'r', 'you're', 'your'.

19 As in Middleton's Epistle, l. 24; see R. H. Barker, 'The Authorship of *The Second Maiden's Tragedy* and *The Revenger's Tragedy*', *Shakespeare Association Bulletin*, XX (1945), 55.

20 'The Shares of Fletcher and his Collaborators in the Beaumont and Fletcher Canon (V)', *S.B.*, XIII (1960), 91.

21 Similar images occur in *Michaelmas Term* (I.i.137, 155–7, and II.iii.223–5), and in *Fair Quarrel* (II.i.188–9, III.ii.123), though R. V. Holdsworth considers the latter instances to be in Rowley passages (New Mermaid edition (1974), p. xx); cf. G. R. Price's Regents Renaissance Drama edition (Lincoln, Nebr., 1976), p. xvi. Evidence which suggests

that Middleton and Rowley worked more or less independently on parts of individual scenes has potential significance for *The Roaring Girl*.

22 Lake (p. 61, n. 1, and Band 1 (i)) notes the occurrence of this trait unique to Middleton here and at I.ii.234 and III.i.124, but omits it from his tabulations.

23 The word is not used in the sense common in Middleton in any of the citations listed in V. A. Small, R. P. Corballis, J. M. Harding, *A Concordance to the Dramatic Works of Thomas Dekker* (Salzburg, 1984).

24 Possibly the moralising tone of ll. 121–4 more strongly supports Dekker. Bawdy songs occur in both dramatists' other work, e.g. *Chaste Maid*, IV.i.152–77 (Revels ed.), and the Dekker ballad reprinted in F. D. Hoeniger, 'Thomas Dekker, the Restoration of St Paul's, and J.P. Collier, Forger', *Renaissance News*, XVI (1963), 193–4.

25 'The Shares of Middleton and Dekker in a Collaborated Play', p. 611.

26 Small, *et al.*, *Concordance*, list two mistaken instances of 'i' the'.

27 *Introductions*, III, 12–13.

28 *The Profession of Dramatist in Shakespeare's Time 1590–1642* (Princeton, 1971), p. 232.

29 The following summarises material presented in this editor's 'The Date of *The Roaring Girl*', *R.E.S.*, new ser., XXVIII (1977), 18–31.

30 The *Correction Book* entry was first brought to light by F. W. X. Fincham in *Transactions of the Royal Historical Society*, 4th ser., IV (1921), 111–13, but was misdated 1605; the incorrect date was then reproduced by E. K. Chambers in 'Elizabethan Stage Gleanings', *R.E.S.*, I (1925), 77–8.

31 If any connection exists between Sir Beauteous Ganymede and Robert Carr, Carr's creation as Viscount of Rochester on 25 March 1611 may figure in the pattern of topical dates also.

32 'The Sources of Middleton's City Comedies', *J.E.G.P.*, XXXIII (1934), 373.

33 *Letters*, ed. N. E. McClure (Philadelphia, 1939), I, 334 (quoted in this editor's 'The Date of *The Roaring Girl*', *R.E.S.*, new ser., XXVIII (1977), 24).

34 In addition to others which have come to light is a citation in the Middlesex Gaol Delivery Register for 19 and 20 Feb. 1617 under 'Came and committed because indicted', reproduced in *Calendar to the Sessions Records*, new ser., IV, ed. William Le Hardy (1941), p. 107. Mary Frith is here linked with John Cummins of Old Street, a thief soon to be executed, whose name appears elsewhere in the Sessions Records. Mary's examination has unfortunately been lost.

35 Margaret Dowling, 'A Note on Moll Cutpurse – "The Roaring Girl"', *R.E.S.*, X (1934), 67–71.

36 See 'The Date of *The Roaring Girl*', p. 28, n. 1.

37 The life expectancy of a whore in the 17th century was very short indeed, so it is unlikely that she engaged in prostitution. She is most frequently cited as a receiver of stolen goods.

38 In addition to the references cited, various accounts of Mary Frith exist, e.g. Capt. Alexander Smith, *A Complete History of the Lives and Robberies of the Most Notorious Highwaymen, Footpads, Shoplifts, & Cheats of Both Sexes*, ed. A. L. Hayward (1730, repr. 1933), Arthur Vincent (ed.), *The Lives of Twelve Bad Women* (1897), F. W. Chandler, *The*

Literature of Roguery, 2 vols. (Boston and New York, 1907), vol. I, and Arthur Freeman, *Elizabeth's Misfits* (New York, 1978). These are all in some measure indebted to *The Life and Death of Mrs. Mary Frith* (1662) which survives in an apparently unique copy in the British Library (shelf-mark 1079.b.11). A single-sheet quarto published in the same year, *The Womans Champion*, is entirely derivative of *The Life and Death*. The Stationers' Register tantalisingly lists two books which either were never printed or, if they were, do not survive: John Day's *Madde Pranckes of Mery Mall of the Banckside* (7 Aug. 1610) and the anonymous *The Merry Conceits of Mrs Mary ffrith, Comonly Called by the name of Mal Cuttpurse* (30 Sept. 1671). Moll appears also in Nathan Field's *Amends for Ladies*, II.i, but not to advantage.

39 Parallel citations are given in the Commentary.

40 A situation involving malpractice of apparators occurs in *A Quip for an Upstart Courtier* (1592), sig. E2v (see Appendix D). The stage representation of a fraudulent apparator in 1611 would have been topical. In July 1610 a petition of the House of Commons drawing attention to offences committed by 'base' apparators was presented to King James (*Select Statutes and Other Constitutional Documents ... of Elizabeth and James I*, ed. G. W. Prothero (Oxford, 1913), p. 301).

41 'Sources', p. 387.

42 *The Plays of Nathan Field*, ed. W. Peery (Austin, 1950). See *Henslowe's Diary*, ed. R. A. Foakes and R. T. Rickert (Cambridge, 1961), pp. 27, 28, 30, 31, 54, 55, 56, concerning performances of the play, *Long Meg of Westminster*.

43 Although a Stationers' Register entry records what is almost certainly this prose work in Aug. 1590, the earliest extant edition is dated 1620. F. P. Wilson in 'The English Jestbooks of the Sixteenth and Early Seventeenth Centuries', *H.L.Q.*, II (1939), 155, shows that the supposed 1582 edition is spurious. Clearly some account of Long Meg's exploits, however, antedated our play.

44 In his University of London doctoral dissertation, *A Critical Study of Thomas Middleton's Borrowings and of his Imitations of Other Authors in his Prose, Poetry and Dramatic Work* (1966), ch. iv, D. F. George examines briefly the jest-biography of *Long Meg*, *The Batchelars Banquet* and some supposed details of Moll's life, drawn mainly from *The Life and Death of Mrs. Mary Frith* (1662).

45 While Moll's rescue of Jack may be indebted to *Long Meg*, the motive behind the ambush may be derived from III.ii and iii of *The London Prodigal* (c. 1605). Although arrests attempted or successful occur in several plays connected with Middleton and Dekker (e.g. *Westward Ho, Northward Ho, The Puritan*), the notion of arrest and imprisonment designed by a father as a lesson and punishment distinguishes the treatments in *The London Prodigal* and *The Roaring Girl*.

46 In addition to that in *A Trick of Catch the Old One*, precontracts figure in *A Mad World* (1604–7), *The Witch* (c. 1609–16), *The Widow* (c. 1615–17), *The Spanish Gipsy* (1623) and *A Game at Chess* (1624); *A Fair Quarrel* (c. 1615–17) contains a secret marriage.

47 The Knight in *The Phoenix* gives a clear indication of the financial base of his affair by calling the Jeweller's Wife his 'Revenue' (III.ii.21); cf. also *The Family of Love*, I.iii.161–70.

48 R. C. Bald in 'Sources' (p. 384) overlooks the appearance of Bellafront as a female page in *1 Honest Whore* (IV.i), and Mary Fitzallard in our play (IV.i).

49 George E. Rowe has drawn attention to Middleton's deliberate use of structural tension springing from the opposing pulls of conventional New Comedy and the prodigal play in 'Prodigal Sons, New Comedy, and Middleton's *Michaelmas Term*', *English Literary Renaissance*, VII (1977), 90–107, and *Thomas Middleton and the New Comedy Tradition* (Lincoln, Nebr., and London, 1979); neither makes specific reference to the present play, however. Dramatic treatments of the prodigal figure are found in both Middleton's and Dekker's earlier work. Lacy's profligacy is a major pretext for disallowing the match with Rose in *The Shoemaker's Holiday*; and in the prodigal vein, the rake Matheo in *2 Honest Whore* callously advises his wife, the reformed prostitute, Bellafront, to return to whoredom to support his licentiousness. Middleton had shown interest in the character in his early group of satires, *Micro-Cynicon* (1599), and later in *Father Hubburd's Tales* (1604), and in citizen comedies for the children's companies.

50 New Mermaid edition, p. xxix.

51 *Elizabethan Dramatists* (1963), p. 92.

52 More recently, although *The Roaring Girl* conforms to the scheme of their studies, A. Covatta, *Thomas Middleton's City Comedies* (Lewisburg, Pa., 1973), Dorothy Farr, *Thomas Middleton and the Drama of Realism* (Edinburgh, 1973) and George E. Rowe, Jr., *Thomas Middleton and the New Comedy Tradition*, choose not to include it in their discussions. Norman A. Brittin touches very lightly on the play in *Thomas Middleton* (New York, 1972), pp. 77–9; but neither J. H. Conover, *Thomas Dekker: An Analysis of Dramatic Structure* (The Hague and Paris, 1969), nor George E. Price, *Thomas Dekker* (New York, 1969), gives it more than passing reference. The play barely merits a mention in *'Accompaninge the players': Essays Celebrating Thomas Middleton, 1580–1980*, ed. Kenneth Friedenreich (New York, 1983). Normand Berlin discusses the play in relation to Dekker's work in *The Base String: the Underworld in Elizabethan Drama* (Rutherford, Madison, Teaneck, 1968), p. 115–18.

53 *The Art of Thomas Middleton* (Oxford, 1970).

54 *Amazons and Warrior Women* (Brighton, 1981). Margot Heinemann in *Puritanism and Theatre: Thomas Middleton and Opposition Drama under the Early Stuarts* (Cambridge, 1980), pp. 99–100, also sees Moll as a prototypal feminist. The brief discussion attempts to maintain a historical perspective, however.

55 See, for example, II.i.316–22, II.ii.38–45, III.i.138 (each of these for obvious reasons has suffered the fate of excision from modern productions). Moll nowhere invites married women to follow her example; she rather sees herself set apart from them, though in a position to comment on imperfections. So far as womankind is concerned the play is traditional in its attitudes. Even when dressed as a man in IV.i, Mary Fitzallard assumes a submissive role relative to Sebastian. A central interest revolves around the precept *nosce teipsum* (know thyself), but in this the men no less than the women are implicated. If Moll is treated as a model for the other women, an ironic interpretation contrary to the spirit of the

play is practically inevitable. Against such an approach Richard Levin's pertinent and entertaining *New Readings vs. Old Plays* (Chicago and London, 1979) is perhaps the best antidote.

56 'Moll Cutpurse as Hermaphrodite in Dekker and Middleton's *The Roaring Girl*', *Renaissance and Reformation*, new ser., VII (1983), 121.

57 *Thomas Dekker and the Traditions of English Drama* (New York, Berne, Frankfurt am Main, 1985).

58 The association of gold with iron-age rapacity is a common figure. On the apparent paradox, George Sandys in his commentary on Book I of Ovid's *Metamorphoses* (1632) remarks, citing a passage from the *Amores: 'But surely we slander this in calling it the Iron:* Now is the true stil'd Golden Age: for Gold / Honour is bought, and loue itself is sould.' (sig. D2r.)

59 Inga-Stina Ewbank has discussed similar matters in 'Realism and Morality in "Women Beware Women"', *E. & S.*, XXII (1969), 57–70.

60 As G. B. Shand has remarked in 'The Elizabethan Aim of *The Wisdom of Solomon Paraphrased*' ('*Accompaninge the Players*', pp. 73–4), Middleton in that work praises not merely chastity but barrenness, and regards it as a source of the highest joy: 'The field which never was ordainde to beare, / Is happier farre, then a still tilled ground, / This sleepes with quietnes in every yeare, / The other curst if any tares bee found: / The barren happier then shee that beares, / This brings foorth joye, the other tares and teares.' (III.xiii.)

61 Middleton's realism has been variously described; T. S. Eliot exaggerates when he terms Middleton's documentary quality 'photographic' in its realism (*Elizabethan Dramatists*, p. 92); Inga-Stina Ewbank elaborates on the idea in 'Realism and Morality in "Women Beware Women"'. L. C. Knights, in contrast, claims that Middleton's realism was of a very general nature (*Drama and Society in the Age of Jonson* (1937), pp. 257ff.). Madeleine Doran terms the same tragedy 'atmospheric' (*Endeavors of Art* (Madison, Wis., 1954), p. 168).

62 See V.i.283–4n.

63 Cf. the Consistory Court record of 1612 (Appendix E).

64 Under Elizabeth especially, and then James, J.P.s prospered to become a wealthy and influential element of the upper middle class (see, for example, A. L. Rowse, *The England of Elizabeth* (1962), pp. 344–59, and J. H. Gleason, *The Justices of the Peace in England 1558 to 1640* (Oxford, 1969)). Many London J.P.s were successful merchants; the dramatists seem to have cast Sir Alexander in this mould. Covetousness, avarice, materialism and social ambition are qualities which Middleton among other writers associates with the rapid acquisition of wealth by prosperous London merchants. See R. H. Tawney, 'The Rise of the Gentry, 1558–1640', *Economic History Review*, XI (1941), 1–38, and 'The Rise of the Gentry: a Postscript', *Economic History Review*, 2nd ser., VII (1954), 91–7, and Lawrence Stone, *The Crisis of the Aristocracy* (Oxford, 1965, rev. 1979).

65 The size of marriage portions among the aristocracy and wealthy gentry of the time place Mary's 5,000 marks (£3,333) in an appropriate perspective. Lawrence Stone in *The Crisis of the Aristocracy*, Appendix xxxi, p. 790, gives £3,800 as the average portion offered by Peers for the period 1600–24; the evidence advanced by J. H. Gleason in *The Justices of the Peace*, Appendix H, p. 264, produces an average of £1,777 for the gentry

for the years 1600–19; and Brian P. Levack in *The Civil Lawyers in England 1603–41* (Oxford, 1973), records in his 'Biographical Dictionary' numerous bequests to unmarried daughters in the range of £200 to £600, and an exceptional £1,500 (p. 242).

66 In a sense, Sebastian's pursuit of Moll is an inversion of this; the dramatists may reasonably have felt that yet another alternative to Mary would unduly complicate the plotting.

67 Dekker had inveighed against this in his chapter on 'Crueltie' in *Seven deadly Sinnes* (1606).

68 Nathan Field presents her in roughly these terms in *Amends for Ladies* (c. 1610–11).

69 Sir Alexander several times plays pathetically on the humours psychology association of grief with the breaking of heart-strings (I.ii.68–9, V.ii.5–6, 148–9). See R. L. Anderson, *Elizabethan Psychology and Shakespeare's Plays* (New York, 1966), pp. 12–13.

70 Madeleine Doran, *Endeavors of Art*, p. 310; see also L. C. Knights, 'Rhetoric and Insincerity', *Shakespeare's Styles*, ed. Philip Edwards, *et al.* (Cambridge, 1980), pp. 1–8.

71 See R. B. Parker, 'Middleton's Experiments with Comedy and Judgement', *Jacobean Theatre*, ed. J. R. Brown and Bernard Harris (1960, repr. 1972), pp. 179–99.

72 See Lawrence Stone, *The Family, Sex and Marriage in England 1500–1800* (1977, repr. 1979), chs. 3–5.

73 Though not elaborated in any detail in the play, a political dimension underlies the traditional plan; see Lawrence Stone, *The Family, Sex and Marriage*, ch. 5.

74 Caroline Lockett Cherry in *The Most Unvaluedst Purchase: Women in the Plays of Thomas Middleton* (Salzburg, 1973), p. 105, finds ironic Moll's adoption of male dress; but it is reasonable that she should take on the dress of the role model of authority. Modern experience accords with Moll's precedent.

75 *The Womans Champion* (1662).

76 *Citizen Comedy in the Age of Shakespeare* (Toronto, 1974), p. 110.

77 *The Art of Thomas Middleton*, p. 103.

78 William Power argues that the doubled names point to confusion in 'Double, double', *N. & Q.*, CCIV (1960), 4–6; R. B. Parker's remarks on the change in speech prefixes from Mary to Moll in the quarto of *Chaste Maid* (Revels ed., Dramatis Personae, l. 4n.) are apt here also. A. H. Gomme in his New Mermaid edition comments on the deliberate play on names (pp. xxxiv–v).

79 M. C. Bradbrook admires the poignancy and dramatic effectiveness of Mary's brief soliloquy at I.i.28–36, in *The Growth and Structure of Elizabethan Comedy* (1955, repr. Harmondsworth, 1963), p. 165.

80 *Elizabethan Dramatists*, p. 90. Other commentators have objected to Eliot's description, e.g. L. C. Knights, *Drama and Society in the Age of Jonson*, p. 268n., and Gomme, p. xxvi.

81 Though the references may be unspecific, the 'mistress' of the first song recalls Mistress Gallipot; and the wench in the second, like Mistress Openwork, ignores her own infidelity as she hypocritically calls Moll a whore.

82 *The Art of Thomas Middleton*, p. 109.

83 Other prominent treatments are Jonson's *The Gypsies Metamorphosed* (1621) and Fletcher and Massinger's *Beggars' Bush* (c. 1615–22).

84 The idea of honour among the lower orders occurs in Plato, *The Republic*, Book I, 351–2, and doubtless in numerous Renaissance commentaries also.

85 Moll's influence may in this respect be drawn from life: see V.i.305n.

86 James I's would-be secret visit to the Exchange in March 1604, which has been noticed in connection with *Meas.*, may be pertinent here also; see J. W. Lever's New Arden ed. (1966), pp. xxxiii–iv.

87 Heinemann in *Puritanism and Theatre*, pp. 98ff., remarks on Middleton's distinctive 'cross-class' marriages.

88 See Inga-Stina Ewbank, 'Realism and Morality in "Women Beware Women"', pp. 57–70.

89 Inga-Stina Ewbank discusses these and similar functions of masques in '"These Pretty Devices": A Study of Masques in Plays', *A Book of Masques*, ed. T. J. B. Spencer and S. W. Wells (Cambridge, 1967), pp. 407–48.

90 Chivalric tradition is touched on through his name and through repeated reference to embodiment of old values: both support his claim to the position. The medieval romance of *Guy of Warwick*, which Dekker and Day gave a dramatic treatment to in a now lost play of 1620, may well underlie the choice of name. References to Sir Guy in Shakespeare, *Henry VIII*, V.iv.20, and Beaumont, *The Knight of the Burning Pestle*, II.505–12 (*Dramatic Works*, I, ed. F. Bowers (Cambridge, 1966)), for example, attest to the figure's place in the popular imagination.

91 Cf. the exchange between Mistresses Openwork and Gallipot at IV.ii.147–8.

92 The First Player (as King) in *Hamlet* provides a gloss on the conventional psychology: '*What to ourselves in passion we propose, / The passion ending, doth the purpose lose. / The violence of either grief or joy / Their own enactures with themselves destroy. / Where joy most revels grief doth most lament; / Grief joys, joy grieves, on slender accident.*' (III.ii.189–194.) Cf. also Joseph Hall, *The King's Prophecie* (1603), stanzas 3–6.

93 The reference may be intended to recall the situation in *Sir Thomas More*, I.ii, in which More arranges with a cutpurse the theft of a justice's purse; cf. also *Bartholomew Fair*, III.v.87–8 (Revels ed.): '*Then why should the judges be free from this curse, / More than my poor self, for cutting the purse?*'

94 Citing Thomas Wright, *The Passions of the minde in generall* (2nd ed., 1604), Lily B. Campbell in *Shakespeare's Tragic Heroes* (1930, repr. New York, 1965), notes the following as one of the four effects of inordinate passion, 'Of the first, the blinding of understanding, he said that passion is like a pair of green glasses to the soul' (p. 78).

95 See Ian Donaldson, *The World Upside-Down* (Oxford, 1970), pp. 1–23 and 64–5.

96 To undermine the nature of the offer by questioning its genuineness or by suggesting that Sir Alexander merely kowtows to Lord Noland runs contrary to all signals of the play's spirit. Sir Alexander is after all given the play's final speech; if he were to be recognised as a figure of mockery, it would be more appropriate for another character – perhaps Sebastian or Lord Noland – to end the play. If conventionality is stressed the mood

and tone of the play's ending are seriously undermined and attended by a disturbing atmosphere of falseness and irony. Sebastian has already promised that Moll will not go unrequited for her part in assisting him (l. 207); his father's gesture is a continuation of the pattern.

97 It is prominent, for example, in his part of *The Magnificent Entertainment*, and appears in the following: *Honorable Entertainments*, ed. R. C. Bald (Oxford, 1953), vi.67–8, *The Triumphs of Truth* (Bullen, VII, 241ff.), *The Triumphs of Honour and Industry* (Bullen, VII, 303–4), *An Invention* (Bullen, VII, 376–7); also Dekker, *Whore of Babylon*, Prologue, ll. 20–6, *Troia-Nova Triumphans*, ll. 274ff. and 528ff.

98 Whether either dramatist may have known Lucian's essay on slander, which contains a description of *The Calumny* of Apelles, an allegorical representation of the administration of justice, is impossible to know. It was at least accessible in Sir Thomas Elyot's version in *The Governor*, III, xxvii. In many respects the allegorical elements and theme of Apelles' painting have dramatic counterparts in *The Roaring Girl*. While these may not specifically inform the play's action, some form of the tradition may be present. See David Cast, *The Calumny of Apelles* (New Haven and London, 1981). Other, more contemporary works such as Shakespeare's *Measure for Measure* explore similar themes.

99 Justice as the guardian of man is common in Middleton's pageant writing: it is one of the themes of *The World Tost at Tennis*, and appears also in *The Triumphs of Honour and Industry* (Bullen, VII, 303–4), and *The Triumphs of Love and Antiquity* (Bullen, VII, 318–20), for example.

100 Noland if understood literally as 'no-land' undermines the point about Moll's noble acquaintances. Gomme accepts 'no-land' (p. xxviii); most other commentators have remained silent on the matter. When 'Hadland' occurs in Middleton's *Michaelmas Term*, V.i.20, and *A Trick to Catch the Old One*, I.ii.4, for example, it serves a mocking or satirical purpose. Lord Noland and Sir Beauteous by contrast seem meant to be regarded as figures of honour and respect.

101 Middleton and Rowley, *The World Tost at Tennis*, l. 234.

102 Although his name did not appear in the 1604 edition, the setting of the work by the King's Printer barely concealed his authorship. (The pamphlet is included in the collection of James's *Workes* (1616).) The king's opposition to tobacco was in any case widely known. He gave a speech against it at Oxford which is quoted in Isaak Wake, *Rex Platonicus* (1607), sigs. L2v–4v. The subtlety of Middleton's references to James may be measured by his provision of an age for the Duke in *Women Beware Women* which corresponds to the king's age. J. R. Mulryne discusses the point first raised by Baldwin Maxwell ('The Date of Middleton's *Women Beware Women*', *P.Q.*, XXII (1943), 338–42) in his Revels edition, pp. xxxiv–v, and cites also a similar reference in *No Wit, No Help* (p. xxxv, n. 3). The association of James with Jove is commonplace.

103 James many times in his political writings cites the image of the head and the body in reference to his relation to the body politic (e.g. in his first speech to Parliament, March 1604, *The Political Works of James I*, ed. C. H. McIlwain (1918, repr. New York, 1965), p. 272). The image may of course be no more than a commonplace of political writing.

104 The meteoric rise to prominence of the handsome young Scot, Robert

Carr, who had by 1608 established for himself a place of special favour in the circle of James's intimates, may be pertinent to Lord Noland's companion, Sir Beauteous Ganymede. His rapid ascent and personal attractiveness resonate suggestively with Jupiter's carrying off of Ganymede to Olympus. The homosexual association of Jupiter and Ganymede seems also to be answered by James and Carr, though whether the dramatists intended this we cannot know: 'That [Carr's] attraction for the King was physical there can be no doubt; and though one must suspect the scandalmongers of the court, there is something in Osborne's remark that when James pawed his favourites so fondly in public he was not likely to restrain himself in private', D. H. Willson, *King James VI and I* (1956), p. 337.

105 The topical and allegorical aspects of Middleton's *The Witch* perhaps provide a perspective for such speculation, however. See Anne Lancashire, '*The Witch*: Stage Flop or Political Mistake?' in '*Accompaninge the Players*', pp. 161–81.

106 Though their actual status is left unspecific, it would probably have declared itself immediately to a contemporary audience: the gallants very likely represent some combination of younger brothers of nobility or gentry, would-be or manqués courtiers, or some manner of Inns-of-Court men. In courting prestige by aping the tradition of aristocratic hospitality (see Lawrence Stone, *The Crisis of the Aristocracy*, pp. 555–562), Sir Alexander, like Sir Bounteous Progress in *A Mad World*, seeks a reputation for largess; the arrangement, like that between the gallants and citizens' wives, is in some measure reciprocal.

107 Class tension and interaction in Middleton have been the subjects of many studies from L. C. Knights onward: *Drama and Society in the Age of Jonson* (1937), Brian Gibbons, *Jacobean City Comedy* (2nd ed., London and New York, 1980), and Heinemann, *Puritanism and Theatre*, ch. 6; also Don E. Wayne, '*Drama and Society in the Age of Jonson*: An Alternative View', *Renaissance Drama*, new ser., XIII (1982), 103–29.

108 Gomme interprets the sexual imagery in the wives' speeches as an undercurrent which runs counter to their declared intentions (p. xxx and IV.ii.49n.). This is the first time, however, that they show mastery over such imagery, and they use it, like Moll, against their adversaries.

109 Since under 17th-century law a husband from a previous match would be entitled to dispose of his wife's estate as he wished, he is understandably anxious to settle the matter. See Lawrence Stone, *The Family, Sex and Marriage*, pp. 550–1.

110 See A. Leggatt, *Citizen Comedy in the Age of Shakespeare*, ch. 7.

111 The circumstances touch on ground explored by Harold Pinter's treatment of a possible infidelity in *The Collection*.

112 She says nothing after IV.ii.296. Just how she reacts to Laxton's account or her husband's acceptance of it is a matter for surmise.

113 Laxton makes reference to returning Gallipot's gold, but we are given no reason to trust him. Unless he has other irons in the fire, he would be hard-pressed to repay even the ten angels he earlier lost to Moll. His account, moreover, contradicts the testimony of earlier asides, and runs counter to the convention that attitudes and feelings so expressed are genuine. Gomme (p. xxx) accepts D. M. Holmes's view (*The Art of*

Thomas Middleton, p. 109), that the apparent confusion resulted from a hasty winding up of the citizen action to make way for material for the canting scene.

114 Richard Hosley, 'A Reconstruction of the Fortune Playhouse: Part I', *Elizabethan Theatre*, ed. G. R. Hibbard, VI (1978), 1–20, and 'Part II', *Elizabethan Theatre*, ed. G. R. Hibbard, VII (1980), 1–20; and Leonie Star, 'The Middle of the Yard', *Theatre Notebook*, XXX (1976), 5–9 and 65–9.

115 N. E. McClure (ed.), *The Letters of John Chamberlain*, (Philadelphia, 1939), II, 415.

116 Whether or not the printer's copy was theatrical in origin, Henslowe's advance payment to Middleton and Dekker for this play suggests that the Fortune Theatre was in their minds during composition.

117 The Prologue refers to the Fortune's distinctive square shape in the opening lines and the Preface plays on the theatre's name at ll. 24–7.

118 Robert Yarington's *Two Lamentable Tragedies* is unlikely to reflect stage conditions at the Fortune since, as A. H. Baugh established in his 1917 edition of Haughton's *Englishmen for My Money*, *Two Lamentable Tragedies* was written no later than 1598.

119 Some staging irregularities discussed below may be a reflection of the nature of the manuscript, since they would probably have been cleared up in prompt copy. By the time of this play both authors were experienced dramatists, and the general fulness of the stage directions confirms this.

120 'The Themes and Staging of *Bartholomew Fair*', *University of Toronto Quarterly*, XXXIX (1970), 293–309.

121 Construction of such a piece or pieces would probably also have been too costly.

122 Stage directions in both parts of *The Honest Whore* (Part I: I.ii; Part II: I.i, V.i) refer to 'one door' and 'another door', and suggest, as in several Blackfriars and Red Bull plays, the existence of more than two doors; a similar direction occurs in *The Roaring Girl* (III.iii.0.1–2). A discovery-space is called for in *1 Honest Whore*, I.iii.10ff., where at the drawing of a curtain, Infaelice is revealed on a bed. 'The other door' occurs in none of the Fortune plays. Despite its considerably larger surviving repertoire, only one Blackfriars play (*Eastward Ho*) refers to a middle door: that theatre is generally acknowledged to have been equipped with three doors. Apart from *The Roaring Girl*'s II.i stage direction, perhaps the strongest explicit evidence for three entranceways at the Fortune is the initial direction to III.iii of *2 Honest Whore*, which involves discovery of a shop: '*Enter at one doore* Lodouico *and* Carolo; *at another* Bots, *and* Mistris Horsleach; Candido *and his wife appeare in the Shop*.' Later, Infaelice hides during a lengthy conference on stage during which two doors are used: she presumably conceals herself in the discovery-space. *1 Honest Whore* calls for three doors in its initial I.i stage direction, and the dumb-shows before I.i and IV.i of *The Whore of Babylon* point to the use of a discovery-space. Richard Hosley discusses these and other features in connection with the theatres cited in 'The Discovery-Space in Shakespeare's Globe', *Sh.S. 12*, (1959), 35–46, and 'The Playhouses', *The Revels History of Drama in English*, III, ed. C. Leech and T. W. Craik

(1975), 121–235. In 'A Reconstruction of the Fortune Playhouse: Part II', p. 17, n. 9, he postulates three doors in the tiring-house façade, citing the III.iii direction in *2 Honest Whore* and II.i direction in *The Roaring Girl*; in 'The Discovery-Space in Shakespeare's Globe', p. 46, he presents the latter as an instance of a multiple discovery.

123 Hosley, 'The Playhouses', suggests a space seven feet by three feet for the second Blackfriars (p. 222), and seven by two for the First Globe (p. 188).

124 'Elizabethan Architecture', *Shakespeare's England*, II, 63. 18th-century illustrations of Shakespeare's birthplace depict similar arrangements.

125 William Creizenach casually suggested this in *The English Drama in the Age of Shakespeare* (1916), p. 374, but did not engage with the details or consequent problems.

126 'Passing over the Stage', *Sh.S. 12*, (1959), 47–55. R. Southern endorses and extends Nicoll's argument in *The Staging of Plays before Shakespeare* (1973), pp. 584–91. He goes so far as to suggest that steps may have been incorporated into the downstage corners of the stage to facilitate such entrances from the yard.

127 See Appendix E.

128 I am grateful to Richard Hosley for this suggestion.

129 Cf. *Every Man Out of His Humour*, III.ix.78ff. and *The Poetaster*, IV.iii.52ff.

130 See, for example, Francis Lenton, *The young Gallants Whirligigg: or Youths Reakes* (1629), and ch. vi of Dekker, *The Gull's Horn-book* (ed. Pendry, pp. 98ff.).

131 A fuller account of the productions dealt with here appears in Paul Mulholland's 'Let her roar again: *The Roaring Girl* revived', *Research Opportunities in Renaissance Drama*, XXVIII (1985), 15–25.

132 See Bentley, *J. & C.S.*, V, 1401–2.

133 A programme and theatre reviews are preserved in the Harvard Theatre Collection. Some speeches of omitted characters may have been redistributed to other characters, but omissions reveal at least shifts of emphasis and the general nature of the altered effect.

134 *Boston Traveler*, 3 May 1951, and *Variety*, 16 May 1951, respectively.

135 Miss Walker had to leave to take up a previous commitment and the role was taken over by Jenny Lou Law in the latter part of the run.

136 *Boston Globe*, 3 May 1951, and *Variety*, 16 May 1951, respectively.

137 No sound recording has been preserved by the B.B.C., but the script is on file at the B.B.C. Drama Library.

138 The lines are quoted by Cordelia Oliver in *The Guardian*, 29 June 1970.

139 e.g. Cordelia Oliver, *Guardian*, 29 June 1970; *Stage*, 2 July 1970; *Dundee Courier*, 19 June 1970.

140 I am grateful to the director for notes on this production and for generously supplying a copy of her script.

141 Character omissions give some idea of the extent of the reworking: Sir Guy, Sir Thomas, Sir Beauteous, Lord Noland, Goshawk, Greenwit, Gallipot, Openwork, Tiltyard, Tearcat, the Coachman, Curtalax, Hanger and the Cutpurses were deleted. In addition, 'Old Adam Appleton' was doubled with 'Adam Appleton', his son, who took over a collection of lines assigned to Goshawk and Greenwit in II.i.

142 I am grateful to the director for supplying me with a copy of her prompt-book.

143 'Miss Arden does not rave or shout or swagger, or fight for attention. . . . she brings with her a chortling enjoyment of life, the kind of roly-poly happiness that instantly fills a hall with sympathetic laughter', John Barber, *Daily Telegraph*, 26 Aug. 1980.

144 Two lines incorporating an image from marriage were cut from Moll's speech after the departure of Laxton, III.i.137–8 (New Mermaid ed. – the edition used), ('Base is that mind that kneels unto her body, / As if a husband stood in awe on's wife.'), for example; and the removal of the second and third citizen scenes prevented the resolution of marital strife among the shopkeepers.

145 I am grateful to the director for comments on his production and for lending me a copy of his prompt-book.

146 A box-office discount scheme also aimed to encourage theatre patrons to attend both productions.

147 His stance on this matter is set out in *The Sunday Times*, 24 Apr. 1983.

148 This change was introduced in the course of the Stratford trial run; the scenes had been rehearsed and played until then in the regular order. Among other things, the alteration gave more time for Miss Mirren's costume change.

THE ROARING GIRL

[THE EPISTLE]

To the Comic Play-readers: Venery and Laughter.

The fashion of play-making I can properly compare to nothing
so naturally as the alteration in apparel: for in the time of the
great-crop doublet, your huge bombasted plays, quilted with
mighty words to lean purpose, was only then in fashion; and as   5
the doublet fell, neater inventions began to set up. Now in the
time of spruceness, our plays follow the niceness of our garments: single plots, quaint conceits, lecherous jests, dressed up
in hanging sleeves; and those are fit for the times and the termers. Such a kind of light-colour summer stuff, mingled with   10

THE EPISTLE] *as running-title to second page of Dedication in Q.*   1. *Play-readers:*] *This ed.; Play-readers, Q.*   9–10. termers.] *Dyce;* Tearmers: *Q.*

---

1. Play-readers:] 17th-century punctuation permitted ambiguity (frequently deliberate) where modern pointing is more specific. The Epistle in an alternative reading may be dedicated to the play-reader's venery and laughter.

Venery] 'Good hunting'; but 'practice or pursuit of sexual pleasure' is also prominent here and elsewhere (II.i.25, 36, 140, III.i.43). See Intro., p. 23.

3–4. *great-crop doublet*] *O.E.D.* defines a 'crop-doublet' as 'a short doublet' citing a contextually uninformative passage from Shirley's *Constant Maid* (1640); possibly 'crop' referred to the length of the skirts, which altered with the fashion (Linthicum, pp. 198–9), but it can also mean 'stomach', a sense which sits better with 'great' and prompts identification with Falstaff's 'great-belly doublet' (*H5*, IV.vii.46). Cf. Stubbes, *Anatomie of Abuses* (1583), sig. E2r: 'Their dublettes are noe lesse monstrous than the reste: For now the fashion is, to haue them hang downe to the middest of their theighes, or at least to their priuie members, beeing so harde-quilted, and stuffed, bombasted and sewed, as they can verie hardly eyther stoupe downe, or decline them selues to the grounde.' He also remarks that these doublets were 'stuffed with foure, five or six pound of Bombast at the least'.

4. *bombasted*] (1) stuffed; (2) rendered grandiose.

quilted] (1) padded; (2) joined together as in a quilt.

5. *was*] plural subject with singular verb: common in Jacobean English; see Abbott, § 333.

7. *spruceness*] neatness.

niceness] elegance.

8. *single*] separate? The description does not otherwise appear to apply either to *The Roaring Girl* or other plays of this time.

quaint conceits] fanciful expressions.

9. *hanging sleeves*] 'long, open sleeve[s] hanging to the knee or foot' (Linthicum, p. 172).

9–10. *termers*] persons who came to London during term-time for business, amusement or intrigue.

diverse colours, you shall find this published comedy – good to
keep you in an afternoon from dice, at home in your chambers;
and for venery, you shall find enough for sixpence, but well
couched an you mark it. For Venus, being a woman, passes
through the play in doublet and breeches: a brave disguise and 15
a safe one, if the statute untie not her codpiece point! The book
I make no question but is fit for many of your companies, as
well as the person itself, and may be allowed both gallery-room
at the playhouse and chamber-room at your lodging. Worse
things, I must needs confess, the world has taxed her for than 20
has been written of her; but 'tis the excellency of a writer to
leave things better than he finds 'em; though some obscene
fellow, that cares not what he writes against others, yet keeps a
mystical bawdy-house himself, and entertains drunkards to

14. it.] *Q;* it: *Reed.*   15. breeches:] *M. Thesis;* breeches, *Q.*   19. lodging.]
Dyce; lodging: *Q.*

13. *sixpence*] the normal price of a printed play; see Jonson, *Every Man in
his Humour*, IV.ii.103–4.
14. *couched*] (1) hidden (looks forward to 'brave disguise', l. 15); (2) 'embroidered with gold thread ... laid flat on the surface' (*O.E.D.*, 4b); cf.
Middleton, *Black Book* (Bullen, VIII), p. 42, '... under the plain frieze of
simplicity, thou mayest finely couch the wrought velvet of knavery' (cited in
O.E.D.).
an] if.
16. *statute*] Prof. O. Hood Phillips has advised me in correspondence that
Moll 'could have been prosecuted in an ecclesiastical court for indecency or
uncleanness, which was an offence both under the *ius commune* of the Church
and the English common law'. *Hic Mulier or, The Man-Woman* (1620), sig.
clv, contains a similar reference: 'Let therefore the powerfull Statute of apparel but lift vp his Battle-Axe, and rush the offenders in pieces ...' Prynne in
Histrio-Mastix (1633) cites numerous canons against women dressing as men
founded on Deut. xxii.5. Hoy considers the reference to be to 'the sumptuary
law that forbade women to wear male attire'; but the sumptuary laws were
repealed in 1603. See F. E. Baldwin, *Sumptuary Legislation and Personal
Regulation in England* (Baltimore, 1926); also this editor's 'The Date of *The
Roaring Girl*', *R.E.S.*, new ser., XXVIII (1977), 21–4, for further discussion of
the reference in relation to the real Moll's circumstances.
untie not ... codpiece point] i.e. does not discover her true sex. The codpiece
point held up the breeches (cf. III.i.62).
22. *obscene*] offensive.
24. *mystical*] secret, concealed; common in Middleton, frequently linked to
a sexually suggestive term (cf. II.i.21). See Intro., p. 10.

make use of their pockets and vent his private bottle-ale at   25
midnight – though such a one would have ripped up the most
nasty vice that ever hell belched forth and presented it to a
modest assembly, yet we rather wish in such discoveries where
reputation lies bleeding, a slackness of truth than fulness of
slander. ·   30

THOMAS MIDDLETON.

28. assembly,] *Dyce;* Assembly; *Q.*

---

25. *vent*] discharge (with a sexual entendre?), perhaps punning on
vent = vend (*O.E.D.*, v.3); cf. Jonson, *Volpone*, II.ii.5–6 (Revels ed.). F. P.
Wilson, 'Some English Mock-prognostications' (*Shakespearian and Other
Studies,* ed. H. Gardner (Oxford, 1969), p. 276n.), remarks, 'The difficulty of
bottling beer, which was hopped, is suggested by Jack Daw: "the which being
once let loose, will furiously flie in any mans face".'
    26. *ripped up*] exposed.

The Roaring Girle.

OR
Moll Cut-Purse.

As it hath lately beene Acted on the Fortune-stage by
the Prince his Players.

Written by *T. Middleton* and *T. Dekkar.*

My case is alter'd, I must worke for my liuing.

Printed at *London* for *Thomas Archer*, and are to be sold at his
shop in Popes head-pallace, neere the Royall
Exchange. 1611.

Title-page of the 1611 quarto

72 THE ROARING GIRL

[DRAMATIS PERSONAE

SIR ALEXANDER WENGRAVE.
SEBASTIAN WENGRAVE, *his son*
SIR DAVY DAPPER.
JACK DAPPER, *his son*.
SIR ADAM APPLETON.   5
SIR GUY FITZALLARD.
LORD NOLAND.
SIR BEAUTEOUS GANYMEDE.

DRAMATIS PERSONAE] *placed after Prologue in Q.*   1. WENGRAVE] *Reed; Went-graue Q.*   2. SEBASTIAN WENGRAVE] *Dyce;* Yong *Wentgraue Q.*   6. FITZALLARD] *Dyce; Fitz-Allard Q.*

The names have been rearranged for the sake of clarity. A facsimile of the Q version is given in Appendix C. The Dramatis Personae in Q follows the Prologue; the order has been reversed.

1. *WENGRAVE*] so spelt in the text, but given as 'Went-graue' in the Dramatis Personae, which suggests the derivation: he 'went grave' in response to Mary Fitzallard's dowry. A character in Middleton's *Your Five Gallants* is named Fitsgrave.

3. *DAVY DAPPER*] William Power ('Middleton's Way with Names', *N. & Q.*, ccv (1960), 58) sees in the name 'a ludicrous picture of an old man who tries to seem young'.

4. *JACK DAPPER*] an inversion of 'dapper jack' (not recorded in *O.E.D.*), usually used in mockery or scorn: cf. Marlowe, *Edward II*, I.iv.412 (*Works*, ed. F. Bowers (Cambridge, 1973, II), 'I have not seene a dapper jack so briske'; and as a deprecatory term used of an upstart in Nashe, *Pierce Penilesse* (*Works*, ed. R. B. McKerrow (Oxford, 1958), 1, p. 169, ll. 19–20), 'You shall see a dapper Iacke, that hath been but ouer at *Deepe*'.

5. *ADAM APPLETON*] presumably derived from 'Adam's-apple'.

6. *SIR GUY FITZALLARD*] Middleton seems to have been fond of the *Fitz* prefix: a Fitzallen appears in *A Fair Quarrel* and a Fitsgrave in *Y.F.G.*; *Guy* had chivalric associations: see Intro., n. 90.

7. *NOLAND*] possibly a simple linking of 'no' and 'land', but no suggestion of prodigality attends this character (cf. Laxton), and he is further a figure who commands general respect. The name may be derived from a conflation of 'noll' (head) or 'know' and 'land', see Intro., p. 38.

8. *BEAUTEOUS GANYMEDE*] The name of Jove's cupbearer and page suits this character's function in assisting the marriage at the play's close. Ganymede performs his traditional role in Middleton's *Women Beware Women*; cf. also Middleton's *A Mad World, My Masters*, II.i.137–9, and Dekker's *Satiromastix*, V.ii.5–6. The homosexual suggestion of the name may have particular significance: see Intro., n. 104.

SIR THOMAS LONG.

LAXTON.   10

GOSHAWK.

GREENWIT.

HIPPOCRATES GALLIPOT, *an apothecary,*⎫

OPENWORK, *a sempster,*   ⎬*Citizens.*

TILTYARD, *a feather-seller.*   ⎭   15

NEATFOOT, *Sir Alexander's man.*

GULL, *Jack Dapper's page.*

---

9. SIR THOMAS LONG] *Collier; not in Q.*   16. NEATFOOT] *Reed; Neats-foot Q.*

---

9. *THOMAS LONG*] 'Tom Long' appears to have been a proverbial name for a carrier in catch-phrases and the like (Tilley, J71; cf. also Jonson's *A Tale of a Tub*, IV.i.96). Several ballads entitled 'Tom Longe the Caryer' are listed in Hyder Rollins, *An Analytical Index to the Ballad Entries (1557–1709)* (1924, repr. Hatboro, Penn., 1967), one of them indecent. Some joke, now lost, may have attended the character name.

10. *LAXTON*] a double play on 'lack-stone', as Sir Alexander makes clear at I.ii.55–7. He has sold all his land (III.i.50) and he is, ironically, impotent (see Intro., p. 39). Cf. 'Cockstone' in Middleton's *Michaelmas Term* and 'Singlestone' in *M.W.M.M.*; also 'Featherstone' in Dekker and Webster's *Northward Ho*.

11. *GOSHAWK*] a large short-winged hawk, often used in falconry; cf. Dekker's *Whore of Babylon*, IV.ii.88ff.

12. *GREENWIT*] *Green*= immature, inexperienced, gullible. Cf. William Fennor, *The Compters Common-wealth* (1617), p. 19: 'I will strip naked ... such as enrich themselves by fraud, deceipt and sinister meanes, working vpon the infirmity of youth, and green-witted Gallants ...'

13. *HIPPOCRATES GALLIPOT*] The name of the father of modern medicine sits loosely and ironically on this character. A *gallipot* is a small earthen pot for ointments and medicines.

14. *OPENWORK*] The implied honesty and straightforwardness extends apparently to his wares, the operation of his shop and the dealings between husband and wife (IV.ii.43–4).

15. *TILTYARD*] so named for the abundant use of feathers by tiltyard combatants; cf. Webster, *White Devil*, I.ii.28–9 (Revels ed.): 'The great barriers moulted not more feathers ...'

16. *NEATFOOT*] Q's presentation in the Dramatis Personae suggests the derivation: 'Neats-foot' (an ox foot prepared as food).

17. *GULL*] fool, simpleton.

RALPH TRAPDOOR.

TEARCAT.

CURTALAX, *a sergeant.*   20

HANGER, *his yeoman.*

MOLL CUTPURSE, *the Roaring Girl.*

MARY FITZALLARD, *Sir Guy's daughter.*

MISTRESS PRUDENCE GALLIPOT, ⎫

MISTRESS ROSAMOND OPENWORK, ⎬ *Citizens' wives.*   25

MISTRESS TILTYARD. ⎭

Gentlemen.

19. TEARCAT] *Collier; not in Q.*   20. CURTALAX] *M. Thesis; Curtilax Q;* Cur-
tleax *Dyce.*   24–6.] *Dyce;* Vxores *Q.*   27–33.] *Dyce subst.;* Ministri *Q.*

---

18. *RALPH TRAPDOOR*] 'Ralph' incorporates the familiar pun on 'raff'
(refuse, trash) as, for example, in *Mankind,* l. 51 (*Four Tudor Interludes,* ed. J.
A. B. Somerset (1974)). 'Rafe' was a common spelling of the name ('Raph'
occurs twice in *R.G.,* sig. C2v). The implication of 'Trapdoor' is made clear at
I.ii.241–2.

19. *TEARCAT*] 'To tear a cat' means 'to play the part of a roistering hero,
to rant and bluster' *O.E.D.,* 'tear', v.1, 1d); the adjectival form, *tear-cat,*
signifies 'swaggering, bombastic'. Cf. *M.N.D.,* I.ii.23–4.

20. *CURTALAX*] a cutlass.

21. *HANGER*] (1) 'a loop or strap on a sword belt from which the sword
was hung' (*O.E.D.,* 2, 4b): such a hanger is pictured in the title-page engraving of Moll; (2) 'a kind of short sword, originally hung from the belt' (*O.E.D.,*
3). In Overbury, *Characters* (*A Book of 'Characters',* ed. R. Aldington (n.d.),
p. 165) the yeoman is described as 'the hanger that a sergeant wears by his
side'.

22. *MOLL*] For reference to the real Mary Frith's life, see Intro., pp. 13–14,
and Appendix E. 'Moll' as a general name for whores appears in Middleton's
Father Hubburd's Tales: '. . . to bring them a whole dozen of taffeta punks at a
supper, and they should be none of these common Molls neither . . .' (Bullen,
VIII, 78). 'Moll' is the name of the wanton daughter in *The Puritan* and of the
title character in *A Chaste Maid in Cheapside.* The name's proper form,
'Mary', which is also used in reference to Moll, signifies chastity and links her
with Mary Fitzallard (see Intro., pp. 30–1). Moll makes a brief appearance in
Nathan Field's *Amends for Ladies,* II.i, but the depiction is less to her advantage. She apparently still had drawing power in 1639 when a later edition
advertised 'the merry prankes of Moll Cut-purse' on its title-page, though the
text remained unaltered.

23. *MARY*] See l. 22n.

24. *PRUDENCE GALLIPOT*] Cf. Dekker, *2 Honest Whore,* I.ii.139–40,
'[a whore] is the Gally-pot to which these Drones flye: not for loue to the pot,
but for the sweet sucket within it, her money, her money'.

27–33.] covered by the term 'Ministri' (Lat. for servants, attendants) in Q.

Three or four Servingmen of Sir Alexander's household.
Fellow with a long rapier.
Porter.   30
Tailor.
Coachman.
Five or six Cutpurses.]

---

28. *Three or four*] See I.ii.42.1.
Servingmen] presumably doubled with the citizens' servants who appear at II.i.398.3.
33. *Five or six*] See V.i.267.1.

Prologue

A play expected long makes the audience look
For wonders – that each scene should be a book
Composed to all perfection. Each one comes
And brings a play in's head with him; up he sums
What he would of a roaring girl have writ –   5
If that he finds not here, he mews at it.
Only we entreat you think our scene
Cannot speak high, the subject being but mean.
A roaring girl, whose notes till now never were,
Shall fill with laughter our vast theatre: 10
That's all which I dare promise; tragic passion,
And such grave stuff, is this day out of fashion.
I see attention sets wide ope her gates
Of hearing, and with covetous listening waits
To know what girl this roaring girl should be –   15
For of that tribe are many. One is she
That roars at midnight in deep tavern bowls,
That beats the watch, and constables controls;
Another roars i'th' day-time, swears, stabs, gives braves,
Yet sells her soul to the lust of fools and slaves: 20

Prologue] Dyce; Prologus Q; placed before Dramatis Personae in Q.   3. perfection.] M. Thesis; perfection; Q.   8. mean.] M. Thesis; meane) Q; mean;)
Reed.   20. slaves:] Dyce; slaues. Q.

---

1. *expected long*] The play was apparently overdue in reaching the stage,
a notion fortified by the elaborate apologies in the Prologue and Epilogue,
especially for the treatment of Moll.

6. *mews*] derides with cat-like mewing. Dekker in *The Gull's Horn-book*
advises his would-be gallant to 'mew at passionate speeches, blare at merry'
(ed. Pendry, p. 101).

8. *high ... mean*] playing on the musical senses picked up in *notes*, l. 9,
meaning (1) musical notes; (2) cries.

10. *vast theatre*] i.e. the Fortune.

17. *bowls*] broad, round drinking vessels.

18. *watch*] guard.

controls] rebukes, takes to task; cf. V.i.151n.

19. *gives braves*] makes a show of defiance.

Both these are suburb-roarers. Then there's besides
A civil, city-roaring girl, whose pride,
Feasting, and riding, shakes her husband's state,
And leaves him roaring through an iron grate.
None of these roaring girls is ours: she flies   25
With wings more lofty. Thus her character lies –
Yet what need characters, when to give a guess
Is better than the person to express?
But would you know who 'tis? Would you hear her name? –
She is called Mad Moll; her life our acts proclaim!   30

21. besides] *Q; beside Collier.*   26. lies –] *Reed; lyes, Q.*

---

21. *suburb-roarers*] The suburbs lay immediately outside the walls of
London; 'As the city-gates were closed during the night, the suburbs were left
very much to themselves' (Sugden, p. 491). Brothels and the like flourished
there.

besides] Although other editors have emended to *beside*, the imperfect
rhyme is not obtrusive; other irregular rhymes occur in the play (e.g. V.i.349).

24. *roaring . . . grate*] i.e. begging for food or money from a grate of one of
the debtors' prisons; cf. III.iii.48.

26. *character*] presumably 'distinctive trait' as given above for other
roarers. The 'fictional personality' sense was not yet current.

30. *Mad*] probably combining the senses 'wild' and 'eccentric'.

acts] i.e. stage actions or portions of the play; no reference to act/scene
division is implied, which Q does not in any case give.

Act I

Enter MARY FITZALLARD *disguised like a sempster, with a case for*
bands, and NEATFOOT, *a servingman, with her, with a napkin on*
his shoulder and a trencher in his hand, as from table.

Neatfoot. The young gentleman, our young master, Sir
　　Alexander's son – it is into his ears, sweet damsel, emblem
　　of fragility, you desire to have a message transported, or to
　　be transcendent?
Mary. A private word or two, sir, nothing else.　　　　　　　　　5
Neatfoot. You shall fructify in that which you come for: your
　　pleasure shall be satisfied to your full contentation. I will,
　　fairest tree of generation, watch when our young master is
　　erected – that is to say, up – and deliver him to this your
　　most white hand.　　　　　　　　　　　　　　　　　　　　10
Mary. Thanks, sir.

---

7. contentation.] *Dyce;* contentation: *Q.*

I.i] This is the only scene heading in Q. Except for the split of Act I into two
scenes by Bowers, all act/scene divisions were introduced by Dyce.

0.1. *sempster*] Though applicable to men or women at this time (*-ster* endings originally designated women only), the use of *needlewoman* at l. 50 below
possibly makes the question of sex comically explicit.

0.1–2. *case for bands*] a box for neck-bands or collars.

0.3. *trencher*] a wooden plate or shallow dish, common in noble and fashionable households before the introduction of pewter.

4. *transcendent*] an affected word, typical of Neatfoot, of uncertain meaning
as used, presumably intended to convey the private meeting that Mary seems
to understand by it.

6. *fructify*] The bawdy quibbles on this and 'come for' extend through the
speech. As Hoy notes, the word is affected: cf. Nathaniel in *L.L.L.*, IV.ii.27,
and Middleton's *Family of Love*, III.iii.21–2.

9. *erected*] i.e. from table; but with an inevitable sexual quibble, set off by
'that is to say, up'.

78

Neatfoot. And withal, certify him, that I have culled out for
    him, now his belly is replenished, a daintier bit or
    modicum than any lay upon his trencher at dinner. – Hath
    he notion of your name, I beseech your chastity?   15

Mary. One, sir, of whom he bespake falling-bands.

Neatfoot. Falling-bands: it shall so be given him. – If you
    please to venture your modesty in the hall, amongst a curl-
    pated company of rude servingmen, and take such as they
    can set before you, you shall be most seriously, and in-   20
    genuously welcome –

Mary. I have dined indeed already, sir.

Neatfoot. Or will you vouchsafe to kiss the lip of a cup of rich
    Orleans in the buttery amongst our waiting-women?

Mary. Not now in truth, sir.   25

Neatfoot. Our young master shall then have a feeling of your
    being here presently. It shall so be given him.

Mary. I humbly thank you, sir.

                         Exit NEATFOOT.

                    But that my bosom
Is full of bitter sorrows, I could smile
To see this formal ape play antic tricks;   30
But in my breast a poisoned arrow sticks,
And smiles cannot become me. Love woven slightly,
Such as thy false heart makes, wears out as lightly,
But love being truly bred i'th' soul, like mine,
Bleeds even to death at the least wound it takes.   35
The more we quench this fire, the less it slakes.
O me!

20–1. ingenuously] *This ed.;* ingeniously *Q.*   22. dined] *Reed;* dyed
Q.   27. here presently.] *Bowers subst.;* here presently *Q;* here; presently
Reed.   28. s.d.] *after l. 27 Q.*   34. i'th'] *Reed;* ith the *Q.*   36. fire] *Dyce;*
not in Q.

12. *withal*] besides, moreover.

14. *dinner*] mid-day meal.

16. *falling-bands*] bands or collars 'worn falling flat round the neck'
(*O.E.D.*), with puns on *band* = bond (in reference to the state of her precontract with Sebastian), and perhaps also banns.

19. *rude*] (1) ignorant; (2) unmannerly.

24. *Orleans*] wine from this wine-growing region.

27. *presently*] immediately. I have followed Bowers's punctuation for the
sake of the comic repetition: cf. ll. 17 and 52.

28. *But*] except, if it were not.

32. *slightly*] loosely, slackly.

36. *fire*] In support of this emendation first proposed by Dyce, Bowers cites
I.ii.175–6.

Enter SEBASTIAN WENGRAVE *with* NEATFOOT.

Sebastian. A sempster speak with me, sayst thou?

Neatfoot. Yes, sir, she's there, *viva voce*, to deliver her auricular confession.

Sebastian. With me, sweetheart? What is't?   40

Mary. I have brought home your bands, sir.

Sebastian. Bands? – Neatfoot!

Neatfoot. Sir?

Sebastian. Prithee look in, for all the gentlemen are upon
rising.   45

Neatfoot. Yes, sir, a most methodical attendance shall be given.

Sebastian. And, dost hear, if my father call for me, say I am
busy with a sempster.

Neatfoot. Yes, sir, he shall know it that you are busied with a
needlewoman.   50

Sebastian. In's ear, good Neatfoot.

Neatfoot. It shall be so given him.   *Exit*.

Sebastian. Bands? You're mistaken, sweetheart, I bespake
none. When, where, I prithee? What bands? Let me see
them.   55

Mary. Yes, sir, a bond fast sealed with solemn oaths,
Subscribed unto, as I thought, with your soul,
Delivered as your deed in sight of heaven.
Is this bond cancelled? Have you forgot me?

Sebastian. Ha! Life of my life! Sir Guy Fitzallard's daughter!   60
What has transformed my love to this strange shape? –
Stay, make all sure [*Shuts doors*.] – so. Now speak and be
brief,

37. sayst] *Qc;* saith *Qu.*   52. s.d.] *Exit Neat-foote. Q.*

---

38. viva voce] by word of mouth (Lat.).

38–9. *auricular confession*] a term normally used of the confession of sins to a
priest; Neatfoot insinuates confession of sexual misdemeanours.

50. *needlewoman*] *Needle* at this time had a bawdy sense (penis): see J. T.
Henke, *Renaissance Dramatic Bawdy* (*Exclusive of Shakespeare*), (Salzburg,
1974). Neatfoot may well load his remark with this innuendo. *Needlewoman* as
slang for 'harlot' is not recorded until the 19th century.

54–6. *bands . . . bond*] The two forms were used indiscriminately, often, as
here, with quibbles on different senses.

62. Shuts doors] Sebastian possibly locks the doors providing access to the
stage; a corresponding action of unlocking would presumably follow at the
end of the scene.

Because the wolf's at door that lies in wait
To prey upon us both. Albeit mine eyes
Are blessed by thine, yet this so strange disguise					65
Holds me with fear and wonder.
Mary.						Mine's a loathed sight. –
Why from it are you banished else so long?
Sebastian. I must cut short my speech: in broken language,
Thus much, sweet Moll, I must thy company shun –
I court another Moll; my thoughts must run					70
As a horse runs that's blind: round in a mill,
Out every step, yet keeping one path still.
Mary. Um! Must you shun my company? – In one knot
Have both our hands by th'hands of heaven been tied
Now to be broke? I thought me once your bride –					75
Our fathers did agree on the time when –
And must another bedfellow fill my room?
Sebastian. Sweet maid, let's lose no time. 'Tis in heaven's book
Set down that I must have thee; an oath we took
To keep our vows; but when the knight, your father,					80
Was from mine parted, storms began to sit
Upon my covetous father's brows, which fell

---

64. both.] *Reed subst.;* both *Q.*   82. brows,] *Dyce;* brow: *Q.*

63. *wolf's at door*] proverbial: cf. Tilley, W605.

71.] proverbial: Tilley, H697; cf. Dekker and Webster, *N.H.*, I.iii.128–9.

73. *Um*] a Dekker trait (spelt 'vmh' in Q); the earliest usage recorded by *O.E.D.* is 1614.

73–80. *one knot ... vows*] Sebastian and Mary have apparently entered into a precontract known as 'spousals *de futuro*' (H. Swinburne, *Treatise of Spousals* (1686, but written about 1600), pp. 213ff.). If *bedfellow*, l. 77, implies 'carnal Copulation' (Swinburne, p. 226), their spousals have become the equivalent of matrimony. See E. Schanzer, 'The Marriage Contracts in *Measure for Measure*', *Sh.S. 13* (1960), 81–9 and *Meas.*, ed. J. W. Lever (1965), pp. liii–v. An exchange of oaths constituting a precontract occurs in Chapman's *The Gentleman Usher*, IV.ii.

78. *heaven's book*] Cf. V.ii.174. The term occurs also in Dekker, *Sat.*, II.i.197 and V.ii.68, *The Witch of Edmonton*, I.i.202.

80–93.] 'A father seeking a wife for his son looked first at the girl's parentage and the size of her dowry, and only if these were satisfactory did he embark on the complicated negotiations and lawyers' discussions then needed for the making of a match', Christina Hole, *The English Housewife in the Seventeenth Century* (1953), p. 7.

81–2. *storms ... brows*] Cf. I.i.79ff.; also Middleton and Rowley, *The Spanish Gipsy*, V.i.64–6, Middleton, Massinger and Rowley, *Old Law*, III.ii.208–10.

82. *brows*] countenance (cf. *O.E.D.*, 5c). Emendation to the plural is adopted to agree with *them*, l. 83.

From them on me. He reckoned up what gold
This marriage would draw from him – at which he swore,
To lose so much blood could not grieve him more. 85
He then dissuades me from thee, called thee not fair,
And asked, 'What is she but a beggar's heir?'
He scorned thy dowry of five thousand marks.
If such a sum of money could be found,
And I would match with that, he'd not undo it, 90
Provided his bags might add nothing to it;
But vowed, if I took thee – nay more, did swear it –
Save birth from him I nothing should inherit.
Mary. What follows then – my shipwreck?
Sebastian.   Dearest, no.
Though wildly in a labyrinth I go, 95
My end is to meet thee: with a side wind
Must I now sail, else I no haven can find,
But both must sink forever. There's a wench
Called Moll, Mad Moll, or Merry Moll, a creature
So strange in quality, a whole city takes 100
Note of her name and person. – All that affection
I owe to thee, on her, in counterfeit passion,
I spend to mad my father; he believes
I dote upon this roaring girl, and grieves
As it becomes a father for a son 105
That could be so bewitched; yet I'll go on
This crooked way, sigh still for her, feign dreams
In which I'll talk only of her: these streams
Shall, I hope, force my father to consent
That here I anchor, rather than be rent 110
Upon a rock so dangerous. Art thou pleased,
Because thou seest we are waylaid, that I take
A path that's safe, though it be far about?
Mary. My prayers with heaven guide thee!
Sebastian.   Then I will on.

---

88. *five thousand marks*] A mark was an amount, not a coin, worth two-thirds of one pound or 13*s*. 4*d*. Five thousand marks was a considerable sum: see Intro., p. 25, and n. 65.

91. *bags*] money-bags.

108. *streams*] currents; a continuation of the nautical imagery begun at l. 81 above.

My father is at hand; kiss and be gone.   115
Hours shall be watched for meetings. I must now,
As men for fear, to a strange idol bow.
Mary. Farewell!
Sebastian.   I'll guide thee forth. When next we meet,
A story of Moll shall make our mirth more sweet.

                                        Exeunt.

[I.ii]

Enter SIR ALEXANDER WENGRAVE, SIR DAVY DAPPER, SIR ADAM
      APPLETON, GOSHAWK, LAXTON, *and* Gentlemen.

All. Thanks, good Sir Alexander, for our bounteous cheer.
Sir Alexander. Fie, fie, in giving thanks you pay too dear!
Sir Davy. When bounty spreads the table, faith, 'twere sin,
      At going off, if thanks should not step in.
Sir Alexander. No more of thanks, no more. – Ay, marry, sir,   5
      Th'inner room was too close; how do you like
      This parlour, gentlemen?
All.   O passing well!
Sir Adam. What a sweet breath the air casts here – so cool!
Goshawk. I like the prospect best.
Laxton.   See how 'tis furnished.
Sir Davy. A very fair sweet room.
Sir Alexander.   Sir Davy Dapper,   10
      The furniture that doth adorn this room
      Cost many a fair grey groat ere it came here;
      But good things are most cheap when they're most dear.

I.ii] *Bowers; not in Q.*   1. *All*] *Omnes Q passim.*   2. *Sir Alexander*] *Alex. Q*
passim.   8. *Sir Adam*] *Adam Q passim.*   10. *Sir Davy*] *Q uses forms of S.*
Dap. throughout this scene.

---

115. *My father is at hand*] Cf. ll. 44–5 above.
117. *strange idol bow*] Cf. I.ii.152.

I.ii.] Although the action seems more or less continuous, I have followed
Bowers's division of Act I into two scenes since the stage is cleared before the
entrance of Sir Alexander and the others, and the progress of the act con-
stitutes a new movement from this point.
7. *passing*] surpassingly.
11–32.] recognised as an impressionistic description of the Fortune
Theatre by M. W. Sampson, *M.L.N.*, XXX (1915), 195. Cf. Dekker, *Wonder of*
a Kingdom, III.i.12–29.
12. *grey groat*] 'an emphatic equivalent of *groat*' (*O.E.D.*, 'grey', 8). A groat,
worth 4*d.*, was often used to express a small sum; cf. Tilley, G458.
13.] Cf. 'The best is best cheap' (Tilley, B319).

Nay, when you look into my galleries –
How bravely they are trimmed up – you all shall swear   15
You're highly pleased to see what's set down there:
Stories of men and women, mixed together
Fair ones with foul, like sunshine in wet weather –
Within one square a thousand heads are laid
So close that all of heads the room seems made;   20
As many faces there, filled with blithe looks,
Show like the promising titles of new books
Writ merrily, the readers being their own eyes,
Which seem to move and to give plaudities;
And here and there, whilst with obsequious ears   25
Thronged heaps do listen, a cutpurse thrusts and leers
With hawk's eyes for his prey – I need not show him:
By a hanging villainous look yourselves may know him,
The face is drawn so rarely. Then, sir, below,

---

14. *galleries*] (1) apartments for the exhibition of art works; (2) the tiered balconies of the Fortune Theatre.

15. *bravely*] finely, handsomely.

trimmed up] arrayed, decorated.

19. *one square*] The Fortune was built on a square plan, measuring 80 ft. sq. externally and 55 ft. sq. internally. Cf. Dekker, *W.B.*, Prologue, 1.

19–21. *a thousand ... there*] Many reports claim that Elizabethan theatres could accommodate as many as 3,000 spectators; see R. Hosley, 'The Playhouses', *Revels History of the Drama in English*, III (1975), 143. Perhaps 'a thousand heads' here refers to the groundlings, while 'as many faces there' refers to a gallery or the galleries collectively.

23. *readers ... eyes*] The spectators described as though in a painting view both the action on the stage and themselves.

24. *plaudities*] peals of applause.

26. *heaps*] multitudes.

cutpurse] Cf. V.i.283–4 and 303–5. *Middlesex County Records*, ed. J. C. Jeaffreson (1886–92), II, 83, gives the order from 1 Oct. 1612 touching the Fortune Theatre: 'by reason of certayne lewde Jigges songes and daunces vsed and accustomed at the play-house called the Fortune in Gouldinglane divers cutt-purses and other lewde and ill disposed persons in greate multitudes doe resort thither at th'end of euerye playe many tymes causinge tumultes and outrages ...' Chambers (*E.S.*, II, 545) notes that William Kempe in *Nine Days Wonder* mentions that pickpockets were pilloried by being tied to the main posts of the stage; and Bentley regards *R.G.*'s references to cutpurses as evidence that the 'Fortune was willing to advertise its dubious audience' (*J. & C.S.*, VI, 147). They may alternatively have been intended to keep the audience on the alert.

The very floor, as 'twere, waves to and fro,   30
And, like a floating island, seems to move
Upon a sea bound in with shores above.

     Enter SEBASTIAN *and* M[ASTER] GREENWIT.

All. These sights are excellent!
Sir Alexander.   I'll show you all;
   Since we are met, make our parting comical.
Sebastian. This gentleman – my friend – will take his leave, sir.   35
Sir Alexander. Ha? Take his leave, Sebastian? Who?
Sebastian.   This gentleman.
Sir Alexander. Your love, sir, has already given me some time,
   And if you please to trust my age with more,
   It shall pay double interest – good sir, stay.
Greenwit. I have been too bold.
Sir Alexander.   Not so, sir. A merry day   40
   'Mongst friends being spent, is better than gold saved. –
   Some wine, some wine! Where be these knaves I keep?

     Enter three or four Servingmen *and* NEATFOOT.

Neatfoot. At your worshipful elbow, sir.
Sir Alexander.   You are
   Kissing my maids, drinking, or fast asleep.
Neatfoot. Your worship has given it us right.
Sir Alexander.   You varlets, stir!   45
   Chairs, stools, and cushions.
             [*Servants bring on wine, chairs, etc.*]
               – Prithee, Sir Davy Dapper,

---

45. stir!] *Dyce;* stir, *Q.*   46. s.d.] *Dyce subst.*

30–1. *The very floor ... island*] the stage surrounded on three sides by masses of seething spectators likened to an island.

34. *comical*] happy, fortunate (*O.E.D.*, 3).

44. *drinking*] Cf. Jonson, Chapman and Marston, *Eastward Ho*, II.i.39–41.
fast asleep] Cf. Middleton, *Phoenix*, III.i.1–10, where Falso complains of his 'sluggish soporiferous villains'.

45–6.] *varlets ... cushions*] Cf. Dekker, *Sat.*, II.i.1ff. The bringing on of chairs etc. is similarly incorporated into the dialogue in *How a Man May Choose a Good Wife from a Bad*, ed. A. E. H. Swaen (Louvain, 1912), ll. 1511ff.

45. *varlets*] (1) servants; (2) 'knaves' (used abusively).

> Make that chair thine.

Sir Davy.   'Tis but an easy gift,
> And yet I thank you for it, sir; I'll take it.

Sir Alexander. A chair for old Sir Adam Appleton.

Neatfoot. A backfriend to your worship.

Sir Adam.   Marry, good Neatfoot,   50
> I thank thee for it: backfriends sometimes are good.

Sir Alexander. Pray make that stool your perch, good Master
> Goshawk.

Goshawk. I stoop to your lure, sir.

Sir Alexander.   Son Sebastian,
> Take Master Greenwit to you.

Sebastian.   Sit, dear friend.

Sir Alexander. Nay, Master Laxton. – [*To Servant*] Furnish
> Master Laxton   55
> With what he wants – a stone – a stool, I would say,
> A stool.

Laxton.   I had rather stand, sir.

Sir Alexander. I know you had, good Master Laxton. So, so –
                          Exeunt [NEATFOOT *and*] Servants.
> Now here's a mess of friends; and gentlemen,
> Because time's glass shall not be running long,   60
> I'll quicken it with a pretty tale.

Sir Davy.   Good tales do well
> In these bad days, where vice does so excel.

Sir Adam. Begin, Sir Alexander.

58.1] *to the right of l. 57 Q.*

---

50. *backfriend*] (1) a backer, supporter; (2) a pretended or false friend; (3) a sergeant (alluding to his method of making an arrest).

Marry] 'to be sure'; originally, 'By Mary', a mild oath.

52–3. *perch . . . stoop to your lure*] playing on Goshawk's name. 'Stoop to the lure' is a technical expression for hawks in training to come down to their food.

56. *what . . . stone*] a play on Laxton's name (i.e. 'lack-stone'), making clear its sexual and landless implications: see Dramatis Personae, l. 10n., and Intro., p. 39.

57. *stand*] with an ironic sexual quibble.

59. *mess*] a company of four; cf. Tilley, F621; also, *3H6*, I.iv.73, *L.L.L.*, IV.iii.203.

60.] 'so that the passage of time shall not seem long'.

61. *pretty*] (1) cleverly wrought; (2) pleasing.

Sir Alexander.   Last day I met
   An agèd man upon whose head was scored
   A debt of just so many years as these   65
   Which I owe to my grave – the man you all know.
All. His name, I pray you, sir?
Sir Alexander.   Nay, you shall pardon me. –
   But when he saw me, with a sigh that brake,
   Or seemed to break, his heart-strings, thus he spake:
   'O my good knight,' says he – and then his eyes   70
   Were richer even by that which made them poor,
   They had spent so many tears, they had no more –
   'O sir,' says he, 'you know it, for you ha' seen
   Blessings to rain upon mine house and me:
   Fortune, who slaves men, was my slave; her wheel   75
   Hath spun me golden threads, for, I thank heaven,
   I ne'er had but one cause to curse my stars.'
   I asked him then what that one cause might be.
All. So, sir.
Sir Alexander. He paused, and as we often see
   A sea so much becalmed there can be found   80
   No wrinkle on his brow, his waves being drowned
   In their own rage; but when th'imperious winds
   Use strange invisible tyranny to shake
   Both heaven's and earth's foundation at their noise,
   The seas, swelling with wrath to part that fray,   85
   Rise up and are more wild, more mad, than they:
   Even so this good old man was by my question
   Stirred up to roughness; you might see his gall
   Flow even in's eyes; then grew he fantastical.
Sir Davy. Fantastical? – Ha, ha!
Sir Alexander.   Yes, and talked oddly.   90

82. winds] *Scott;* wind, *Q.*   90. talked] *Dyce;* talke *Q.*

75–6. *Fortune ... threads*] apparently a confusion of the wheel of Fortune
with the spinning wheel of the Fates, as noted by J. G. McManaway in
'Fortune's Wheel', *Times Literary Supplement,* 16 Apr. 1948, p. 264; cf.
Middleton, *Ghost of Lucrece,* l. 402, 'That string of Fortune's wheel'; also ll.
235–6. The confusion does not occur in Dekker, *W.B.,* II.i.254–5, and *If This
Be Not a Good Play, the Devil Is In It,* V.iii.157.
   82. *winds*] Emendation is prompted by 'their' (l. 84) and 'they' (l. 86).
   85. *part that fray*] i.e. end the disturbance begun by the winds.
   88. *gall*] (1) bile; (2) bitterness, rancour.

Sir Adam. Pray, sir, proceed. How did this old man end?
Sir Alexander. Marry, sir, thus:
    He left his wild fit to read o'er his cards;
    Yet then, though age cast snow on all his hairs,
    He joyed, 'Because,' says he, 'the god of gold   95
    Has been to me no niggard. That disease
    Of which all old men sicken, avarice,
    Never infected me – '
Laxton. [*Aside*] He means not himself, I'm sure.
Sir Alexander.   'For like a lamp
    Fed with continual oil, I spend and throw   100
    My light to all that need it, yet have still
    Enough to serve myself. O but,' quoth he,
    'Though heaven's dew fall thus on this agèd tree,
    I have a son that's like a wedge doth cleave
    My very heart-root.'
Sir Davy.   Had he such a son?   105
Sebastian. [*Aside*] Now I do smell a fox strongly.
Sir Alexander. Let's see – no, Master Greenwit is not yet
    So mellow in years as he, but as like Sebastian,
    Just like my son Sebastian – such another.
Sebastian. [*Aside*] How finely, like a fencer, my father fetches 110

93. cards] *Q;* cares *Bowers.*   104. that's] *Q(*thats*);* that, *Dyce.*

---

93. *cards*] Although Bowers's emendation ('cares') has appeal, the sense of
the Q reading better fits the context, since the 'old man' takes stock not only of
cares, but of blessings also.

96–8. *disease . . . me*] Cf. *Mer.V.*, IV.i.262–7.

99.] The aside interrupts Sir Alexander's blank verse line; cf. Sebastian's
interjected prose asides below.

98–102. *For . . . myself*] Cf. Middleton, *More Dissemblers Besides Women*,
I.iii.38–41; also *Meas.*, I.i.33–6.

100. *continual*] inexhaustible.

103. *heaven's*] one syllable.

104. *that's*] Emendation is unnecessary if an ellipsis of 'that' after *wedge* is
allowed (Abbott, § 244).

105. *heart-root*] the seat of deepest emotion.

106. *smell a fox*] given by *O.D.E.P.* as a variant of 'smell a rat'. And, as the
fencing terms in Sebastian's next aside make clear, *fox* also signifies a kind of
sword. Pistol threatens with such a sword in *H5* (IV.iv.9); cf. also Beaumont
and Fletcher, *Philaster*, IV.v.130 (Revels ed.), and Webster, *White Devil*,
V.vi.235 (Revels ed.). The exact phrase with similar word-play occurs in
Locrine, II.v.93 (ed. Brooke).

his by-blows to hit me; but if I beat you not at your own
    weapon of subtlety –
Sir Alexander. 'This son,' saith he, 'that should be
    The column and main arch unto my house,
    The crutch unto my age, becomes a whirlwind   115
    Shaking the firm foundation – '
Sir Adam.   'Tis some prodigal.
Sebastian. [*Aside*] Well shot, old Adam Bell!
Sir Alexander. No city monster neither, no prodigal,
    But sparing, wary, civil, and – though wifeless –
    An excellent husband; and such a traveller,   120
    He has more tongues in his head than some have teeth.
Sir Davy. I have but two in mine.
Goshawk.   So sparing and so wary:
    What then could vex his father so?
Sir Alexander.   O, a woman.
Sebastian. A flesh-fly: that can vex any man!
Sir Alexander. A scurvy woman,   125
    On whom the passionate old man swore he doted.
    'A creature,' saith he, 'nature hath brought forth

---

111. *by-blows*] side-blows or side-strokes (with a sword).

111–12. *at your own weapon*] a common phrase (see Tilley, W204), meaning 'with the weapon you are expert in' (*O.E.D.*, 'weapon', 2c).

112. *subtlety*] craftiness, guile.

117. *Adam Bell*] 'a celebrated archer and outlaw' (Reed) who figures in the anonymous ballad, *Adam Bell, Clim of the Clough, and William of Cloudesly* (*The English and Scottish Popular Ballads*, ed. F. J. Child (New York, 1957), III, 14ff.). Cf. Dekker, *Sat.*, IV.iii.118–19; also *Ado*, I.i.222–4.

120. *excellent husband*] playing on the two senses suggested by 'wifeless' and 'sparing, wary, civil'.

124. *flesh-fly*] a blow-fly: a fly which lives on and lays its eggs in dead flesh. Parker (*C.M. in C.*, II.i.52n. (Revels ed.)) remarks, 'Lust is frequently emblematized as a flesh-fly in Middleton'; cf. *W.B.W.*, II.ii.398–400 (Revels ed.); also *Ham.*, II.ii.180–6.

129–30. *birth ... made*] suggestive of an abortion, which Sir Alexander seems to feel explains her alleged hermaphroditism. Both abortions and hermaphrodites were regarded by the Elizabethans as monsters.

127–32.] apparently imitated in N. Field, *Amends for Ladies*, II.i.32–9 (*Plays*, ed. W. Peery (Austin, Tex., 1950)): 'Hence lewd impudent / I know not what to tearme thee man or woman, / For nature shaming to acknowledge thee / For either; hath produc'd thee to the World / Without a sexe, some say thou art a woman, / Others a man; and many thou art both / Woman and man, but I thinke rather neither / Or man and horse, as the old Centaures were faign'd.'

To mock the sex of woman.' It is a thing
One knows not how to name: her birth began
Ere she was all made. 'Tis woman more than man,   130
Man more than woman, and – which to none can hap –
The sun gives her two shadows to one shape;
Nay, more, let this strange thing walk, stand, or sit,
No blazing star draws more eyes after it.

Sir Davy. A monster! 'Tis some monster!

Sir Alexander.   She's a varlet!   135

Sebastian. [*Aside*] Now is my cue to bristle.

Sir Alexander. A naughty pack.

Sebastian.   'Tis false!

Sir Alexander.   Ha, boy?

Sebastian.   'Tis false!

Sir Alexander. What's false? I say she's naught.

Sebastian.   I say that tongue
That dares speak so – but yours – sticks in the throat
Of a rank villain. – Set yourself aside –   140

Sir Alexander. So, sir, what then?

Sebastian.   Any here else had lied.
– (*Aside*) I think I shall fit you.

Sir Alexander. Lie?

Sebastian.   Yes.

Sir Davy.   Doth this concern him?

---

140. villain. – Set] *This ed.;* villaine, set *Q;* villain: set *Dyce.*

---

132. *two shadows*] possibly meaning a different shadow for each sex.
    shape] semblance, appearance; cf. *Gent.*, V.iv.108–9: 'It is the lesser blot,
modesty finds, / Women to change their shapes than men their minds.'

134. *blazing star*] comet; a favourite Dekker image: see this editor's 'The
Date of *The Roaring Girl*', *R.E.S.*, new ser., XXVIII (1977), 20.

137. *naughty pack*] person of worthless or bad character.

138. *naught*] immoral; cf. Middleton and Rowley, *F.Q.*, V.i.93.

138–9. *tongue ... throat*] a charge of lying; cf. III.i.89–90 and n.

139. *but*] except.

140. *set yourself aside*] He appears to mean physically.

142. Aside] This s.d., which follows a dash at the end of the line in Q (sig.
c1r), seems to have been confused with the text, probably because of the
word's use within the speech at l. 140. On sig. D4r 'aside' as a s.d. is set on the
right side of the page in roman instead of the more usual italics.
    fit you] (1) provide what you need; (2) requite you as you deserve; cf. Kyd,
Spanish Tragedy, IV.i.70 (Revels ed.); Beaumont and Fletcher, *Philaster*,
II.ii.143 (Revels ed.).

Sir Alexander.   Ah, sirrah boy,
   Is your blood heated? Boils it? Are you stung?
   I'll pierce you deeper yet. – O my dear friends,   145
   I am that wretched father, this that son
   That sees his ruin, yet headlong on doth run.
Sir Adam. Will you love such a poison?
Sir Davy.   Fie, fie!
Sebastian.   You're all mad!
Sir Alexander. Thou'rt sick at heart, yet feel'st it not. Of all
   these,
   What gentleman, but thou, knowing his disease   150
   Mortal, would shun the cure? O Master Greenwit,
   Would you to such an idol bow?
Greenwit.   Not I, sir.
Sir Alexander. Here's Master Laxton: has he mind to a woman
   As thou hast?
Laxton.   No, not I, sir.
Sir Alexander.   Sir, I know it.
Laxton. Their good parts are so rare, their bad so common,   155
   I will have naught to do with any woman.
Sir Davy. 'Tis well done, Master Laxton.
Sir Alexander.   O thou cruel boy,
   Thou wouldst with lust an old man's life destroy;
   Because thou seest I'm half-way in my grave,
   Thou shovel'st dust upon me: would thou mightest have   160
   Thy wish, most wicked, most unnatural!
Sir Davy. Why sir, 'tis thought Sir Guy Fitzallard's daughter
   Shall wed your son Sebastian.
Sir Alexander.   Sir Davy Dapper,
   I have upon my knees wooed this fond boy
   To take that virtuous maiden.
Sebastian.   Hark you a word, sir.   165
   You on your knees have cursed that virtuous maiden,
   And me for loving her; yet do you now

155. Their ... their] *Reed;* There ... there *Q.*

156.] Laxton slyly equivocates; he appears to say that he will have nothing
to do with women, but the pun on *naught* in a sense allied to that at l. 138 above
(*O.E.D.*, sb. 2a, and adj., 2c) suggests that he is willing to deal immorally with
any woman.
   164. *fond*] foolish.

Thus baffle me to my face? Wear not your knees
In such entreats! Give me Fitzallard's daughter!
Sir Alexander. I'll give thee ratsbane rather!
Sebastian.   Well then you know   170
What dish I mean to feed upon.
Sir Alexander.   Hark, gentlemen,
He swears to have this cutpurse drab to spite my gall.
All. Master Sebastian!
Sebastian.   I am deaf to you all!
I'm so bewitched, so bound to my desires,
Tears, prayers, threats, nothing can quench out those fires   175
That burn within me!   *Exit.*
Sir Alexander. [*Aside*]   Her blood shall quench it then.
 – [*To them*] Lose him not: O dissuade him, gentlemen!
Sir Davy. He shall be weaned, I warrant you.
Sir Alexander.   Before his eyes
Lay down his shame, my grief, his miseries.
All. No more, no more; away!
                    Exeunt all but Sir Alexander.
Sir Alexander.   I wash a negro,   180
Losing both pains and cost. But take thy flight:
I'll be most near thee when I'm least in sight.
Wild buck, I'll hunt thee breathless: thou shalt run on,
But I will turn thee when I'm not thought upon.

---

176. s.d.] *Exit Sebastian. Q.*

---

168. *baffle*] (1) hoodwink, cheat (*O.E.D.*, 4); (2) disagree (*O.E.D.*, 1); originally 'to baffle' meant to degrade an unworthy knight by hanging him, his effigy or his shield upside down. Cf. III.i.17.

Wear not your knees] Cf. 'Weare not your cloathes thred-bare at knees for me', Dekker, *2 H.W.*, IV.i.33.

169. *entreats*] entreaties, supplications.

171. *dish ... upon*] Cf. III.ii.245–7.

172. *drab*] slut, whore.

180.1. Exeunt all but] The same construction appears in Dekker and Webster, *Sir Thomas Wyatt*, III.i.156, IV.ii.18.

180–1. *I wash ... cost*] proverbial: 'To wash an Ethiop (blackamoor, moor) white' (Tilley, E186), 'He that washes an Ass's head loses both his soap and labour' (A370); cf. Jer. xiii.23, 'Can the blacke More change his skin? or the leopard his spottes?' (Geneva); common in Dekker.

184. *turn*] check, or divert from a course of action.

Enter RALPH TRAPDOOR [*with a letter*].

Now, sirrah, what are you? Leave your ape's tricks and
    speak.   185
Trapdoor. A letter from my captain to your worship.
Sir Alexander. O, O, now I remember, 'tis to prefer thee into
    my service.
Trapdoor. To be a shifter under your worship's nose of a clean
    trencher, when there's a good bit upon't.   190
Sir Alexander. Troth, honest fellow. – [*Aside*] Hm – ha – let me
    see –
    This knave shall be the axe to hew that down
    At which I stumble: 'has a face that promiseth
    Much of a villain; I will grind his wit,
    And if the edge prove fine, make use of it.   195
    – [*To him*] Come hither, sirrah. Canst thou be secret, ha?
Trapdoor. As two crafty attorneys plotting the undoing of their
    clients.
Sir Alexander. Didst never, as thou hast walked about this
    town,
    Hear of a wench called Moll – Mad, Merry Moll?   200
Trapdoor. Moll Cutpurse, sir?
Sir Alexander. The same; dost thou know her then?
Trapdoor. As well as I know 'twill rain upon Simon and Jude's

193. 'has] *Reed subst.* (he has); has Q.

186.] Numerous statutes in the reigns of Elizabeth and James dealt with
problems associated with discharged soldiers turned beggars and other
vagrants; J.P.s were responsible for administering them.

193. *'has*] Q's 'has' is a contracted form of 'he has', found often in Middleton and occasionally in Dekker.

197–8.] Cf. Middleton, *M.T.*, III.i.158–61.

203–4. *rain . . . Simon and Jude's day*] Cf. II.i.154. Simon and Jude's day, 28
October, is closely associated with the annual Lord Mayor's Pageants held the
following day. In 1605 the show was postponed 'by reason of ye greate rayne
and fowle weather hapnyng, and falling vpon the morrowe after *Symon and
Iudes Day*' (J. Robertson and D. J. Gordon (edd.), *M.S.C.*, III (1954), 69).
John Chamberlain speaks in 1606 (when no Lord Mayor's Show is recorded)
of 'fowle weather' on 28 October (*Letters*, ed. N. E. McClure (Philadelphia,
1939), I, 236). Rain on Simon and Jude's day may have acquired a quasi-
proverbial status after several successive years' inclement weather. But *R.G.*'s
are oddly unique references: W. C. Hazlitt, *Faiths and Folklore of the British
Isles* (New York, 1870), II, 549–50, A. R. Wright *British Calendar Customs*,
ed. T. E. Lones (1940), III, 105, and V. S. Lean, *Collectanea* (1902–4), I, 381,
cite its allusions as their only creditable authorities.

day next. I will sift all the taverns i'th' city, and drink half-
pots with all the watermen o'th' Bankside, but if you   205
will, sir, I'll find her out.

Sir Alexander. That task is easy; do't then. – Hold thy hand up.
What's this? Is't burnt?

Trapdoor. No, sir, no: a little singed with making fireworks.

Sir Alexander. There's money: spend it; that being spent, fetch
more.   210

Trapdoor. O sir, that all the poor soldiers in England had such a
leader! For fetching, no water-spaniel is like me.

Sir Alexander. This wench we speak of strays so from her kind,
Nature repents she made her; 'tis a mermaid
Has tolled my son to shipwreck.   215

Trapdoor. I'll cut her comb for you.

Sir Alexander. I'll tell out gold for thee then; hunt her forth,

---

205. *watermen o'th' Bankside*] i.e. boatmen operating boats for hire. John
Taylor, the water poet, in *The Water-mens suite concerning Players* (*Works*,
1630) states, 'the number of Water-men, and those that liue and are maintained by them, and by the onely labour of the Oare and the Scull, betwixt the
Bridge of Windsor and Grauesend, cannot be fewer then forty thousand; the
cause of the greater halfe of which multitude, hath beene the Players playing
on the Banke-side' (sig. Pp4v). The *Bankside* is 'the district in Southwark
running along the Surrey side of the Thames from St. Saviour's Church and
Winchester House to the point where Blackfriars Bridge now stands. The row
of houses on the river-side was a series of brothels, and was known as the
Bordello, or Stews' (Sugden, p. 44).

208. *burnt*] i.e. branded as a felon (with an F): a common punishment for a
first offence; see William Harrison, *Description of England*, ed. Georges
Edelen (Ithaca, N.Y., 1968), pp. 191–2.

214–15. *mermaid . . . shipwreck*] Mermaids were commonly associated by
the Elizabethans with sirens; cf. Dekker, *Penny-Wise* (ed. Pendry), p. 120,
'This woman . . . is some mermaid enticing me to run upon the rocks of
destruction'; also *Tit.*, II.i.23–5, *3H6*, III.ii.186, *Err.*, III.ii.44–7. 'Mermaid'
could also mean 'whore', as in Middleton, *C.M. in C.*, IV.iv.26 (Revels ed.),
F.Q., IV.iv.114–16.

215. *tolled*] attracted, allured.

216. *cut . . . comb*] lower the pride of, humiliate; proverbial (Tilley, C526),
and common in Middleton (e.g., *A Trick to Catch the Old One*, IV.iv.32,
Hengist, King of Kent, III.iii.215). Gomme notes, 'cutting a cock's comb was
a usual accompaniment of gelding. So Trapdoor will destroy Moll's
masculinity.'

217. *tell out*] count out.

　　　　Cast out a line hung full of silver hooks
　　　　To catch her to thy company: deep spendings
　　　　May draw her that's most chaste to a man's bosom.　　　220
Trapdoor. The jingling of golden bells, and a good fool with a ·
　　　　hobby-horse, will draw all the whores i'th' town to dance
　　　　in a morris.
Sir Alexander. Or rather – for that's best – they say sometimes
　　　　She goes in breeches: follow her as her man.　　　225
Trapdoor. And when her breeches are off, she shall follow me!
Sir Alexander. Beat all thy brains to serve her.
Trapdoor. Zounds, sir, as country wenches beat cream, till
　　　　butter comes.
Sir Alexander. Play thou the subtle spider: weave fine nets　　　230
　　　　To ensnare her very life.
Trapdoor.　　　　　　　　Her life?
Sir Alexander.　　　　　　　　Yes, suck
　　　　Her heart-blood if thou canst. Twist thou but cords
　　　　To catch her; I'll find law to hang her up.
Trapdoor. Spoke like a worshipful bencher!
Sir Alexander. Trace all her steps; at this she-fox's den　　　235

218.] Cf. III.i.98; a common image in Dekker; also proverbial (Tilley, H591).

219–20. *deep spendings ... bosom*] Cf. II.i.195–7; also *Cym.*, II.iii.66–73, *Rom.*, I.i.212.

221–3.] Morris-dancing originally incorporated characters from the Robin Hood legend. The hobby-horse (a dancer with the figure of a horse attached to his waist) wore bells and capered lewdly (it was suppressed by the Puritans after the Reformation); *hobby-horse* could also mean 'whore', as in *Ham.*, III.ii.127–30, *L.L.L.*, III.i.26–9, *Oth.*, IV.i.151.

225. *man*] i.e. manservant.

227. *Beat all thy brains*] proverbial: Tilley, B602.

228. *Zounds*] a euphemistic abbreviation of 'by God's (i.e. Christ's) wounds', 'Apparently thought profane and excised in many prompt-books after the Act of Abuses, 1606' (E. A. J. Honigmann, ed., *John*, (1967), II.i.466n.).

228–9. *country wenches ... comes*] with a bawdy quibble.

230–1.] Cf. III.iii.41 and IV.ii.204–9 and n.; spider images are common in Middleton (e.g., *M.W.M.M.*, I.i.153ff., *W.B.W.*, II.ii.398–9 (Revels ed.)), and Dekker (e.g., *2 H.W.*, II.i.195–8, *W.B.*, I.i.66–8, III.i.120–4, *The Seven deadly Sinnes*, sig. B4r, *Foure Birds of Noahs Arke* (ed. Wilson), p. 36).

232. *heart-blood*] life-blood, vital energy.

234. *bencher*] magistrate.

Watch what lambs enter; let me play the shepherd
To save their throats from bleeding, and cut hers.
Trapdoor. This is the goll shall do't.
Sir Alexander.   Be firm, and gain me
Ever thine own. This done, I entertain thee.
How is thy name?   240
Trapdoor. My name, sir, is Ralph Trapdoor – honest Ralph.
Sir Alexander. Trapdoor, be like thy name: a dangerous step
For her to venture on; but unto me –
Trapdoor. As fast as your sole to your boot or shoe, sir.
Sir Alexander. Hence then; be little seen here as thou canst;   245
I'll still be at thine elbow.
Trapdoor.   The trap-door's set:
Moll, if you budge, you're gone. This me shall crown:
A roaring boy the Roaring Girl puts down.
Sir Alexander. God-a-mercy, lose no time.   *Exeunt.*

---

241. Ralph . . . Ralph] *Reed; Raph . . . Raph Q.*   243. me –] *Reed;* me. *Q.*

---

238. *goll*] hand; because a cant term, generally regarded as a sign of Dekker, but it is common in Middleton also (e.g. *Blurt, Master Constable*, I.i.7, *C.M. in C.*, II.ii.64 (Revels ed.), *H.K.K.*, V.i.188).

239. *entertain*] take into service.

242–4.] playing on Trapdoor's name; cf. a similar play in Dekker, *Patient Grissil*, IV.i.227–8.

248. *roaring boy*] roisterer; 'The Cheating Age', a broadside ballad, gives a depiction of roarers (*A Pepysian Garland*, ed. H. E. Rollins (Cambridge, 1922), pp. 244–7); see also the portrait given in Overbury, *Characters* (*A Book of 'Characters'*, ed. R. Aldington (n.d.), pp. 139–40); and cf. the 'Roaring School' in Middleton and Rowley, *F.Q.*

puts down] (1) drops down, with a play on his name; (2) in a sexual sense (Partridge, p. 170); (3) kills (*O.E.D.*, 41d).

249. *God-a-mercy*] 'God have mercy' in the sense of 'God reward you'; used as an exclamation of thanks.

Act II

[II.i]

The three shops open in a rank: the first a pothecary's shop, the next a feather shop, the third a sempster's shop. MISTRESS GALLIPOT *in the first,* MISTRESS TILTYARD *in the next,* MASTER OPENWORK *and his* Wife *in the third. To them enters* LAXTON, GOSHAWK, *and* GREENWIT.

Mistress Openwork. Gentlemen, what is't you lack? What is't you buy? See find bands and ruffs, fine lawns, fine cambrics. What is't you lack, gentlemen, what is't you buy?

II.i] *Dyce; not in* Q.

II.i.] See Intro., pp. 42–6, for a discussion of staging.

0.1. shops] An illustration of the kind of shop probably intended is given in J. A. Comenius, *Orbis Pictus* (1659, ed. J. E. Sadler, 1968), p. 364.

rank] line.

pothecary's shop] *pothecary* = aphetic form of apothecary. See Richard Brathwait, *A Solemne Iouiall Disputation* (1617) for an illustration of a tobacco-shop interior (reproduced in Pendry, opposite p. 88). 'Pothecary's shop' becomes 'tobacco shop' in subsequent s.dd. In addition to herbs, drugs, etc., apothecaries sold tobacco at this time; cf. Dekker, *G.H.* (ed. Pendry), p. 95: 'And here you must observe to know in what state tobacco is in town better than the merchants, and to discourse of the pothecaries where it is to be sold and to be able to speak of their leaves as readily as the pothecary himself reading the barbarous hand of a doctor.'

0.2. feather shop] Philip Stubbes, *Anatomie of Abuses* (1583), sig. D7v, remarks, 'many get good liuing by dying and selling of [feathers]'.

0.2–4.] Women used to attract custom were frequently satirised: e.g. Francis Lenton, *Characterismi; or, Lenton's Leasures* (1631), sigs. E3v–4v, 'Shee is very neatly spruc'd vp, and placed in the frontispice of her shop, of purpose, (by her curious habit) to allure some Custome, which still encraseth and decreaseth as her beauty is in the full, or the wane.' Cf. Middleton, *F. of L.*, II.i.2–6; also Marston, *Dutch Courtesan*, ed. M. L. Wine (1965), III.iii.10–13.

0.4. enters] singular verb with plural subject: common in Jacobean English; see Abbott, § 335.

1–4. *what . . . buy*] traditional street cries; see F. P. Wilson, 'Illustrations of Social Life III: Street Cries', *Sh.S. 13* (1960), 106ff.

Laxton. Yonder's the shop.   5
Goshawk. Is that she?
Laxton. Peace!
Greenwit. She that minces tobacco?
Laxton. Ay: she's a gentlewoman born, I can tell you, though it
   be her hard fortune now to shred Indian pot-herbs.   10
Goshawk. O sir, 'tis many a good woman's fortune, when her
   husband turns bankrupt, to begin with pipes and set up
   again.
Laxton. And indeed the raising of the woman is the lifting up of
   the man's head at all times: if one flourish, t'other will bud   15
   as fast, I warrant ye.
Goshawk. Come, thou'rt familiarly acquainted there, I grope
   that.
Laxton. An you grope no better i'th' dark, you may chance lie
   i'th' ditch when you're drunk.   20
Goshawk. Go, thou'rt a mystical lecher!
Laxton. I will not deny but my credit may take up an ounce of
   pure smoke.
Goshawk. May take up an ell of pure smock! – Away, go! –
   [*Aside*] 'Tis the closest striker! Life, I think he commits   25

---

10. *Indian pot-herbs*] *Pot-herb* is used normally of any herb grown for boil-
ing in the pot; the reference here, however, is presumably to tobacco.

11–13.] The swift increase in tobacco consumption in the early 1600's
caused tradesmen to flock to the new commodity; cf. Middleton, *No Wit, No
Help Like a Woman's*, II.ii.186ff., Dekker, *Penny Wise, Pound Foolish* (ed.
Pendry), p. 139, and John Earle, *Microcosmography* (*A Book of 'Characters'*,
ed. R. Aldington), p. 216.

14–15. *raising . . . head*] with a bawdy quibble.

17. *grope*] (1) understand; (2) handle, feel.

19. *An*] if.

19–20. *lie i'th' ditch*] i.e. as a reward for groping (in a bawdy sense).

21. *mystical*] Cf. Epistle, l. 24.

22. *credit*] (1) reputation; (2) sale on trust.

24. *ell*] a measure of length: 45 inches.

smock] 'a shirt-like garment worn as underwear, and as a sleeping garment'
(Linthicum, p. 189). The reference is to lifting up a woman's underskirt for a
sexual encounter.

25. *'Tis*] i.e. he is.

closest] (1) most secret, hence, most imperceptible; (2) most intimate.

striker] fornicator, wencher.

venery forty foot deep: no man's aware on't. I, like a palpable smockster, go to work so openly with the tricks of art
that I'm as apparently seen as a naked boy in a vial; and
were it not for a gift of treachery that I have in me to betray
my friend when he puts most trust in me – mass, yonder   30
he is, too – and by his injury to make good my access to
her, I should appear as defective in courting as a farmer's
son the first day of his feather, that doth nothing at Court
but woo the hangings and glass windows for a month together, and some broken waiting-woman for ever after. I   35
find those imperfections in my venery that, were't not for
flattery and falsehood, I should want discourse and impudence; and he that wants impudence among women is
worthy to be kicked out at bed's feet. – He shall not see
me yet.   40

[*At the tobacco shop.*]

40.1.] *M. Thesis.*

---

27. *smockster*] bawd.
28. *apparently*] clearly.

naked boy in a vial] Steevens (Reed) conjectured, 'I suppose he means an
abortion preserved in spirits.' Abortions were regarded as monsters in
Jacobean times and put on display in this manner. But 'to look a naked boy in
the eyes' meant 'to look amorously' (see J. S. Farmer (ed.), *Proverbs, Epi-
grams, and Miscellanies of John Heywood* (1906), p. 414); this secondary sense
may underlie Goshawk's statement.

30. *my friend*] i.e. Openwork.

mass] 'Asseverations like "by the mass" and "Birlady" survived the
Reformation and still came naturally to Protestant lips' (F. P. Wilson (ed.),
The Batchelars Banquet (Oxford, 1929), p. xix).

32-3. *farmer's son ... feather*] Middleton writes of a foolish young farmer's
son who squanders his patrimony in *F.H.T.* (Bullen, VIII), pp. 65ff.; feathers
are among his first purchases. Cf. 'the first day of his plumage' (= introduction to Court).

33-5. *nothing ... after*] i.e., once the neophyte at Court's expectations or
ambitions are dashed and his money exhausted, he contents himself with
whatever he can get.

34. *hangings*] drapery with which a bedstead or the walls of a room is hung.
Cf. Dekker and Webster, *Westward Ho*, V.i.246–9: 'I ha not beene so often at
Court, but I know what the back-side of the Hangings are made of. Ile trust
none vnder a peece of Tapistry, *viz.* a Couerlet.'

35. *broken*] violated, defiled.
38. *impudence*] Cf. Middleton, *Y.F.G.*, IV.v.69–73.

Greenwit. Troth, this is finely shred.

Laxton. O, women are the best mincers!

Mistress Gallipot. 'T had been a good phrase for a cook's wife,
     sir.

Laxton. But 'twill serve generally, like the front of a new   45
     almanac, as thus: calculated for the meridian of cooks'
     wives, but generally for all Englishwomen.

Mistress Gallipot. Nay, you shall ha't, sir: I have filled it for
     you.   *She puts it to the fire.*

Laxton. The pipe's in a good hand, and I wish mine always so.   50

Greenwit. But not to be used o' that fashion!

Laxton. O pardon me, sir, I understand no French. I pray be
     covered. Jack, a pipe of rich smoke?

Goshawk. Rich smoke: that's sixpence a pipe, is't?

Greenwit. To me, sweet lady.   55

---

42. *mincers*] playing on chopping small, and mincing words.

43. *'T had*] i.e. it would have been.

46. *almanac*] Almanacs giving astrological and other predictions were sold
cheaply to the gullible.

46–7. *calculated ... Englishwomen*] parodying the conventional formula on
the title-pages of almanacs to reach the widest possible market. *Calculated to
the meridian* = suited to the special tastes.

48. *Nay ... ha't*] presumably in response to a weak gesture of refusal from
Laxton.

50. *pipe's ... hand*] with the common bawdy play, taken up in the ensuing
exchange. Cf. Middleton, *B.M.C.*, II.ii.338ff., *F.Q.*, IV.i.240–2, Dekker,
Sat., I.ii.176ff.

51.] i.e. put to the fire: alluding to the burning effects of syphilis.

52. *French*] 'bawdy language', as well as the common reference to venereal
diseases, or the means of acquiring them; cf. Dekker and Webster, *W.H.*,
I.i.127–8: 'you [Birdlime] may speake French, most of your kinds can vnder-
stand French'.

52–3. *be covered*] possibly directed in aside to Mist. Gallipot alerting her to
his wish for a secret conference, but more probably addressed to Goshawk,
who has just rejoined them, to replace the hat he has removed either in salute
or to waft away tobacco smoke. Cf. *Mer.V.*, II.ix.44, *A.Y.L.*, III.iii.67.

53. *Jack*] in reference to Goshawk; a generic name for a man. Cf. Jack used
for Moll when dressed as a man, V.i.1, 30, 55, *passim*.

54. *sixpence a pipe*] Tobacco is half this price (though adulterated) in
Jonson, *Bartholomew Fair*, II.ii.89–92. Goshawk may be fishing for credit.

55. *To me*] i.e. a pipe for me; cf. Middleton, *C.M. in C.*, I.i.22 (Revels ed.),
for a similar use of *to* = for.

Mistress Gallipot. [*Aside to Laxton*] Be not forgetful; respect
      my credit; seem strange: art and wit makes a fool of sus-
      picion; pray be wary.
Laxton. [*Aside to Mistress Gallipot*] Push, I warrant you. – [*To
      them*] Come, how is't gallants?   60
Greenwit. Pure and excellent.
Laxton. I thought 'twas good, you were grown so silent. You
      are like those that love not to talk at victuals, though they
      make a worse noise i' the nose than a common fiddler's
      prentice, and discourse a whole supper with snuffling. –   65
      [*Aside to Mistress Gallipot*] I must speak a word with you
      anon.
Mistress Gallipot. [*Aside to Laxton*] Make your way wisely
      then.
Goshawk. O what else, sir? He's perfection itself: full of man-   70
      ners, but not an acre of ground belonging to 'em.
Greenwit. Ay, and full of form; 'has ne'er a good stool in's
      chamber.
Goshawk. But above all religious: he preyeth daily upon elder
      brothers.   75
Greenwit. And valiant above measure: 'has run three streets
      from a sergeant.

72, 76. 'has] *Reed subst.;* h'as *Q.*

---

57. *seem strange*] 'do not appear too familiar'.
59. *Push*] Middleton's characteristic form of the interjection, 'pish'.
Though so written throughout Middleton's holograph manuscript of *A Game
at Chess*, Ralph Crane in his transcript consistently renders it 'pish'.
64–5. *worse noise ... snuffling*] Fiddle and cognate terms commonly carried
bawdy significations (cf. Lyly, *Midas* (ed. A. Lancashire (Lincoln, Nebr.,
1969), I.ii.8); *noise i' the nose* and *snuffling* may accordingly refer to the effects
of venereal disease, and *fiddler's prentice* may be the equivalent of 'assistant to
a bawd' (see IV.ii.237n.); cf. Dekker, Rowley and Ford, *W. of E.*, IV.i.38–9,
'... which trick as surely proves her a Witch, as the Pox in a snuffling nose, is a
sign a Man is a Whore-master'. *Prentice* is an aphetic form of 'apprentice'.
70–1. *manners*] punning on 'manors'; cf. Heywood, *Woman Killed with
Kindness*, xvi.7–10 (Revels ed.).
72. *form*] punning on (1) etiquette, code of manners; (2) bench. The second
sense explains the remainder of the speech; cf. *Rom.*, H.iv.33–4.
72–3. *ne'er ... chamber*] reasserts his lack of property; cf. III.i.50–1.
76–7. *run ... sergeant*] belies Laxton's valour and suggests impecunious-
ness: sergeants generally arrested for debt.

Laxton. (*Blows tobacco-[smoke] in their faces.*) Pooh, pooh.

Greenwit, Goshawk. [*Coughing*] O, pooh, ho, ho!

> [*They move away.*]

Laxton. So, so.   80

Mistress Gallipot. What's the matter now, sir?

Laxton. I protest I'm in extreme want of money. If you can
supply me now with any means, you do me the greatest
pleasure, next to the bounty of your love, as ever poor
gentleman tasted.   85

Mistress Gallipot. What's the sum would pleasure ye, sir? –
Though you deserve nothing less at my hands.

Laxton. Why, 'tis but for want of opportunity, thou knowest. –
[*Aside*] I put her off with opportunity still! By this light I
hate her, but for means to keep me in fashion with gal-   90
lants; for what I take from her I spend upon other
wenches, bear her in hand still. She has wit enough to rob
her husband, and I ways enough to consume the money. –
[*To Gallants*] Why, how now? What, the chincough?

Goshawk. Thou hast the cowardliest trick to come before a   95
man's face and strangle him ere he be aware. I could find
in my heart to make a quarrel in earnest.

Laxton. Pox, an thou dost – thou knowest I never use to fight
with my friends – thou'll but lose thy labour in't.

78. *Blows*] Q *(he blowes) ; s.d. to the right of the speech in Q.*   79. s.dd.] *M.
Thesis.*

---

87. *nothing less*] i.e. 'anything but that' – an early signal that Mist. Gallipot
is dissatisfied with Laxton. Middleton seems to have favoured the expression;
cf. *W.B.W.*, II.i.133 and II.ii.281 (Revels ed.).

88. *opportunity*] Cf. Middleton, *M.T.*, II.iii.1ff., Dekker and Webster,
W.H., I.i.124–6; also *Lucr.*, 876ff.; Jonson, *Every Man in his Humour*,
III.iii.13–17.

thou] Laxton modulates from *you* to the more familiar *thou/thee* forms.

89–93.] This private declaration betrays the character's true thoughts and
undermines the improvised account given at the end of IV.ii.

89. *By this light*] an asseveration referring to daylight, as in *Ado*, V.iv.93.

91–3. *for . . . money*] Cf. Middleton, *F. of L.*, I.iii.166–70: 'Let me tell you in
private that the doctor cuckolds Purge oftener than he visits one of his patients: what 'a spares from you 'a spends lavishly on her. These 'pothecaries
are a kind of panders: look to it: if 'a keep Maria long close, it is for some
lascivious end of his own.'

92. *bear her in hand*] delude her with false hopes, lead her on; proverbial:
Tilley, H94.

94. *chincough*] whooping cough: referring to the coughing fit precipitated
by Laxton's blowing smoke in their faces.

Enter J[ACK] DAPPER *and his man* GULL.

– Jack Dapper!   100

Greenwit. Monsieur Dapper, I dive down to your ankles.

Jack Dapper. Save ye, gentlemen, all three, in a peculiar salute.

Goshawk. He were ill to make a lawyer: he dispatches three at
    once!

Laxton. So, well said! – [*Receiving purse from Mistress Gal-*   105
    lipot.] But is this of the same tobacco, Mistress Gallipot?

Mistress Gallipot. The same you had at first, sir.

Laxton. I wish it no better: this will serve to drink at my
    chamber.

Goshawk. Shall we taste a pipe on't?   110

Laxton. Not of this, by my troth, gentlemen; I have sworn
    before you.

Goshawk. What, not Jack Dapper?

Laxton. Pardon me, sweet Jack, I'm sorry I made such a rash
    oath, but foolish oaths must stand. – Where art going,   115
    Jack?

Jack Dapper. Faith, to buy one feather.

Laxton. One feather? – [*Aside*] The fool's peculiar still!

Jack Dapper. Gull.

Gull. Master?   120

99.1.] *on l. 100* Q.   102. *Jack Dapper*] Q *uses* I. Dap., Iac. Dap., *and* Iack
Dap. *throughout.*   105–6. s.d.] *This ed.*

---

101. *dive . . . ankles*] i.e. in a bow; playing on 'dive-dapper', a dabchick.

102. *peculiar*] (1) single; (2) special.

103. *He were . . . lawyer*] either 'He had better not become a lawyer', or 'He
would make a wicked (or poor) lawyer'.

106. *But . . . tobacco*] 'She gives him money, and he pretends that he receives
only tobacco from Mist. Gallipot' (Collier).

108. *drink*] smoke.

117–18. *feather . . . still*] Stubbes reviles the extravagant use of feathers in
hats in *Anatomie of Abuses* (1583), sig. D8r–v. The association of fools with
feathers was proverbial; cf. *O.D.E.P.*, 'Fool with a feather', which cites in
addition to the present passage Marston, *Malcontent*, V.iii.40 (Revels ed.), 'no
fool but has his feather'. The Revels editor, G. K. Hunter, notes also Sir John
Davies, Epigram xlvii, 'his great black feather / By which each gull is now a
gallant deemed'. J. Crow, 'Some Jacobean Catchphrases and Some Light on
Thomas Bretnor', *Elizabethan and Jacobean Studies presented to F. P. Wilson*
(Oxford, 1959), p. 263, no. 232, records 'a feather for a foole' as a catch-phrase
for an evil day.

118. *peculiar*] playing on Jack's single feather (l. 117), and 'odd' or 'queer'.

Jack Dapper. Here's three halfpence for your ordinary, boy;
    meet me an hour hence in Paul's.
Gull. [*Aside*] How? Three single halfpence? Life, this will
    scarce serve a man in sauce: a ha'p'orth of mustard, a
    ha'p'orth of oil, and a ha'p'orth of vinegar – what's left   125
    then for the pickle herring? This shows like small beer
    i'th' morning after a great surfeit of wine o'ernight. He
    could spend his three pound last night in a supper
    amongst girls and brave bawdy-house boys – I thought his
    pockets cackled not for nothing: these are the eggs of three   130
    pound. I'll go sup 'em up presently.   *Exit.*

131. s.d.] *Exit Gul. Q.*

121–6. *three . . . herring*] An ordinary could be an eating-house which served
fixed-price meals, or the meal itself. Bullen noted the allusion to a three-
halfpenny ordinary in *F.H.T.* (Bullen, VIII), p. 80; but Gull seems to lament
that three halfpence will purchase the dressing but not the main part of the
meal. He then consoles himself through word-play with the idea that he will
sup up 'the eggs of three pound'. A threepenny ordinary is the cheapest mentioned by Dekker in *G.H.* (ed. Pendry), p. 96. Cf. *W.B.*, II.i.88–92; 'your
Ordinary is your Isle of Gulles, your ship of fooles, your hospitall of incurable
madmen: it is the field where your captaine and braue man is cal'd to the last
reckoning, and is ouerthrown horse and foot: it is the onely schoole to make an
honest man a knaue.'
    122. *Paul's*] probably Paul's Walk (the middle aisle of St Paul's Cathedral),
a general meeting place for both high and low life. See Dekker, *G.H.* ch. iv
(ed. Pendry), pp. 88–92.
    123. *Life*] a shortened form of 'God's life', a mild oath.
    124. *ha'p'orth*] halfpennyworth.
    126–7. *small beer . . . o'ernight*] Small (i.e. thin or weak) beer was sometimes
recommended as a morning draught after a night of heavy drinking; cf.
Middleton, Massinger and Rowley, *Old Law*, II.i.229–32: '*Sim.* . . . I shall
ne'er drink at home, I shall be so drunk abroad.   *But.* But a cup of small beer
will do well next morning, sir.'
    127. *o'ernight*] the night before.
    128. *supper*] 'taken about 5:30. . . . a modified version of dinner' (*Shake-
speare's England*, II, 134).
    129. *brave*] handsome.
    130. *cackled*] playing on the normal cackling of a hen after laying an egg, and
referring to the chinking of coins in Jack's pockets or purse – the residue of
small change from his three pounds.
    131. *presently*] at once.

Laxton. [*Aside*] Eight, nine, ten angels. Good wench, i'faith,
    and one that loves darkness well: she puts out a candle
    with the best tricks of any drugster's wife in England; but
    that which mads her, I rail upon opportunity still, and   135
    take no notice on't. The other night she would needs lead
    me into a room with a candle in her hand to show me a
    naked picture, where no sooner entered, but the candle
    was sent of an errand; now I, not intending to understand
    her, but like a puny at the inns of venery, called for an-   140
    other light innocently: thus reward I all her cunning with
    simple mistaking. I know she cozens her husband to keep
    me, and I'll keep her honest, as long as I can, to make the
    poor man some part of amends. – An honest mind of a
    whoremaster! – [*To Gallants*] How think you amongst   145
    you? What, a fresh pipe? Draw in a third man.
Goshawk. No, you're a hoarder: you engross by th'ounces!

At the feather shop now.

Jack Dapper. Pooh, I like it not.
Mistress Tiltyard.   What feather is't you'd have, sir?
    These are most worn and most in fashion
    Amongst the beaver gallants, the stone-riders,   150

---

132. *Eight, nine, ten angels*] 'He is reckoning the money he received from
Mist. Gallipot' (Ellis). An angel was a gold coin worth ten shillings at this time
(so called because it was stamped with a design of St Michael slaying the
dragon).

133. *puts . . . candle*] i.e. like a prostitute.

134. *drugster*] apothecary.

135. *rail . . . still*] i.e. always find excuses.

139. *understand*] with a bawdy entendre on 'under-stand'.

140. *puny*] freshman at a university or an Inn of Court.

inns of venery] playing on 'Inns of Court'.

145. *whoremaster*] lecher, fornicator.

147.] Goshawk's churlish response is prompted by Laxton's refusal to
share the 'tobacco' he received earlier from Mist. Gallipot.

engross] (1) monopolise; (2) fatten.

150. *beaver gallants*] gallants who wore the fashionable and expensive
beaver hats. A sexual suggestion may also be intended: the beaver was thought
'a very hot Beaste of nature . . . his stones are much vsed in Physicke, and of
great esteeme' (Henry Cockeram, *English Dictionarie* (1626), sig. T3r).

stone-riders] riders of stallions (more spirited as a rule than geldings or
mares); cf. ll. 268–9 below. *Stone* also carried the sexual sense, 'lascivious' or
'lustful'.

The private stage's audience, the twelvepenny-stool
    gentlemen:
I can inform you 'tis the general feather.
Jack Dapper. And therefore I mislike it – tell me of general!
    Now a continual Simon and Jude's rain
    Beat all your feathers as flat down as pancakes!   155
    Show me – a – spangled feather.
Mistress Tiltyard.   O, to go a-feasting with! –
    You'd have it for a hench-boy; you shall.

          At the sempster's shop now.

Openwork. Mass, I had quite forgot!
    His honour's footman was here last night, wife:
    Ha' you done with my lord's shirt?
Mistress Openwork.   What's that to you, sir?   160
    I was this morning at his honour's lodging
    Ere such a snail as you crept out of your shell.
Openwork. O, 'twas well done, good wife.

---

158. Openwork] *Maist. Open.* Q *passim.*   162. snail] *M. Thesis, Gomme;*
snake *Q.*

---

    151. *twelvepenny-stool*] A. Harbage (*Shakespeare and the Rival Traditions*
(New York, 1952), p. 45) suggests that this reference 'may mean that a shilling
above the ordinary maximum was charged for a stool on the stage'; but William A. Armstrong in 'The Audience of the Elizabethan Private Theatres'
(*The Seventeenth Century Stage*, ed. G. E. Bentley (Chicago, 1968), p. 224)
rejects the idea, citing numerous references to sixpence. *Twelvepenny-stool
gentlemen* may not refer to the private stage's audience at all, but perhaps to
those who attended the best rooms in the public playhouses (see Chambers,
E.S., II, 534).
    154. *Simon . . . rain*] See I.ii.203–4n.
    155. *as flat . . . pancakes*] proverbial (Tilley, P39).
    156. *spangled*] (1) decorated with spangles; (2) speckled; cf. Marlowe, *I
Tamburlaine*, IV.i.50–1 (*Complete Works*, ed. F. Bowers (Cambridge, 1973)),
'. . . and on his silver crest / A snowy Feather spangled white he beares' (cited
by *O.E.D.*).
    157. *hench-boy*] page.
    you shall] i.e. you shall have it (ellipsis).
    162. *snail*] Q's 'snake' may have resulted from a simple misreading of the
MS. Emendation improves the sense; cf. Dekker, *S.D.S.*, sig. D2r: '. . . all that
owed any mony, and for feare of arrests, or Iustices warrants, had like so many
Snayles kept their houses ouer their heads al the day before, began now to
creep out of their shels . . .'; and *2 H.W.*, III.iii.51.

Mistress Openwork.   I hold it better, sir,
    Than if you had done't yourself.
Openwork.   Nay, so say I;
    But is the countess's smock almost done, mouse?   165
Mistress Openwork. Here lies the cambric, sir, but wants I fear
    me.
Openwork. I'll resolve you of that presently.
Mistress Openwork. Heyday! O audacious groom,
    Dare you presume to noblewomen's linen?
    Keep you your yard to measure shepherd's holland! –   170
    I must confine you, I see that.

                    At the tobacco shop now.

Goshawk. What say you to this gear?
Laxton. I dare the arrantest critic in tobacco to lay one fault
    upon't.

            Enter MOLL *in a frieze jerkin and a black safeguard.*

Goshawk. Life, yonder's Moll.   175
Laxton. Moll? Which Moll?
Goshawk. Honest Moll.
Laxton. Prithee let's call her. – Moll!
All Gallants. Moll, Moll, pist, Moll!
Moll. How now, what's the matter?   180
Goshawk. A pipe of good tobacco, Moll?

---

168. Heyday] *Reed;* Haida *Q.*   173. arrantest] *Reed (*arrant'st*);* arrants
Q.   179. *All Gallants*] *All Q.*

---

165. *mouse*] a term of endearment.
168. *Heyday*] an exclamation of surprise or wonder.
groom] fellow.
170. *yard*] (1) measuring stick; (2) penis.
shepherd's holland] a coarse variety of linen fabric first made in Holland.
171. *confine*] limit, restrict.
172. *gear*] 'stuff' (in reference to the tobacco).
174.1. frieze jerkin] The jerkin (a short coat with a collar, usually with
sleeves) was normally worn by men. Moll's dress is hermaphroditic in combining elements of the dress of both sexes.
safeguard] 'Its name probably arose from its purpose: to protect the lady's
costume from dust and soiling by the horse' (Linthicum, pp. 188–9). Moll's
safeguard may also have served a practical function in facilitating her later
costume change.

Moll. I cannot stay.

Goshawk. Nay, Moll – pooh – prithee hark, but one word,
     i'faith.

Moll. Well, what is't?   185

Greenwit. Prithee come hither, sirrah.

Laxton. [*Aside*] Heart, I would give but too much money to be
     nibbling with that wench. Life, sh'has the spirit of four
     great parishes, and a voice that will drown all the city!
     Methinks a brave captain might get all his soldiers upon   190
     her, and ne'er be beholding to a company of Mile End
     milksops, if he could come on and come off quick enough.
     Such a Moll were a marrowbone before an Italian: he

---

193. marrowbone] *Collier;* maribone *Q.*

---

186. *sirrah*] often used in addressing women: cf. III.ii.160, IV.ii.10, *passim.*
187. *Heart*] abbreviation of 'God's heart'.
     but too much] i.e. any amount of.
190-2. *Methinks . . . milksops*] Cf. *The Life of Long Meg of Westminster* (ed.
1620), sig. B2v: '. . . she [Long Meg] shall be kept for breede: for if the King
would marry her to Long *Sanders* of the Court, they would bring foorth none
but Souldiers'; soldierly offspring from mannish women may have been a
common jest: cf. Beaumont and Fletcher, *Love's Cure*, IV.ii.193-4 (*Dramatic
Works*, III, ed. F. Bowers (Cambridge, 1976)).
     190. *get*] beget.
     191. *Mile End*] The green (now Stepney Green), south of Mile End Road,
was used as a drill ground for London citizens under training; most contemporary references, as here, mock the military exercises held there: cf. *2H4*,
III.ii.270ff.
     192. *come on . . . come off*] battle terms meaning 'advance' and 'retire',
continuing the military imagery which carries also a secondary bawdy sense;
cf. Middleton, *B.M.C.*, I.i.141-6: "S light, methinks a Frenchman should
have a good courage to wine, for many of them be exceeding hot fiery whore-
sons, and resolute as Hector, and as valiant as Troilus; then come off and on
bravely, and lie by it, and sweat for't too, upon a good and a military advantage'; also, Jonson, Chapman and Marston, *Eastward Ho*, II.i.19-23.
     193. *marrowbone*] bone containing edible marrow: considered a great deli-
cacy and held to be an aphrodisiac; cf. Middleton, *M.W.M.M.*, I.ii.46-9, 'I
have conveyed away all her wanton pamphlets; as *Hero and Leander*, *Venus
and Adonis*; O, two luscious marrow-bone pies for a young married wife!', and
Dekker and Middleton's *1 Honest Whore*, IV.i.95-6, 'If it be a woman, mary-
bones and Potato pies keepe me for medling with her, for the thing has got the
breeches.' Marston makes a similar allusion in *The Scourge of Villainie*, Satyre
ii.31-7 (*Poems*, ed. A. Davenport (Liverpool, 1961), p. 107); see also *How a
Man May Choose a Good Wife from a Bad*, ed. A. E. H. Swaen (Louvain,
1912), ll. 682-5.
     Italian] Italians had a reputation for lust and perverse sexual desires: cf.
Middleton, *M.W.M.M.*, III.iii.63-5. Sugden (p. 276) cites Heylyn: 'in their
lusts they are unnatural'.

would cry bona-roba till his ribs were nothing but bone.
I'll lay hard siege to her – money is that *aquafortis* that eats   195
into many a maidenhead: where the walls are flesh and
blood, I'll ever pierce through with a golden auger.
Goshawk. Now thy judgement, Moll – is't not good?
Moll. Yes, faith, 'tis very good tobacco. How do you sell an
ounce? Farewell. God buy you, Mistress Gallipot.   200
Goshawk. Why Moll, Moll!
Moll. I cannot stay now, i'faith; I am going to buy a shag ruff –
the shop will be shut in presently.
Goshawk. 'Tis the maddest, fantasticalest girl! – I never knew
so much flesh and so much nimbleness put together!   205
Laxton. She slips from one company to another like a fat eel
between a Dutchman's fingers. – [*Aside*] I'll watch my
time for her.
Mistress Gallipot. Some will not stick to say she's a man, and
some, both man and woman.   210
Laxton. That were excellent: she might first cuckold the husband and then make him to as much for the wife!

The feather shop again.

---

194. *bona-roba*] 'Buonarobba, as we say, good stuffe, a good wholesome
plum-cheeked wench' (Florio, *A Worlde of Words* (1598)); cf. Dekker, *2
H.W.*, I.i.55–6; and Shallow's reminiscence of 'bona-robas' in *2H4*, III.ii.22.

ribs ... bone] possibly an allusion to the popular belief that the passions (love
in particular) were supposed by their excessive heat to burn or melt the marrow, the seat of animal vitality and strength; cf. *Ven.*, 'My flesh is soft and
plump, my marrow burning' (l. 142). Richard Lovelace reproduces the rather
forced puns on 'rib' (roba) and 'bone' (bona) in 'La Bella Bona Roba', *Poems*,
ed. C. H. Wilkinson (Oxford, 1930), p. 96; 'I Cannot tell who loves the
Skeleton / Of a poor Marmoset, nought but boan, boan. / Give me nakednesse
with her cloth's on. / . . . . . / Sure it is meant good Husbandry in men, / Who
do incorporate with Aëry leane, / T'repair their sides, and get their Ribb
agen.'

195–6. *money ... maidenhead*] Cf. I.ii.219–20.

195. *aquafortis*] 'The early scientific, and still the popular, name of the
Nitric Acid of commerce (dilute HNO_3), a powerful solvent and corrosive'
(*O.E.D.*, 3, citing this reference).

199. *How*] At what price (*O.E.D.*, 6).

200. *God buy you*] a phrase possibly meaning 'God redeem you', equivalent
to the modern 'good-bye'; see H. Jenkins (ed.), *Ham.* (1982), II.i.69n.

202. *shag ruff*] a ruff made of shag, a cloth with a velvet nap on one side,
usually of worsted, sometimes of silk.

206–7. *eel. ... fingers*] Cf. 'as slippery as an eel' (Tilley, E60); in Holland, eel
then as now was a favourite dish.

Moll. Save you – how does Mistress Tiltyard?

Jack Dapper. Moll!

Moll. Jack Dapper!   215

Jack Dapper. How dost, Moll?

Moll. I'll tell thee by and by – I go but to th'next shop.

Jack Dapper. Thou shalt find me here this hour about a
      feather.

Moll. Nay, an a feather hold you in play a whole hour, a goose   220
      will last you all the days of your life!

                        The sempster['s] shop.

Let me see a good shag ruff.

Openwork. Mistress Mary, that shalt thou, i'faith, and the best
      in the shop.

Mistress Openwork. How now? – Greetings! Love terms, with a   225
      pox between you! Have I found out one of your haunts? I
      send you for hollands, and you're i' the low countries with
      a mischief. I'm served with good ware by th'shift that
      makes it lie dead so long upon my hands, I were as good
      shut up shop, for when I open it, I take nothing.   230

Openwork. Nay, an you fall a-ringing once, the devil cannot

221.1.] *to the right of* shag ruffe, *l. 222 Q.*   227. i' the] *Scott;* ith the *Q.*

226–30. *I send . . . nothing*] All of the key terms in the passage have secondary (mostly sexual) senses, which considerably extend the reference of Mist.
Openwork's colourful rebuke: she seems indeed to speak two languages at
once. *Low countries*, playing on *hollands* (linen), puns on (1) the Netherlands,
(2) the low haunts (the stews where Mist. Openwork suspects foul play of her
husband), and (3) the lower parts of the body, especially the sexual organs;
served with signifies both 'supplied with' and 'covered' (in a sexual sense);
ware, 'goods' and 'genitals'; and *shift* carries the senses, 'subterfuge' or
'evasive device', and 'underclothing'. The first element of the passage echoes
2H4, II.ii.19–20, 'because the rest of thy low countries have made a shift to eat
up thy holland'. Within the scheme of primary senses naturally appropriate
for a seamstress, Mist. Openwork complains, 'I am supplied with good linen
merely as a device to attract customers (i.e. so that my husband can make love
to them), with the result that I sell nothing and I might as well shut up the
shop'; and among various other permutations, she charges also that her own
bodily wares, next to her shift (underclothing), are ignored so that, left to
unsatisfying self-stimulation, she might as well renounce sexual activity
altogether. Cf. 'When the wares be gone shut up shop' (Tilley, W68). As R. B.
Parker has observed, 'Ware usually has a bawdy implication in Middleton'
(*C.M. in C.*, II.i.100 n. (Revels ed.)); he cites also *R.G.*, IV.ii.139, *F. of L.*,
II.i.22, V.i.28–9, *N.W.N.H.*, I.i.209–10. The same suggestion is found in
Dekker, *I.T.B.N.*, II.ii.72.

231–2. *a-ringing . . . belfry*] Cf. 'Her tongue goes like a hand bell' (Tilley,
T386).

stop you; I'll out of the belfry as fast as I can. – Moll.

Mistress Openwork. Get you from my shop!

Moll. I come to buy.

Mistress Openwork. I'll sell ye nothing; I warn ye my house and   235
    shop.

Moll. You, goody Openwork, you that prick out a poor living
    And sews many a bawdy skin-coat together,
    Thou private pandress between shirt and smock,
    I wish thee for a minute but a man: 240
    Thou shouldst never use more shapes; but as th'art,
    I pity my revenge. Now my spleen's up,
    I would not mock it willingly.

       Enter a Fellow *with a long rapier by his side.*

243.1.] *two lines to the right of l. 242 Q.*

---

232. – *Moll*] Openwork apparently does not leave the stage since he re-
emerges in conversation (l. 300 below) with Goshawk, possibly at the tobacco
shop. As no exit or entrance is given, at some point he presumably crosses the
stage to get there. Towards the end of the scene, he meets up with Moll, and
they leave the stage together.

235. *warn ye*] deny you entry to.

235–6. *house and shop*] the shop is at the front of Openwork's house: see
Intro., p. 43.

237. *goody*] goodwife.

prick out] Moll's sewing image extends the bawdy reference of Mist.
Openwork's speech, ll. 226–30.

238. *skin-coat*] a coat of skins, but also a person's skin.

239. *shirt and smock*] man and woman (metonymy); cf. *Rom.*, II.iv.99.

241. *shapes*] Cf. I.ii.132.

th'art] The Q form has been preserved against the general normalisation
policy here because 'thou'rt' is too weak. The shift from *you* to *thee/thou* forms
signifies contempt: see R. Quirk, 'Shakespeare and the English Language', *A
New Companion to Shakespeare Studies*, ed. K. Muir and S. Schoenbaum
(Cambridge, 1971), pp. 70–3.

242. *spleen*] fiery temper.

243. *willingly*] i.e. if I were you.

243.1. long rapier] Proclamation 542 (1562), *Tudor Royal Proclamations*,
ed. P. L. Hughes and J. F. Larkin (New Haven and London, 1969), II, 191,
which attempted to regulate sword length, may be apt, 'And whereas an usage
is crept in, contrary to former orders, of wearing long swords and rapiers,
sharpened in such sort as may appear the usage of them can not tend to
defense . . . but to murder and evident death.' Harcourt's quip in Wycherley's
Country Wife, I.i.285–6 (Revels ed.), may also be pertinent, 'Most men are
the contraries to that they would seem: your bully, you see, is a coward with a
long sword.' Either this or the later incident involving Trapdoor (ll. 366–71
below) is depicted in a conjectural reconstruction in *Illustrated London News*,
12 Aug. 1911, p. 277.

                                        – Ha, be thankful,
      Now I forgive thee.

Mistress Openwork. Marry, hang thee! I never asked forgive-   245
      ness in my life.

Moll. You, goodman swine's face!

Fellow. What, will you murder me?

Moll. You remember, slave, how you abused me t'other night
      in a tavern?   250

Fellow. Not I, by this light.

Moll. No, but by candlelight you did: you have tricks to save
      your oaths, reservations have you, and I have reserved
      somewhat for you. [*Strikes him.*] – As you like that, call for
      more: you know the sign again.   255

Fellow. Pox on't! Had I brought any company along with me to
      have borne witness on't, 'twould ne'er have grieved me;
      but to be struck and nobody by, 'tis my ill fortune still.
      Why, tread upon a worm, they say 'twill turn tail; but
      indeed a gentleman should have more manners.   *Exit.*   260

Laxton. Gallantly performed, i'faith, Moll, and manfully! I
      love thee forever for't. Base rogue, had he offered but the
      least counterbuff, by this hand, I was prepared for him.

Moll. You prepared for him? Why should you be prepared for
      him? Was he any more than a man?   265

Laxton. No, nor so much by a yard and a handful, London
      measure.

Moll. Why do you speak this, then? Do you think I cannot ride
      a stone-horse unless one lead him by th'snaffle?

Laxton. Yes, and sit him bravely, I know thou canst, Moll.   270

---

254. s.d.] *Dyce.*   260. s.d.] *Exit fellow. Q.*

---

247. *goodman*] title given to yeomen and others under the rank of gentleman; here contemptuous.

257. *borne witness*] presumably in support of an action against her.

259. *tread ... tail*] proverbial: Tilley, W909; i.e. even the humblest person
will resent ill treatment.

263. *counterbuff*] blow in return.

266. *yard and a handful*] = London measure: 'full measure with a little over,
as the London mercers used to give' (Sugden, p. 314).

269. *stone-horse*] (1) stallion: cf. l. 150 above; (2) applied figuratively to a
man (with special significance for Laxton).

270. *bravely*] (1) finely; (2) valiantly.

'Twas but an honest mistake through love, and I'll make
amends for't any way; prithee, sweet plump Moll, when
shall thou and I go out o' town together?

Moll. Whither? To Tyburn, prithee?

Laxton. Mass, that's out o' town indeed! Thou hangest so   275
many jests upon thy friends still. – I mean honestly to
Brentford, Staines, or Ware.

Moll. What to do there?

Laxton. Nothing but be merry and lie together; I'll hire a coach
with four horses.   280

Moll. I thought 'twould be a beastly journey; you may leave
out one well: three horses will serve if I play the jade
myself.

Laxton. Nay, push, thou'rt such another kicking wench.
Prithee be kind and let's meet.   285

Moll. 'Tis hard but we shall meet, sir.

Laxton. Nay, but appoint the place then – there's ten angels in
fair gold, Moll: you see I do not trifle with you – do but say
thou wilt meet me, and I'll have a coach ready for thee.

Moll. Why, here's my hand I'll meet you, sir.   290

Laxton. [*Aside*] O good gold! – [*To her*] The place, sweet Moll?

Moll. It shall be your appointment.

---

277. Brentford] *Q* (Brainford) *passim.*   291. s.dd.] *Dyce.*

272–5. *when . . . indeed*] Cf. *Ham.*, II.ii.204–7: '*Pol.* . . . Will you walk out of
the air, my lord?   *Ham.* Into my grave?   *Pol.* Indeed, that's out of the air.'
Also Dekker and Webster, *N.H.*, I.ii.61–2.

274. *Tyburn*] the place of execution for Middlesex criminals, roughly near
the present-day Marble Arch.

275. *hangest*] Laxton continues the gallows humour.

277. *Brentford, Staines, or Ware*] *Brentford* is a town on the north bank of
the Thames, eight miles west of London; *Staines*, also on the north bank of the
Thames, lies seventeen miles west of London; *Ware*, a town in Hertfordshire
on the Lea, is twenty miles north of London. All three were favourite resorts
of Londoners out for a day's excursion to the country and famous as rendez-
vous. Brentford (Brainford) is the place of assignation in Dekker and
Webster's *W.H.*; and the opening of *N.H.* is set in Ware. The Saracen's Head
Inn at Ware housed the famous great bed of Ware (now in the Victoria and
Albert Museum); cf. Middleton, *C.M. in C.*, III.iii.108 (Revels ed.).

282. *jade*] (1) ill-conditioned horse; (2) whore: cf. Middleton, *C.M. in C.*,
V.iv.85 (Revels ed.).

Laxton. Somewhat near Holborn, Moll.

Moll. In Gray's Inn Fields then.

Laxton. A match.   295

Moll. I'll meet you there.

Laxton. The hour?

Moll. Three.

Laxton. That will be time enough to sup at Brentford.

Fall from them to the other.

Openwork. I am of such a nature, sir, I cannot endure the house   300
when she scolds; sh'has a tongue will be heard further in a
still morning than St Antholin's bell. She rails upon me
for foreign wenching, that I, being a freeman, must needs
keep a whore i'th' suburbs, and seek to impoverish the
liberties. When we fall out, I trouble you still to make all   305
whole with my wife.

302. St Antholin's] *Q (*Saint Antlings*)*.

---

293. *Holborn*] The main road from Wales and one of the main thorough-
fares in London. It was a great lawyers' quarter, flanked on the north side by
Furnival's and Gray's Inns, and on the south by Thavies', Barnard's and
Staple Inns. 'Holborn had not a good reputation, especially towards the west
end of it, where the gardens lent themselves to loose behaviour' (Sugden,
p. 252).

294. *Gray's Inn Fields*] 'The open fields north of Gray's Inn Gardens, used
as a practice ground for archers, and afterwards frequented by footpads and
other undesirable chatacters' (Sugden, p. 232).

299.1.] Cf. Middleton, *Honorable Entertainments*, viii, 194–5, '*Then fals
into the former speech of* Flora . . .' The s.d. apparently signals the shift of focus
from one group to another.

302. *St Antholin's*] an ancient church in Watling St. (destroyed in the Great
Fire). 'A number of clergymen of Puritan views established a morning lecture
here in 1599, the bell for which began to ring at 5 a.m. and was a great nuisance
to the neighbourhood' (Sugden, p. 21).

303. *foreign*] perhaps playing on 'low countries', l. 227 above.
that] in that.

303–5. *freeman . . . liberties*] Mist. Openwork seems to wonder why her
husband must go to the suburbs and so deny his custom to the liberties (i.e.
nearer home) over which his privileges as a freeman extend. Brothels flourished in the suburbs (see Prologue, l. 21), where the city had no control; the
liberties (with a quibble on 'freedom') were districts which extended beyond
the bounds of the city and were subject to its control.

305. *fall out*] quarrel.

305–6. *make all whole*] restore to health (with a play on *fall out*, extended by
Goshawk in *join things*, l. 307).

Goshawk. No trouble at all: 'tis a pleasure to me to join things
   together.

Openwork. Go thy ways. – [*Aside*] I do this but to try thy
   honesty, Goshawk.   310

                        The feather shop.

Jack Dapper. How likest thou this, Moll?

Moll. O singularly: you're fitted now for a bunch. – [*Aside*] He
   looks for all the world with those spangled feathers like a
   nobleman's bedpost. The purity of your wench would I
   fain try: she seems like Kent unconquered, and I believe   315
   as many wiles are in her. – O the gallants of these times are

309. s.d.] *Dyce.*

---

307. *things*] for Goshawk the bawdy sense is dominant.

309. *ways*] 'old genitive of "way" used in adverbial expressions *come your
ways, go thy ways*' (C. T. Onions, *Shakespeare Glossary* (2nd ed., Oxford,
1958)).

312. *singularly*] possibly playing on Jack's intention to buy one feather.
fitted for a bunch] fitted out with a bunch.

314. *nobleman's bed-post*] Elizabeth Burton, *The Jacobean Home* (1962), p.
112, remarks on 'great or State beds', 'Four slender posts also covered with
material supported the tester. Finials of various shapes surmounted the four
corners. Vase-shaped finials were popular and often contained great plumes
of feathers . . . or alternatively, feathers were just clumped at the corners and
tied with ribbon bows.'
purity] chastity. Middleton uses *try* in a sexual sense in *Changeling*,
II.ii.97–100 (Revels ed.).

315. *Kent unconquered*] a common Kentish boast. Hoy cites Deloney's
Strange Histories (1602) which celebrates 'The valiant courage and policie of
the Kentishmen with long tayles, whereby they kept their ancient Lawes and
Customes, which *William* the Conquerer sought to take from them' (p. 383),
and the account given by Selden in his commentary on Drayton's *Poly-
Olbion*, Song xviii.735. He adds, 'The phrase "Kent unconquered" was
something of a byword', and notes 'a bawdy quibble on "Kent"/"cunt".' Cf.
also George Peele, *The Merry Conceited Jests of George Peele* (*Works*, ed. A. H.
Bullen (1888), II, 395), 'a climate as yet unconquered, the fruitful county of
Kent'; and Drayton, *The Barons' Wars*, i. 323–4, 'Then those of Kent, unconquered of the rest, / That to this day maintain their ancient right' (cited by
Gomme).

316. *wiles*] Hoy notes 'a quibble on "wild" or "Weald", referring to the
district of Kent "formerly covered with forest, between the chalk hills and the
border of Sussex" (Sugden). It was notorious for highway robberies.' He
cites *1H4*, II.i.55–6, Middleton, *M.T.*, II.iii.334–5, and J. Howell, *Instructions for Forreine Travell* (1642), p. 61, 'The Earth is the Lords, and all the
corners thereof, he created the Mountaines of *Wales*, as well as the *Wiles* of
Kent.'

shallow lechers: they put not their courtship home enough
to a wench; 'tis impossible to know what woman is
throughly honest, because she's ne'er thoroughly tried. I
am of that certain belief there are more queans in this town   320
of their own making than of any man's provoking: where
lies the slackness then? Many a poor soul would down,
and there's nobody will push 'em!
Women are courted but ne'er soundly tried,
As many walk in spurs that never ride.   325

The sempster's shop.

Mistress Openwork. O abominable!

Goshawk. Nay, more, I tell you in private, he keeps a whore
i'th' suburbs.

Mistress Openwork. O spittle dealing! I came to him a gentlewoman born: I'll show you mine arms when you please,   330
sir.

Goshawk. [*Aside*] I had rather see your legs, and begin that
way!

Mistress Openwork. 'Tis well known he took me from a lady's
service where I was well-beloved of the steward. I had my   335
Latin tongue and a spice of the French before I came to

---

317. *put . . . home*] a term relating to weapons, with a bawdy quibble.

319. *throughly . . . thoroughly*] Though they share other senses, a fine distinction seems worth preserving here; *throughly*: 'through the whole thickness,
substance, or extent' (*O.E.D.*, 2); *thoroughly*: 'in a thorough manner or degree' (*O.E.D.*, 2).

322-3. *Many . . . push 'em*] Cf. Dekker and Webster, *W.H.*, I.i.89-91,
'Many are honest, either because they haue not wit, or because they haue not
opportunity to be dishonest.'

322. *down*] fall from chastity; the earliest recorded use in an intransitive
sense in *O.E.D.* is 1825.

326. *O abominable*] Cf. *Per.*, IV.vi.133, where the outburst similarly effects
a shift of the centre of interest.

329. *spittle*] aphetic form of 'hospital', probably in reference to St Mary's
Spittle (which chiefly treated those afflicted with venereal disease) or the
neighbourhood around it, which became the haunt of thieves and prostitutes.

330. *arms*] i.e. her mark of gentle birth: shield of arms. Goshawk takes up in
aside a common word-play. Cf. Middleton, *M.T.*, V.iii.6-8.

336. *spice of the French*] 'In a woman a knowledge of French was regarded
with some suspicion, as an indication of questionable morality' (Sugden, p.
208); the secondary bawdy sense (venereal disease) also seems likely.

him, and now doth he keep a suburbian whore under my
nostrils.

Goshawk. There's ways enough to cry quit with him – hark in
thine ear.   [*Whispers.*]   340

Mistress Openwork. There's a friend worth a million.

[*Before the feather shop.*]

Moll. [*Aside*] I'll try one spear against your chastity, Mistress
Tiltyard, though it prove too short by the burr.

Enter RALPH TRAPDOOR.

Trapdoor. [*Aside*] Mass, here she is! I'm bound already to serve
her, though it be but a sluttish trick. – [*To her*] Bless my   345
hopeful young mistress with long life and great limbs,
send her the upper hand of all bailiffs and their hungry
adherents!

Moll. How now, what art thou?

Trapdoor. A poor ebbing gentleman that would gladly wait for   350
the young flood of your service.

Moll. My service! What should move you to offer your service
to me, sir?

340. s.d.] *M. Thesis.*

---

337. *suburbian*] suburban (often so spelt in reference to the licentious life of
the London suburbs); cf. Prologue, l. 21, and l. 304 above. The spelling was
still current in the Restoration: see Dryden, *The Kind Keeper, or Mr. Limberham*, IV.i (*Dramatic Works*, IV, ed. Montague Summers (1932)).

339. *cry quit with*] repay, make full retaliation on.

341. *friend ... million*] proverbial: 'Your love is worth a million' (Tilley,
L553).

342–3.] possibly a fossil of a third citizen plot.

343. *burr*] 'a broad ring of iron behind the handle [of a tilting lance], which
burre is brought into the sufflue or rest [on the breastplate], when the tilter is
ready to run against his enimy', R. Holme, *Academy of Armoury* (cited by
Dyce). Moll's imagery plays on the suggestions of 'Tiltyard'.

346. *hopeful*] i.e. Trapdoor hopes Moll will hire him.

350. *ebbing gentleman*] Cf. Middleton, *N.W.N.H.*, III.i.268–9, 'water will
ebb and flow, so will a gentleman', and the characters, Master and Mistress
Low-water.

351. *young flood*] the flow of the tide up river; cf. Middleton, *C.M. in C.*,
II.ii.174 (Revels ed.), *N.W.N.H.*, II.ii.81.

352–60. *What ... use me*] C. Ricks ('The Moral and Poetic Structure of *The
Changeling*', *E. in C.*, X (1960), 296) remarks in reference to this passage that
'service' has a 'cruder sexual sense, linked ... with the farmyard sense', as well
as 'the duty of a servant'. Bawdy innuendo runs throughout the passage,
playing also on *stand, parts, use, movable* and *immovable*.

Trapdoor. The love I bear to your heroic spirit and masculine
    womanhood.   355

Moll. So, sir, put case we should retain you to us: what parts
    are there in you for a gentlewoman's service?

Trapdoor. Of two kinds right worshipful: movable and im-
    movable – movable to run of errands, and immovable to
    stand when you have occasion to use me.   360

Moll. What strength have you?

Trapdoor. Strength, Mistress Moll? I have gone up into a
    steeple and stayed the great bell as 't has been ringing,
    stopped a windmill going.

Moll. And never struck down yourself?   365

Trapdoor. Stood as upright as I do at this present.

                        Moll trips up his heels; he falls.

Moll. Come, I pardon you for this: it shall be no disgrace to
    you; I have struck up the heels of the high German's size
    ere now. – What, not stand?

Trapdoor. I am of that nature where I love, I'll be at my   370
    mistress' foot to do her service.

Moll. Why, well said! But say your mistress should receive
    injury: have you the spirit of fighting in you – durst you
    second her?

Trapdoor. Life, I have kept a bridge myself, and drove seven at   375
    a time before me.

Moll. Ay?

Trapdoor. (*Aside*) But they were all Lincolnshire bullocks, by
    my troth.

366.1.] *to the right of* going. *l. 364 Q.*   *Moll*] *Collier; Mols Q.*

---

356. *put case*] suppose.

368. *high German's size*] Cf. III.i.90. 'This would appear to have been a
German fencer of great height and strength, who was in London at the time'
(Sugden, p. 221); another allusion occurs in *The Owl's Almanac*, p. 7, 'The
German fencer cudgell'd most of our English fencers now about a month
past.' Hoy cites references in Dekker, *Newes from Hell* (1606), sig. Blv,
S.D.S., sig. Clv, and *The Noble Spanish Soldier*, II.ii.29–30; and Bullen notes
a reference in Shirley, *The Opportunity*, III.i (*Dramatic Works and Poems*, ed.
W. Gifford (1833), III, 407).

369–71. *What ... service*] Trapdoor on the ground jokes on being at his
'mistress' foot'; sexual quibbles on *stand* and *service* continue.

378. *Lincolnshire bullocks*] 'The wide grazing lands of the county have been
long famous, and the breeds of bullocks and sheep are well known' (Sugden,
p. 309).

Moll. Well meet me in Gray's Inn Fields between three and   380
    four this afternoon, and upon better consideration, we'll
    retain you.
Trapdoor. I humbly thank your good mistress-ship. – [*Aside*]
    I'll crack your neck for this kindness.   *Exit.*

            Moll meets Laxton.

Laxton. Remember three.   385
Moll. Nay, if I fail you, hang me.
Laxton. Good wench, i'faith.

          Then [Moll meets] Openwork.

Moll. Who's this?
Openwork. 'Tis I, Moll.
Moll. Prithee tend thy shop and prevent bastards!   390
Openwork. We'll have a pint of the same wine, i'faith, Moll.
               [*Exit* OPENWORK *with* MOLL.]
                    The bell rings.

Goshawk. Hark, the bell rings; come, gentlemen. Jack Dapper,
    where shall's all munch?
Jack Dapper. I am for Parker's Ordinary.
Laxton. He's a good guest to'm, he deserves his board: he   395

---

384. s.d.] *Exit Trapdore Q.*   384.1.] *to the right of* three *l. 385 Q.*   387.1.]
to the right of i'faith *Q.*   391.1.] *Dyce subst.*

---

388. *Who's this*] presumably indicates that Openwork has somehow disguised or hidden himself to escape his wife's notice.

391. *same wine*] punning on *bastard*, a sweet Spanish wine; the joke was common: cf. Middleton, *M.W.M.M.*, II.i.67–72; *F.Q.*, V.i.123–5, Dekker and Middleton, *1 H.W.*, II.i.232–4.

391.2.] Possibly the bell of the Royal Exchange is intended. Leonora in Webster's *Devil's Law Case*, I.i.149 (ed. F. L. Lucas, II), complains, 'th'Exchange bell makes us dine so late'.

393. *shall's*] i.e. shall us = shall we: see Abbott, § 215; cf. III.ii.172, V.i.351.

394. *Parker's Ordinary*] H. B. Wheatley, 'Signs of Booksellers in St. Paul's Churchyard' (*Transactions of the Bibliographical Society*, IX (1906–8), 67–106) notes some shops and houses adjacent to St Paul's which were condemned in 1630. Among these is 'a shead adjoining to the library (Parker's Alehouse)': possibly this is the ordinary to which Jack refers.

395. *to'm*) i.e. to him.

draws all the gentlemen in a term time thither. We'll be
your followers, Jack: lead the way. – Look you, by my
faith, the fool has feathered his nest well.

Exeunt Gallants.

Enter MASTER GALLIPOT, MASTER TILTYARD, *and* Servants, *with
water-spaniels and a duck.*

Tiltyard. Come, shut up your shops. Where's Master
Openwork?   400
Mistress Openwork. Nay, ask not me, Master Tiltyard.
Gallipot. Where's his water-dog? Pooh – pist – hurr – hurr –
pist.
Tiltyard. Come wenches, come, we're going all to Hogsden.
Mistress Gallipot. To Hogsden, husband?   405
Gallipot. Ay, to Hogsden, pigsney.
Mistress Tiltyard. I'm not ready, husband.
Tiltyard. Faith, that's well. (*Spits in the dog's mouth.*) Hum –

401. *Mistress Openwork.*] Q *2nd stage cor. (Mist Open.); Mist. Gal.* Q *1st stage
cor. and uncor.*   402. *Gallipot.*] Q *2nd stage cor. (Maist. Gal.); Maist. Tilt.* Q
1st stage cor. and uncor.   404, 408. *Tiltyard.*] Q *2nd stage cor. (Maist. Tilt.);
Maist. Gal.* Q *1st stage cor. and uncor.*   407. *Mistress Tiltyard.*] Q *2nd stage
cor. (Mist. Tilt.); Mist. Gal.* Q *1st stage cor. and uncor.*   408. s.d.] *to the right
of l. 407* Q.

398. *the fool ... well*] Cf. ll.117–18 above, and 'To feather one's nest'
(Tilley, N125–6).

398.2. water-spaniels and a duck] 'This [duck-hunting] is another barbarous pastime, and for the performance it is necessary to have recourse
to a pond of water sufficiently extensive to give the duck plenty of room for
making her escape from the dogs when she is closely pursued; which she does
by diving as often as any of them come near to her', Joseph Strutt, *Sports and
Pastimes of the People of England* (ed. 1850), p. 284.

401–10.] See this editor's '*The Roaring Girl*: New Readings and Further
Notes', *S.B.*, XXXVII (1984), 159–70, for a discussion of the Q variants.

402. *Pooh – pist*] presumably whistling or other sounds to call the dog.
O.E.D.'s citations of *pist* are exclusively from Middleton.

hurr] a dog-like snarling sound: *O.E.D.* cites Jonson's *English Grammar*
(1640), '*R* Is the Dogs Letter, and hurreth in the sound.'

404. *Hogsden*] Hoxton, a district in the north of London. 'The Hogsden
Fields were a favourite place for afternoon jaunts' (Sugden, p. 251); *Parlous
Pond* (l. 413) would be on the way.

406. *pigsney*] darling, pet; possibly playing on *Hogs*den.

408. s.d. Spits ... mouth] apparently a not uncommon expression of affection and means of befriending a dog; cf. William Fennor, *Compters Common-*

pist – pist.

Gallipot. Come Mistress Openwork, you are so long.   410

Mistress Openwork. I have no joy of my life, Master Gallipot.

Gallipot. Push, let your boy lead his water-spaniel along, and
    we'll show you the bravest sport at Parlous Pond. Hey
    Trug, hey Trug, hey Trug! Here's the best duck in
    England, except my wife. Hey, hey, hey! Fetch, fetch,   415
    fetch!

    Come, let's away:

    Of all the year, this is the sportful'st day.   [*Exeunt.*]

---

wealth (1617), p. 73, '. . . when a poore man comes nigh a churlish mastiffe he
must not spurne at him if he meane to goe quietly by him, but flatter and
stroake him on the backe, and spit in his mouth'. Support is given by the
proverbial saying, 'Spit in his mouth and make him a mastiff (as men do with
dogs)' (Tilley, M1259); cf. Dekker, Ford and Rowley, *W. of E.*, IV.i.256–7, 'a
Pox, that Morrice makes me spit in thy mouth' (cited by Tilley). *O.D.E.P.*
cites Ulpian Fulwell, *Ars Adulandi*, viii, sig. I3v, 'I thinke those men of
Honour and worship, vse you as men vse their waterspaniels: that is, they
make you their instrument to fetch and bringe vnto them such commodities,
as you by the corrupting of your conscience may compasse, and . . . for your
labour they spitte in your mouth.' Littlewit in Jonson's *Bartholomew Fair*,
III.vi.14–15 (Revels ed.), enumerates 'the lady . . . that desir'd to spit i' the
great lawyer's mouth, after an eloquent pleading'.

408–9. *Hum – pist – pist*] possibly representing the action of spitting in the
dog's mouth; but cf. ll. 402–3.

413. *Parlous Pond*] 'A pool of water lying behind St. Luke's Hospital off
City Road, London . . . It was a favourite bathing place . . .' (Sugden, p. 392).
Parlous is a corruption of 'perilous': Stow (*Survey*, I, 16) explained, 'called
Perillous Pond, because diverse youthes swimming therein haue beene
drowned'. The Pond was not far from the Fortune Theatre.

414. *Trug*] possibly the name of the spaniel, as Steevens (Reed) supposed
(Hoy cites numerous instances in contemporary works), though the sense of
Trug ('prostitute, trull') better accords with common associations of *duck*; cf.
III.ii.238 and n. Gallipot may first refer to the duck, and then with *Fetch,
fetch, fetch!* call to the spaniel.

418. *sportful'st day*] possibly Shrove Tuesday or May Day, though the
reference may simply be general. If Shrove Tuesday, the bell of l. 391.2 would
be the pancake bell, described by John Taylor, the water-poet, in *Jack a Lent*
(*Works* (1630), sig. L4r), 'At [Shrove Tuesday's] entrance in the morning, all
the whole Kingdome is in quiet, but by that time the clocke strikes eleuen,
which (by the helpe of a knauish Sexton) is commonly before nine, then there
is a bell rung, cald *The Pancake Bell*, the sound whereof makes thousands of
people distracted, and forgetfull either of manner or humanitie'. Cf. also
Dekker, *Shoemaker's Holiday*, xvii.52–5 (Revels ed.), 'I have procured that
upon every Shrove Tuesday, at the sound of the pancake bell, my fine dapper
Assyrian lads shall clap up their shop windows, and away.'

[II.ii]

Enter SEBASTIAN *solus.*

Sebastian. If a man have a free will, where should the use
 More perfect shine than in his will to love?
 All creatures have their liberty in that;

Enter SIR ALEXANDER *and listens to him.*

 Though else kept under servile yoke and fear,
 The very bondslave has his freedom there.   5
 Amongst a world of creatures voiced and silent,
 Must my desires wear fetters? – [*Aside*] Yea, are you
 So near? Then I must break with my heart's truth,
 Meet grief at a back way. – [*Aloud*] Well: why, suppose
 The two-leaved tongues of slander or of truth   10
 Pronounce Moll loathsome; if before my love
 She appear fair, what injury have I? –
 I have the thing I like. In all things else
 Mine own eye guides me, and I find 'em prosper;
 Life, what should ail it now? I know that man   15
 Ne'er truly loves – if he gainsay't, he lies –

II.ii] *Dyce; not in Q.* 7. fetters?] *Reed;* fetters – – – – *Q.* s.d.] *M.
Thesis.* 9. why, suppose] *Reed subst.;* why suppose. *Q.* 10. two-leaved]
Q subst. (two leaud)*;* two-lewd *Collier.*

0.1.] Cf. IV.i.o.1; the construction appears also in the opening s.d. of
Middleton, *T.C.O.O.*, I.i (not preserved by Bullen).

1–5.] Cf. Middleton, *F. of L.*, III.i.19–26.

10. *two-leaved tongues*] In suport of 'the comparison of the tongue to the two
hinged parts of a door or gate', Hoy instances two passages additional to
Bowers's: Dekker, *Worke for Armorours* (1606), sig. E2r, and *W.B.*, I.ii.172–3;
O.E.D. notes also Isaiah xlv.1. The image is not restricted to this association,
however. *Two-leaved* occurs in Marlowe's translation of Ovid, *Elegies*,
III.xiii.43–4 (Revels ed.), 'Though while the deed be doing you be took, /
And I see when you ope the two-leav'd book', and George Sandys, *Christ's
Passion*, iv.304–5 (*Poetical Works*, ed. Richard Hooper (1872), II, 477), 'Those
two-leav'd Tables, wherein God reveal'd / His Sacred Laws', both apparently
renderings of 'tabellae duplices' of *Elegies*, I.xii. The image of *R.G.*, is suggestive of a forked tongue, like the tongue of a snake, and as F. D. Hoeniger
has remarked to me, 'The devil as serpent has a double or forked tongue
because he speaks a mixture of truth and falsehood or slander. Virgil's Fama
(false fame) in *Aeneid*, iv.181–90, sings alike of truth and falsehood, and has
many tongues, but the image of Satan as serpent is closer still.'

That winks and marries with his father's eyes;
I'll keep mine own wide open.

Enter MOLL *and a* Porter *with a viol on his back.*

Sir Alexander. [*Aside*]   Here's brave wilfulness.
 A made match: here she comes; they met o' purpose.
Porter. Must I carry this great fiddle to your chamber,   20
 Mistress Mary?
Moll. Fiddle, goodman hog-rubber? Some of these porters
 bear so much for others, they have no time to carry wit for
 themselves.
Porter. To your own chamber, Mistress Mary?   25
Moll. Who'll hear an ass speak? – Whither else, goodman pa-
 geant bearer? – They're people of the worst memories.
               Exit Porter.
Sebastian. Why, 'twere too great a burden, love, to have them
 carry things in their minds and o' their backs together.
Moll. Pardon me, sir, I thought not you so near.   30
Sir Alexander. [*Aside*] So, so, so.
Sebastian. I would be nearer to thee, and in that fashion
 That makes the best part of all creatures honest.
 No otherwise I wish it.
Moll. Sir, I am so poor to requite you, you must look for no-   35

27. They're] *M. Thesis;* the're *Q.*

---

17. *winks*] 'keeps his eyes closed' in the figurative sense of 'is complacent'.
19. *made match*] arranged meeting.
22. *Fiddle*] possibly with a bawdy entendre: cf. II.i.64–5 and n.
 hog-rubber] apparently an abusive term for a swineherd; cf. Jonson, *Bartholomew Fair*, V.iv.169 (Revels ed.) (cited by Hoy).
22–4. *Some ... themselves*] Moll may draw on a tradition that porters were deemed weak-witted: cf. the porter's opening speech of 'The Queen's Entertainment at Wimbledon' (1599), transcribed in *Records of Early English Drama Newsletter*, X (1985), 1.
26. *ass*] fool, with a quibble on the Porter as a beast of burden.
26–7. *pageant bearer*] Porters were employed to carry the spectacular structures in municipal shows. '"Pageant" was first used to signify the scaffolding whether stationary or portable on which the scene or exhibition was built or carried ... later the word was transferred to the exhibition itself'; 'About 8 to 16 porters were needed to carry each pageant', J. Robertson and D. J. Gordon (edd.), *M.S.C.*, III (1954), xxii, nn. 3 and 4.
32–3. *fashion ... honest*] i.e. in marriage. Cf. l. 132 below.
33. *the best part*] most.

thing but thanks of me: I have no humour to marry. I love
to lie o' both sides o'th' bed myself; and again, o' th'other
side, a wife, you know, ought to be obedient, but I fear me
I am too headstrong to obey, therefore I'll ne'er go about
it. I love you so well, sir, for your good will, I'd be loath   40
you should repent your bargain after, and therefore we'll
ne'er come together at first. I have the head now of myself,
and am man enough for a woman; marriage is but a chopping and changing, where a maiden loses one head, and
has a worse i'th' place.   45

Sir Alexander. [*Aside*] The most comfortablest answer from a
          roaring girl
     That ever mine ears drunk in.

Sebastian.   This were enough
     Now to affright a fool forever from thee,
     When 'tis the music that I love thee for.

Sir Alexander. [*Aside*] There's a boy spoils all again!

Moll.   Believe it, sir,   50
     I am not of that disdainful temper,
     But I could love you faithfully.

Sir Alexander. [*Aside*]   A pox
     On you for that word. I like you not now;
     You're a cunning roarer, I see that already.

Moll. But sleep upon this once more, sir; you may chance shift   55
     a mind tomorrow: be not too hasty to wrong yourself.
     Never while you live, sir, take a wife running: many have
     run out at heels that have done't. – You see, sir, I speak

---

37–8. myself; . . . side,] *Q;* myself, . . . side; *Gomme.*

---

36. *humour*] disposition, mood.

37. *again*] besides.

37–8. *o' th'other side*] on the other hand.

42. *I have . . . myself*] figurative use of a term from horsemanship which
picks up the metaphor of 'too headstrong to obey', l. 39. 'To give a horse his
head' means to allow him to go freely, unchecked. Moll is in charge of herself
and has no wish to surrender her freedom; the image suggests an element of
wildness.

44–5. *loses . . . place*] i.e. exchanges a maidenhead for a head of household
(with a pun also on *head*, l. 42).

57. *running*] in haste, on the run.

58. *out at heels*] with the heels of stockings or shoes worn through: hence, in
debt or dire circumstances; proverbial: Tilley, H389.

against myself, and if every woman would deal with their
suitor so honestly, poor younger brothers would not be so   60
often gulled with old cozening widows that turn o'er all
their wealth in trust to some kinsman, and make the poor
gentleman work hard for a pension. Fare you well, sir.
Sebastian. Nay, prithee one word more!
Sir Alexander. [*Aside*] How do I wrong this girl; she puts him
off still.   65
Moll. Think upon this in cold blood, sir; you make as much
haste as if you were a-going upon a sturgeon voyage. Take
deliberation, sir, never choose a wife as if you were going
to Virginia.   [*Moves away from him.*]
Sebastian. And so we parted, my too cursèd fate!   [*Retires.*]   70

---

69. s.d.] *This ed.*   70. s.d.] *M. Thesis; Stands aloofe. Bowers.*

---

60. *younger brothers*] i.e. those with modest or no inheritance.

61-2. *widows ... kinsman*] Cf. Jonson, *Epicoene*, II.ii.140-3, 'This too, with
whom you are to marry, may haue made a conuayance of her virginity afore-
hand, as your wise widdowes doe of their states, before they marry, in trust to
some friend, sir.' In *Introducing Shakespeare* (Harmondsworth, 3rd ed.,
1973), p. 95, G. B. Harrison remarks, 'On marriage, a woman's goods and
money passed into the possession of her husband unless special settlements
were made by the lawyers.' Wary widows accordingly used their wealth as an
enticement, but placed it in the hands of a relative as a precaution. Middleton
would have known about the problems of widows since he and his mother had
been involved in considerable litigation against his adventurer step-father,
mainly over possession of the estate left by his father. Several of his plays
feature the predicament of suitors vying for the hand of a rich widow. Cf.
Middleton?, *The Second Maiden's Tragedy*, IV.ii.51-2 (Revels ed.).

67. *sturgeon voyage*] *O.E.D.* queries, 'a fishing voyage for sturgeon', citing
only this instance. 'The point here, and in what follows, seems to be: don't
choose a wife as if you were going to be away from home and would never have
to live with her, or as if you were going to a barbaric country where any female
will do' (Hoy).

68-9. *never ... Virginia*] Cf. Middleton, *W.B.W.*, I.ii.59-61 (Revels ed.):
''Tis fit i'faith she should have one sight of him, / And stop upon't, and not be
joined in haste, / As if they went to stock a new-found land.' Also Jonson,
Chapman and Marston, *Eastward Ho*, II.ii.163-9. Middleton may have had
first-hand knowledge of such matches; his step-father had been with Sir
Francis Drake on a voyage to Virginia: see M. G. Christian, 'A Sidelight on
the Family History of Thomas Middleton', *S.P.*, XLIV (1947), 490-6.

70. *And ... fate*] If a quotation, as Dyce suggested, it has not been identified. Sebastian strikes the attitude of a dejected lover for his father's benefit.

Retires] Although Moll breaks off from Sebastian, he does not leave the
stage.

Sir Alexander. [*Aside*] She is but cunning, gives him longer
time in't.

Enter a Tailor.

Tailor. Mistress Moll, Mistress Moll! So ho ho, so ho!
Moll. There boy, there boy. What dost thou go a-hawking after
me with a red clout on thy finger?
Tailor. I forgot to take measure on you for your new breeches.   75

[*Takes measurements.*]

Sir Alexander. [*Aside*] Heyday, breeches! What, will he marry
a monster with two trinkets? What age is this? If the wife
go in breeches, the man must wear long coats like a fool.

75.1.] *This ed.*   76. Heyday] *This ed.;* Hoyda *Q*.

---

72. *So ho ho, so ho*] a cry in hare-hunting and falconry, which explains
Moll's responses in the following speech; cf. Middleton, *T.C.O.O.*,
IV.iv.45–8: '*Fal.* A falconer, an't please your worship.   *Hoa.* Sa ho, sa ho, sa
ho! – And you, sir?   *Hunt.* A huntsman, sir.   *Hoa.* There, boy, there, boy,
there, boy!'

73. *There boy*] i.e. as to a dog.
What] why.

74. *red clout*] a piece of cloth probably used for measuring, or containing
pins and needles.

76. *Heyday*] Q's 'hoyda' (also at III.ii.13 and V.ii.15).

77. *monster*] Cf. I.ii.135; also Stubbes, *Anatomie of Abuses* (1583), sig. F5v,
'Our Apparell was giuen vs as a signe distinctiue to discern betwixt sex and
sex, & therfore one to weare the Apparel of another sex, is to participate with
the same, and to adulterate the veritie of his owne kinde. Wherefore these
Women may not improperly be called *Hermaphroditi*, that is, Monsters of
bothe kindes, half women, half men.'

two trinkets] possibly signifying the sexual organs of both sexes; but cf.
John Chamberlain's quotation of King James in *Letters*, ed. N. E. McClure
(Philadelphia, 1939), II, 286–7, '... the insolencie of our women, and theyre
wearing of brode brimd hats, pointed dublets, theyre haire cut short or
shorne, and some of them stillettaes or poinards, and such other trinckets of
like moment ...'

77–8. *wife ... breeches*] Cf. 'She wears the breeches' (Tilley, B645).

78. *long coats*] petticoats such as were worn by women, idiots and jesters; cf.
T. Nashe, *Saffron Walden* (*Works*, ed. R. B. McKerrow (Oxford, 1958), III, p.
17, ll. 18–21), 'it is a garment for the woodcocke *Gabriel Haruey*, and fooles,
ye know, alwaies for the most part (especiallie if they bee naturall fooles) are
suted in long coates'. See E. W. Ives, 'Tom Skelton – A Seventeenth-Century
Jester', *Sh.S. 13* (1960), 90–105, for further discussion and illustrations.

Moll. What fiddling's here? Would not the old pattern have
    served your turn?   80
Tailor. You change the fashion, you say you'll have the great
    Dutch slop, Mistress Mary.
Moll. Why sir, I say so still.
Tailor. Your breeches then will take up a yard more.
Moll. Well, pray look it be put in then.   85
Tailor. It shall stand round and full, I warrant you.
Moll. Pray make 'em easy enough.
Tailor. I know my fault now: t'other was somewhat stiff be-
    tween the legs; I'll make these open enough, I warrant
    you.   90
Sir Alexander. [*Aside*] Here's good gear towards! I have
    brought up my son to marry a Dutch slop and a French
    doublet: a codpiece daughter.
Tailor. So, I have gone as far as I can go.
Moll. Why then, farewell.   95
Tailor. If you go presently to your chamber, Mistress Mary,
    pray send me the measure of your thigh by some honest
    body.

---

79. *fiddling*] fidgeting, with a sexual innuendo: cf. II.i.64–5n. Bawdy suggestion runs throughout Moll's exchange with the Tailor. 'Tailor' could mean
the male or female sexual organ: see Hilda Hulme, 'Three Notes on
Shakespeare's Plays', *J.E.G.P.*, LVII (1958), 722–4.

82. *Dutch slop*] wide, baggy breeches; 'the Dutch slops . . . were the loose
type that would hold a "bushell of wheate"' (Linthicum, p. 210). See title-
page woodcut of Moll.

84. *yard*] with a play on *yard* = penis, continued in the following lines; cf.
II.i.170. Cf. Dekker and Middleton, *1 H.W.*, V.ii.259–61, 'this was her
Tailer, – you cut out her loose-bodied gowne, and put in a yard more then I
allowed her.'

85.] Moll's insistence is founded on a common complaint that tailors stole
cloth in making up breeches. See F. P. Wilson, 'Some English Mock-
prognostications', *Shakespearian and Other Studies*, ed. Helen Gardner
(Oxford, 1969), pp. 271–2; also Beaumont, *Knight of the Burning Pestle*,
II.ii.437–9 (*Dramatic Works*, I, ed. F. Bowers (Cambridge, 1966)).

91. *gear*] (1) business, doings; (2) genitals (*O.E.D.*, 5b): cf. Middleton,
C.M. in C., II.i.17 (Revels ed.), *F.H.T.* (Bullen, VIII), p. 91.

    towards] coming, about to take place.

92–3. *Dutch . . . daughter*] metonymically playing on Moll's supposed com-
posite sexuality.

94.] i.e. in taking measurements, with an underlying sexual quibble.

97. *thigh*] Thighs were considered the source of sexual potency: cf.
Webster, *Duchess of Malfi*, II.v.42 (Revels ed.), 'Happily with some strong
thigh'd bargeman'.

Moll. Well sir, I'll send it by a porter presently.   *Exit.*

Tailor. So you had need: it is a lusty one. Both of them would   100
    make any porter's back ache in England!   *Exit.*

Sebastian. [*Comes forward.*] I have examined the best part of
    man –
          Reason and judgement – and in love, they tell me,
          They leave me uncontrolled. He that is swayed
          By an unfeeling blood, past heat of love,   105
          His springtime must needs err: his watch ne'er goes right
          That sets his dial by a rusty clock.

Sir Alexander. [*Comes forward.*] So – and which is that rusty
    clock, sir, you?

Sebastian. The clock at Ludgate, sir, it ne'er goes true.

Sir Alexander. But thou goest falser; not thy father's cares   110
          Can keep thee right, when that insensible work
          Obeys the workman's art, lets off the hour,

---

99. s.d.] *Exit Mol. Q.*   101. s.d.] *Exit Taylor. Q.*   102.s.d.] *This
ed.*   108.s.d.] *Dyce subst.*

---

100. *lusty*] (1) healthy; (2) lustful.

100–1. *Both ... England*] a bawdy jest.

105. *unfeeling blood ... love*] *Blood* is the source of vitality, passion and
temperamental disposition, and more particularly of love passion. *Unfeeling
blood* is cold, i.e. dominated by cold humours, and therefore unresponsive to
the *heat of love.* Because when people age the sanguine humour in their blood
decreases while the melancholy cold humour increases, they are 'past heat of
blood', past love passion. However, Sebastian also alludes to his blood-
kinship with his father; cf. *blood* in l. 121 below (F. D. Hoeniger).

106. *springtime ... err*] *Springtime* alludes both to youth and the time-
keeping of the watch or clock of the following lines. But the phrase is deliberately ambiguous. Those who by natural disposition and not only by age
have *unfeeling blood* must *needs err* in their springtime when it is natural and
healthy to have very warm blood and to experience *uncontrolled* (l. 104) love
passion. Yet when one is swayed by uncontrolled passion rather than *reason
and judgement* (l. 103) one also must needs err. Sebastian quibbles cleverly (F.
D. Hoeniger).

106–16.] Sebastian's word-plays on *blood, springtime* and *err* prepare his
stubborn father for his insistence that the metaphor of the rusty clock applies
to his son rather than himself. The *clock at Ludgate* may be old and may not go
perfectly *true*, but it goes a lot better than Sebastian's (F. D. Hoeniger). Cf.
Middleton, *N.W.N.H.*, I.i.253–7: 'Why, now the clocks / Go right again: it
must be a strange wit / That makes the wheels of youth and age so hit; / The
one are dry, worn, rusty, furr'd, and soil'd, / Love's wheels are glib, ever kept
clean and oil'd.' Also *W.B.W.*, IV.i.11–15 (Revels ed.); Dekker, 2 *H.W.*,
III.i.111–25.

And stops again when time is satisfied;
But thou run'st on, and judgement, thy main wheel,
Beats by all stops as if the work would break,   115
Begun with long pains for a minute's ruin,
Much like a suffering man brought up with care,
At last bequeathed to shame and a short prayer.
Sebastian. I taste you bitterer than I can deserve, sir.
Sir Alexander. Who has bewitched thee, son? What devil or
          drug   120
Hath wrought upon the weakness of thy blood
And betrayed all her hopes to ruinous folly?
O wake from drowsy and enchanted shame,
Wherein thy soul sits with a golden dream
Flattered and poisoned! I am old, my son –   125
O let me prevail quickly,
For I have weightier business of mine own
Than to chide thee – I must not to my grave
As a drunkard to his bed, whereon he lies
Only to sleep, and never cares to rise;   130
Let me dispatch in time: come no more near her.
Sebastian. Not honestly? Not in the way of marriage?
Sir Alexander. What sayst thou? Marriage? In what place? –
          The sessions-house?
And who shall give the bride, prithee? – An indictment?
Sebastian. Sir, now ye take part with the world to wrong her.   135
Sir Alexander. Why, wouldst thou fain marry to be pointed at?
Alas the number's great, do not o'erburden't.

---

120. bewitched] *Reed subst.;* bewitch *Q.*

114–16. *judgement ... ruin*] *Judgement* (i.e. malfunctioning judgement
because beclouded by love passion) threatens to wreck speedily the whole
work Begun (i.e. created or made) *with long pains* by *the workman's art* (i.e. *thy
father's cares*, l. 110).

120. *bewitched*] Although Q prints 'bewitch', the full form occurs at I.i.106,
I.ii.174 and IV.i.200, so emendation seems justified. But cf. Dekker and
Webster, *W.H.*, I.i.139, 'haue you dispatch?' and *N.H.*, IV.i.148, '. . . thou
hast be witch me'.

121. *blood*] See l. 105n. above.

122. *betrayed*] (1) given over, exposed; (2) led astray.

her] in reference to 'blood', l. 121.

125. *flattered*] encouraged with false hopes (*O.E.D.*, 7a).

133. *sessions-house*] court house.

Why, as good marry a beacon on a hill,
Which all the country fix their eyes upon,
As her thy folly dotes on. If thou long'st   140
To have the story of thy infamous fortunes
Serve for discourse in ordinaries and taverns,
Thou'rt in the way; or to confound thy name,
Keep on, thou canst not miss it; or to strike
Thy wretched father to untimely coldness,   145
Keep the left hand still, it will bring thee to't.
Yet if no tears wrung from thy father's eyes,
Nor sighs that fly in sparkles from his sorrows,
Had power to alter what is wilful in thee,
Methinks her very name should fright thee from her,   150
And never trouble me.

Sebastian. Why is the name of Moll so fatal, sir?

Sir Alexander. Many one, sir, where suspect is entered,
Forseek all London from one end to t'other
More whores of that name than of any ten other.   155

Sebastian. What's that to her? Let those blush for themselves;
Can any guilt in others condemn her?
I've vowed to love her: let all storms oppose me
That ever beat against the breast of man,

---

153. Many one,] *Q subst.;* Mary, one *Bowers.* entered,] *Q;* entered;
Reed.   154. Forseek] *This ed.;* For seeke *Q;* For, seek *Dyce.*

---

143. *name*] (1) family; (2) reputation.

146. *left hand*] sinister way; possibly in allusion also to the allegory of
Heracles in which the right path led to virtue and the left to vice. Hoy cites
Kyd, *Spanish Tragedy*, I.i.63–4 (Revels ed.), 'The left hand path, declining
fearfully, / Was ready downfall to the deepest hell.'

148. *sparkles*] Cf. Dekker and Middleton, *1 H.W.*, V.ii.366–8, 'Let it be
rugged still and flinted o're, / What can come forth but sparkles, that will
burne, / Your selfe and vs?' and Dekker, *W.B.*, IV.ii.172–3, 'For from their
flintie hearts what sparkes I got, / Were but to fire themselues.'

153–5.] Though previous editors have introduced various emendations, the
sense of the passage is best served by reading Q's 'For seeke' as *forseek* in
either of its meanings: (1) seek thoroughly, seek out; (2) weary (oneself) with
seeking. *Many one* = many or many a one (*O.E.D.*, 'many', 1c), presumably in
reference to constables or other arresting officers (*suspect* = suspicion). The
sense is, 'After a legal entry of suspicion, many (e.g. constables) scour London
for more whores called Moll than by ten other names.' Cf. Middleton,
M.W.M.M., V.ii.160–2, where the Constable speaks: 'Did not I tell your
worship this before? / Brought 'em before you for suspected persons? / Stay'd
'em at town's end upon warning given?'

Nothing but death's black tempest shall divide us.   160
Sir Alexander. O folly that can dote on nought but shame!
Sebastian. Put case a wanton itch runs through one name
    More than another: is that name the worse
    Where honesty sits possessed in't? It should rather
    Appear more excellent and deserve more praise   165
    When through foul mists a brightness it can raise.
    Why, there are of the devil's, honest gentlemen,
    And well descended, keep an open house;
    And some o'th' good man's that are arrant knaves.
    He hates unworthily that by rote contemns,   170
    For the name neither saves nor yet condemns;
    And for her honesty, I have made such proof on't
    In several forms, so nearly watched her ways,
    I will maintain that strict against an army,
    Excepting you, my father. Here's her worst: 175
    Sh'has a bold spirit that mingles with mankind,
    But nothing else comes near it, and oftentimes
    Through her apparel somewhat shames her birth;
    But she is loose in nothing but in mirth:
    Would all Molls were no worse!   180
Sir Alexander. [*Aside*] This way I toil in vain and give but aim
    To infamy and ruin: he will fall,
    My blessing cannot stay him; all my joys
    Stand at the brink of a devouring flood

167. Why,] *Dyce;* Why *Q.*   devil's] *Gomme;* diuels *Q.*   175. father.]
Collier; father: *Q.*

---

168. *keep*] elliptical: who keep; see Abbott, § 244.
169. *good man's*] Cf. 'God is a good man' (Tilley, G195) (cited by Dyce).
172. *for*] as for.
174. *strict*] i.e. strictly, rigorously: adverbial use of adjective; see Abbott,
§ 1.
176. *mankind*] male sex; as an adjective the term often denotes a masculine,
virago quality in a woman; cf. *Life of Long Meg of Westminster* (ed. 1620), sig.
D4r, 'for that he had heard she was so mankinde as to beat all she met withall,
he would try her manhoode'; also *Wint.*, II.iii.67 ('A mankind witch'), *Cor.*,
IV.ii.16 ('Are you mankind?').
177. *But . . . it*] Sebastian's defence concentrates on Moll's chastity, so the
sense is apparently, 'but nothing besides her spirit comes near mankind'.
181. *give . . . aim*] an archery term: 'guide one's aim by signalling the result
of a previous shot'; cf. Middleton and Rowley, *S.G.*, II.i.92–3, 'I myself gave
aim, thus, – wide, four bows; short, three and a half.'

And will be wilfully swallowed, wilfully!   185
But why so vain let all these tears be lost? –
I'll pursue her to shame, and so all's crossed.   *Exit.*
Sebastian. He is gone with some strange purpose whose effect
        Will hurt me little if he shoot so wide
        To think I love so blindly: I but feed   190
        His heart to this match to draw on th'other,
        Wherein my joy sits with a full wish crowned –
        Only his mood excepted, which must change
        By opposite policies, courses indirect:
        Plain dealing in this world takes no effect.   195
        This mad girl I'll acquaint with my intent,
        Get her assistance, make my fortunes known:
        'Twixt lovers' hearts she's a fit instrument,
        And has the art to help them to their own.
        By her advice, for in that craft she's wise,   200
        My love and I may meet, spite of all spies.   *Exit.*

187. s.d.] *Exit Sir Alexander Q.*   191. th'other,] *Reed;* th'other. *Q.*   193.
change] *Reed;* change. *Q.*   201. s.d.] *Exit Sebastian. Q.*

---

189. *shoot so wide*] Cf. l. 181.
193. *mood*] anger, displeasure.
195.] Cf. 'Plain dealing is a jewel but they that use it die beggars' (Tilley,
P382).
201. *spite of*] in spite of.

Act III

Enter LAXTON *in Gray's Inn Fields with the* Coachman.

Laxton. Coachman!

Coachman. Here, sir.

Laxton. [*Gives money*.] There's a tester more; prithee drive thy
    coach to the hither end of Marybone Park – a fit place for
    Moll to get in.   5

Coachman. Marybone Park, sir?

Laxton. Ay, it's in our way, thou knowest.

Coachman. It shall be done, sir.

Laxton. Coachman.

Coachman. Anon, sir.   10

Laxton. Are we fitted with good frampold jades?

Coachman. The best in Smithfield, I warrant you, sir.

Laxton. May we safely take the upper hand of any coached

III.i] *Dyce; not in Q.*   3. s.d.] *M. Thesis.*   12. you,] *Reed;* your *Q.*
13. coached] *Q subst.;* couched *Gomme.*

---

    3. *tester*] sixpence; originally a small coin (the teston of Henry VIII) worth a
shilling.

    4. *Marybone Park*] i.e. Marylebone Park: now Regent's Park, at this time a
centre of prostitution; 'Marybone' (marrow-bone) carries with it the bawdy
senses of II.i.193, as in Middleton and Rowley, *F.Q.*, IV.iv.217–20: '*He that
the reason would know, let him hark, | Why these three were buried near
Marybone Park; | These three were a pander, a bawd, and a whore, | That suck'd
many dry to the bones before.*'

    11. *frampold*] fiery, spirited; see Intro., p. 10.

    12. *Smithfield*] West Smithfield was a famous market for horses and cattle,
with by this time a poor reputation: cf. *2H4*, I.ii.48; William Fennor,
Compters Common-wealth (1617), p. 72; Tilley, W276.

    13. *coached*] Possibly Gomme's emendation ('couched') should be adopted;
but the Q reading makes good sense, and Laxton's subsequent lines amplify
the reference. 'Couched' means 'embroidered with gold thread or the like laid
flat on the surface'; cf. Middleton, *B.B.* (Bullen, VIII), p. 42, cited in reference
to Epistle, l. 14n. The same Q form ('coacht') occurs at V.ii.221.

velvet cap or tuftaffety jacket? For they keep a vile swaggering in coaches nowadays – the highways are stopped   15
with them.

Coachman. My life for yours, and baffle 'em too, sir! – Why,
they are the same jades – believe it sir – that have drawn all
your famous whores to Ware.

Laxton. Nay, then they know their business; they need no   20
more instructions.

Coachman. They're so used to such journeys, sir, I never use
whip to 'em; for if they catch but the scent of a wench
once, they run like devils. *Exit* Coachman *with his whip.*

Laxton. Fine Cerberus! That rogue will have the start of a   25
thousand ones, for whilst others trot afoot, he'll ride
prancing to hell upon a coach-horse! – Stay, 'tis now about
the hour of her appointment, but yet I see her not. (*The
clock strikes three.*) Hark, what's this? – One, two, three:
three by the clock at Savoy; this is the hour, and Gray's   30

28–9. s.d.] *in left-hand margin in Q.*

---

14. *velvet ... jacket*] With the repeal of the sumptuary laws in 1603, the
merchant class was able to display its affluence in clothing. *Tuftaffety* (tuftaf-
feta) was a favoured fabric: 'plain taffeta was not rich enough for Elizabethan
taste. It must be "tufted", i.e. woven with raised stripes or spots. These
stripes, upon being cut, left a pile like velvet, and, since the tufted parts were
always a different colour from the ground, beautiful colour combinations
were possible' (Linthicum, p. 124). Cf. Middleton, *M.T.*, IV.i.78.

15. *coaches*] Stow remarks, 'but now of late yeares the vse of coatches
brought out of Germanie is taken vp, and made so common, as there is neither
distinction of time, nor difference of persons obserued: for the world runs on
wheeles with many, whose parents were glad to goe on foote' (*Survey*, I, p.
84); Kingsford, II, p. 282, quotes from Stow's *Annals* (ed. 1631), 'Lastly, even
at this time, 1605, began the ordinary use of Caroaches'. Cf. Dekker, *Newes
from Hell*, sig. H2r, 'he doubts there is some secrete Bridge made ouer to Hell,
and that they steale thither in coaches, for euery Iustices wife, and the wife of
euerie Cittizen must be iolted now' (all cited by Hoy); also John Taylor, the
water-poet, *The World runnes on Wheeles* (*Works* (1630)).

17. *baffle*] disgrace; cf. I.ii.168.

18. *jades*] Cf. II.i.282 and n.

25. *Cerberus*] mythological three-headed dog, porter of Hades; cf.
III.iii.146.

start] head-start, advantage; cf. Tilley, S828.

30. *Savoy*] a hospital built by Henry VII on the site of the destroyed Savoy
Palace on the north bank of the Thames between the Strand and the river.
Sugden (p. 453) notes this to be the only allusion to a striking clock in its
tower.

Inn Fields the place, she swore she'd meet me. Ha,
yonder's two Inns-o'-Court men with one wench: but
that's not she; they walk toward Islington out of my way. I
see none yet dressed like her: I must look for a shag ruff, a
frieze jerkin, a short sword, and a safeguard, or I get none.   35
Why, Moll, prithee make haste or the coachman will curse
us anon.

Enter MOLL *like a man.*

Moll. [*Aside*] O here's my gentleman! – If they would keep
their days as well with their mercers as their hours with
their harlots, no bankrupt would give sevenscore pound   40
for a sergeant's place; for would you know a catchpole
rightly derived: the corruption of a citizen is the generation of a sergeant. – How his eye hawks for venery! – [*To
him*] Come, are you ready, sir?
Laxton. Ready? For what, sir?   45
Moll. Do you ask that now, sir? Why was this meeting
'pointed?
Laxton. I thought you mistook me, sir.
You seem to be some young barrister;
I have no suit in law – all my land's sold,   50

32–3. *two* ... *Islington*] a joke aimed at Inns-of-Court men? Islington, one
of London's northern suburbs, was a favourite resort for outings and assig-
nations; the wench is probably to be understood as a prostitute.

32. *Inns-o'-Court*] legal societies in London, frequently referred to as the
third university of England at this time.

34–5. *shag ruff* ... *safeguard*] Laxton is thoroughly unprepared for Moll.

37.1. *like a man*] i.e. dressed as a man: her first appearance in the play in
man's apparel.

39. *mercers*] 'The mercer's book' proverbially referred to the debts of a
gallant. See Middleton?, *S.M.T.*, I.i.92 and n. (Revels ed.).

40–3. *bankrupt* ... *sergeant*] proverbial: cf. 'A sergeant is the spawn of some
decayed shop-keeper' (Tilley, S226: the earliest citation is from Overbury's
Characters (1615)); also Dekker and Webster, *W.H.*, III.ii.8–10, where
Ambush, the Sergeant, remarks, 'I haue bin a Broker already; for I was first a
Puritan, then a Banquerout, then a Broker, then a Fencer, and then a Ser-
geant, were not these Trades woulde make a man honest?'

41. *catchpole*] a sherriff's officer or sergeant who arrests for debt.

42–3. *corruption* ... *generation*] alchemical terms which evolved into a
quasi-proverbial construction; cf. Tilley, C667. See *Shakespeare's England*, I,
464.

47. *'pointed*] appointed.

50. *all* ... *sold*] a further allusion to the derivation of Laxton's name.

I praise heaven for't, 't has rid me of much trouble.

Moll. Then I must wake you, sir; where stands the coach?

Laxton. Who's this? – Moll? Honest Moll?

Moll. So young, and purblind? You're an old wanton in your
    eyes, I see that.   55

Laxton. Thou'rt admirably suited for the Three Pigeons at
    Brentford. I'll swear I knew thee not.

Moll. I'll swear you did not: but you shall know me now!

Laxton. No, not here: we shall be spied i'faith! – The coach is
    better; come.   60

Moll. Stay!   *She puts off her cloak and draws [her sword].*

Laxton. What, wilt thou untruss a point, Moll?

Moll.   Yes, here's the point
    That I untruss: 't has but one tag, 'twill serve though
    To tie up a rogue's tongue!

Laxton.   How?

Moll.   There's the gold
    With which you hired your hackney, here's her pace: 65

61. s.d.] *Bowers; after* Moll?, *l. 62 Q; Puts off her cloak. to the right of l. 61,
Draws her sword. to the right of l. 62 Dyce.*

---

54. *purblind*] totally blind.

56. *suited*] (1) dressed; (2) fitted, appropriate.

Three Pigeons] a famous tavern at Brentford and a favourite resort of
Londoners. 'At a later period, when Puritanism had silenced the stage, it was
kept by the celebrated actor, Lowin' (Dyce). It is mentioned by Jonson in
Alchemist, V.iv.89, and is the scene of one of George Peele's jests (*Works*, ed.
A. H. Bullen (1888, repr. Port Washington, 1966), II, 395ff.).

59. *No, not here*] Moll possibly removes her hat (see title-page of Middleton
and Rowley's *F.Q.*) and then her cloak. Laxton misinterprets these actions as
preliminaries to a sexual encounter of a different sort.

59–60. *coach is better*] Cf. John Taylor, the water-poet, *The World runnes on
Wheeles*, (*Works* (1630), sig. Bbb3r), '[A coach] is neuer vnfurnished of a
bedde and curtaines, with shop-windowes of leather to buckle Bawdry vp as
close in the midst of the street, as it were in the Stewes ...'; also Middleton,
Phoenix, II.iii.17–18. Knockem comments on the use of coaches for sexual
purposes in Jonson's *Bartholomew Fair*, IV.v.97–100 (Revels ed.).

62. *untruss a point*] *Points* (laces) fastened the hose to the doublet; Laxton
may refer to the codpiece point, but Moll refers to the point of her sword.

63. *untruss*] i.e. unsheath.

64. *tongue*] with bawdy innuendo.

65. *hackney*] (1) horse used for ordinary riding; (2) prostitute.

pace] extending the horse imagery; (1) rate of speed; (2) gait (of a horse) in
which both fore and hind legs move together on one side, then the other. Cf.
Per., IV.v.62–3, where the training of a prostitute is involved.

She racks hard and perhaps your bones will feel it.
Ten angels of mine own I've put to thine:
Win 'em and wear 'em!
Laxton.   Hold, Moll! Mistress Mary –
Moll. Draw, or I'll serve an execution on thee
    Shall lay thee up till doomsday.   70
Laxton. Draw upon a woman? Why, what dost mean, Moll?
Moll. To teach thy base thoughts manners! Thou'rt one of
    those
    That thinks each woman thy fond flexible whore:
    If she but cast a liberal eye upon thee,
    Turn back her head, she's thine; or, amongst company,   75
    By chance drink first to thee, then she's quite gone,
    There's no means to help her; nay, for a need,
    Wilt swear unto thy credulous fellow lechers
    That thou'rt more in favour with a lady

---

78. lechers] *Bowers;* letchers. *Q.*

---

66. *racks hard*] paces (at the gait described above, l. 65n.). The rack or pace
when fast would be very rough or bone-shaking.

68. *win . . . wear*] proverbial (Tilley, W408). *O.E.D.* ('wear', v.1, 8b), '*To
win and wear* (a lady as one's wife)', notes 'the literal reference may have been
to a favour won in the tilt, or to a king's crown'.

69. *serve . . . on*] normally a formula used of 'making a legal delivery of (a
process or writ)' (*O.E.D.*, 'serve', v.1, 50a), which connects with Judgement
Day.

70. *Shall*] i.e. that shall (ellipsis); see Abbott, § 244.

lay thee up] (1) put you away; (2) incapacitate you.

73. *fond*] foolish, infatuated.

flexible] manageable, impressionable.

74–7. *If . . . her*] Cf. Joseph Swetnam, *The araignment of lewd, idle, froward
and unconstant women* (1615), p. 32, 'Some thinke that if a woman smile on
them she is presently ouer head and eares in loue, one must weare her gloue,
another her garter, another her coulers of delight, and another shall spend and
liue vpon the spoile which she getteth from all the rest.' Nashe, *Anatomie of
Absurditie* (*Works*, ed. R. B. McKerrow (Oxford, 1966), I, p. 17, ll. 17–23),
gives the reverse construction: 'But women through want of wisedome are
growne to such wantonnesse, that vppon no occasion they will crosse the
streete, to haue a glaunce of some Gallant, deeming that men by one looke of
them, shoulde be in loue with them, and will not stick to make an errant ouer
the way, to purchase a Paramour to helpe at a pinche . . .'

74. *liberal*] (1) generous; (2) licentious.

77. *for a need*] in an emergency, at a pinch.

At first sight than her monkey all her lifetime.   80
How many of our sex by such as thou
Have their good thoughts paid with a blasted name
That never deserved loosely or did trip
In path of whoredom beyond cup and lip?
But for the stain of conscience and of soul,   85
Better had women fall into the hands
Of an act silent than a bragging nothing:
There's no mercy in't. – What durst move you, sir,
To think me whorish? – A name which I'd tear out
From the high German's throat if it lay ledger there   90
To dispatch privy slanders against me!
In thee I defy all men, their worst hates
And their best flatteries, all their golden witchcrafts
With which they entangle the poor spirits of fools:

---

80. *monkey*] Monkeys were common as ladies' pets: cf. Middleton, *B.M.C.*,
I.ii.9–10, 'For as your tame monkey is your only best, and most only beast to
your Spanish lady . . .'; also the s.d. at the opening of I.ii of Jonson, Chapman
and Marston's *Eastward Ho, 'Bettrice leading a Monkey after her'*. 'Old maids
[or, Coy maids] lead apes in hell' (Tilley, M37) proverbially referred to the
plight of spinsters, possibly obliquely alluded to here. Cf. Middleton, *M.T.*,
I.i.326–8, *F.H.T.* (Bullen, VIII), pp. 66, 70, *S.G.*, II.i.135; Dekker and
Webster, *N.H.*, II.i.267–8 and III.i.27–8.

81–4.] Cf. Middleton, *N.W.N.H.*, III.i.59–63, 'Marry, sir, I'll give it out
abroad that I have lain with the widow myself, as 'tis the fashion of many a
gallant to disgrace his new mistress when he cannot have his will of her, and lie
with her name in every tavern, though he ne'er came within a yard of her
person.'

84. *beyond cup and lip*] The allusion is to a betrothal; cf. Middleton,
N.W.N.H., II.i.390–3: 'Have I so happily found / What many a widow has
with sorrow tasted, / Even when my lip touch'd the contracting cup, / Even
then to see the spider?'

85. *But for*] were it not for.

89–90. *tear . . . throat*] Cf. 'To lie in the throat' (Tilley, T268), meaning 'to
lie foully'. A. R. Humphreys, *2H4* (1966), I.ii.80–1n., cites the following
distinction: '*The lie in the throat* was a lie uttered deliberately; *the lie in the
teeth* was one for which some excuse was allowed on the ground of its having
proceeded from haste or some palliating cause.'

90. *high German's*] See II.i.368 and n.

ledger] ambassador; *dispatch privy slanders*, l. 91, extends the image.

92. *defy*] (1) challenge; (2) reject, despise.

93. *flatteries . . . golden*] Cf. II.ii.124–5.

witchcrafts] bewitching charms.

Distressèd needlewomen and trade-fallen wives –   95
Fish that must needs bite, or themselves be bitten –
Such hungry things as these may soon be took
With a worm fastened on a golden hook:
Those are the lecher's food, his prey. He watches
For quarrelling wedlocks and poor shifting sisters: 100
'Tis the best fish he takes. But why, good fisherman,
Am I thought meat for you, that never yet
Had angling rod cast towards me? – 'Cause you'll say
I'm given to sport, I'm often merry, jest;
Had mirth no kindred in the world but lust?   105
O shame take all her friends then! But howe'er
Thou and the baser world censure my life,
I'll send 'em word by thee, and write so much
Upon thy breast, 'cause thou shalt bear't in mind:
Tell them 'twere base to yield where I have conquered.   110
I scorn to prostitute myself to a man,
I that can prostitute a man to me! –
And so I greet thee.
Laxton.   Hear me!
Moll.   Would the spirits
Of all my slanderers were clasped in thine,

95. wives –] *This ed.;* wiues. *Q.*   98. hook:] *Dyce;* hooke. *Q.*   114. slanderers] *Collier;* slanders *Q.*

95.] Though unspecific, the references recall Mist. Openwork and Mist. Gallipot (cf. II.i.9–13).

96.] Cf. III.iii.141–3.

98. *worm . . . hook*] a favourite Dekker image; but also proverbial (Tilley, H691). Cf. Middleton, *M.T.*, I.i.137, 155–7, and II.iii.223–5, and *F.Q.*, I.i.188, III.ii.123. See Intro., p. 10.

100. *wedlocks*] wives.

shifting] deceitful.

101. *fish . . . fisherman*] Fish commonly means 'prostitute'; cf. 'fishmonger', *Ham.*, II.ii.173.

102. *meat*] suggestive of 'whore', and punning on 'meet' (suitable, fit, proper).

103. *'Cause*] because.

113. *greet*] (1) assail, attack; (2) accost.

114. *slanderers*] Collier first proposed this emendation (from Q's 'slanders') because 'both the sense and the metre' require it. But cf. three instances of *slander* 'applied to persons who cause disgrace or bring reproach' in C. T. Onions, *A Shakespeare Glossary* (2nd ed., Oxford, 1958).

That I might vex an army at one time!   *They fight.*   115
Laxton. I do repent me; hold!
Moll. You'll die the better Christian then.
Laxton. I do confess I have wronged thee, Moll.
Moll. Confession is but poor amends for wrong,
     Unless a rope would follow.
Laxton.   I ask thee pardon.   120
Moll. I'm your hired whore, sir!
Laxton.   I yield both purse and body.
Moll. Both are mine and now at my disposing.
Laxton. Spare my life!
Moll.   I scorn to strike thee basely.
Laxton. Spoke like a noble girl, i'faith.
     – [*Aside*] Heart, I think I fight with a familiar, or the ghost   125
     of a fencer! Sh'has wounded me gallantly. Call you this a
     lecherous voyage? Here's blood would have served me
     this seven year in broken heads and cut fingers, and it now
     runs all out together! Pox o' the Three Pigeons! I would
     the coach were here now to carry me to the chirurgeon's.   130
                                                      Exit.

Moll. If I could meet my enemies one by one thus,
     I might make pretty shift with 'em in time,
     And make 'em know, she that has wit and spirit
     May scorn to live beholding to her body for meat,

---

115. s.d.] *to the right of l. 116 Q.*   127. voyage] *Dyce subst.;* viage *Q;* visage
Reed.   130.1.] *Exit Laxton. Q.*

119–20. *Confession . . . follow*] Cf. the proverbial 'Confession of a fault is half amends' (Tilley, C589; also C590).

122. *disposing*] disposal.

123. *I scorn*] I would not condescend.

125. *familiar*] 'a familiar spirit, a demon or evil spirit supposed to attend at a call (*O.E.D.*, 3).

126. *gallantly*] (1) excellently, finely; (2) in the manner of a gallant.

127. *voyage*] 'sexual adventure' (cf. II.ii.67 and n.); cf. Middleton, *W.B.W.*, II.ii.471–3 and IV.i.163 (Revels ed.).

128. *broken*] cut open.

129. *together*] at once.

130. *chirurgeon's*] surgeon's.

134–6. *scorn . . . shame*] Cf. Dekker, *S.D.S.*, sig. B4v, 'She liues basely by the abuse of that body, to maintaine which in costly garments, thou didst wrong to thine owne soule.'

134. *beholding*] beholden; a confusion common in Middleton, less so in Dekker. See Abbott, § 372.

Or for apparel, like your common dame   135
That makes shame get her clothes to cover shame.
Base is that mind that kneels unto her body
As if a husband stood in awe on's wife;
My spirit shall be mistress of this house
As long as I have time in't.

Enter TRAPDOOR

– O,   140
Here comes my man that would be: 'tis his hour.
Faith, a good well-set fellow, if his spirit
Be answerable to his umbles. He walks stiff,
But whether he will stand to't stiffly, there's the point!
'Has a good calf for't, and ye shall have many a woman   145
Choose him she means to make her head by his calf;
I do not know their tricks in't. Faith, he seems
A man without; I'll try what he is within.
Trapdoor. [*Aside*] She told me Gray's Inn Fields 'twixt three
          and four.
I'll fit her mistress-ship with a piece of service: 150

145. 'Has] *Bowers subst.;* Has Q.

---

135. *common dame*] whore.
138. *husband ... wife*] Cf. Low-water marvelling over his wife's subservience in Middleton, *N.W.N.H.*, II.iii.214–18, 'How few women are of thy mind! she thinks it took much to keep me in subjection for one day; whereas some wives would be glad to keep their husbands in awe all days of their lives, and think it the best bargain that e'er they made.' *Stood in awe* = dreaded, greatly feared (*O.E.D.*, 'awe', sb.1, 4a).
on's] on his.
139–40.] Cf. Beaumont and Fletcher, *Maid's Tragedy*, V.iii.179 (*Dramatic Works*, II, ed. F. Bowers (Cambridge, 1970)), 'My soule growes weary of her house', and Middleton and Rowley, *S.G.*, III.i.1–4.
141. *my man that would be*] i.e. he who wishes to be my manservant.
142–8.] Cf. Phillipa's remarks on Francisco in Middleton, *Widow*, I.i.88–94.
143. *umbles*] 'the edible inward parts of an animal, usually a deer' (*O.E.D.*, 1a), used figuratively for 'insides'.
stiff] resolute, steadfast (with bawdy innuendo).
145–6. *many ... calf*] Cf. Middleton, *N.W.N.H.*, III.i.176–8, 'by my faith, one may pick a gentleman out of his calves and a scholar out on's cheeks; one may see by his looks what's in him'.
146. *head*] i.e. of the household; husband (cf. II.ii.43–5).
147. *tricks*] knacks, skills.
150. *fit*] furnish.

I'm hired to rid the town of one mad girl. *She jostles him.*
    – [*To her*] What a pox ails you, sir? –
Moll. He begins like a gentleman.
Trapdoor. Heart, is the field so narrow, or your eyesight? –
    Life, he comes back again!   *She comes towards him.*
Moll.   Was this spoke to me, sir?   155
Trapdoor. I cannot tell, sir.
Moll.   Go, you're a coxcomb!
Trapdoor. Coxcomb?
Moll.   You're a slave!
Trapdoor.   I hope there's law for you, sir!
Moll. Yea, do you see, sir?   *Turn[s] his hat.*
Trapdoor. Heart, this is no good dealing. Pray let me know
    what house you're of.   160
Moll. One of the Temple, sir.   *Fillips him.*
Trapdoor.   Mass, so methinks.
Moll. And yet, sometime I lie about Chick Lane.
Trapdoor. I like you the worse because you shift your lodging
    so often; I'll not meddle with you for that trick, sir.
Moll. A good shift, but it shall not serve your turn.   165
Trapdoor. You'll give me leave to pass about my business, sir?
Moll. Your business? – I'll make you wait on me
    Before I ha' done, and glad to serve me too!
Trapdoor. How sir, serve you? Not if there were no more men
    in England!   170
Moll. But if there were no more women in England,

158. Yea] *Dyce;* Ye *Q;* Yes *Reed.*

152.] Cf. Middleton, *Y.F.G.*, IV.viii.21, 'What a pox ail you, sir?'
156. *coxcomb*] fool.
157. *law for you*] i.e. a law to deal with such as you.
161. *One ... Temple*] i.e. a lawyer; in reference to the Middle or the Inner Temple, two Inns of Court.
Fillips him] 'strikes him with the nail of a finger forced from the thumb with a sudden jerk'; or perhaps in a wider sense, 'strikes him with a smart blow'.
162. *Chick Lane*] or Chicken Lane, a street in the London suburb of Smithfield. Sugden (p. 115) notes that the notorious Red Lion Inn, 'an infamous haunt of thieves and ruffians', was here and that 'the whole district had a most evil reputation'.
164.] Trapdoor shrinks from the prospect of an encounter with one from Chick Lane; *trick* means 'habit' or 'custom'.
165. *shift*] punning on the sense, 'change', at l. 163 and 'device, stratagem' (i.e. for withdrawing from confrontation).
serve your turn] suit your purpose, help you.

I hope you'd wait upon your mistress then.

Trapdoor. Mistress!

Moll. O you're a tried spirit at a push, sir.

Trapdoor. What would your worship have me do?   175

Moll. You a fighter?

Trapdoor. No, I praise heaven, I had better grace and more manners.

Moll. As how, I pray, sir?

Trapdoor. Life, 't had been a beastly part of me to have drawn   180
    my weapons upon my mistress; all the world would ha'
    cried shame of me for that.

Moll. Why, but you knew me not.

Trapdoor. Do not say so, mistress; I knew you by your wide
    straddle as well as if I had been in your belly.   185

Moll. Well, we shall try you further; i'th' meantime,
    We give you entertainment.

Trapdoor. Thank your good mistress-ship.

Moll. How many suits have you?

Trapdoor. No more suits than backs, mistress.   190

Moll. Well, if you deserve, I cast off this next week,
    And you may creep into't.

Trapdoor.   Thank your good worship.

Moll. Come, follow me to St Thomas Apostles:
    I'll put a livery cloak upon your back
    The first thing I do.

Trapdoor.   I follow my dear mistress.   *Exeunt.*   195

195. s.d.] *Exeunt omnes Q.*

---

174. *at a push*] (1) in an emergency; (2) possibly bawdy: *push* = copulate
(Farmer and Henley (edd.), *Slang and its Analogues* (1890–1904), v, 331).

180. *part*] action, piece of conduct.

180–1. *drawn my weapons*] with a bawdy innuendo.

180–5.] Cf. Falstaff to Hal, *1H4*, II.iv.258–61.

182. *cried shame of*] bitterly reproached.

187. *give you entertainment*] engage you.

190.] Cf. 'All his wardrobe is on his back' (Tilley, W61). Bullen misprinted
'blacks', and Ellis compounded the error by glossing, 'mourning garments'!

193. *St Thomas Apostles*] a church in London in Knightrider St., destroyed
in the Great Fire and not rebuilt. Sugden (p. 52) notes that 'The clothiers'
shops were in this neighbourhood.'

194. *livery cloak*] Cf. Middleton, *T.C.O.O.*, II.i.155–9, 'There's more true
honesty in such a country serving-man than in a hundred of our cloak companions: I may well call 'em companions, for since blue coats have been
turned into cloaks, we can scarce know the man from the master.'

[III.ii]

Enter MISTRESS GALLIPOT *as from supper, her* Husband *after her.*

Gallipot. What, Prue! Nay, sweet Prudence!

Mistress Gallipot. What a pruing keep you! I think the baby
      would have a teat, it kyes so. Pray be not so fond of me,
      leave your city humours. I'm vexed at you to see how like a
      calf you come bleating after me.   5

Gallipot. Nay, honey Prue, how does your rising up before all
      the table show? – And flinging from my friends so un-
      civilly? Fie, Prue, fie! – Come.

Mistress Gallipot. Then up and ride, i'faith.

Gallipot. Up and ride? Nay, my pretty Prue, that's far from my   10
      thought, duck. Why mouse, thy mind is nibbling at some-
      thing. Whats' is't? What lies upon thy stomach?

Mistress Gallipot. Such an ass as you! – Heyday, you're best
      turn midwife or physician; you're a pothecary already, but
      I'm none of your drugs.   15

Gallipot. Thou art a sweet drug, sweetest Prue, and the more
      thou art pounded, the more precious.

III.ii] *Dyce; not in Q.*   12. Whats'] *Q subst.;* what *Reed.*   13. Heyday] *This
ed.;* hoyda *Q.*

0.1. *as from supper*] presumably the late afternoon or evening of the same
day as II.i.

2. *pruing*] a nonce word derived from Prudence; the phrase means 'stop
pestering me'.

3. *kyes*] baby-talk = cries; 'she imitates the jargon talked by nurses to infants' (Steevens).

4. *humours*] moods, dispositions.

9. *up and ride*] bawdy: cf. Middleton, *B.M.C.*, IV.i.42, *F. of L.*, I.ii.105–6,
III.iii.15–16, *M.D.B.W.*, I.iv.11. J. Crow, 'Some Jacobean Catch-phrases',
cites 'vp and ride' for a good day (no. 612, p. 275), and 'Nothing but up and
ride' is recorded by Tilley (N284), though the earliest usage he cites is 1639.

11. *duck ... mouse*] terms of affection.

12. *Whats'*] Though other editors emend to *what*, the Q reading ('whats')
may be defended as an elided form of *whatso* = whatever (*O.E.D.*, 1a).

What ... stomach] 'What has upset your stomach?', possibly in literal reference to her sudden departure from supper. *Stomach* had also the bawdy
sense, 'sexual appetite'.

13–14. *Heyday ... physician*] Gallipot has presumably made some physical
advance.

15. *drugs*] playing on 'drudge' (frequently spelt 'drugge' or 'drug'), a menial
servant, and in a bawdy sense, a willing lover.

16–17. *more ... pounded*] with a bawdy innuendo.

Mistress Gallipot. Must you be prying into a woman's secrets?
    Say ye?

Gallipot. Woman's secrets?   20

Mistress Gallipot. What? I cannot have a qualm come upon me
    but your teeth waters till your nose hang over it.

Gallipot. It is my love, dear wife.

Mistress Gallipot. Your love? Your love is all words; give me
    deeds! I cannot abide a man that's too fond over me – so   25
    cookish! Thou dost not know how to handle a woman in
    her kind.

Gallipot. No, Prue? Why, I hope I have handled –

Mistress Gallipot. Handle a fool's head of your own! – Fie, fie!

Gallipot. Ha, ha, 'tis such a wasp, it does me good now to have 30
    her sting me, little rogue.

Mistress Gallipot. Now fie how you vex me! I cannot abide
    these apron husbands: such cotqueans! You overdo your
    things; they become you scurvily.

---

29. Fie, fie] *Dyce;* fih – – – fih *Q.*   31. sting] *Reed;* sing *Q.*

---

18. *secrets*] with a play on the bawdy sense, 'privates'.

22. *teeth waters*] proverbial: Tilley, T430.

24–5. *words . . . deeds*] proverbial: cf. 'From words to deeds is a great space'
(Tilley, W802) and 'Not words but deeds' (W820). The rebuke might equally
be served to Laxton.

25. *fond*] foolish, silly, infatuated.

26. *cookish*] like a cook; i.e. like a woman.

26–7. *in her kind*] in the manner she desires.

28. *handled*] Gallipot presumably acts on the sexual suggestion of *handle*.

29. *fool's head . . . own*] i.e. handle your own foolish head: proverbial (Tilley,
F519); cf. IV.ii.89–90; *Wiv.*, I.iv.114–15.

30–1. *wasp . . . me*] Cf. Middleton, *F. of L.*, V.iii.392–5, 'Your wife is an
angry honeyless wasp, whose sting, I hope, you need not fear, – and yours
carries honey in her mouth, but her sting makes your forehead swell.' The
emendation *sting* better fits the image than Q's 'sing'. But cf. *C.M. in C.*,
II.i.51–2 and n. (Revels ed.) for a similar occurrence. Both terms have a
secondary bawdy sense.

32–4.] The bawdy by-play prompted the editor of the Pearson reprint to
remark: 'The exclamations of Mistress Gallipot evidently refer to some action
on the part of her husband: this portion of the scene is very adroitly *written*,
requiring to be read *entre les lignes* . . . but how it can have been represented
publicly on the stage it is difficult to imagine' (III, 375).

33. *cotqueans*] 'men who meddle with female affairs' (Dyce).

34. *things*] (1) attentions; (2) sexual organs.
    scurvily] meanly, sorrily.

Gallipot. [*Aside*] Upon my life, she breeds. Heaven knows how   35
    I have strained myself to please her night and day. I won-
    der why we citizens should get children so fretful and
    untoward in the breeding, their fathers being for the most
    part as gentle as milch kine. – [*To her*] Shall I leave thee,
    my Prue?   40
Mistress Gallipot. Fie, fie, fie!
Gallipot. Thou shalt not be vexed no more, pretty kind rogue;
    take no cold, sweet Prue.   *Exit.*
Mistress Gallipot. As your wit has done! Now Master Laxton,
    show your head: what news from you? [*Produces a letter.*]   45
    Would any husband suspect that a woman crying, 'Buy
    any scurvy-grass,' should bring love letters amongst her
    herbs to his wife? Pretty trick! Fine conveyance! Had jea-

---

43. s.d.] *Exit Maist. Gallipot. Q.*   45. s.d.] *M. Thesis.*

---

37. *get*] beget.

38. *untoward*] difficult to manage.

39. *milch kine*] milk-cows.

42. *not . . . no*] double negative for emphasis: see Abbott, § 406.

43. *take no cold*] (1) do not catch cold (he has in mind the reason his wife
gave for leaving the table as well as the pregnancy he suspects); (2) don't
become dispirited, depressed.

44. *As your wit has done*] i.e. taken cold.

46–8. *Would . . . wife*] Cf. Middleton, *F.H.T.* (Bullen, VIII), pp. 91–2; also
Fennor, *Compters Common-wealth*, p. 37.

47. *scurvy-grass*] spoonwort (*Cochlearia officinalis*) used in anti-scorbutic
preparations; the figurative senses of *scurvy* ('shabby, worthless') are perhaps
intended also. *Scurvy-grass* is mentioned as a 'diet-drink' for April in
Middleton, *N.W.N.H.*, II.i.29–30. John Gerard, who figured in Middleton's
family history (see M. Eccles, 'Thomas Middleton a Poett', *S.P.*, LIV (1957),
517), in *The Herball* (1597), Bk II, ch. 82, p. 325, describes the plant's use:
'The iuice of Spoonewoort giuen to drinke in ale or beere, is a singular
medicine against the corrupt and rotten vlcers, and stench of the mouth: it
perfectly cureth the disease called . . . in English the Scuruie.' He also notes
that the common variety of the plant grows along the shores of the Thames
near London.

48. *herbs*] possibly in allusion to 'herb-woman', a term for a bawd or whore:
cf. *Per.*, IV.vi.84.

trick] device, deception.

conveyance] underhand dealing, trickery.

48–9. *jealousy . . . eyes*] *jealousy* = suspicion. The reference is to Argus, an
earthborn giant who had eyes all over his body. According to different accounts he had a hundred or simply many eyes. Prompted by Zeus' love for Io,

lousy a thousand eyes, a silly woman with scurvy-grass
blinds them all.   50
Laxton, with bays
Crown I thy wit for this: it deserves praise.
This makes me affect thee more, this proves thee wise;
'Lack, what poor shift is love forced to devise? –
To the point.   *She reads the letter.*   55
    O sweet creature – a sweet beginning *– pardon my long*
    absence, for thou shalt shortly be possessed with my pre-
    sence. Though Demophon was false to Phyllis, I will be to
    thee as Pan-da-rus was to Cres-sida; though Aeneas made

---

the jealous Hera turned her into a cow and set Argus to watch over her; but
Hermes at Zeus' bidding bewitched his sight and killed him. To honour
Argus, Hera set his eyes in the tail of her sacred bird, the peacock. Cf. Spen-
ser, *Faerie Queene*, III.ix.7, 'For who wotes not, that womans subtiltyes / Can
guilen *Argus*, when she list misdonne?'
    49. *silly*] (1) plain, simple; (2) helpless, defenceless.
    53. *affect*] fond of, love.
    54. *'Lack*] alack.
    shift] subterfuge, stratagem.
    58. Demophon ... Phyllis] Demophon, son of Theseus and Phaedra, on his
return from Troy fell in love with and married Phyllis, daughter of the Bisal-
tian king. Demophon later left her to sail for Athens, promising to return at a
specified time. At his departure, Phyllis presented him with a box containing,
she claimed, an object sacred to the goddess Rhea, which he was not to open
unless he had given up all intentions of returning to her. Demophon went
instead to Cyprus and settled there. When he failed to return at the appointed
time, Phyllis hanged herself; and Demophon, prompted to open the box, was
maddened by its contents. Charging away wildly on his horse, he was thrown,
and died by falling on his own sword. The story is often confused with that
concerning Demophon's brother, Acamas. In another version, Demophon's
return passage was delayed by storms, and Phyllis died and was transformed
into an almond tree. When he embraced the tree, it burst into flower instead of
leaf – a peculiarity of almond trees ever since.
    59. Pan-da-rus ... Cres-sida] According to mediaeval tradition, Pandarus
acted as the intermediary in the love relationship of Troilus and Cressida. Q's
presentation of the names indicates not only 'the difficulty with which such
hard names were read by mistress Gallipot', as Dyce noted, but also that she
misses the implication that their relationship is to remain unconsummated.
    59–60. Aeneas ... Dido] after Aeneas left Carthage in accordance with the
will of the gods, Dido, pining from unrequited love, killed herself. The allusion like the others characterises Laxton's lack of regard for Mist. Gallipot,
though its significance goes over her head. Ovid's *Heroides* includes epistles
from Phyllis to Demophon and from Dido to Aeneas.

    an ass of Dido, I will die to thee ere I do so. O sweetest   60
    creature, make much of me, for no man beneath the silver
    moon shall make more of a woman than I do of thee. Fur-
    nish me therefore with thirty pounds – you must do it of
    necessity for me. I languish till I see some comfort come
    from thee. Protesting not to die in thy debt, but rather to   65
    live so, as hitherto I have and will,

                            Thy true Laxton ever.

Alas, poor gentleman! Troth I pity him.
How shall I raise this money? Thirty pound?
'Tis thirty sure: a three before an O –   70
I know his threes too well. My childbed linen?
Shall I pawn that for him? Then if my mark
Be known, I am undone! It may be thought
My husband's bankrupt. Which way shall I turn?
Laxton, what with my own fears, and thy wants,   75
I'm like a needle 'twixt two adamants.

        Enter MASTER GALLIPOT *hastily.*

Gallipot. Nay, nay, wife, the women are all up – *[Aside]* Ha?
    How? Reading o' letters? I smell a goose, a couple of
    capons, and a gammon of bacon from her mother out of
    the country, I hold my life –   80

---

    60. ass] punning on Aen*ass*; cf. Dekker's dedication to *G.H.* (ed. Pendry),
p. 69, 'my most worthy Maecen*asses*'.

    die to] In addition to the normal sense, a forced pun on 'Dido' is probably
intended, as well as the sexual meaning, 'experience orgasm'.

    62. make more] deliberately ambivalent: Mist. Gallipot no doubt interprets
personally, while Laxton is interested in her money. Cf. his protest to live in
her debt, ll. 65–6.

    70. *three before an O*] possibly with a bawdy entendre: cf. Middleton, *F. of
L.*, III.i.54–5, for *O* = pudend, 'Lastly, take *O*, in *re* stands all my rest, /
Which I, in Chaucer-style, do term a jest.' Gerardine plays on 'amore': the
joke depends on *re*, the Latin for 'thing' (penis). Possibly 'th*ree*' functions
similarly.

    71. *childbed linen*] bed linen used for childbirth and confinement.

    72. *mark*] device or character used as a sign of ownership or identification;
cf. T. Heywood, *Woman Killed with Kindness*, xiii.164 (Revels ed.).

    76. adamants] extremely hard stones frequently confused or identified with
loadstones or magnets.

    78. *Reading o' letters*] reading letters: 'of' was often used to separate a
gerund and its object: see Abbott, § 178.

    80. *hold*] bet, wager.

    Steal – steal –   [*Sneaks behind her.*]
Mistress Gallipot.   O beshrew your heart!
Gallipot.   What letter's that? –
    I'll see't.
Mistress Gallipot. O would thou hadst no eyes to see
                         She tears the letter.
    The downfall of me and thyself! I'm for ever,
    For ever I'm undone.
Gallipot.   What ails my Prue?
    What paper's that thou tear'st?
Mistress Gallipot   Would I could tear   85
    My very heart in pieces, for my soul
    Lies on the rack of shame that tortures me
    Beyond a woman's suffering.
Gallipot.   What means this?
Mistress Gallipot. Had you no other vengeance to throw down,
    But even in height of all my joys –
Gallipot.   Dear woman!   90
Mistress Gallipot. When the full sea of pleasure and content
    Seemed to flow over me?
Gallipot.   As thou desirest
    To keep me out of Bedlam, tell what troubles thee!
    Is not thy child at nurse fallen sick, or dead?
Mistress Gallipot. O no!
Gallipot.   Heavens bless me! Are my barns and houses   95
    Yonder at Hockley Hole consumed with fire? –
    I can build more, sweet Prue.

81. s.d.] *This ed.*   82.1.] *This ed.; to the right of* I'll see't. *Q.*

---

81. *Steal*] i.e. intending to read the letter over her shoulder.

beshrew your heart] a common imprecation, often used lightly, meaning,
'devil take your heart' or 'evil befall you'.

82–138.] Mist. Gallipot in dealing with her husband adopts a rhetorical
style, self-parodying in its extravagance.

93. *Bedlam*] a corruption of Bethlehem, originally used in allusion to the
Hospital of St Mary of Bethlehem situated outside Bishopsgate in which were
lodged 'people that bee distraight in wits' (Stow, *Survey*, I, 165). The term
came to mean a mad-house of any kind.

94. *child . . . sick*] Cf. Dekker and Webster, *W.H.*, II.iii.85ff., where a false
report of sickness is proposed.

96. *Hockley Hole*] Hockley in the Hole, 'A village lying in the Fleet Valley in
London, north-west of Clerkenwell Green' (Sugden, p. 251).

Mistress Gallipot.   'Tis worse, 'tis worse!

Gallipot. My factor broke? Or is the *Jonas* sunk?

Mistress Gallipot. Would all we had were swallowed in the
     waves,
  Rather than both should be the scorn of slaves!   100

Gallipot. I'm at my wit's end!

Mistress Gallipot.   O my dear husband,
  Where once I thought myself a fixèd star
  Placed only in the heaven of thine arms,
  I fear now I shall prove a wanderer. –
  O Laxton, Laxton, is it then my fate   105
  To be by thee o'erthrown?

Gallipot.   Defend me, wisdom,
  From falling into frenzy! On my knees,
  Sweet Prue, speak! What's that Laxton who so heavy
  Lies on thy bosom?

Mistress Gallipot.   I shall sure run mad!

Gallipot. I shall run mad for company then. Speak to me –   110
  I'm Gallipot, thy husband – Prue! – Why, Prue!
  Art sick in conscience for some villainous deed
  Thou wert about to act? Didst mean to rob me?
  Tush, I forgive thee. Hast thou on my bed
  Thrust my soft pillow under another's head?   115
  I'll wink at all faults, Prue; 'las, that's no more
  Than what some neighbours near thee have done before.
  Sweet honey Prue, what's that Laxton.

---

98. *factor*] agent, commission merchant.

Jonas] trade vessel named after the biblical Jonas (Jonah): possibly intended as a joke since the cargo of the ship in which the prophet sailed was cast
overboard in the storm (see Jonah, i.5). A ship so named is recorded in Marc
Lescarbot, *Nova Francia*, tr. P. Erondelle (1609), sig. H2r.

99. *swallowed in the waves*] prompted by the mention of *Jonas*.

101. *at my wit's end*] continuing the 'madness' suggestion of *Bedlam* (l. 93)
which peaks at ll. 106ff.

102. *Where*] whereas.

102–4. *fixèd star . . . wanderer*] A *fixed star* is one 'which appears always to
occupy the same position in the heavens' (*O.E.D.*, 'fixed', 6b); and so distinguished from a wandering star or planet (*wanderer*). The earliest usage of
wanderer in this sense recorded by *O.E.D.* (1b) is 1614. A play on 'a person of a
roving nature' (1a) may also be intended.

107. *On my knees*] i.e. in supplication.

116. *wink at*] seem not to see.

'las] alas.

Mistress Gallipot.   O!

Gallipot. Out with him!

Mistress Gallipot.   O, he's born to be my undoer!
 This hand which thou call'st thine, to him was given; 120
 To him was I made sure i'th' sight of heaven.

Gallipot. I never heard this thunder!

Mistress Gallipot.   Yes, yes, before
 I was to thee contracted, to him I swore.
 Since last I saw him, twelve months three times told
 The moon hath drawn through her light silver bow; 125
 For o'er the seas he went, and it was said –
 But rumour lies – that he in France was dead.
 But he's alive; O he's alive! He sent
 That letter to me, which in rage I rent,
 Swearing with oaths most damnably to have me 130
 Or tear me from this bosom. O heavens save me!

Gallipot. My heart will break – shamed and undone forever!

Mistress Gallipot. So black a day, poor wretch, went o'er thee
  never!

Gallipot. If thou shouldst wrestle with him at the law,
 Thou'rt sure to fall; no odd sleight, no prevention. – 135
 I'll tell him thou'rt with child.

Mistress Gallipot.   Um!

Gallipot.   Or give out
 One of my men was ta'en abed with thee.

Mistress Gallipot. Um, um!

Gallipot.   Before I lose thee, my dear Prue,
 I'll drive it to that push.

Mistress Gallipot.   Worse, and worse still!

---

121. *sure ... heaven*] betrothed, contracted.

122. *thunder*] prompted by *heaven*, l. 121.

124–5. *twelve ... bow*] Cf. Dekker, *W.B.*, I.i.47, 'Fiue Summers haue scarce drawn their glimmering nights / Through the Moons siluer bowe' (cited by Dyce), IV.ii.2–4, 'The Moone that from your beames did borrow light, / Hath from her siluer bow shot pitchy clowds', *2 H.W.*, V.ii.25–6, 'The Moone hath thorow her Bow scarce drawn to'th head, / (Like to twelue siluer Arrowes) all the Moneths'.

135. *odd sleight*] devious trickery or device (i.e. to counter Laxton's 'claim'); cf. Middleton, *Y.F.G.*, II.iii.41, *M.D.B.W.*, IV.i.212.

136, 138. *Um!*] Mist. Gallipot guides her husband in the desired direction.

139. *to that push*] (1) to that extremity; (2) in a sexual sense: cf. III.i.174 and n.

You embrace a mischief to prevent an ill.   140
Gallipot. I'll buy thee of him, stop his mouth with gold:
    Think'st thou 'twill do?
Mistress Gallipot.   O me! Heavens grant it would!
    Yet now my senses are set more in tune,
    He writ, as I remember in his letter,
    That he in riding up and down had spent,   145
    Ere he could find me, thirty pounds: send that,
    Stand not on thirty with him.
Gallipot.   Forty, Prue.
    Say thou the word, 'tis done. We venture lives
    For wealth, but must do more to keep our wives.
    Thirty or forty, Prue?
Mistress Gallipot.   Thirty, good sweet;   150
    Of an ill bargain let's save what we can:
    I'll pay it him with my tears; he was a man,
    When first I knew him, of a meek spirit:
    All goodness is not yet dried up, I hope.
Gallipot. He shall have thirty pound: let that stop all;   155
    Love's sweets taste best when we have drunk down gall.

Enter MASTER TILTYARD *and his* Wife, MASTER GOSHAWK, *and*
                MISTRESS OPENWORK.

    Gods-so, our friends! – Come, come, smooth your cheek;
    After a storm, the face of heaven looks sleek.
Tiltyard. Did I not tell you these turtles were together?
Mistress Tiltyard. How dost thou, sirrah? Why, sister   160
    Gallipot! –
Mistress Openwork. Lord, how she's changed!
Goshawk. Is your wife ill, sir?

    140.] Cf. 'Better once a mischief than always an inconvenience' (Tilley,
M995).
    147. *Stand not on*] do not scruple over.
    151.] proverbial: Tilley, B326.
    156.] Cf. 'Sweet meat must have sour sauce' (Tilley, M839), and 'He de-
serves not the sweet that will not taste of the sour' (S1035).
    gall] bile, with special reference to its bitterness.
    157. *Gods-so*] said to be a corruption of 'catso' ('a man's privy member',
Giovanni Florio, *A World of Words* (1598)); but cf. *Uds-so* (V.i.10), a corruption of 'By God's soul' or 'God save my soul'.
    158. *sleek*] tranquil.
    159. *turtles*] i.e. turtle-doves.

Gallipot. Yes indeed, la, sir, very ill, very ill, never worse.

Mistress Tiltyard. How her head burns; feel how her pulses   165
    work.

Mistress Openwork. Sister, lie down a little: that always does
    me good.

Mistress Tiltyard. In good sadness, I find best ease in that too.
    Has she laid some hot thing to her stomach?   170

Mistress Gallipot. No, but I will lay something anon.

Tiltyard. Come, come, fools, you trouble her. – Shall's go,
    Master Goshawk?

Goshawk. Yes, sweet Master Tiltyard.
                        [*Talks apart with Mistress Openwork.*]
    Sirrah Rosamond, I hold my life Gallipot hath vexed his   175
    wife.

Mistress Openwork. She has a horrible high colour indeed.

Goshawk. We shall have your face painted with the same red
    soon at night, when your husband comes from his rubbers
    in a false alley; thou wilt not believe me that his bowls run   180
    with a wrong bias?

Mistress Openwork. It cannot sink into me that he feeds upon
    stale mutton abroad, having better and fresher at home.

Goshawk. What if I bring thee where thou shalt see him stand
    at rack and manger?   185

174.1.] *This ed.*

164.] Gallipot's overemphatic response betrays a wish to avoid any suggestion of strife or scandal.

169. *In good sadness*] in earnest, in all seriousness.

170. *hot thing ... stomach*] (1) i.e. as medication; (2) with conscious or
unconscious bawdy innuendo: *hot, thing* and *stomach* all have secondary
sexual senses; cf. Middleton, *B.M.C.*, I.ii.6–8, *F. of L.*, II.iii.57–8,
N.W.N.H., II.iii.133–7, *C.M. in C.*, I.i.141 (Revels ed.).

179. *rubbers*] (1) a set of (usually) three games; (2) playing bawdily on the
normal sense of *rub*, in combination with *false alley*: cf. Dekker, *O Per Se O*
(ed. Pendry), p. 302, 'I met a drab, I liked her well / (My bowls did fit her
alley).'

181. *with a wrong bias*] i.e. with unnatural crookedness. The bias is the
bulge or weight in one side of a bowl which gives it an oblique motion.

182–3. *feeds ... home*] Cf. 'Dry bread at home is better than roast meat
abroad' (Tilley, B618). *Mutton* is slang for 'whore'; cf. Middleton, *B.M.C.*,
I.ii.6–8, *C.M. in C.*, I.i.185, II.i.81, IV.i.145–6 (Revels ed.).

185. *at rack and manger*] in the midst of abundance; a proverbial tag: cf.
Tilley, R4. The suggestion is followed up with a series of word-plays on terms
from horsemanship.

Mistress Openwork. I'll saddle him in's kind and spur him till
    he kick again!

Goshawk. Shall thou and I ride our journey then?

Mistress Openwork. Here's my hand.

Goshawk. No more. – [*To Tiltyard*] Come Master Tiltyard,   190
    shall we leap into the stirrups with our women and amble
    home?

Tiltyard. Yes, yes; come wife.

Mistress Tiltyard. In troth, sister, I hope you will do well for all
    this.   195

Mistress Gallipot. I hope I shall. Farewell good sister, sweet
    Master Goshawk.

Gallipot. Welcome, brother; most kindly welcome, sir.

All Guests. Thanks, sir, for our good cheer.

                Exeunt all but Gallipot and his Wife.

Gallipot. It shall be so, because a crafty knave   200
    Shall not outreach me, nor walk by my door
    With my wife arm in arm, as 'twere his whore.
    I'll give him a golden coxcomb: thirty pound.
    Tush, Prue, what's thirty pound? Sweet duck, look
    cheerly.

Mistress Gallipot. Thou art worthy of my heart, thou buy'st it
    dearly.   205

           Enter LAXTON *muffled.*

190. s.d.] *M. Thesis.*   199. *All Guests*] *M. Thesis.; Omnes Q.*

---

186. *in's kind*] in the same manner.

188. *journey*] Cf. *voyage*, III.i.127 and n.

191. *leap ... stirrups*] Cf. *up and ride*, l. 9 above and n.

   amble] a leisurely version of the gait, 'pace': see III.i.65n. 'The favourite
pace in Elizabethan days' (*Shakespeare's England*, II, 416).

201. *walk by my door*] possibly glancing at 'to keep a door' = to act as pander.

205.1. *muffled*] Laxton is so described at each of his entrances after III.i;
any or all of three reasons explain this appearance: (1) he is ashamed to show
his face after his drubbing by Moll (he may be hiding the wounds he received); (2) the loss of ten angels to Moll has left him vulnerable to creditors,
and he goes muffled to escape arrest for debt. Cf. Middleton, *F. of L.*,
II.iv.150–2, 'I thought it was a gallant that walked muffled: come, let me
behold you at full; here are no sergeants, man'; and Dekker, *A Rod for Run-
awayes* (ed. Wilson), p. 152, Middleton and Rowley, *F.Q.*, I.i.313, Dekker
and Webster, *N.H.*, I.i.185–6, and *Wonder of a Kingdom*, I.iii.69–71; (3) he
muffles his face to approach the Gallipots' house incognito as might a lover or

Laxton. [*Aside*] Uds light, the tide's against me! A pox of your
   pothecaryship! O for some glister to set him going! 'Tis
   one of Hercules' labours to tread one of these city hens,
   because their cocks are still crowing over them. There's
   no turning tail here; I must on.   210

Mistress Gallipot. O husband, see, he comes!

Gallipot.   Let me deal with him.

Laxton. Bless you, sir.

Gallipot. Be you blessed too, sir, if you come in peace.

Laxton. Have you any good pudding-tobacco, sir?

Mistress Gallipot. O pick no quarrels, gentle sir! My husband   215
   Is not a man of weapon, as you are.
   He knows all: I have opened all before him
   Concerning you.

Laxton. [*Aside*]   Zounds, has she shown my letters?

Mistress Gallipot. Suppose my case were yours, what would
      you do?
   At such a pinch, such batteries, such assaults,   220
   Of father, mother, kindred, to dissolve
   The knot you tied, and to be bound to him?
   How could you shift this storm off?

Laxton.   If I know, hang me!

---

a patron at a brothel; Bellarius does so, for example, in Middleton?, *S. M.T.*,
I.ii.293.1–306, and II.ii.100–2: 'What's his business? / His face half darkened,
stealing through the house / With a whoremaster's pace – ' and II.ii.120–1.

   206. *Uds light*] corruption of 'by God's light', a mild oath: common in
Dekker.

   207. *glister*] (1) suppository, enema; Greene in *A Quip for an Upstart Courtier* (1592), sig. D4r, mocks their use as affectations of the aspiring gallant; (2)
whore? In reference to Jonson, *Alchemist*, V.v.13, Herford and Simpson cite
this as a sense of 'suppository', referring also to Marston, *Dutch Courtesan*,
I.ii.

   208. *Hercules' labours*] Cf. Dekker and Middleton, *1 H.W.*, III.iii.102.

   tread] copulate with (used to a male bird with a hen); cf. Dekker and
Webster, *W.H.*, V.i.184–6.

   210. *turning tail*] with a bawdy innuendo on *tail* = pudend.

   214. *pudding-tobacco*] 'compressed tobacco, made in rolls resembling a
pudding or sausage' (*O.E.D.*, 'pudding', sb., 11c). Not yet caught up with
events, Laxton pretends to be a customer.

   218. *letters*] evidence suggesting that the affair has been going on for some
time.

   219–23.] Mist. Gallipot cunningly apprises Laxton of the new situation by
assuming his position in her account.

Mistress Gallipot. Besides, a story of your death was read
    Each minute to me.

Laxton. [*Aside*]   What a pox means this riddling?   225

Gallipot. Be wise, sir, let not you and I be tossed
    On lawyers' pens: they have sharp nibs and draw
    Men's very heart-blood from them; what need you, sir,
    To beat the drum of my wife's infamy,
    And call your friends together, sir, to prove   230
    Your precontract, when sh'has confessed it?

Laxton.   Um, sir –
    Has she confessed it?

Gallipot.   Sh'has, faith, to me, sir,
    Upon your letter sending.

Mistress Gallipot.   I have, I have.

Laxton. [*Aside*] If I let this iron cool, call me slave!
    – [*To her*] Do you hear, you dame Prudence? Think'st
      thou, vile woman,   235
    I'll take these blows and wink?

Mistress Gallipot.   Upon my knees. –

Laxton. Out, impudence!

Gallipot.   Good sir –

Laxton.   You goatish slaves! –
    No wild fowl to cut up but mine?

226–8. *tossed … them*] Cf. Dekker, *Dead Tearme* (1608), sig. C3v, 'In the
handes of badde and vnconscionable Lawyers, *Pens* are forkes of yron, vpon
which poore Clients are tossed from one to another, till they bleede to death:
yea the nebs of them are like the *Beakes* of *Vultures*, (who so they may glutte
their appetite with flesh) care not from whose backes they teare it.' Also *W.H.*,
II.i.81 (Hoy).

229. *beat the drum of*] i.e. make public; continuing the military imagery
begun at l. 220.

231. *precontract*] i.e. of marriage. Spousals *de futuro* could not normally be
dissolved without the mutual consent of both parties; see I.i.73–80n.

233. *iron cool*] Cf. 'It is good to strike while the iron is hot' (Tilley, 194).

237. *goatish*] lascivious, lustful; goats, like monkeys, were regarded as particularly sexually active.

238. *No … mine*] *Wild fowl* = prostitute; Hoy cites a passage from Dekker,
Newes from Hell, sig. C3r–v, in which the Post from hell is seated in a tavern at
'the vpper end of the boord: you must take out your writing tables, and note
by the way, that euery roome of the house was a Cage full of such wild fowle,
Et crimine ab vno disce omnes, cut vp one, cut vp all, they were birds all of a
beake, not a Woodcocks difference among twenty dozen of them; euery man
had before him a bale of dice, by his side a brace of Punks, and in his fist a nest
of bowles.' Cf. also H. Shirley, *Martyr'd Soldier* (*A Collection of Old English*

Gallipot.   Alas, sir,
　　You make her flesh to tremble: fright her not;
　　She shall do reason, and what's fit.
Laxton.   I'll have thee,   240
　　Wert thou more common than an hospital
　　And more diseased –
Gallipot.   But one word, good sir!
Laxton.   So, sir.
Gallipot. I married her, have lien with her, and got
　　Two children on her body: think but on that.
　　Have you so beggarly an appetite,   245
　　When I upon a dainty dish have fed,
　　To dine upon my scraps, my leavings? Ha, sir?
　　Do I come near you now, sir?
Laxton.   Be lady, you touch me.
Gallipot. Would not you scorn to wear my clothes, sir?
Laxton.   Right, sir.
Gallipot. Then pray, sir, wear not her, for she's a garment   250
　　So fitting for my body, I'm loath
　　Another should put it on: you will undo both.
　　Your letter, as she said, complained you had spent
　　In quest of her, some thirty pound: I'll pay it;
　　Shall that, sir, stop this gap up 'twixt you two?   255
Laxton. Well, if I swallow this wrong, let her thank you.
　　The money being paid, sir, I am gone;
　　Farewell. O women, happy's he trusts none!
Mistress Gallipot. Dispatch him hence, sweet husband.

Plays, ed. A. H. Bullen (1882–9, repr. New York, 1964), I, 235), 'Come, wench; Ile teach thee how to cut up wild fowle.'

　242. *diseased*] Those afflicted with venereal disease accounted for most of the patients in hospitals at this time.

　243. *lien*] lain (an old form).

　248. *Be lady*] a corruption of 'by our Lady'.

　touch] punning on the literal and figurative senses of *come near you*.

　249. *Right, sir*] undoubtedly with some comic gesture or intonation designed to mock Gallipot's dress.

　253. *complained*] stated the grievance.

　258. *O women ... none*] Cf. 'No trust is to be given to a woman' (Tilley, T551).

　259. *Dispatch him hence*] 'Settle the business and send him away' (*O.E.D.*, 3).

Gallipot.   Yes, dear wife. –
     Pray, sir, come in; – [*To Wife*] ere Master Laxton part,   260
     Thou shalt in wine drink to him.
Mistress Gallipot.   With all my heart. –
                                             Exit GALLIPOT.
     How dost thou like my wit?
Laxton.   Rarely: that wile
     By which the serpent did the first woman beguile
     Did ever since all women's bosoms fill:
     You're apple-eaters all, deceivers still!   *Exeunt.*   265

[III.iii]

Enter SIR ALEXANDER WENGRAVE, SIR DAVY DAPPER, SIR ADAM
     APPLETON *at one door, and* TRAPDOOR *at another door.*

Sir Alexander. Out with your tale, Sir Davy, to Sir Adam –
     A knave is in mine eye deep in my debt.
Sir Davy. Nay, if he be a knave, sir, hold him fast.
                    [*Sir Alexander talks apart with Trapdoor.*]
Sir Alexander. Speak softly; what egg is there hatching now?
Trapdoor. A duck's egg, sir; a duck that has eaten a frog. I have   5
     cracked the shell and some villainy or other will peep out
     presently. The duck that sits is the bouncing ramp, that

---

261.1.] *Dyce; Exit* Maister Gallipot *and his wife.* Q (*after* him. *l. 261*).   265.
s.d.] *Exit Laxton.* Q.   III.iii] *Dyce; not in* Q.   3. *Sir Davy.*] Q *uses forms of*
Sir Da. or *S. Dauy. throughout this scene.*   3.1.] *This ed.;* Sir D. Dapper *and*
Sir A. Appleton *talk apart. Dyce.*

261.1, 265. s.d.] The Q s.dd. indicate a premature exit for Gallipot and his
wife. The proposed arrangement, which follows Dyce, allows Gallipot to hear
his wife's response at l. 243 before his exit, and Mist. Gallipot to be present for
Laxton's final cynical quip. Alternatively, Mist. Gallipot might leave the
stage after Laxton's *Rarely.*

III.iii]
     3.] possibly with a play on the knave or jack, the lowest court card.
     5. *duck . . . frog*] Trapdoor may simply mean that Moll has swallowed the
bait. *Duck* probably carries the suggestion of *wild fowl*, III.ii.238.
     6. *shell . . . villainy*] Cf. Dekker and Webster, *W.H.*, II.i.193–4, 'why, euen
now must you and I hatch an egge of iniquity.'
     7. *bouncing ramp*] *Bouncing* (blustering, swaggering) intensifies the sense of
ramp: 'A bold, vulgar, ill-behaved woman or girl' (*O.E.D.*).

roaring girl, my mistress; the drake that must tread is your
son, Sebastian.

Sir Alexander. Be quick.   10

Trapdoor. As the tongue of an oyster-wench.

Sir Alexander. And see thy news be true.

Trapdoor. As a barber's every Saturday night. – Mad Moll –

Sir Alexander. Ah!

Trapdoor. Must be let in without knocking at your back gate.   15

Sir Alexander. So.

Trapdoor. Your chamber will be made bawdy.

Sir Alexander. Good!

Trapdoor. She comes in a shirt of mail.

Sir Alexander. How, shirt of mail?   20

Trapdoor. Yes, sir, or a male shirt, that's to say, in man's
apparel.

Sir Alexander. To my son?

Trapdoor. Close to your son: your son and her moon will be in
conjunction if all almanacs lie not. Her black safeguard is   25
turned into a deep slop, the holes of her upper body to

---

11. *oyster-wench*] Oysters were regarded as a delicacy and aphrodisiac (see
reference to Marston, *The Scourge of Villainy*, II, at II.i.193n.); cf. Dekker
and Massinger, *The Virgin Martyr*, III.iii.102–3.

13. *barber's ... night*] presumably referring to the busiest time, and hence
the freshest news. Cf. Dekker, *A Strange Horse-Race* (1613), sig. D2r,
'*Barbers* had neuer such vtterance of a newes.' In support of 'barbers' reputation as news-mongers', Hoy cites *Newes from Hell*, sig. F4r, 'he was more
busie in his prating then a Barber, with thee my seruant, about my houshold
affaires'; and *G.H.*, sig. F4r, 'if you itch, to step into the Barbers, a whole
Dictionary cannot afford more words to set downe notes what *Dialogues* you
are to maintaine whilest you are Doctor of the Chaire there.'

15. *back gate*] with a bawdy entendre alluding to perverse sexual practices:
see R. K. Turner, Jr., 'Dekker's "Back-door'd Italian": *1 H.W.*, II.i.355', *N.
& Q.*, CCV (1960), 25–6, R. Levin, *N. & Q.*, CCVIII (1963), 338–9, and M. P.
Jackson, *N. & Q.*, CCIX (1964), 37, citing passages from Middleton, *M.T.*,
and Tourneur, *Atheist's Tragedy*. Cf. also *M.W.M.M.*, III.iii.63–7.

24–5. *son ... conjunction*] playing on the terminology of astrological prophecy found in almanacs; *in conjunction* = in apparent proximity, as two
heavenly bodies (with a bawdy innuendo).

26. *deep slop*] possibly the 'great Dutch slop' of II.ii.82: see title-page woodcut of Moll.

26–7. *holes ... button-holes*] The *upper body*, or bodice, was a garment very
similar to the male doublet, and the object of much satire on this account.
Here the eyelets used for fastening with points and tags in the female garment
are set against the buttons and button-holes of the doublet. Cf. Phillip

button-holes, her waistcoat to a doublet, her placket to the
ancient seat of a codpiece; and you shall take 'em both with
standing collars.

Sir Alexander. Art sure of this?   30

Trapdoor. As every throng is sure of a pickpocket; as sure as a
whore is of the clients all Michaelmas Term, and of the
pox after the term.

Sir Alexander. The time of their tilting?

Trapdoor. Three.   35

Stubbes, *Anatomy of Abuses* (ed. 1879), p. 73, 'The Women also there haue
dublets & Ierkins, as men haue heer, buttoned vp the brest, and made with
wings, welts, and pinions on the shoulder points, as mans apparel is for all the
world.' In the title-page cut, Moll's doublet or jerkin is fastened with buttons.
Cf. Middleton, *M.W.M.M.*, III.iii.108–16.

27. *waistcoat*] 'A woman did not appear in waistcoat unless she were a
strumpet' (Linthicum, p. 214, citing references from Beaumont and Fletcher,
Woman Hater, II.i.252, *Love's Cure*, III.i.19, and Massinger, *City Madam*,
III.i.43).

27–8. *placket . . . codpiece*] The *placket* referred to here is probably the slit at
the top of a skirt or petticoat to facilitate putting on and removal, though the
term could also mean 'apron or petticoat' and 'a pocket in a woman's skirt'. As
a typical feature of women's dress it evolved into a term for a woman and, by
its physical proximity, as Partridge notes (p. 161), the pudend: cf. Middleton,
Anything for a Quiet Life, II.ii.204–10: '*Geo*. . . . between which is discovered
the open part, which is now called the placket.   *Frank. jun*. Why, was it ever
called otherwise?   *Geo*. Yes; while the word remained pure in his original,
the Latin tongue, who have no K's, it was called the *placet*; *a placendo*, a thing
or place to please.' A *codpiece* was 'a bagged appendage to the front of the
close-fitting hose or breeches worn by men from the 15th to the 17th century;
often conspicuous and ornamental' (*O.E.D.*). The term developed in reference to men as did the *placket* for women.

29. *standing collars*] 'The standing collar was a high straight collar fastened
in the front' (Linthicum, pp. 168–9). Cf. Dekker, *S.D.S.*, sig. E4r, 'For as man
is Gods Ape, striuing to make artificiall flowers, birdes, &c. like to the naturall: So for the same reason are women, Mens *Shee Apes*, for they will not bee
behind them the bredth of a Taylors yard (which is nothing to speake of) in
anie new-fangled vpstart fashion. If men get vp French standing collers,
women will haue the French standing coller too.' See title-page cut of Moll.

32–3. *whore . . . term*] Cf. Dekker and Webster, *W.H.*, III.iii.13–14, '. . .
there were many Punkes in the Towne (as you know our Tearme is their
Tearme . . .', and 20–5, 'Captains, Schollers, Seruingmen, Iurors, Clarks,
Townesmen, and the Blacke-guarde vsed all to one Ordinarye, and most of
them were cald to a pittifull reckoning, for before two returnes of Michaelmas, Surgeons were full of busines, the cure of most secresie grew as common as Lice in *Ireland*, or as scabbes in *France*.'

34. *tilting*] encounter (possibly prompted by *shirt of mail*, l. 19 above).

Sir Alexander. The day?

Trapdoor. This.

Sir Alexander. Away, ply it; watch her.

Trapdoor. As the devil doth for the death of a bawd, I'll watch
    her; do you catch her.   40

Sir Alexander. She's fast; here, weave thou the nets. Hark –

Trapdoor. They are made.

Sir Alexander. I told them thou didst owe me money: hold it
    up, maintain't.

Trapdoor. Stiffly, as a Puritan does contention. – [*As in a quar-*   45
    rel] Fox, I owe thee not the value of a halfpenny halter!

Sir Alexander. Thou shalt be hanged in't ere thou 'scape so!
    Varlet, I'll make thee look through a grate!

Trapdoor. I'll do't presently: through a tavern grate. Drawer!
    Pish!   *Exit.*   50

Sir Adam. Has the knave vexed you, sir?

Sir Alexander.   Asked him my money;
    He swears my son received it! O that boy
    Will ne'er leave heaping sorrows on my heart
    Till he has broke it quite!

Sir Adam.   Is he still wild?

Sir Alexander. As is a Russian bear.

Sir Adam   But he has left   55
    His old haunt with that baggage.

Sir Alexander.   Worse still and worse!
    He lays on me his shame, I on him my curse.

Sir Davy. My son, Jack Dapper, then shall run with him
    All in one pasture.

45–6. s.d.] *M. Thesis.*   46. Fox] *Q (*Foxe*)*; For *Reed;* Pox *Dyce.*   50.s.d.]
Exit Trapdore Q.

---

46. *halter*] rope with a noose used for hanging.

47. *'scape*] escape.

48. *grate*] Cf. Prologue, l. 24. 'The prison-grating, through which the poor
prisoners let down their boxes or baskets to receive money or food from the
charitable' (Bullen).

49. *tavern grate*] i.e. the red lattices which signified the windows of an
alehouse; cf. Dekker, *S.D.S.*, sig. E2r.

    Drawer] tapster.

55. *Russian bear*] 'Bears were imported into England from Russia for the
bear-baitings which were so popular in London' (Sugden, p. 444); cf. Dekker,
W.B., II.i.42–3; also *Mac.*, III.iv.100, *H5*, III.vii.141–2.

56. *baggage*] strumpet.

Sir Adam.   Proves your son bad too, sir?
Sir Davy. As villainy can make him: your Sebastian   60
  Dotes but on one drab, mine on a thousand!
  A noise of fiddlers, tobacco, wine, and a whore,
  A mercer that will let him take up more,
  Dice, and a water-spaniel with a duck; O,
  Bring him abed with these: when his purse jingles,   65
  Roaring boys follow at's tail, fencers and ningles –
  Beasts Adam ne'er gave name to – these horse-leeches
    suck
  My son; he being drawn dry, they all live on smoke.
Sir Alexander. Tobacco?
Sir Davy.   Right; but I have in my brain
  A windmill going that shall grind to dust   70
  The follies of my son, and make him wise
  Or a stark fool. Pray lend me your advice.
Sir Alexander, Sir Adam. That shall you, good Sir Davy.
Sir Davy.   Here's the springe
  I ha' set to catch this woodcock in: an action
  In a false name – unknown to him – is entered   75
  I'th' Counter to arrest Jack Dapper.

73, 76, 113. *Sir Alexander, Sir Adam.*] *Dyce; Both. Q.*

---

62. *noise*] company (of musicians),
63. *take up more*] i.e. buy more on credit.
65. *Bring him abed with these*] 'Let him be delivered of these parasites'.
66. *at's*] at his.
fencers] Dekker comments on bets laid on fencers in *G.H.* (ed. Pendry),
p. 79.
ningles] ingles: (1) favourites; (2) catamites.
67. *Adam ... name to*] in reference to Gen. ii.19–20.
horse-leeches] (1) extortioners; (2) whores; cf. Mist. Horseleech in Dekker *2*
H.W. (Partridge, *Dictionary of Historical Slang* (Harmondsworth, 1972)).
70. *windmill*] playing on the figurative sense, 'a fanciful notion, a visionary
scheme or project'; *O.E.D.* (4a) cites Webster, *White Devil* (1612), II.ii.12, as
the earliest recorded usage in this sense; cf. also 'He has windmills in his head'
(Tilley, W455: earliest reference 1612), and Dekker and Massinger, *V.M.*,
II.ii.11, and Dekker, Rowley and Ford, *W. of E.*, IV.ii.85.
73. *shall you*] shall you have (ellipsis); cf. II.i.157.
73–4. *springe ... woodcock*] proverbial: 'A springe to catch a woodcock'
(Tilley, S788); cf. Dekker, *G.H.* (ed. Pendry), p. 83; *Ham.*, I.iii.115. A *springe*
is a snare for catching small birds, and a *woodcock*, a bird easily caught.

Sir Alexander, Sir Adam.　　　　　　　　　Ha, ha, he!

Sir Davy. Think you the Counter cannot break him?

Sir Adam.　　　　　　　　　　　　　　　Break him?
　　Yes, and break's heart too, if he lie there long!

Sir Davy. I'll make him sing a counter-tenor, sure.

Sir Adam. No way to tame him like it; there shall he learn　　80
　　What money is indeed, and how to spend it.

Sir Davy. He's bridled there.

Sir Alexander.　　　　　　　Ay, yet knows not how to mend it!
　　Bedlam cures not more madmen in a year
　　Than one of the counters does; men pay more dear
　　There for their wit than anywhere. A counter,　　85
　　Why, 'tis an university! Who not sees?
　　As scholars there, so here men take degrees
　　And follow the same studies, all alike.
　　Scholars learn first logic and rhetoric;

---

77. *Counter*] 'A prison for debtors connected with the City court in London' (Sugden, p. 133). There were two Counters within the city walls at this time: the Poultry Counter and Wood Street Counter, both named after the streets in Cheapside in which they stood.

78. *break's*] i.e. break his.

79. *counter-tenor*] with the common pun on 'Counter'.

82. *He's bridled*] The present tense in Sir Davy's speech here and at other points has the force of the future.

83. *Bedlam*] See III.ii.93n.

85–6. *counter . . . university*] Middleton was fond of the analogy: cf. *Phoenix*, IV.iii.16–22, '. . . nay, we have been scholars, I can tell you, – we could not have been knaves so soon else; for as in that notable city called London stand two most famous universities Poultry and Wood-street, where some are of twenty years' standing, and have took all their degrees, from the Master's side down to the Mistress' side, the Hole, so in like manner – '; and *M.T.*, III.iv.91–3, 'Has at least sixteen at this instant proceeded in both the counters; some bachelors, some masters, some doctors of captivity of twenty years' standing'. Similar comparisons occur in Greene, *Defence of Cony-Catching* (ed. Grosart (1886, repr. New York, 1964), XI, 43), Overbury, in his character of a prison (*A Book of 'Characters'*, ed. R. Aldington, p. 160), Dekker, *O.P.* (ed. Pendry), p. 300, and Fennor, *Compters Common-wealth*, p. 4, but none as developed as Middleton's.

89. *logic and rhetoric*] C. R. Thompson in 'Universities in Tudor England' (*Life and Letters in Tudor and Stuart England* (Ithaca, N.Y., 1962), p. 345) observes, 'In his first two years an undergraduate studied mostly rhetoric and Aristotelian logic and some arithmetic and music.'

So does a prisoner: with fine honeyed speech   90
At's first coming in he doth persuade, beseech
He may be lodged with one that is not itchy,
To lie in a clean chamber, in sheets not lousy;
But when he has no money, then does he try
By subtle logic and quaint sophistry   95
To make the keepers trust him.
Sir Adam.   Say they do?
Sir Alexander. Then he's a graduate!
Sir Davy.   Say they trust him not?
Sir Alexander. Then is he held a freshman and a sot,
    And never shall commence; but, being still barred,
    Be expulsed from the Master's Side to th'Twopenny
        Ward,   100

90–6.] In *Compters Common-wealth*, pp. 4 and 11, William Fennor charts the decline of the well-provided prisoner from the most expensive to the poorest ward as his money runs out; cf. also J. Cooke, *Greene's Tu Quoque* (*A Select Collection of Old Plays*, ed. Collier (1825), VII, 71).

92–3. *lodged ... lousy*] Fennor describes the conditions in *Compters Common-wealth* (pp. 68–9), 'What a strange thing is it when a man is arrested & puts himselfe to the *knightsward* must pay a groat a night for his lodging, and a groate for euery paire of sheetes hee lies in, what conscience haue they [the jailers] to exact so much when the best bedde in that side is not worth a Seruing-mans yearely wages; but I haue heard their due is but twopence a night if a man lie alone, and a penny a night if he haue a bedfellow, and that in the twopenny-ward where they receiue fourteene pence a weeke their due is but seuenpence' (cited by Hoy).

95. *subtle*] cunning, crafty.

quaint] ingeniously elaborated.

99. *commence*] 'take the full degree of Master or Doctor at a University.' (*O.E.D.*, 4).

barred] obstructed from graduating (with a pun on the prison bars).

100–1. *Master's Side ... Hole*] with a play on 'Master of Arts'; E. D. Pendry, *Elizabethan Prisons and Prison Scenes*, unpublished doctoral dissertation, University of Birmingham (1954), p. 83, remarks, 'There were three basic paying-wards in the Counter, varying in both comfort and expense: the Master's Side, the Knight's Ward, and the Twopenny Ward; and there was one for the destitute – the Hole. ... The Gallant who came in for the first time might well be as high-handed and contemptuous as he pleased – with all the confidence of a full purse – and he would be welcomed and tolerated; porters, cooks, clerks and others would swarm about him ready to be of service. ... Kindness would be shown to a man dressed in rags – if it was certain he had criminal associates able to pay for him.' Fennor, as Reed noted, in *Compters Common-wealth* (p. 79) describes the horrors of the Hole: 'hee that would see the miseries of man let him come into this place the Hole, that stinkes many

Or else i'th' Hole be placed.

Sir Adam.   When then, I pray,
Proceeds a prisoner?

Sir Alexander.   When, money being the theme,
He can dispute with his hard creditors' hearts
And get out clear, he's then a Master of Arts!
Sir Davy, send your son to Wood Street College;   105
A gentleman can nowhere get more knowledge.

Sir Davy. There gallants study hard.

Sir Alexander.   True: to get money.

Sir Davy. 'Lies by th'heels, i'faith. Thanks, thanks; I ha' sent
For a couple of bears shall paw him.

Enter SERGEANT CURTALAX *and* YEOMAN HANGER.

Sir Adam.   Who comes yonder?

Sir Davy. They look like puttocks; these should be they.

Sir Alexander.   I know 'em;   110
They are officers. Sir, we'll leave you.

Sir Davy.   My good knights,
Leave me; you see I'm haunted now with sprites.

101. be placed] *Dyce conj.; beg plac't Q; beg place Reed (Steevens's note).*
112. sprites] *Dyce; spirits Q.*

---

men to death, and is to all that liue in it, as the Dog daies are to the world, a causer of diseases, except a few whom I haue seene so stout and tough (stinkeproofe, nay plagueproof I thinke) that no infection could pierce their hearts.'

101. *be placed*] The Q reading, 'beg plac't', was altered by Reed to 'beg place' (adopted also by Gomme); but in view of the Hole's wretched conditions, the idea of a prisoner begging for a place there makes little sense, even if as a refuge from further debt (it was the only non-paying ward).

102. *Proceeds*] 'advance[s] from graduation as B.A. to some higher degree, as master or doctor' (*O.E.D.*, 4).

108. *'Lies by th'heels*] 'He lies, shall lie' (Dyce); *by th'heels* refers to placement in irons, or the stocks, here used more generally: 'in jail'. Cf. V.i.262.

110. *puttocks*] (1) kites; (2) sergeants, catchpoles: cf. V.i.3; also Sergeant Puttock in *Puritan*.

112. *sprites*] i.e. sergeants. Cf. Shortyard disguised as a sergeant in Middleton, *M.T.*, III.iii.1–7, 'So, no man is so impudent to deny that: spirits can change their shapes, and soonest of all into sergeants, because they are cousin-germans to spirits; for there's but two kind of arrests till doomsday, – the devil for the soul, the sergeant for the body; but afterward the devil arrests body and soul, sergeant and all, if they be knaves still and deserve it.' The rhyme with 'knights' makes clear the pronunciation of Q's 'spirits'; 'sprites' and 'spirits' were used indiscriminately.

Sir Alexander, Sir Adam. Fare you well, sir.

                    Exeunt [SIR] ALEX[ANDER] *and* [SIR] ADAM.

Curtalax. This old muzzle chops should be he by the fellow's
    description. – [*To Sir Davy*] Save you, sir.   115

Sir Davy. Come hither, you mad varlets; did not my man tell
    you I watched here for you?

Curtalax. One in a blue coat, sir, told us that in this place an old
    gentleman would watch for us: a thing contrary to our
    oath, for we are to watch for every wicked member in a   120
    city.

Sir Davy. You'll watch, then, for ten thousand! What's thy
    name, honesty?

Curtalax. Sergeant Curtalax, I sir.

Sir Davy. An excellent name for a sergeant, Curtalax;   125
    Sergeants indeed are weapons of the law:
    When prodigal ruffians far in debt are grown,
    Should not you cut them, citizens were o'erthrown.
    Thou dwell'st hereby in Holborn, Curtalax?

Curtalax. That's my circuit, sir; I conjure most in that circle.   130

Sir Davy. And what young toward whelp is this?

Hanger. Of the same litter: his yeoman, sir; my name's Hanger.

Sir Davy. Yeoman Hanger.
    One pair of shears, sure, cut out both your coats;
    You have two names most dangerous to men's throats.   135

---

123. honesty] *Q;* honestly *Gomme.*

---

114. *muzzle chops*] 'nickname for a man with prominent nose and mouth'
(*O.E.D.*, 'muzzle', sb.1, 8, citing this instance).

116. *mad*] foolish.

varlets] sergeants (*O.E.D.*, 1d).

118. *One in a blue coat*] i.e. a servant.

123. *honesty*] 'an honourable or respectable man'; though *O.E.D.* gives this
sense only collectively, another singular example occurs in Middleton,
T.C.O.O., II.i.30, 'A good, blunt honesty; I like him well.'

126. *weapons*] See Dramatis Personae, l. 20n.

128. *cut*] playing on Curtalax's name and the sense, 'strike sharply'
(*O.E.D.*, 3).

130. *conjure ... circle*] Cf. l. 112 above; an expression common in Dekker.

131. *toward*] (1) bold; (2) docile, willing.

132. *Of the same litter*] a proverbial tag: see Tilley, W293.

134.] proverbial: 'There went but a pair of shears between them' (Tilley,
P36); cf. Dekker, *G.H.* (ed. Pendry), p. 77, and *A strange Horse-Race*, sig. E3v.

You two are villainous loads on gentlemen's backs;
Dear ware, this Hanger and this Curtalax.

Curtalax. We are as other men are, sir; I cannot see but he who
  makes a show of honesty and religion, if his claws can
  fasten to his liking, he draws blood. All that live in the   140
  world are but great fish and little fish, and feed upon one
  another: some eat up whole men; a sergeant cares but for
  the shoulder of a man. They call us knaves and curs, but
  many times he that sets us on worries more lambs one year
  than we do in seven.   145

Sir Davy. Spoke like a noble Cerberus! – Is the action entered?

Hanger. His name is entered in the book of unbelievers.

Sir Davy. What book's that?

Curtalax. The book where all prisoners' names stand; and not
  one amongst forty when he comes in believes to come out   150
  in haste!

Sir Davy. Be as dogged to him as your office allows you to be.

Curtalax, Hanger. O sir!

153, 166, 169, 171. *Curtalax, Hanger*] *This ed.; Both Q.*

---

140. *liking*] i.e. the object of his desire.

140–2. *All ... another*] proverbial: Tilley, F311; cf. III.i.96. Bullen cites
Day, *Law Tricks* (*Works*, ed. Bullen, p. 15), and *Per.*, II.i.26–34; cf. also
Fennor, *Compters Common-wealth*, p. 54.

142–3. *sergeant ... man*] alluding to the manner in which a sergeant made
his arrest: by laying his hand or mace on his victim's shoulder; they were
frequently referred to as 'shoulder-clappers'.

144. *worries*] in reference to dogs or wolves attacking sheep (extending the
image suggested by 'cur'): 'seize by the throat with the teeth and tear or
lacerate' (*O.E.D.*, 3a); see I.ii.236–7.

146. *Cerberus*] Cf. III.i.25 and n.; also Fennor, *Compters Common-wealth*,
p. 4, 'But heere is one serious point not to be slipt ouer, for the *Cerberus* that
turned the key of the Compter-gate, no sooner saw those hell-guides bringing
me in ...' A prison of the king's debtors was named Hell and may have
generated the image: see Herford and Simpson, x, 112.

147. *book of unbelievers*] possibly the 'Black Book' (cf. Middleton's
pamphlet of this name) described by Fennor, *Compters Common-wealth*, p. 4,
'I no sooner was entred into this *Infernal Iland* (where many men lie winde-
bound sometimes foure of fiue yeeres together) but a fellow ... called mee to a
booke (no Bible of Diuinity, but rather of Negromancy, for all the Prisoners
called it the *Blacke-booke*) comming to it, hee demanded my name, I told him,
and then hee set it downe as horses are in Smithfield at the Tole-booth.'

152. *dogged*] playing on *Cerberus*, l. 146.

153.] i.e. 'As if we need to be told that'.

Sir Davy. You know the unthrift Jack Dapper?

Curtalax. Ay, ay, sir, that gull? – As well as I know my yeoman.   155

Sir Davy. And you know his father too, Sir Davy Dapper?

Curtalax. As damned a usurer as ever was among Jews! If he
    were sure his father's skin would yield him any money, he
    would, when he dies, flay it off and sell it to cover drums
    for children at Barthol'mew Fair!   160

Sir Davy. [*Aside*] What toads are these to spit poison on a man
    to his face! – [*To them*] Do you see, my honest rascals?
    Yonder Greyhound is the dog he hunts with: out of that
    tavern, Jack Dapper will sally. Sa, sa! Give the counter!

---

163. Greyhound] *Dyce;* gray-hound *Q.*

---

157. *usurer ... Jews*] 'During the Middle Ages the Jews were largely engaged in money lending, and Jew came to mean a money-lender, a usurer,
with the added suggestion of craft and unscrupulousness' (Sugden, p. 285).

157–60.] Cf. Jonson, Chapman and Marston, *Eastward Ho*, II.ii.211–15, 'O
'tis a notable Iewes trump! I hope to liue to see dogs meate made of the old
Vsurers flesh; Dice of his bones; and Indentures of his skinne: and yet his
skinne is too thicke to make Parchment, 'twould make good Bootes for a
Peeter man to catch Salmon in'; also Dekker and Massinger, *V.M.*,
II.i.140–3.

160. *Barthol'mew Fair*] 'The great Fair held in Smithfield on August 24, St.
Bartholomew's Day, was the most famous in England. Originally established
as a cloth-fair, it became in course of time a popular carnival, and after flour-
ishing for 7½ centuries was abolished in 1855. ... Drums, gingerbread, and
ugly dolls were to be bought for children' (Sugden, p. 48).

161. *toads ... poison*] proverbial: 'Full as a toad of poison' (Tilley, T360); cf.
IV.ii.207–9 and n.

163. *Greyhound*] probably the name of a tavern. Sugden notes that a Grey-
hound tavern was situated in Fleet St., 'evidently ... close to Fleet Bridge,
at the east end of the street'. Cf. Dekker and Webster, *W.H.*, II.iii.104–5,
'The Grey-hound, the Greyhound in Black-fryers, an excellent *Randeuous*'.
The present scene is set in Holborn, however (ll. 129 and 180), so the reference may be to another establishment.

164. *Sa, sa*] said to derive from the French exclamation *ça, ça*, formerly
used by fencers when delivering a thrust (*O.E.D.*); cf. *Revenger's Tragedy*,
V.i.62 (Revels ed.), 'Sa, sa, sa; thump. There he lies' (cited by *O.E.D.*). Cf.
also Middleton, *B.M.C.*, III.i.17–20, and *S.G.*, III.ii.87–8.

counter] (1) '*Fencing*. A name applied to all circular parries, i.e. parries in
which, while the hand retains the same position, the point is made to describe
a circle, passing under the adverse blade so as to meet it again when the latter
is "disengaged"' (*O.E.D.*, sb.5, 1); cf. *O.E.D.*, 'give', 14b; (2) encounter
(*O.E.D.*, sb.1); (3) possibly the hunting term, 'the opposite direction to the
course taken by the game': i.e. the hunter hunted. Sir Davy, apparently in
reprisal for Curtalax's abusive remarks, sternly puts the officers through their
paces in drill.

On, set upon him!   165
Curtalax, Hanger. We'll charge him upo'th' back, sir.
Sir Davy. Take no bail; put mace enough into his caudle.
  Double your files! Traverse your ground!
Curtalax, Hanger. Brave, sir!
Sir Davy. Cry arm, arm, arm!   170
Curtalax, Hanger. Thus, sir.
Sir Davy. There boy, there boy, away: look to your prey, my
  true English wolves and – and so I vanish.   *Exit.*
Curtalax. Some warden of the sergeants begat this old fellow,
  upon my life! – Stand close.   175
Hanger. Shall the ambuscado lie in one place?
Curtalax. No, nook thou yonder.

---

173. and – and] *M. Thesis;* and and *Q;* and *Reed.*   s.d.] *Exit S. Dauy Q.*

---

167. *mace ... caudle*] punning on *mace*, the staff carried by sergeants as a badge of their office and with which they often made their arrests, and the spice; similar puns occur in Middleton, *M.W.M.M.*, III.ii.75–6, *A.F.Q.L.*, III.ii.20–1, and Dekker and Webster, *W.H.*, V.iv.205ff. *Caudle* is a spiced warm drink of thin gruel, mixed with wine or ale, given mainly to the sick.

168. *Double your files*] increase the file to twice its length by marching other files up into them; the simplest of military drills, but comical in reference to two men.

Traverse your ground] move from side to side in fencing or fighting.

169. *Brave*] bravo, excellent.

170. *Cry arm*] either 'be ready for fight', or 'take up arms'; cf. *Mac.*, V.v.46.

172. *There boy*] i.e. as to a dog (a hunting cry): cf. II.ii.73 and n.

173. *English wolves*] In *S.D.S.*, sig. C1r, Dekker uses the term in reference to 'Politick Bankrupts'.

176. *ambuscado*] a force lying in ambush. Similar ambushes are laid in Dekker and Webster, *W.H.*, III.ii, and Middleton?, *Puritan*, III.iii; cf. Middleton, *B.B.* (Bullen, VIII), p. 38, 'And because I take pity on thee [a catchpole], waiting so long as thou usest to do, ere thou canst land one fare at the Counter, watching sometimes ten hours together in an alehouse, ever and anon peeping forth and sampling thy nose with the red lattice; let him whosoever that falls into thy clutches at night pay well for thy standing all day ...' and Dekker and Wilkins, *Jests to make you Merie* (1607), sig. H1v, '... passing by a *Tauerne* doore, he might behold a tumultuous crew, (like drunken waues) reeling from one side to the other; the whirlewinde that raiz'd this tempest, beeing nothing else then the clapping of one on the shoulders that was watcht for when he came out of his cup'.

177. *nook*] hide in a corner; see Intro., p. 48.

Enter MOLL *and* TRAPDOOR.

Moll. Ralph.

Trapdoor. What says my brave captain, male and female?

Moll. This Holborn is such a wrangling street.   180

Trapdoor. That's because lawyers walks to and fro in't!

Moll. Here's such jostling as if everyone we met were drunk
    and reeled.

Trapdoor. Stand, mistress, do you not smell carrion?

Moll. Carrion? No, yet I spy ravens.   185

Trapdoor. Some poor wind-shaken gallant will anon fall into
    sore labour; and these men-midwives must bring him to
    bed i' the Counter: there all those that are great with child
    with debts lie in.

Moll. Stand up.   190

Trapdoor. Like your new maypole!

Hanger. [*To Curtalax*] Whist, whew!

Curtalax. [*To Hanger*] Hump, no!

Moll. Peeping? – It shall go hard, huntsmen, but I'll spoil your
    game. They look for all the world like two infected malt-   195
    men coming muffled up in their cloaks in a frosty morning
    to London.

---

180. *Holborn ... street*] Hoy cites Dekker, *The Belman of London*, sig. F2v,
'when Countrie Clyents ... trauell from Lawyer to Lawyer, through Chan-
cerie lane, Holborne, and such like places', *Ravens Almanacke*, sig. A3r, as a
scene for the arrest of 'wind-shaken gallants'. See also III.ii.205.1n. above.

181. *lawyers*] See III.i.32–3 and n.

walks] singular verb with plural subject: common in Jacobean English; see
Abbott, § 333.

186. *wind-shaken*] flawed or cracked at heart, as timber by high winds.

187–9. *men-midwives ... lie in*] Cf. Dekker, *W.B.*, II.i.61–4, 'Doe not you
know (mistresse) what Serieants are? a number of your courtiers are deare in
their acquaintance: why they are certaine men-midwiues, that neuer bring
people to bed, but when they are sore in labour, that no body els can deliuer
them' (cited by Dyce).

191.] proverbial tag: cf. 'As tall as a maypole' (Tilley, M778).

192–3.] Hanger's sounds may be intended to indicate a whistle. *Whist*,
normally like 'hush' an exclamation demanding silence, is possibly used here
to get Curtalax's attention; cf. Middleton?, *Puritan*, III.iii.23 (ed. Brooke).
Whew commonly represents a whistling sound. *Hump* may simply be a re-
turned signal.

194. *Peeping*] See l. 176n. above.

195–6. *infected maltmen*] F. P. Wilson in *The Plague in Shakespeare's
London* (Oxford, 1963), p. 36, remarks in connection with goods infected with

Trapdoor. A course, captain: a bear comes to the stake!

Enter JACK DAPPER *and* GULL.

Moll. It should be so, for the dogs struggle to be let loose.
Hanger. [*To Curtalax*] Whew!   200
Curtalax. [*To Hanger*] Hemp!
Moll. Hark Trapdoor, follow your leader.
Jack Dapper. Gull.
Gull. Master?
Jack Dapper. Didst ever see such an ass as I am, boy?   205
Gull. No, by my troth, sir, to lose all your money, yet have false
    dice of your own! Why, 'tis as I saw a great fellow used
    t'other day: he had a fair sword and buckler, and yet a
    butcher dry-beat him with a cudgel!
Moll, Trapdoor. Honest sergeant! – [*To Jack*] Fly! Fly, Master   210
    Dapper, you'll be arrested else!
Jack Dapper. Run, Gull, and draw!

210. *Moll, Trapdoor*] *M. Thesis; Both. Q.*   Honest ... Fly,] *M. Thesis;*
Honest Serieant fly, flie *Q;* Honest Gull fly; fly *Scott;* Trap. Honest servant,
fly! *Moll.* Fly, *Dyce;* Honest Sir fly, flie *Bowers.*

---

the plague, 'In 1630 it came to the notice of the Privy Council that those who
carried malt into the City were accustomed to return home with rags "for
manuring of the soiling of the ground" and the practice was forbidden.'
Maltsters by their handling of such infected rags were particularly susceptible
to the plague.

    198. *course*] 'the animal pursued', in reference to the practice of coursing or
pursuing game with hounds (*O.E.D.*, 7b).

    stake] the post to which a bear was tethered for baiting.

    199. *dogs*] Cf. ll. 131–2 above.

    206–7. *lose ... dice*] Cf. Dekker and Webster, *W.H.*, V.iv.113–14, 'O you are
proper Gamsters to bring false dice with you from *London* to cheat your
selues', and *2 H.W.*, III.ii.18–24.

    207–9. *great fellow ... cudgel*] See this editor's 'The Date of *The Roaring
Girl*', *R.E.S.*, new ser., XXVIII (1977), 27–8, concerning a recorded incident
involving butchers outside the Fortune Theatre.

    209. *dry-beat*] inflicted blows which bruise but do not draw blood.

    210. *Honest Sergeant*] I have retained the Q reading in contrast to other
editors; stage business of some sort could clear up the apparent difficulty. The
statement could be part of the diversionary tactics which Moll prepares about
l. 194. Bowers suggests that an abbreviated form may have been mistakenly
expanded by a compositor to 'Serieant'; but 'Honest Sergeant' occurs in
Dekker and Webster, *W.H.*, III.ii.92, where there is no doubt of the
reference.

Gull. Run master! Gull follows you!

                  Exit [JACK] DAPPER *and* GULL.

Curtalax. [*Moll holding him.*] I know you, well enough: you're
    but a whore to hang upon any man.   215

Moll. Whores then are like sergeants: so now hang you! – [*To
    Trapdoor*] Draw, rogue, but strike not: for a broken pate
    they'll keep their beds and recover twenty marks
    damages.

Curtalax. You shall pay for this rescue! – [*To Hanger*] Run   220
    down Shoe Lane and meet him!

Trapdoor. Shoo! Is this a rescue, gentlemen, or no?

                [*Exeunt* CURTALAX *and* HANGER.]

Moll. Rescue? A pox on 'em! – Trapdoor, let's away;
    I'm glad I have done perfect one good work today.
    If any gentleman be in scrivener's bands,   225
    Send but for Moll, she'll bail him by these hands!

                    Exeunt.

214. s.d.] *Dyce.*   216–17. s.d.] *M. Thesis.*   220. s.d.] *M. Thesis.*   222.1.]
Dyce subst. (after l. 223).

---

    216. *Whores . . . sergeants*] playing on the sergeant's method of arrest: see ll.
142–3 and n., above.

    217–19. *a broken . . . damages*] Cf. Fennor, *Compters Common-wealth*, p. 49,
'If any man they arrest, in his struggling to make an escape from them, chance
to hit any of them, either on the legs, face or brest, so that they haue no hurt at
all, they will gripe, beat and pinch the poore man so miserably, that hee shall
not bee able to lift his arme to his head, and then enter an action of battery
against him, which will more vex and disturbe him then all the rest'; *a broken
pate* = a cut open or bleeding head. Moll warns that catchpoles make much of
the slightest wound by taking to their beds on the pretence of convalescing. A
mark was an amount (not a coin) valued at two-thirds of a pound.

    221. *Shoe Lane*] 'A street in London, running north from Fleet Street
opposite St. Bride's Church, to Holborn' (Sugden, p. 464); with a probable
quibble on *Run.*

    222. *Shoo*] a contemptuous exclamation, probably playing on *Shoe* Lane.

    225. *in scrivener's bands*] i.e. in debt. *Scrivener* could mean 'a notary', or a
kind of broker who 'received money to place out at interest, and who supplied
those who wanted to raise money on security': cf. Dekker and Webster, *N.H.*,
II.i.140–2, 'here was a scriuener but euen now, to put my father in minde of a
bond, that wilbe forfit this night if the mony be not payd Maister *Allom*' (cited
by *O.E.D.*).

    226. *by these hands*] (1) with these hands; (2) a mild oath.

Act IV

Enter SIR ALEXANDER WENGRAVE *solus*.

Sir Alexander. Unhappy in the follies of a son,
　　Led against judgement, sense, obedience,
　　And all the powers of nobleness and wit –
　　O wretched father!

Enter TRAPDOOR.

　　　　　　　　 – Now, Trapdoor, will she come?
Trapdoor. In man's apparel, sir; I am in her heart now,　　　　5
　　And share in all her secrets.
Sir Alexander. 　　　　　　 Peace, peace, peace.
　　Here, take my German watch, hang't up in sight
　　That I may see her hang in English for't.
Trapdoor. I warrant you for that now, next sessions rids her,
　　sir. –
　　This watch will bring her in better than a hundred
　　constables.　　　　　　　　　　　　　　　　　　　　10
Sir Alexander. Good Trapdoor, sayst thou so? Thou cheer'st
　　my heart

IV.i] *Dyce; not in Q.*　　4.1.] *to the right of l. 3 Q.*

0.1. solus] Cf. II.ii.0.1 and n.
　4.1.] Only three and a half lines separate Trapdoor's exit in the previous
scene and his entrance here: possibly an indication of an interval between the
two acts during which the court-cupboard and viol could have been set.
　5. *heart*] confidence.
　7. *German watch*] Cf. Dekker and Webster, *W.H.*, I.i.78 (cited by Hoy).
　8. *hang in English*] i.e. be hanged under English law.
　10. *watch*] playing on 'timepiece' and 'a body of soldiers constituting the
guard of a town'; cf. Prologue, l. 18.

After a storm of sorrow. – My gold chain, too:
Here, take a hundred marks in yellow links.
Trapdoor. That will do well to bring the watch to light, sir,
And worth a thousand of your headborough's lanterns.   15
Sir Alexander. Place that o' the court-cupboard, let it lie
Full in the view of her thief-whorish eye.
Trapdoor. She cannot miss it, sir; I see't so plain
That I could steal't myself.
Sir Alexander.   Perhaps thou shalt, too;
That or something as weighty. What she leaves,   20
Thou shalt come closely in and filch away,
And all the weight upon her back I'll lay.
Trapdoor. You cannot assure that, sir.
Sir Alexander.   No? – What lets it?
Trapdoor. Being a stout girl, perhaps she'll desire pressing;
Then all the weight must lie upon her belly.   25
Sir Alexander. Belly or back, I care not, so I've one.
Trapdoor. You're of my mind for that, sir.
Sir Alexander. Hang up my ruff band with the diamond at it:
It may be she'll like that best.
Trapdoor. It's well for her that she must have her choice –   30

---

12. *gold chain*] '. . . every well-dressed gentleman wore a gold chain' (*Shakespeare's England*, III, 115). Gomme suggests this is 'his chain of office as magistrate', citing Middleton, *M.W.M.M.*, V.i.132 and V.ii.187–8, where a chain of the same value 'for a justice's hat' is stolen. *A hundred marks* = £66 13s. 4d.: see I.i.88n.

15. *headboroughs' lanterns*] lanterns carried at night by the parish peace officers or constables.

16. *court-cupboard*] a movable sideboard or cabinet used to display plate, and to store 'wine, fruit, cordials, spoons, and table linen' (*Shakespeare's England*, II, 123).

23. *lets*] hinders, prevents.

24. *pressing*] double entendre on (1) the *peine forte et dure* which involved the loading of weights upon accused persons to induce them to answer a charge (described by S. Chidley in *A Cry against a Crying Sin* (1652), *The Harleian Miscellany* (1811), VIII, 482); and (2) a bawdy sense in reference to coitus. Trapdoor makes numerous related sexual jokes and puns in the ensuing dialogue.

28. *ruff band*] probably a ruff collar (smaller than a full ruff), in contrast to the new fashion of falling bands: see I.i.16n. and II.i.2.

30–1.] An aside seems called for here by the nature of Trapdoor's remarks and the shift from *he* to *you* in reference to Sir Alexander. Other plausible arrangements besides that offered are possible; e.g. the first statement could also be included.

[*Aside*] he thinks nothing too good for her! – [*To him*] If
you hold on this mind a little longer, it shall be the first
work I do to turn thief myself: would do a man good to be
hanged when he is so well provided for!

Sir Alexander. So, well said! All hangs well; would she hung so
   too: 35
   The sight would please me more than all their glisterings.
   O that my mysteries to such straits should run,
   That I must rob myself to bless my son!   *Exeunt.*

Enter SEBASTIAN *with* MARY FITZALLARD *like a page, and* MOLL
   [*dressed as a man*].

Sebastian. Thou hast done me a kind office, without touch
   Either of sin or shame: our loves are honest.   40
Moll. I'd scorn to make such shift to bring you together else.
Sebastian. Now have I time and opportunity
   Without all fear to bid thee welcome, love.
                                                Kiss[es Mary].
Mary. Never with more desire and harder venture!
Moll. How strange this shows, one man to kiss another.   45
Sebastian. I'd kiss such men to choose, Moll;
   Methinks a woman's lip tastes well in a doublet.
Moll. Many an old madam has the better fortune then,
   Whose breaths grew stale before the fashion came:
   If that will help 'em, as you think 'twill do,   50
   They'll learn in time to pluck on the hose too!

---

33. would] *Q;* 'twould *Reed.*   37. mysteries] *Q;* miseries *Dyce conj.*

32–3. *it shall . . . do to*] i.e. before I do anything else I will.
37. *mysteries*] skills, craft (*O.E.D.*, 'mystery' 2, 2a and c).
39. *office*] service.
41. *shift*] effort (*O.E.D.*, 6).
45–7. *How . . . doublet*] Cf. Dekker and Middleton *1 H.W.*, IV.i.95–7, 'If it
be a woman, mary-bones and Potato pies keepe me for medling with her, for
the thing has got the breeches, 'tis a male-varlet sure my Lord, for a womans
tayler nere measurd him.'
48. *madam*] bawd, whore. Monticelso in Webster's *White Devil*, IV.i.57–8
(Revels ed.), remarks, 'These are for impudent bawds, / That go in men's
apparel'; see also Jonson, *Volpone*, IV.ii.8 and n. (Revels ed.).
50. *that*] i.e. male dress.

Sebastian. The older they wax, Moll. Troth, I speak seriously:
　　　　As some have a conceit their drink tastes better
　　　　In an outlandish cup than in our own,
　　　　So methinks every kiss she gives me now   55
　　　　In this strange form is worth a pair of two.
　　　　Here we are safe, and furthest from the eye
　　　　Of all suspicion: this is my father's chamber,
　　　　Upon which floor he never steps till night.
　　　　Here he mistrusts me not, nor I his coming;   60
　　　　At mine own chamber he still pries unto me:
　　　　My freedom is not there at mine own finding,
　　　　Still checked and curbed; here he shall miss his purpose.
Moll. And what's your business, now you have your mind, sir?
　　　　At your great suit I promised you to come: 65
　　　　I pitied her for name's sake, that a Moll
　　　　Should be so crossed in love, when there's so many
　　　　That owes nine lays apiece, and not so little. –
　　　　My tailor fitted her: how like you his work?
Sebastian. So well, no art can mend it for this purpose;   70
　　　　But to thy wit and help we're chief in debt,

---

52. Moll. Troth ... seriously:] *This ed.; Moll,* troth ... seriously, *Q.*   56. of]
Q; or *Bowers.*   two.] *Reed;* two, *Q.*   64. business, now] *Dyce;* business
now, *Q.*

52.] Sebastian's *they* refers to the 'old madams' of l. 48. He insists that what
he said previously was serious: Mary's kisses in her doublet taste like pairs of
two, particularly well. Moll turned that into a joking comment on old bawds,
and Sebastian refuses to accept it. He emphasises his joy. As for old bawds,
they grow old whether they dress themselves in pants or not (F. D. Hoeniger).

　　53. *conceit*] fancy, whim.
　　54. *outlandish*] (1) foreign; (2) unfamiliar, strange.
　　56. *pair of two*] i.e. a set of two; cf. 'pair of stairs'.
　　68. *owes nine lays*] meaning uncertain. Though the normal sense of *owes*
is possible, 'owns' seems more probable. Of the many meanings of *lays*, the two
following would fit the context best: (1) wagers (*O.E.D.*, sb.7, 1), in the sense
of 'prizes won in a contest' (*O.E.D.*, 'wager', sb.2, 2b); (2) lodgings (*O.E.D.*,
'lay', sb. 7, 2a), but in the particular sense of those owned or used by prostitutes as in Beaumont and Fletcher, *Philaster,* II.iv.155–6, 'I know her and
her haunts, / Her lays, leaps, and outlays, and will discover all', which Andrew
Gurr in his Revels ed. glosses: lodgings, fornications and places of assignment. While *O.E.D.* does not record bawdy senses of the noun so early as
1611, verbal uses of the term were common, and the association here with
'Moll' (as a whore's name) supports a sexual sense (F. D. Hoeniger).

And must live still beholding.

Moll.   Any honest pity

I'm willing to bestow upon poor ring-doves.

Sebastian. I'll offer no worse play.

Moll.   Nay, an you should, sir,

I should draw first and prove the quicker man! [*Draws.*]   75

Sebastian. Hold, there shall need no weapon at this meeting;

But 'cause thou shalt not loose thy fury idle,

[*Takes down and gives her a viol.*]

Here take this viol: run upon the guts

And end thy quarrel singing.

Moll.   Like a swan above bridge:

For, look you, here's the bridge and here am I.   80

Sebastian. Hold on, sweet Moll.

Mary. I've heard her much commended, sir, for one that was
ne'er taught.

Moll. I'm much beholding to 'em. – Well, since you'll needs
put us together, sir, I'll play my part as well as I can: it   85

---

75. s.d.] *M. Thesis.*   77.1.] *Dyce (after* singing. *l.* 79*).*

---

72. *still*] for ever.

72, 84. *beholding*] beholden (as at III.i.134).

73. *ring-doves*] wood pigeons (i.e. lovers).

74. *play*] (1) sport; (2) sexual indulgence.

75–6. *draw . . . weapon*] with sexual entendre.

77–9.] with an underlying sexual joke apparently of the order of that cited
by Gustav Ungerer, 'The Viol da Gamba as a Sexual Metaphor in Elizabethan Music and Literature', *Renaissance and Reformation*, new ser., VIII
(1984), 86, 'No Knight being out of matter shall revenge himself upon a base
Viol.'

77. *loose*] perhaps playing on the term for the discharge of an arrow
(prompted by 'weapon'), with a pun on the viol bow.

fury] fierce passion, wild fit.

idle] quasi-adverbial use (*O.E.D.*, 7): vainly, uselessly.

78. *run upon the guts*] a pun on running through with a weapon and drawing
the bow across the gut strings of the instrument.

79. *swan*] in playful allusion to the proverbial singing of a swan before
dying; cf. Middleton, *C.M. in C.*, V.ii.45–6 (Revels ed.): 'She plays the swan /
And sings herself to death'; also Dekker, *2 H.W.*, I.ii.64, 75–6. In addition,
swans traditionally drew the chariot of Venus. They are very familiar on
English streams now, including the Thames.

bridge] with a pun on the bridge of the viol.

shall ne'er be said I came into a gentleman's chamber and
let his instrument hang by the walls!

Sebastian. Why well said, Moll, i'faith; it had been a shame for
that gentleman then, that would have let it hang still, and
ne'er offered thee it.   90

Moll. There it should have been still then for Moll, for though
the world judge impudently of me, I ne'er came into that
chamber yet where I took down the instrument myself.

Sebastian. Pish, let 'em prate abroad! Thou'rt here where thou
art known and loved; there be a thousand close dames that   95
will call the viol an unmannerly instrument for a woman,
and therefore talk broadly of thee, when you shall have
them sit wider to a worse quality.

Moll. Push, I ever fall asleep and think not of 'em, sir; and thus
I dream.   100

Sebastian. Prithee let's hear thy dream, Moll.

The Song.

Moll.   *I dream there is a mistress,*
                        And she lays out the money;
                    She goes unto her sisters;
                        She never comes at any.   105

89. hang] *M. Thesis;* hung *Q.*   94. Thou'rt] *This ed.;* th'art *Q.*   101.1.
The Song.] *Reed; to the right of l. 103 Q.*

---

87. *instrument . . . walls*] a bawdy joke; cf. Heywood, *Woman Killed With
Kindness*, xvi.20–1 (Revels ed.). See ll. 77–9n. G. H. Cowling, *Music on the
Shakespearian Stage* (Cambridge, 1913), p. 61, observes, 'The viol da gamba,
corresponding to our violoncello, was a fashionable instrument for men, and
was often hung up as a property when the stage represented an interior.'

88. *it had*] it would have.

89–90. *hang . . . it*] with a sexual entendre. In Middleton's orthography 'a'
and 'u' are often indistinguishable, possibly the cause of Q's 'hung'.

93. *took down*] with a bawdy quibble.

95. *close*] reserved, or strict, severe.

96. *viol . . . instrument*] the sexual joke depends on the *viol/vial* (penis) pun,
picked up in *unmannerly instrument*.

98. *sit wider*] i.e. in a sexual sense; with a play on *broadly*.

100. *dream*] In addition to the normal sense, *dream* can signify 'make
melody' (*O.E.D.*, v.1); the substantive form (l. 101) similarly carries the secondary sense, 'music, melody'.

104. *sisters*] (1) neighbours; (2) prostitutes: *O.E.D.* cites 'sisters of the
Bank' (i.e. the Bankside, famous for its brothels); cf. *Revenger's Tragedy*,
II.ii.144–5 (Revels ed.).

105. *comes at*] (1) arrives at; (2) comes into sexual contact with (*O.E.D.*,
38b).

any] i.e. (1) money; (2) sexual partners; (3) sexual fulfilment.

Enter SIR ALEXANDER *behind them.*

> *She says she went to th'Burse for patterns;*
> *You shall find her at Saint Kathern's,*
> *And comes home with never a penny.*

Sebastian. That's a free mistress, faith.

Sir Alexander. [*Aside*] Ay, ay, ay, like her that sings it; one of   110
thine own choosing.

Moll. But shall I dream again?

> *Here comes a wench will brave ye,*
> *Her courage was so great,*
> *She lay with one o' the navy,*   115
> *Her husband lying i' the Fleet.*
> *Yet oft with him she cavilled;*
> *I wonder what she ails:*
> *Her husband's ship lay gravelled*

---

106. Burse] The original name for the Royal Exchange, built by Gresham in 1566. 'The piazzas around it were supported by marble pillars, and were allocated to small shops, 100 in number. They were chiefly taken up by milliners, but all sorts of goods likely to attract fashionable ladies were sold there' (Sugden, p. 85). Cf. also Middleton, *C.M. in C.*, I.ii.33–4 and n. (Revels ed.), 'As if she lay with all the gaudy-shops / In Gresham's Burse about her'. Sugden notes also the silly maid of Middleton's *Micro-Cynicon*, III (Bullen, VIII), 126, who 'Flies to the Burse-gate for a match [= pattern] or two'. *Pattern* probably has a bawdy meaning, perhaps derived from the pun on 'patron' (patron still was sometimes spelt 'pattern' in 1610) (F. D. Hoeniger).

107. Saint Kathern's] 'The dockside district in the east end of London, extending from the Tower to Ratcliffe; it was notorious for its brewhouses and taverns' (Hoy); cf. the ballad, 'John Jarret' (1630), in H. Rollins (ed.), *A Pepysian Garland* (Cambridge, 1922), p. 338: 'They say, at the *Talbot* you runne on the score, / Beside, at S. *Katherines* you keepe a braue whore, / Where you on a night spent an Angell and more: / If you vse such dealings, twill make you full poore.' Sugden (p. 290) cites Jonson, *The Devil is an Ass*, I.i.59–62: 'We will suruay the *Suburbs*, and make forth our sallyes, / Downe *Petticoate-lane*, and vp the *Smock-allies*, / To *Shoreditch, Whitechappell*, and so to Saint *Kathernes*, / To drinke with the *Dutch* there, and take forth their patternes.'

109. *free*] (1) loose; (2) generous.

116. Fleet] with a play on the Fleet Prison, near the junction of Ludgate Hill and Fleet St. 'The prisoners were taken by boat along the Fleet Ditch and entered by a water-gate' (Sugden, p. 194).

118. what she ails] i.e. what ails her.

119. gravelled] beached, stranded (with a bawdy innuendo); cf. Middleton, *N.W.N.H.*, I.i.6–7.

> *When hers could hoise up sails;*   120
> *Yet she began, like all my foes,*
> *To call whore first; for so do those –*
> *A pox of all false tails!*

Sebastian. Marry, amen, say I!

Sir Alexander. [*Aside*] So say I, too.   125

Moll. Hang up the viol now, sir; all this while I was in a dream:
    one shall lie rudely then; but being awake, I keep my legs
    together. – A watch: what's o'clock here?

Sir Alexander. [*Aside*] Now, now, she's trapped!

Moll. Between one and two; nay then I care not. A watch and a   130
    musician are cousin-germans in one thing: they must both
    keep time well or there's no goodness in 'em. The one else
    deserves to be dashed against a wall, and t'other to have
    his brains knocked out with a fiddle-case.

> What? – A loose chain and a dangling diamond!   135
> Here were a brave booty for an evening thief now;
> There's many a younger brother would be glad

---

122. *those* –] *Dyce; those,* Q.   130. not.] *Dyce;* not: Q.   134. case.] *Reed;* case, Q.

---

120. hoise up sails] Cf. Dekker, *2 H.W.*, IV.i.277, 'So does a Strumpet hoist the loftiest saile.' Hoy also cites *Lanthorne and Candle-light* (ed. 1609), sig. H4v, which enumerates a whore's strategies to account for the parade of clients, 'If *Marchants* resort to her, then hoistes she vp these *sayles,* she is wife to the Maister of a shippe, & they bring newes yt her husband put in at the *Straytes,* or at *Venice,* at *Aleppo, Alexandria,* or *Scanderoon,* &c.', and *Magnificent Entertainment,* l. 437, *Lanthorne* (1616), sig. L1V, *P.G.,* III.i.32, *I.T.B.N.,* II.i.154, and *R.G.,* IV.ii.33.

123. tails] sexual organs (*O.E.D.,* sb.1, 5c), and by extension, 'persons'; with a pun on 'tales'.

127–8. *lie . . . together*] with a bawdy joke on playing the viol; cf. Middleton, *T.C.O.O.,* I.i.139ff., 'She now remains at London with my brother, her second uncle, to learn fashions, practise music; the voice between her lips, and the viol between her legs, she'll be fit for a consort very speedily', and *Y.F.G.,* II.i.74–7.

130. *Between one and two*] apparently earlier than planned: cf. III.iii.31.

130–46.] A mixture of prose and verse in a single speech, as here, is fairly common in Middleton. The speech has been set up differently by other editors (see Appendix A); but retention of Q's arrangement seems the most sensible treatment. See Intro., pp. 7–8 and 10–11.

131. *cousin-germans*] punning on 'first cousins' and the German watch.

136. *brave*] splendid, finely arrayed.

137. *younger*] i.e. poor.

137–9. *younger . . . out*] Hoy remarks on a correspondence with 'that type of

To look twice in at a window for't,
And wriggle in and out like an eel in a sandbag.
O, if men's secret youthful faults should judge 'em,   140
'Twould be the general'st execution
That e'er was seen in England!
There would be but few left to sing the ballads: there
would be so much work, most of our brokers would be
chosen for hangmen – a good day for them! – they might   145
renew their wardrobes of free cost then!

Sebastian. [*To Mary*] This is the roaring wench must do us
          good.

Mary. [*To Sebastian*] No poison, sir, but serves us for some
          use,
          Which is confirmed in her.

139. sandbag.] *Reed;* sandbag, *Q.*   143. ballads:] *Bowers;* ballets, *Q.*   144.
work,] *Bowers;* worke: *Q.*   146. wardrobes] *Dyce;* wardrops *Q.*

---

cony-catching known as "The Curbing Law" (whereby a thief angles with a
hooked rod through an open window for valuables that he has previously
spotted)', and quotes from Dekker, *Belman,* sig. G2v.

139. *eel ... sandbag*] Herford and Simpson cite this passage in reference to
Jonson, *Cynthia's Revels,* II.v.23–4, 'no better then a few trowts cast a-shore,
or a dish of eeles in a sand-bagge' (noted by Hoy). Cf. 'As nimble as an eel in a
sandbag' (Tilley, E59).

143. *the ballads*] 'i.e. those commemorating the last words of the condemned, and the manner in which he met his end' (Hoy).

144–6. *brokers ... cost*] Hangmen traditionally received their victims' clo-
thing: cf. Ulpian Fulwell, *Like Will to Like (Four Tudor Interludes,* ed. J. A. B.
Somerset (1974)), ll. 1156–63: '*N. New.* Come, Hankin Hangman, let us two
cast lots / And between us divide a couple of coats. / Take thou the one and the
other shall be mine; / Come, Hankin Hangman, thou cam'st in good time. /
They take off the coats and divide them. / *H. Hang.* Thou should'st have one,
Nichol, I swear by the mass, / For thou bringest work for me daily to pass, /
And through thy means I get more coats in one year / Than all my living is
worth beside, I swear.' Brokers (second-hand dealers) as hangmen could
maintain their inventory at no cost. Hoy cites Jonson, *Devil is an Ass,*
I.i.142–3, 'For clothes imploy your credit, with the Hangman, / Or let our
tribe of Brokers furnish you.'

148. *No poison ... use*] Cf. Middleton, *W.B.W.,* I.ii.179–80 (Revels ed.),
'That Providence that has made ev'ry poison / Good for some use'. The idea
links thematically with I.ii.148 above. N. W. Bawcutt in the Revels ed. of
Changeling, II.ii.44n., cites several other instances of the doctrine of purpose-
fulness in creation. The idea is based in experience: what is poisonous one way
is medicinally useful or pleasant in another (this 'fact' became one of the
cornerstones of Paracelsian pharmacy, but was familiar to the ancients) (F. D.
Hoeniger). Cf. Friar Lawrence in *Rom.,* II.iii.13–14, 19–22.

Sebastian. Peace, peace –

Foot, I did hear him sure, where'er he be. 150

Moll. Who did you hear?

Sebastian. My father:

'Twas like a sigh of his – I must be wary.

Sir Alexander. [*Aside*] No? Will't not be? Am I alone so wretched

That nothing takes? I'll put him to his plunge for't.

Sebastian. [*Aside to Moll and Mary*] Life, here he comes! –

[*Aloud to Moll*] Sir, I beseech you take it. 155

Your way of teaching does so much content me,

I'll make it four pound; here's forty shillings, sir.

I think I name it right. – [*Aside to Moll*] Help me, good Moll.

– [*Aloud*] Forty in hand. [*Offering money.*]

Moll. Sir, you shall pardon me,

I have more of the meanest scholar I can teach: 160

This pays me more than you have offered yet.

Sebastian. At the next quarter,

When I receive the means my father 'lows me,

You shall have t'other forty.

Sir Alexander. [*Aside*] This were well now,

Were't to a man whose sorrows had blind eyes; 165

But mine behold his follies and untruths

With two clear glasses. [*Comes forward.*]

–[*To Sebastian*] How now?

Sebastian. Sir?

Sir Alexander. What's he there?

Sebastian. You're come in good time, sir: I've a suit to you;

I'd crave your present kindness.

Sir Alexander. What is he there?

Sebastian. A gentleman, a musician, sir: one of excellent

---

152. sigh] *Dyce;* sight *Q.* 153. Will't] *Ellis;* wilt *Q.* 167. *Comes forward*] *Dyce subst.*

153. *be*] i.e. be successful, work.

154. *takes*] takes effect, succeeds (*O.E.D.,* 11a, cites 1622 as the earliest recorded usage).

plunge] crisis, dilemma (*O.E.D.,* 5).

160.] Presumably Moll pretends that even poor scholars pay more than Sebastian has offered.

fingering –   170
Sir Alexander. Ay, I think so. – [*Aside*] I wonder how they
      'scaped her?
Sebastian. 'Has the most delicate stroke, sir –
Sir Alexander. A stroke indeed. – [*Aside*] I feel it at my heart!
Sebastian. Puts down all your famous musicians.
Sir Alexander. Ay. – [*Aside*] A whore may put down a hundred
      of 'em!   175
Sebastian. Forty shillings is the agreement, sir, between us;
      Now, sir, my present means mounts but to half on't.
Sir Alexander. And he stands upon the whole.
Sebastian. Ay indeed does he, sir.
Sir Alexander. And will do still; he'll ne'er be in other tale.   180
Sebastian. Therefore I'd stop his mouth, sir, an I could.
Sir Alexander. Hum, true. There is no other way indeed.
      – [*Aside*] His folly hardens; shame must needs succeed.
      – [*To Moll*] Now sir, I understand you profess music.

170. fingering –] *M. Thesis;* fingring. *Q.*   172. 'Has] *M. Thesis;* Has
Q.   sir –] *M. Thesis;* sir, *Q;* sir. *Reed.*   181. an] *Ellis;* and *Q.*

---

170. *fingering*] (1) i.e. in playing an instrument; (2) pilfering; cf. *Gent.*,
I.ii.100–1, *3H6*, V.i.44, *Ham.*, V.ii.15; (3) with a bawdy entendre.

171. *'scaped*] escaped.

172, 173. *stroke*] (1) i.e. in bowing the viol; (2) with a bawdy entendre; cf.
Middleton, *Y.F.G.*, II.i.74–6, 'you shall have 'em sometimes in every corner
of the house, with their viols betwixt their legs, and play the sweetest strokes';
(3) with a play on 'paralytic seizure', perhaps in reference to 'heart-strings'.

174. *Puts down*] Sebastian means 'excel, surpass' (*O.E.D.*, 41f); but Sir
Alexander makes puns, l. 175, on the sexual sense in reference to coitus (Partridge, p. 170), and 'kill' (*O.E.D.*, 41g), probably as a result of venereal disease. Cf. Middleton, *B.M.C.*, III.iii.161–4: '*Imp.* Music there, to close our
stomachs! How do you like him, madonna?   *Second Lady.* O, trust me, I like
him most profoundly! why, he's able to put down twenty such as I am.'

176. *Forty . . . on't*] At l. 157 above, and confirmed by l. 159, Sebastian
pretends (for his father's ears) to offer Moll 40*s.* in ready money, and at l. 164
he promises to pay the remainder when he gets his next quarterly allowance.
But ll.176–7 suggest half the amount: 40*s.* as a whole, of which he can only pay
20 – possibly a careless error by the dramatists or scribe.

177. *mounts*] with a bawdy quib. le; a series of double entendres runs
through the following lines.

180. *he'll . . . tale*] The primary sense seems to be, 'his story will always
agree with yours' (*O.E.D.*, 'tale', 3d); but puns on *tale* = account, reckoning
(*O.E.D.*, 8) – 'he won't accept less' – and 'tail' = penis, pudend (*O.E.D.*, 5c)
are likely.

183. *folly*] (1) foolishness; (2) lewdness, wantonness.

Moll. I am a poor servant to that liberal science, sir.   185
Sir Alexander. Where is it you teach?
Moll.   Right against Clifford's Inn.
Sir Alexander. Hum, that's a fit place for it; you have many
    scholars?
Moll. And some of worth, whom I may call my masters.
Sir Alexander. [*Aside*] Ay, true, a company of whoremasters!
    – [*To Moll*] You teach to sing, too?   190
Moll. Marry, do I, sir.
Sir Alexander. I think you'll find an apt scholar of my son,
    especially for prick-song.
Moll. I have much hope of him.
Sir Alexander. [*Aside*] I am sorry for't, I have the less for that.   195
    – [*To Moll*] You can play any lesson?
Moll. At first sight, sir.
Sir Alexander. There's a thing called 'The Witch' – can you
    play that?
Moll. I would be sorry anyone should mend me in't.
Sir Alexander. Ay, I believe thee. – [*Aside*] Thou has so
    bewitched my son,   200
    No care will mend the work that thou hast done.
    I have bethought myself, since my art fails,

---

201. done.] *Reed;* done, *Q.*

---

186. *against*] next to.
    Clifford's Inn] the oldest of the Inns of Chancery, situated on the north side of Fleet St. between Chancery Lane and Fetter Lane. Fleet St., like Holborn, had a reputation for prostitutes: cf. Middleton, *T.C.O.O.*, IV.v.1–4 (cited by Sugden): '*Let the usurer cram him, in interest that excel,* | *There's pits enow to damn him, before he comes to hell;* | *In Holborn some, in Fleet Street some,* | *Where'er he come there's some, there's some.*'
    190. *sing*] punning on the bawdy sense: see III.ii.30–1n.
    193. *prick-song*] an accompanying melody written or 'pricked' down, as opposed to plain song where the descant was extemporised. The bawdy pun is common.
    198. '*The Witch*'] possibly an allusion to a contemporary ballad or song (several candidates are recorded in H. E. Rollins, *Analytical Index to the Ballad Entries (1557–1709)* (1924, repr. Hatboro, Penn., 1967). The reference may not be specific, however. Cf. Dekker, *W.B.*, IV.i.57ff., for a similar word-play.
    201. *mend*] with a pun on the sense 'improve upon', as at l. 199, and 'set right'.

I'll make her policy the art to trap her.
Here are four angels marked with holes in them,
Fit for his cracked companions: gold he will give her;   205
These will I make induction to her ruin,
And rid shame from my house, grief from my heart.
  – [*To Sebastian*] Here, son, in what you take content and
      pleasure,
  Want shall not curb you; [*Gives money.*] pay the gentleman
  His latter half in gold.
Sebastian.   I thank you, sir.   210
Sir Alexander. [*Aside*] O, may the operation on't end three:
  In her, life; shame in him; and grief in me.   *Exit.*
Sebastian. Faith, thou shalt have 'em; 'tis my father's gift:
  Never was man beguiled with better shift.
Moll. He that can take me for a male musician,   215
  I cannot choose but make him my instrument
  And play upon him!   *Exeunt.*

[IV.ii]

    Enter MISTRESS GALLIPOT *and* MISTRESS OPENWORK.

Mistress Gallipot. Is then that bird of yours, Master Goshawk,
  so wild?
Mistress Openwork. A goshawk, a puttock: all for prey! He
  angles for fish, but he loves flesh better.
Mistress Gallipot. Is't possible his smooth face should have   5
  wrinkles in't, and we not see them?
Mistress Openwork. Possible? Why, have not many handsome

---

207. heart.] *Reed;* heart *Q.*   209. s.d.] *M. Thesis.*   212. s.d.] *Exit Alexander. Q.*   217. s.d.] *Exeunt omnes. Q.*   IV.ii] *Dyce; not in Q.*

---

   203. *policy*] device, stratagem (of posing as a musician).
   205. *cracked*] morally unsound.
   206. *induction*] (1) initial step; (2) preamble to a play.
   215–17.] Cf. Dekker, *2 H.W.*, II.i.191–2; also *Ham.*, III.ii.362–4, and
A.Y.L., IV.iii.68–9.

IV.ii]
   3. *puttock*] kite.

legs in silk stockings villainous splay feet for all their great
roses?

Mistress Gallipot. Troth, sirrah, thou sayst true.   10

Mistress Openwork. Didst never see an archer, as thou'st
walked by Bunhill, look asquint when he drew his bow?

Mistress Gallipot. Yes, when his arrows have fline toward
Islington, his eyes have shot clean contrary towards
Pimlico.   15

Mistress Openwork. For all the world, so does Master Goshawk
double with me.

Mistress Gallipot. O fie upon him! If he double once, he's not
for me.

---

8. *silk stockings*] 'Silk stockings became the "only weare" among gallants,
for they showed off the comeliness of the wearer's leg much better than did the
woollen ones' (Linthicum, p. 261).

8–9. *villainous . . . roses*] *Splay feet* are flat feet which turn outwards, but a
suggestion of cloven feet masked by roses may underlie the reference; cf.
Webster, *White Devil*, V.iii.102–4 (Revels ed.), 'Why 'tis the devil. / I know
him by a great rose he wears on's shoe / To hide his cloven foot'; also Jonson,
Devil is an Ass, I.iii.7–9, '. . . my heart was at my mouth, / Till I had view'd his
shooes well: for, those roses / Were bigge inough to hide a clouen foote.'
Herford and Simpson cite also Chapman, *Caesar and Pompey*, II.i.159–62.
Roses were ornamental knots of ribbon in the shape of a rose tied at the shoe
front (see title-page cut of Moll).

10. *sirrah*] often used in addressing women.

11. *thou'st*] i.e. thou hast.

12. *Bunhill*] 'A street in London on the west side of the Artillery Ground,
near Moorfields. . . . The fields were used for archery practice, and were a
common resort of the young Londoners. The neighbourhood had a somewhat
unsavoury reputation' (Sugden, p. 83). In 1623 in the course of his duties as
City Chronologer, Middleton received 20 marks 'for and towards the charges
of the service latelie performed by him att the shuting at Bunhill' (noted by
Bullen).

asquint] out of the corners of his eyes.

13–15. *when . . . Pimlico*] i.e. when his aim is toward Islington (to the north-
west), his eyes appear to look toward Pimlico (to the north-east). *Pimlico* was
an inn and 'place of entertainment in Hogsden [i.e. Hoxton] much resorted to
by the Londoners of the 17th. century for the sake of the fresh air and the
cakes and ale for which it was famous' (Sugden, p. 412). Terms from archery
lent themselves readily to bawdy use.

13. *fline*] flown (an old form).

14. *Islington*] See III.i.32–3n.

17. *double*] act deceitfully, with a play on the literal suggestion of doing two
things at once, prompted by the archery image.

Mistress Openwork. Because Goshawk goes in a shag-ruff 20
  band, with a face sticking up in't which shows like an agate
  set in a cramp-ring, he thinks I'm in love with him.

Mistress Gallipot. 'Las, I think he takes his mark amiss in thee.

Mistress Openwork. He has, by often beating into me, made me
  believe that my husband kept a whore. 25

Mistress Gallipot. Very good.

Mistress Openwork. Swore to me that my husband this very
  morning went in a boat with a tilt over it to the Three
  Pigeons at Brentford, and his punk with him under his
  tilt! 30

Mistress Gallipot. That were wholesome!

Mistress Openwork. I believed it; fell a-swearing at him, cursing of harlots, made me ready to hoise up sail and be there
  as soon as he.

Mistress Gallipot. So, so. 35

Mistress Openwork. And for that voyage, Goshawk comes
  hither incontinently; but, sirrah, this water-spaniel dives
  after no duck but me: his hope is having me at Brentford to

---

20–2. *shag-ruff . . . cramp-ring*] Cf. Jonson, *Alchemist*, IV.iii.24 (Revels ed.),
'He looks in that deep ruff, like a head in a platter.' *Cramp-rings* were charms
against illness distributed annually by the monarch on Good Friday. The
image is of a small head in the centre of an enormous ruff: by *agate* is very
likely meant 'a very diminutive person, in allusion to small figures cut in agate
for seals' (*O.E.D.*, 2); cf. *Ado.*, III.i.65.

23. *takes his mark amiss*] possibly continuing the archery image, but *mark* is
also a falconry term for the quarry of a hawk (*O.E.D.*, 7b); cf. 'To miss his
mark' (Tilley, M669).

24. *often beating into me*] i.e. repeatedly telling me; suggestive also of beating wings.

27–8. *this very morning*] Except as deliberate foreshortening, this cannot
refer to the action of II.i.

28. *tilt*] an awning over a boat; several kinds are depicted in Visscher's
'View of London' (1616), also G. M. Trevelyan, *Illustrated English Social
History II* (Harmondsworth, 1960), p. 261.

28–9. *Three Pigeons*] the first mention of this inn in this subplot; see
III.i.56n.

29. *punk*] whore.

33. *made me*] i.e. his story made me.

hoise up sail] See IV.i.120n.

36. *voyage*] See III.i.127n.

37. *incontinently*] at once, immediately.

38. *duck*] Cf. 'wild fowl', III.ii.238n.

having] i.e. carnally.

    make me cry quack!

Mistress Gallipot. Art sure of it?   40

Mistress Openwork. Sure of it? My poor innocent Openwork
    came in as I was poking my ruff; presently hit I him i' the
    teeth with the Three Pigeons: he forswore all, I up and
    opened all, and now stands he, in a shop hard by, like a
    musket on a rest, to hit Goshawk i' the eye when he comes   45
    to fetch me to the boat.

Mistress Gallipot. Such another lame gelding offered to carry
    me through thick and thin – Laxton, sirrah – but I am rid
    of him now.

Mistress Openwork. Happy is the woman can be rid of 'em all!   50
    'Las, what are your whisking gallants to our husbands,
    weigh 'em rightly, man for man?

Mistress Gallipot. Troth, mere shallow things.

Mistress Openwork. Idle, simple things: running heads; and yet
    – let 'em run over us never so fast – we shopkeepers, when   55
    all's done, are sure to have 'em in our purse-nets at length,
    and when they are in, Lord, what simple animals they are!

54–5. yet – let] *This ed.;* yet let *Q.*

---

    39. *cry quack*] possibly a variation, continuing the duck image, on 'cry
creak' or 'cry craven', meaning 'to give in, give up the contest'.

    42. *poking my ruff*] 'While the ruff was still wet with starch, the pleats or
"sets" were put in, by folding each pleat over a poking-stick until it dried'
(Linthicum, p. 160).

    42–3. *hit . . . i' the teeth*] proverbial: Tilley, T429.

    44. *hard by*] close at hand.

    45. *musket on a rest*] The early unwieldy and heavy muskets required a
support, usually a wooden pole with a spike for driving into the ground at one
end, and a forked piece for receiving the musket barrel at the other: see G. M.
Trevelyan, *Illustrated English Social History II*, 70.

    48. *thick and thin*] proverbial tag: cf. 'To run through thick and thin'
(Tilley, T101).

    51. *whisking*] (1) brisk, lively, smart; (2) hoaxing? (*O.E.D.*, 5).

    53. *things*] with a play on the bawdy sense.

    54. *Idle*] (1) foolish; (2) useless.

    running heads] (1) footmen, lackeys; (2) bawdy?

    56. *purse-nets*] a bag-shaped net, the mouth of which can be drawn together
with cords, used especially for catching rabbits; the 'cony-catching' suggestion seems deliberate. Cf. 'There I have caught a knave in a purse net' (Tilley,
K138); also Dekker and Webster, *W.H.*, II.iii.34ff., V.i.157ff.

    57. *they are!*] Disruption in the printing process at this point along with
duplicated speech prefixes has led other editors to suppose that a speech or
two was lost here.

Then they hang the head –
Mistress Gallipot. Then they droop –
Mistress Openwork. Then they write letters –   60
Mistress Gallipot. Then they cog –
Mistress Openwork. Then deal they underhand with us, and we
    must ingle with our husbands abed; and we must swear
    they are our cousins, and able to do us a pleasure at Court.
Mistress Gallipot. And yet when we have done our best, all's   65
    but put into a riven dish: we are but frumped at and libel-
    led upon.
Mistress Openwork. O if it were the good Lord's will there were
    a law made, no citizen should trust any of 'em all!

Enter GOSHAWK.

Mistress Gallipot. Hush sirrah! Goshawk flutters.   70
Goshawk. How now, are you ready?
Mistress Openwork. Nay, are you ready? A little thing, you see,
    makes us ready.
Goshawk. Us? – [*To Mistress Openwork*] Why, must she make
    one i' the voyage?   75
Mistress Openwork. O by any means: do I know how my hus-
    band will handle me?

58. the] *Q original setting; not in Q reset.*   head –] *Dyce;* head. *Q.*   59.
droop –] *Dyce;* droupe. *Q.*   60. letters –] *Dyce;* letters. *Q.*   61. cog –]
Dyce; cogge, *Q.*   62. deal they] *Q original setting;* they deale *Q reset.*   68.
will] *Dyce;* will, *Q.*

58. *hang the head*] i.e. in shame or despondency.

59. *droop*] (1) flag, languish; (2) become dejected, despondent; (3) bawdy:
become detumescent.

61. *cog*] (1) cheat; (2) fawn, wheedle.

63. *ingle*] (1) fondle; (2) cajole, wheedle.

64. *able ... Court*] Cf. Middleton, *Phoenix*, IV.ii.82–5, 'Nay, last of all,
which offends me most of all, you told me you could countenance me at court;
and you know we esteem a friend there more worth than a husband here.'

65–6. *all's ... dish*] i.e. all our efforts have gone for nought; *riven* = broken.

66. *frumped at*] mocked.

70. *flutters*] In the R.S.C. production Goshawk fluttered his arms like wings
on entering.

72. *little thing*] (1) perhaps in reference to some article of clothing; (2) with a
bawdy entendre: cf. Jonson, Chapman and Marston, *Eastward Ho*,
III.ii.33–6, 'I, by'r ladie Madam, a little thing does that; I haue seene a little
prick no bigger than a pins head, swell bigger and bigger, til it has come to an
Ancome; & eene so tis in these cases.'

Goshawk. [Aside] Foot, how shall I find water to keep these two
    mills going? – [*To them*] Well, since you'll needs be
    clapped under hatches, if I sail not with you both till all   80
    split, hang me up at the main-yard and duck me. – [*Aside*]
    It's but liquoring them both soundly, and then you shall
    see their cork heels fly up high, like two swans, when their
    tails are above water and their long necks under water,
    diving to catch gudgeons. – [*To them*] Come, come! Oars   85
    stand ready; the tide's with us. On with those false faces.

86. us.] *M. Thesis;* vs, *Q.*   faces.] *M. Thesis;* faces, *Q;* faces; *Reed.*

---

78. *Foot*] abbreviated form of the oath, 'Christ's foot', with a bawdy play on
'foutre', copulation (Partridge, p. 108).

water] with a sexual entendre: semen. Cf. Middleton, *C.M. in C.*, II.i.175
and n. (Revels ed.), and *B.M.C.*, IV.i.28–31.

79. *mills*] For the bawdy innuendo, cf. Dekker, *I.T.B.N.*, II.ii.37–9, 'ther's
little marying, we ha so much whoring. / Grynding milles so much-vsde;
about the citie / Such grinding, yet no more mony'. Hoy cites numerous other
references in his note to *W.H.*, II.i.170.

80. *clapped under hatches*] with a bawdy entendre: copulated with: cf. *Wiv.*,
II.i.81–2, 'if he come under my hatches, I'll never to sea again' (cited by
Partridge, p. 68).

81. *split*] go to pieces: cf. *M.N.D.*, I.ii.22–4 (cited by Reed), *Temp.*, I.i.59.

hang ... duck me] traditional sailors' punishment; cf. Gascoigne, *Complete
Works* (1907), I, 80, 'His eares cut from his head, they set him in a chayre, /
And from a maine yard hoisted him aloft into the ayre' (cited by *O.E.D.*).

82. *liquoring*] plying with liquor.

83. *cork heels fly up*] Cork heels were fashionable in both dress and
overshoes. Wanton behaviour in women is frequently associated with light
heels; cf. Greene, *Black Book's Messenger* (*Works*, ed. Grosart (1886), XI, 16),
'and yet though shee could foyst a pocket well, and get me some pence, and
lifte nowe and then for a neede, and with the lightnes of hir heeles bring mee in
some crownes ...'; also Middleton, *C.M. in C.*, III.ii.187–90 (Revels ed.):
'Look how they have laid them, / E'en as they lie themselves, with their heels
up! / How they have shuffled up the rushes too, Davy, / With their short
figging little shittle-cork-heels!'

84. *tails*] Cf. N. Field, *Amends for Ladies*, V.i.13 (*Plays*, ed. W. Perry),
'Your wife has yeelded, vp-tailes is her song.'

85. *diving to catch gudgeons*] 'To swallow or gape for a gudgeon' (Tilley,
G473) was proverbial for being easily deceived (a *gudgeon* being a small fish
used for bait). Goshawk overconfidently puts the ladies' apparent compliance
down to his own skill and their foolishness.

Oars] i.e. a boat.

86. *false faces*] i.e. masks. Cf. Dekker and Webster, *W.H.*, III.iii.92ff.,
where the voyage is similarly to Brentford, 'In Blacke Friers, there take
Water, keepe a loofe from the shore, on with your Masks, vp with your sails,
and *West-ward Hoe.*'

Blow winds, and thou shalt take thy husband casting out
     his net to catch fresh salmon at Brentford.
Mistress Gallipot. I believe you'll eat of a cod's-head of your
     own dressing before you reach half way thither.   90
                              [*They put on masks.*]
Goshawk. So, so, follow close. Pin as you go.

               Enter LAXTON *muffled.*

Laxton. Do you hear?   [*Talks apart with Mistress Gallipot.*]
Mistress Gallipot. Yes, I thank my ears.
Laxton. I must have a bout with your pothecary-ship.
Mistress Gallipot. At what weapon?   95
Laxton. I must speak with you.
Mistress Gallipot. No!
Laxton. No? You shall!
Mistress Gallipot. Shall? Away soused sturgeon, half fish, half
     flesh!   100
Laxton. Faith, gib, are you spitting? I'll cut your tail, puss-cat,
     for this.
Mistress Gallipot. 'Las poor Laxton, I think thy tail's cut

90.1.] *Dyce subst.*   91. close.] *M. Thesis;* close, *Q;* close; *Reed.*   92. s.d.]
This ed.

---

88. *fresh salmon*] i.e. young whores.

89–90. *eat ... dressing*] The dominant sense seems to be, 'you will find
yourself hoist with your own foolish plans'. A *cod's-head* is a 'blockhead' (cf. 'a
fool's head of your own', III.ii.29). The image, which plays also on the
goshawk's prey, is charged with sexual innuendo, possibly to tantalise Goshawk. Cf. *Oth.*, II.i.153–4, 'She that in wisdom never was so frail / To change
the cod's head for the salmon's tail'. In the R.S.C. production the line was
presumed to be 'about oral sex' (*Sunday Times*, 24 Apr. 1983), and was addressed to Mist. Openwork; but Goshawk seems the likelier recipient.

91. *Pin*] possibly in reference to fastening the masks.

91.1. *muffled*] See III.ii.205.1n.

94. *bout*] Laxton plays deliberately on the bawdy suggestion of the term
(sexual encounter).

99. *soused sturgeon*] a term of opprobrium: cf. 'sous'd gurnet', *1H4*,
IV.ii.12.

99–100. *half fish, half flesh*] i.e. neither one thing nor another: probably in
reference to Laxton's dubious sexuality. Cf. 'Neither fish nor flesh nor good
red herring' (Tilley, F319).

101. *gib*] 'a term of reproach, especially for an old woman' (*O.E.D.*, sb.1, 3,
citing this reference).

103. *tail's cut*] in a bawdy sense, alluding to Laxton's impotence.

  already! – Your worst!
Laxton. If I do not –   *Exit.* 105
Goshawk. Come, ha' you done?

      Enter MASTER OPENWORK.

    [*To Mist. Open.*]'Sfoot, Rosamond, your husband!
Openwork. How now? Sweet Master Goshawk! None more
  welcome!
  I have wanted your embracements. When friends meet,
  The music of the spheres sounds not more sweet
  Than does their conference. Who is this? – Rosamond? 110
  Wife? – [*To Mistress Gallipot*] How now, sister?
Goshawk.   Silence, if you love me!
Openwork. Why masked?
Mistress Openwork. Does a mask grieve you, sir?
Openwork.   It does.
Mistress Openwork. Then you're best get you a-mumming.
Goshawk. [*Aside to Mist. Open.*] 'Sfoot, you'll spoil all!
Mistress Gallipot. May not we cover our bare faces with masks
  As well as you cover your bald heads with hats? 115
Openwork. No masks; why, they're thieves to beauty, that rob
  eyes
  Of admiration in which true love lies.
  Why are masks worn? Why good? Or why desired?

104. Your] *Q; you'r Bowers.* 105. s.d.] *Exit Laxton. Q.* 106.1. *Enter ...*
OPENWORK.] *Reed; to the right of* done? *l. 106 Q; at l. 105.1, Bowers.* 117.
lies.] *Reed; lies, Q.*

---

 104. *Your worst*] a truncated form of *Do your worst*: a challenge to Laxton,
which he picks up in the following line. Cf. Jonson, *Alchemist*, I.i.1, 'Thy
worst', where the shortened form is clear; also J. Cooke, *Greene's Tu Quoque*,
(*A Select Collection of Old Plays*, ed. Collier (1825), VII, 50), 'Well, sir, your
worst', and l. 273 below. Bowers prints 'You'r worst' (i.e. you are worsted);
but the present reading is more idiomatic.
 108. *wanted*] lacked, missed.
 109. *music of the spheres*] The heavenly spheres of the Ptolemaic system
were thought to make music (normally inaudible to human ears) as they
rubbed against one another; cf. Middleton, *F. of L.*, III.i.13–15.
 111. *Silence ... me!*] if not an aside, probably said to Mist. Openwork, Mist.
Gallipot or both.
 113. *a-mumming*] Mummers' plays were mimed and without dialogue;
Mist. Openwork seems to be telling her husband to be silent (perhaps playing
on 'mum').

Unless by their gay covers wits are fired
To read the vil'st looks. Many bad faces –   120
Because rich gems are treasured up in cases –
Pass by their privilege current; but as caves
Damn misers' gold, so masks are beauties' graves.
Men ne'er meet women with such muffled eyes,
But they curse her that first did masks devise,   125
And swear it was some beldame. Come, off with't.

Mistress Openwork. I will not!

Openwork. Good faces, masked, are jewels kept by sprites.
Hide none but bad ones, for they poison men's sights;
Show them as shopkeepers do their broidered stuff: 130

---

123. Damn] *Reed;* Dambe *Q;* Dam *Gomme.*   128. sprites] *Collier subst.;*
spirits *Q.*   130. them] *Bowers;* then *Q.*

120–2. *Many . . . current*] Cf. Dekker and Webster, *N.H.*, V.i.126–9, 'off
with thy maske sweete sinner of the North: these maskes are foiles to good
faces, and to bad ones they are like new sattin out-sides to lousie linings'; also,
Middleton and Rowley, *Changeling*, V.iii.3–5 (Revels ed.), 'The black mask /
That so continually was worn upon't / Condemns the face for ugly ere't be
seen.'

122–3. *caves . . . gold*] Useless hoarding of money was considered morally
reprehensible. Cf. Middleton, *F.H.T.* (Bullen, VIII), pp. 104–5, 'Gold lies
now as prisoner in an usurer's great iron-barred chest, where the prison-
grates are the locks and the key-holes, but so closely mewed, or rather
dammed [Q prints damnd] up, that it never looks to walk abroad again, unless
there chance to come a speedy rot among usurers'; and Dekker, *Troia-Nova
Triumphans*, ll. 232–3, '*no* Misers *kay* / *Has bard the* Gold *vp*'; Marlowe, *Hero
and Leander*, i.234–5 (Revels ed.), 'Then treasure is abus'd, / When misers
keep it.'

126. *beldame*] hag.

128. *sprites*] Q's 'spirits' emended for rhyme: see III.iii.112 and n.

130–1. *broidered . . . wares*] *Stuff* is an ordinary fabric (*O.E.D.*, sb.1, 5b), so
the comparison is between this and first quality wares. *Stuff* is used in this
sense in Middleton, *A.F.Q.L.*, II.ii.191–2, 'but if you'd have a petticoat for
your lady, here's a stuff'. Bawdy senses of *stuff* and *wares* may be present also,
as in Middleton, *M.T.*, III.i.205, 'what piece of stuff comes here?', and
V.iii.131; and see II.i.194n. above (*bona-roba*). Hoy suggests that 'braided',
meaning 'goods that have changed colour, tarnished, faded', may be intended,
and cites passages from Marston and Deloney for support; but the sense is
plain enough. References to dimly lit sempsters' or drapers' shops are common: cf. *A.F.Q.L.*, II.ii.52–4, 'though your shop-wares you vent / With your
deceiving lights, yet your chamber stuff / Shall not pass so with me'; also
M.T., II.iii.35–8, and Quomodo the draper's 'familiar spirit', Falselight.
Dekker in *S.D.S.*, singles out candlelight (i.e. dim light) as one of the sins; see
sig. D2r–v, where he attacks mercers and other shop-keepers for their misuse
of it.

By owl-light; fine wares cannot be open enough.
Prithee, sweet Rose, come strike this sail.

Mistress Openwork.   Sail?

Openwork.   Ha?
Yes, wife, strike sail, for storms are in thine eyes.

Mistress Openwork. They're here, sir, in my brows, if any rise.

Openwork. Ha, brows? – What says she, friend? Pray tell me
    why   135
Your two flags were advanced: the comedy?
Come, what's the comedy?

Mistress Gallipot.   *Westward Ho.*

Openwork.   How?

Mistress Openwork. 'Tis *Westward Ho,* she says.

Goshawk.   Are you both mad?

Mistress Openwork. Is't market day at Brentford, and your
    ware
Not sent up yet?

Openwork.   What market day? What ware?   140

Mistress Openwork. A pie with three pigeons in't – 'tis drawn

---

131. enough.] *Reed;* enough, *Q.*   137. *Mistress Gallipot*] *Scott; Mist. Open.*
Q.   141. in't –] *This ed.;* in't, *Q.*

---

134. *in my brows*] possibly, as Gomme suggests, 'a remote allusion to a
female cuckold's (or cuckquean's) horns'.

136. *flags ... advanced*] 'playhouses flew flags when they were open for
performances, and took them down when Lent or a plague rendered playing
impossible', Chambers, *E.S.,* II, 546). The specific reference is to the masks.
Cf. Middleton, *M.W.M.M.,* I.i.38–9, ''tis Lent in your cheeks, the flag's
down', and III.iii.142–4.

137. Gallipot] Scott's emendation from Mist. Openwork to Mist. Gallipot
solves two problems: it makes sense of Mist. Openwork's speech at l. 138 and
it explains Goshawk's aside in response. A similar effect is achieved
whichever of the two speech-headings assigned by Q to Mist. Openwork is
altered (l. 137 or l. 138). In Scott's arrangement Mist. Gallipot takes the
initiative, while in the alternative arrangement she provides support.

Westward Ho] 'The cry of the Thames watermen, but also of course an
allusion to the title of Dekker and Webster's comedy of 1604, where a westward voyage to Brainford [Brentford] of citizens' wives and their gallants
figures prominently in the plot' (Hoy).

139. *ware*] with a bawdy entendre; see II.i.201–3 and n.

141. *three pigeons*] with a play on the Three Pigeons Inn; *pigeons* may suggest 'wild fowl' (prostitutes), further supported by 'cutting up'; cf. III.ii.238
and n.

drawn] i.e. from the oven (*O.E.D.,* 32).

and stays your cutting up.

Goshawk. As you regard my credit –

Openwork. Art mad?

Mistress Openwork. Yes, lecherous goat! Baboon!   145

Openwork. Baboon? Then toss me in a blanket.

Mistress Openwork. [*To Mistress Gallipot*] Do I it well?

Mistress Gallipot. [*To Mistress Openwork*] Rarely!

Goshawk. [*To Open.*] Belike, sir, she's not well; best leave her.

Openwork.   No,

 I'll stand the storm now, how fierce soe'er it blow.   150

Mistress Openwork. Did I for this lose all my friends? Refuse

 Rich hopes and golden fortunes to be made

 A stale to a common whore?

Openwork.   This does amaze me!

Mistress Openwork. O God, O God! Feed at reversion now?

 A strumpet's leaving?

Openwork.   Rosamond!   155

Goshawk. [*Aside*] I sweat; would I lay in Cold Harbour.

Mistress Openwork. Thou hast struck ten thousand daggers

 through my heart!

143. credit –] *M. Thesis;* credit. *Q.* 147–9. s.dd.] *This ed.*

---

145. *goat! Baboon*] traditionally regarded as the most lustful of animals (cf. III.ii.237); cf. 'As lecherous as a goat' (Tilley, G167); also *Oth.*, 'Goats and monkeys!', IV.i.260.

146. *toss ... blanket*] a rough, humiliating punishment; cf. Dekker, *G.H.* (ed. Pendry), p. 101, 'you shall disgrace him worse than by tossing him in a blanket', *Sat.*, IV.iii.164ff.

151–3. *Refuse ... whore*] Cf. II.i.329–37.

153–90.] printed as prose in Q, but several rhyming couplets and strong rhythms support a verse arrangement. Speeches are twice doubled up on a single line on sig. 13r, which in conjunction with the verse set as prose suggests that the compositor was forced to crowd.

153. *stale*] (1) 'a lover or mistress whose devotion is turned into ridicule for the amusement of a rival or rivals' (*O.E.D.*, sb.3, 6); (2) decoy (sb.3, 3).

154. *reversion*] remains or left-overs of a meal; cf. III.ii.245–7, also *N.H.*, V.i.266–7.

156. *Cold Harbour*] 'a great number of smal tenements letten out for great rents, to people of all sortes' (Stow, *Survey*, I, 237); in Upper Thames St. near London Bridge. It became notorious as a habitation for the needy and a sanctuary for debtors and malefactors: cf. Middleton, *T.C.O.O.*, III.iii.115–16: '*Host.* They have took Cole-Harbour.   *Luc.* The devil's sanctuary!' also *B.B.* (Bullen, VIII), p. 14, *F.H.T.* (Bullen, VIII), p. 96, and Dekker, *L.C.* (ed. Pendry), p. 271. Goshawk also puns on the name, wishing to alleviate his sweating.

Openwork. Not I, by heaven, sweet wife.

Mistress Openwork. Go, devil, go! That which thou swear'st
    by, damns thee!

Goshawk. [*Aside to Mist. Open.*] 'S heart, will you undo me?   160

Mistress Openwork. [*To Openwork*] Why stay you here? The
    star by which you sail
      Shines yonder above Chelsea; you lose your shore.
    If this moon light you, seek out your light whore.

Openwork. Ha?

Mistress Gallipot. Push! Your western pug!

Goshawk. [*Aside*]   Zounds, now hell roars!

Mistress Openwork. With whom you tilted in a pair of oars   165
    This very morning.

Openwork.   Oars?

Mistress Openwork.   At Brentford, sir!

Openwork. Rack not my patience. Master Goshawk,

160, 161. s.dd.] *M. Thesis.*   164. *Mistress Gallipot*] *Q; Mistress Openwork Gomme.*

161–2. *star ... Chelsea*] (1) alluding to a whore at Brentford, eight miles west of London; *Chelsea* was at this time a village west of London on the north side of the Thames. By boat it lies on the way to Brentford. Cf. Dekker, *P.W.* (ed. Pendry), p. 119, 'He had, as he thought, a brighter star of his own to sail by' (in reference here to his wife); also Middleton, *F. of L.*, II.iv.124–5, 'O, I perceive, then, 'tis some city star that attracts your aspect'; (2) referring to Venus (hence, suggestive of wantonness), the morning or evening star?

162. *lose your shore*] probably, 'lose your way'.

163. *moon*] Cf. Dekker, *Sat.*, II.i.206–11: 'I know women to be earthly Moones, / That neuer shine till night, I know they change / Their Orbes (their husbands) and in sickish hearts, / Steale to their sweete Endimions, to be cur'd / With better Phisicke, sweeter dyet drinkes, / Then home can minister.'

164. *western pug*] (1) bargee plying the Thames upriver from London: cf. Dekker, *Wonderful Year* (ed. Pendry), p. 63, 'Insomuch that even the western pugs receiving money here have tied it in a bag at the end of their barge and so trailed it through the Thames lest, plague-sores sticking upon shillings, they should be nailed up for counterfeits when they were brought home' (cited by Dyce); (2) whore (alluding to Brentford to the west): cf. Dekker and Webster, *W.H.*, II.ii.192–3, 'the Westerne-man his Pug, the Seruing-man his Punke'. Old Merri-thought in Beaumont, *Knight of the Burning Pestle*, III.515–16 (*Dramatic Works*, I, ed. F. Bowers (Cambridge, 1966)) sings, '*Begone, begone, my Juggy, my puggy, / Begone my love, my deere.*'

165. *tilted*] playing on the jousting sense (with a bawdy innuendo), and the boat with a tilt.

pair of oars] boat rowed by two men.

Some slave has buzzed this into her, has he not? –
I run a-tilt in Brentford with a woman?
'Tis a lie!   170
What old bawd tells thee this? 'Sdeath, 'tis a lie!

Mistress Openwork. 'Tis one to thy face shall justify
All that I speak.

Openwork.   Ud' soul, do but name that rascal!

Mistress Openwork. No, sir, I will not.

Goshawk. [*Aside*]   Keep thee there, girl. – [*To them*] Then!

Openwork. [*To Mist. Gall.*] Sister, know you this varlet?

Mistress Gallipot.   Yes.

Openwork.   Swear true;   175
Is there a rogue so low damned? A second Judas?
A common hangman? Cutting a man's throat?
Does it to his face? Bite me behind my back?
A cur-dog? Swear if you know this hell-hound!

Mistress Gallipot. In truth I do.

Openwork.   His name?

Mistress Gallipot.   Not for the world,   180
To have you to stab him.

Goshawk. [*Aside*]   O brave girls: worth gold!

Openwork. A word, honest Master Goshawk.

                          Draw[s] out his sword.

Goshawk.   What do you mean, sir?

---

175. Openwork] *Dyce; Mist. Open. Q.*

---

172. *one to*] i.e. one who to (ellipsis); see Abbott, § 244. Dyce inserted 'who' for the metre; but the verse is in any case irregular.

173. *Ud' soul*] corrupted form of 'God bless my soul'; common in Dekker: see III.ii.157n.

175. Openwork] given to Mist. Openwork in Q, but reassignment to her husband makes better sense. The error may have resulted from simple compositorial confusion (possibly a speech-prefix transfer error): see this editor's '*The Roaring Girl*: New Readings and Further Notes', *S.B.*, XXXVII (1984), 163–70.

178. *Bite . . . back*] i.e. a backbiter: one who vilifies another behind his back.

179. *cur-dog*] (1) worthless, low-bred dog: a term of contempt; (2) watch dog, in allusion to the hell-hound, Cerberus.

181. *girls: worth gold*] Dyce remarked on the proverb, 'An honest woman is worth a crown of gold' (Tilley, W628), and the subtitle of Heywood's *Fair Maid of the West, or A Girl Worth Gold* (Part I is dated *c*. 1604 by R. K. Turner in his Regents Renaissance Drama edition (Lincoln, Nebr., 1968)).

Openwork. Keep off, and if the devil can give a name
        To this new fury, holla it through my ear,
        Or wrap it up in some hid character: 185
        I'll ride to Oxford and watch out mine eyes,
        But I'll hear the Brazen Head speak; or else
        Show me but one hair of his head or beard,
        That I may sample it. If the fiend I meet
        In mine own house, I'll kill him – the street,   190
        Or at the church door – there, 'cause he seeks to untie
        The knot God fastens – he deserves most to die!
Mistress Openwork. My husband titles him!
Openwork.   Master Goshawk, pray, sir,
        Swear to me that you know him or know him not,
        Who makes me at Brentford to take up a petticoat   195
        Besides my wife's.
Goshawk.   By heaven, that man I know not.
Mistress Openwork. Come, come, you lie!
Goshawk.   Will you not have all out?

190. – the] *Q;* [in] the *Dyce.*   191. there,] *Dyce;* there – – (Q.   196. Be-
sides] *Q subst., original setting;* beside *Q reset.*

---

183. *and if*] possibly *an if*, an intensified form of *if* = if indeed.
184. *fury*] avenging goodess.
holla] shout.
185. *hid character*] secret cipher; cf. Dekker, *Match Me in London*,
IV.iv.87–8, '... 'twas a letter / Wrap'd vp in hidden Characters'.
186. *watch out mine eyes*] i.e. keep awake; possibly, in addition to the *Brazen
Head* allusion, in reference to the traditional technique of training a hawk in
which the trainer must 'outstare' the bird (see T. H. White, *The Goshawk*
(1951)).
187. *Brazen Head*] referring to the legend of the Brazen Head of Brasenose
College, Oxford, dramatised by Greene in *Friary Bacon and Friar Bungay* (*c.*
1589). By making the Head speak, Friar Bacon intended to wall England with
brass, but through the foolishness of a servant missed hearing its pronounce-
ment. Among Middleton's earliest productions for Henslowe were a new
prologue and epilogue for Greene's play (see R. A. Foakes and R. T. Rickert
(edd.), *Henslowe's Diary*, p. 207).
190. – *the street*] Dyce, followed by other editors, added 'in', apparently for
the metre; but the ellipsis contributes to the impression of disjointed speech.
191–2. *untie ... fastens*] Cf. the speech on the sanctity of marriage in Middleton, *Phoenix*, II.ii.164–96.
193. *titles*] addresses.
197. *Will ... out*] possibly a furtive aside to Mist. Openwork or, alternatively, a bold statement of innocence intended to absolve himself of suspicion
and to control Mist. Openwork's unruly tongue.

　　　　– [*To Openwork*] By heaven, I know no man beneath the
　　　　　　moon
　　　　Should do you wrong, but if I had his name,
　　　　I'd print it in text letters.
Mistress Openwork.　　　　　　Print thine own then;　　200
　　　　Didst not thou swear to me he kept his whore?
Mistress Gallipot. And that in sinful Brentford they would
　　　　commit
　　　　That which our lips did water at, sir? – Ha?
Mistress Openwork. Thou spider, that hast woven thy cunning
　　　　web
　　　　In mine own house t'ensnare me: hast not thou　　205
　　　　Sucked nourishment even underneath this roof
　　　　And turned it all to poison, spitting it
　　　　On thy friend's face, my husband – he as 'twere, sleeping –
　　　　Only to leave him ugly to mine eyes,
　　　　That they might glance on thee?
Mistress Gallipot.　　　　　　Speak, are these lies?　　210

208. husband –] *M. Thesis;* husband?) *Q.*　　　sleeping –] *M. Thesis;* sleeping:
Q.

---

　　199. *Should*] i.e. who should (ellipsis); see Abbott, § 244.
　　200. *text letters*] large or capital letters. Hoy cites Dekker, *Lanthorne* (1609),
sig. E4r, 'They would take vp any commodity whatsoeuer, but their names
stand in too many texted letters all ready in Mercers and Scriueners bookes'.
Also *I.T.B.N.*, I.ii.211, and *W.B.*, V.ii.113.
　　202. *commit*] Hoy notes the word's 'bawdy implications' citing Dekker,
Lanthorne (1609), sig. 11r, 'or if shee bee not in trauell all night, they spend
some halfe an houre together, but what doe they? marry, they doe that, which
the Constable should haue done for them both in the streetes[,] thats to say
commit, commit'.
　　203. *lips . . . water*] with a bawdy entendre. Cf. 'To have one's teeth to water
at anything' (Tilley, T430).
　　204–8. *spider . . . face*] See I.ii.230–1 and n. Cf. Dekker, *2 H.W.*,
II.i.195–200: 'Would thou wouldst leaue my house, thou ne'r shalt please me,
/ Weaue thy nets ne'r so hye, / Thou shalt be but a spider in mine eye. / Th'art
ranke with poyson, poyson temperd well, / Is food for health; but thy blacke
tongue doth swell / With venome, to hurt him that gaue thee bread.' Also
S.D.S., sig. B4r, 'O thou that on thy pillow (lyke a Spider in his loome)
weauest mischeuous nets, beating thy braynes, how by casting downe others,
to rayse vp thy selfe!'
　　209. *leave him ugly*] Cf. Dekker, *L.C.* (ed. Pendry), pp. 200–1, 'a fellow . . .
having sucked what knowledge he can from them, to turn it all into poison and
to spit it in the very faces of the professors with a malicious intent to make
them appear ugly and so to grow hateful and out of favour with the world'.

Goshawk. Mine own shame me confounds.

Openwork.   No more, he's stung.

    Who'd think that in one body there could dwell

    Deformity and beauty, heaven and hell?

    Goodness, I see, is but outside; we all set

    In rings of gold, stones that be counterfeit: 215

    I thought you none.

Goshawk.   Pardon me.

Openwork.   Truth, I do.

    This blemish grows in nature, not in you;

    For man's creation stick even moles in scorn

    On fairest cheeks. – Wife, nothing is perfect born.

Mistress Openwork. I thought you had been born perfect.   220

Openwork. What's this whole world but a gilt rotten pill?

    For at the heart lies the old core still.

    I'll tell you, Master Goshawk, ay, in your eye

    I have seen wanton fire; and then to try

    The soundness of my judgement, I told you   225

    I kept a whore, made you believe 'twas true,

---

211. *Openwork.*] Scott; Mist. Open. Q.   219. cheeks. –] Dyce; cheeks,
Q.   222. core] Reed; chore Q.   223. ay] Dyce; I Q; aye (= even) Reed;
Bowers omits.

---

211. Openwork] assigned to Mist. Openwork in Q, but the speech sits
better with her husband.

216. *Truth*] abbreviated form of 'in truth'.

218. *man's creation*] i.e. mankind.

218–19. *moles ... cheeks*] Moles or patches were 'small pieces of velvet or
silk, cut into various shapes and attached by mastic to the face or fore head to
cover a blemish or attract attention to a beautiful feature' (Linthicum, p. 275).
Cf. Middleton, *B.M.C.*, III.iii.100–4, 'the first principle to learn is, that you
stick black patches for the rheum on your delicate blue temples, though there
be no room for the rheum: black patches are comely in most women, and
being well fastened, draw men's eyes to shoot glances at you.' Also Dekker
and Webster, *W.H.*, II.i.135ff.

221–2. *gilt ... core*] Cf. Dekker, *Sat.*, I.ii.222–3, 'If they take off all gilding
from their pilles, / And onely offer you the bitter Coare'. 'Gilding' (i.e. de-
coration with an edible golden colouring) was often used on sweetmeats such
as marzipan. The pill was probably given a sweet covering before the gilding
was applied: cf. Middleton and Rowley, *F.Q.*, I.i.383–4, 'Your cruel-smiling
father all this while / Has candied o'er a bitter pill for me'.

223. *ay*] yes; *O.E.D.* notes that *ay* in this sense was at first always written 'I'
(as elsewhere in Q), and is so distinguished from *ay/aye* meaning 'ever' or
'even'.

Only to feel how your pulse beat, but find
The world can hardly yield a perfect friend. –
Come, come, a trick of youth, and 'tis forgiven;
This rub put by, our love shall run more even.   230
Mistress Openwork. You'll deal upon men's wives no more?
Goshawk.   No. – You teach me
    A trick for that!
Mistress Openwork. Troth, do not; they'll o'erreach thee.
Openwork. Make my house yours, sir, still.
Goshawk.   No.
Openwork.   I say you shall:
    Seeing, thus besieged, it holds out, 'twill never fall!

Enter MASTER GALLIPOT, *and* GREENWIT *like a sumner*; LAXTON
                muffled, aloof off.

All. How now?   235
Gallipot. [*To Greenwit*] With me, sir?
Greenwit. [*To Gallipot*] You, sir. – I have gone snuffling up and
    down by your door this hour to watch for you.

237. snuffling] *Dyce;* snaffling *Q.*

---

229. *trick*] (1) habit, custom; (2) device, deception; (3) prank, joke.

230. *rub*] obstacle, difficulty: a technical term in the game of bowls, used of touches of a bowl against others in its path, or generally of any unevenness in its passage.

put by] thrust aside.

231. *deal upon*] proceed against, set to work upon.

232. *trick*] knack, art, skill.

o'erreach] overtake, overpower (*O.E.D.*, 2b).

234.1. *sumner*] summoner, apparitor: an officer in an ecclesiastical court who summoned persons to appear there.

234.2. *muffled*] See III.ii.205.1 and n.

aloof off] at a distance. The phrase is characteristic of Middleton, appearing in *M.T.*, I.i.230 and III.i.241, *N.W.N.H.*, IV.i s.d., *1 H.W.*, II.i.117 s.d. (presumed a Middleton section), and in *Meeting of Gallants at an Ordinary* (ed. Wilson), p. 127, ll. 12–15 (Wilson finds this a mark of Middleton's presence in the work).

237. *snuffling*] Bowers defends Q's 'snaffling' as a variant of 'snuffling' = speaking through the nose (see *O.E.D.*, 'snaffle', v.3, also 'snaffler' 2, and 'snaffling', ppl.a.). He rejects *O.E.D.*'s citation of the present passage under 'snaffle', v.2 = to saunter, directing attention to Greenwit's next speech, ll. 240–2. His interpretation is all the more persuasive because sumners seem to have been commonly associated with snuffling as a symptom of venereal disease; cf. Chaucer's Summoner and E. Sharpham, *The Fleire*

Mistress Gallipot. What's the matter, husband?

Greenwit. I have caught a cold in my head, sir, by sitting up late   240
in the Rose Tavern, but I hope you understand my
speech.

Gallipot. So, sir.

Greenwit. I cite you by the name of Hippocrates Gallipot, and
you by the name of Prudence Gallipot, to appear upon   245
Crastino – do you see – *Crastino Sancti Dunstani*, this
Easter Term, in Bow Church.

Gallipot. Where, sir? What says he?

Greenwit. Bow – Bow Church, to answer to a libel of precontract on the part and behalf of the said Prudence and ano-   250
ther; you're best, sir, take a copy of the citation: 'tis but
twelvepence.

All. A citation?

Gallipot. You pocky-nosed rascal, what slave fees you to this?

(1606), sig. Dr, 'What! shall wee embrace? shall we haue red-nos'd Corporals
here: what you rogue? will you turne Sumner? away you whale-nosd rogue
away, goe, snufle, snufle in the Ocean, away you slaue', where 'whale-nosd' is
tantamount to noseless, as a result of syphilis (so G. Williams, 'An Elizabethan Disease', *Trivium*, VI (1971), 51). The joke extends apparently to the
shedding of Greenwit's hair, l. 278 below. *Snuffling* in this text is therefore
to be understood not as a correction but as a modernisation. Cf. II.i.63–5.
Greenwit may yet pun on the word's other meaning.

241. *Rose Tavern*] There were many taverns so named in London at this
time. Probably that at the corner of Thanet Place, outside Temple Bar, is
meant.

244–9. *cite . . . libel*] In ecclesiastical court procedure, the offender was summoned into court by a writ of citation and was issued with the libellum or
charge on his appearance there.

246. Crastino Sancti Dunstani] i.e. the morrow after St Dunstan's Day (19
May): 20 May (Lat.).

247. *Bow Church*] 'At the vpper ende of Hosier [or Bow] Lane, towarde
West Cheape, is the fayre Parish Church of Saint *Marie* Bow. This Church in
the reigne of *William Conqueror*, being the first in this Cittie builded on
Arches of stone, was therefore called newe *Marie* Church, of Saint *Marie de
Arcubus*, or *le Bow* in West Cheaping', Stow, *Survey*, I, 253. 'the Ecclesiastical Court of Arches was so called because it sat in this church' (Sugden, p.
71).

248.] Gallipot apparently has trouble understanding Greenwit through his
snuffling.

252. *twelvepence*] Cf. Middleton, *F. of L.*, IV.iv.135–9.

254. *pocky-nosed*] i.e. as a sign of syphilis: see l. 237n. above. The destruction of the nose by venereal disease was a common, though grotesque, butt of
humour.

Laxton. Slave? [*Comes forward; aside to Goshawk*] I ha'   255
    nothing to do with you, do you hear, sir?

Goshawk. [*Aside to Laxton*] Laxton is't not? What vagary is
    this?

Gallipot. Trust me, I thought, sir, this storm long ago
    Had been full laid, when – if you be remembered –
    I paid you the last fifteen pound, besides   260
    The thirty you had first – for then you swore –

Laxton. Tush, tush, sir, oaths –
    Truth, yet I'm loath to vex you. – Tell you what:
    Make up the money I had an hundred pound,
    And take your bellyful of her.

Gallipot.   An hundred pound?   265

Mistress Gallipot. What, a hundred pound? He gets none!
    What, a hundred pound?

Gallipot. Sweet Prue, be calm; the gentleman offers thus:
    If I will make the moneys that are past
    A hundred pound, he will discharge all courts
    And give his bond never to vex us more.   270

Mistress Gallipot. A hundred pound? 'Las, take, sir, but
    threescore.
    – [*Aside to Laxton*] Do you seek my undoing?

Laxton.   I'll not 'bate one sixpence.
    – [*Aside to Mist. Gall.*] I'll maul you, puss, for spitting.

Mistress Gallipot. [*Aside to Laxton*]   Do thy worst!
    – [*Aloud*] Will fourscore stop thy mouth?

Laxton.   No.

Mistress Gallipot.   You're a slave!

---

261. swore –] *Collier;* swore. *Q.*   272–4. s.dd.] *M. Thesis.*

---

257. *vagary*] devious journey, excursion.

258. *storm*] Cf. III.ii.122, 223.

259. *laid*] allayed, caused to subside.

260. *last fifteen pound*] a transaction not dramatised; presumably Laxton
has bilked Gallipot behind the scenes.

264.] i.e. bring the total sum to a hundred pounds.

269. *courts*] Gallipot apparently perceives a threat of several legal actions.

272. *'bate*] deduct.

273. *maul*] beat, with a pun on 'maule' or 'mawle', to cry like a cat.

Thou cheat; I'll now tear money from thy throat. –   275
Husband, lay hold on yonder tawny-coat.

Greenwit. Nay, gentlemen, seeing your women are so hot,
I must lose my hair in their company, I see.

                              [*Removes hair-piece.*]

Mistress Openwork. His hair sheds off, and yet he speaks not so
     much
In the nose as he did before.

Goshawk.   He has had   280
The better chirurgeon. – Master Greenwit,
Is your wit so raw as to play no better
A part than a sumner's?

Gallipot.   I pray, who plays
A Knack to Know an Honest Man in this company?

Mistress Gallipot. Dear husband, pardon me, I did dissemble,   285
Told thee I was his precontracted wife –
When letters came from him for thirty pound,
I had no shift but that.

275. throat. –] *Dyce;* throat, *Q.*   278.1.] *M. Thesis.*   286. wife –] *This ed.;*
wife, *Q.*

---

275. *cheat*] thief, swindler; the earliest usage recorded by *O.E.D.* for this
sense is 1664; cf. also V.ii.160.

tear . . . throat] Embedded in this challenge is a charge that Laxton is lying:
see III.i.89–90n.

276. *tawny-coat*] i.e. in allusion to Greenwit, who wears the tawny-
coloured livery of a summoner.

277–8. *hot . . . hair*] another joke alluding the effects of venereal disease. *Hot*
carries the sense of 'sexually eager, ardent' (Partridge, p. 124), and perhaps
also an element of the burning effects of syphilis. Cf. Dekker, *2 H.W.*,
II.ii.123–4, 'Nay, if your seruice be so hot, a man cannot keepe his haire on,
Ile serue you no longer', *I.T.B.N.*, II.ii.70–1; and *Revenger's Tragedy*,
I.i.99–101 (Revels ed.).

279–80. *speaks . . . nose*] See l. 237n. above. Cf. 'To speak in the nose'
(Tilley, N242: earliest recorded usage 1636).

281. *The better chirurgeon*] i.e. in 'curing' his apparent malady;
chirurgeon = surgeon.

282. *wit so raw*] playing on Greenwit's name.

284. A Knack to Know an Honest Man] an anonymous comedy of 1594
acted under the auspices of the Admiral's Men, Henslowe's company. In it,
Sempronio, after pretending to be mortally wounded, wanders about in disguise testing the honesty of those he meets, and the title becomes a kind of
catch-phrase in the course of the action.

288. *shift*] Mist. Gallipot uses *shift* in the sense of 'device, strategem', and
her husband puns on it in the senses 'underclothing' and 'change'.

Gallipot.   A very clean shift,
   But able to make me lousy. – On.
Mistress Gallipot.   Husband, I plucked –
   When he had tempted me to think well of him –   290
   Gelt feathers from thy wings, to make him fly
   More lofty.
Gallipot.   O' the top of you, wife. – On.
Mistress Gallipot. He, having wasted them, comes now for
      more,
   Using me as a ruffian doth his whore,
   Whose sin keeps him in breath. By heaven, I vow,   295
   Thy bed he never wronged more than he does now.
Gallipot. My bed? – Ha, ha, like enough! – A shop-board will
      serve
   To have a cuckold's coat cut out upon;
   Of that we'll talk hereafter. – [*To Laxton*] You're a villain!
Laxton. Hear me but speak, sir, you shall find me none.   300
All. Pray, sir, be patient and hear him.
Gallipot.   I am
   Muzzled for biting, sir; use me how you will.
Laxton. The first hour that your wife was in my eye,
   Myself with other gentlemen sitting by

---

291. Gelt] *Dyce;* Get *Q; Gilt* Ellis; Collier omits.   297. enough! –] *This ed.;*
enough, *Q.*

---

   291. *Gelt feathers*] Most editors have expressed uneasiness over the Q reading, 'Get feathers'. The general image is common enough; Bowers cites Dekker, *Lust's Dominion*, I.ii.194–8: '*Alvero. Mendoza* woo's the King to banish thee; / Startle thy wonted spirits, awake thy soul, / And on thy resolution fasten wings, / Whose golden feathers may out-strip their hate. / *Eleazar.* I'le tye no golden fethers to my wings.' Hoy adds *I.T.B.N.*, II.iii.87, and *V.M.*, III.iii.89. Cf. also Middleton, *A.F.Q.L.*, II.ii.175–6. *Gelt*, though not recorded at this date as an adjective in *O.E.D.*, preserves the sense and is closer to the Q reading than 'Gilt'. But Q's 'Get feathers' may yet be correct: 'get' can mean 'booty, earnings, gain' (*O.E.D.*, sb.1) (cf. 'get-penny'), and 'feathers' commonly signifies money (cf. 'To feather one's nest': Tilley, N125–6).
   292. *O' the top of you*] with a bawdy entendre.
   294. *ruffian*] pimp.
   297–8. *shop-board … upon*] Cf. Middleton, *M.T.*, II.iii.35–8, '… my shop is not altogether so dark as some of my neighbours', where a man may be made cuckold at one end, while he's measuring with his yard at t'other.' A *shop-board* is a counter or table for the display of goods or transaction of business.

In your shop tasting smoke, and speech being used   305
That men who have fairest wives are most abused
And hardly 'scaped the horn, your wife maintained
That only such spots in city dames were stained
Justly, but by men's slanders; for her own part,
She vowed that you had so much of her heart,   310
No man by all his wit, by any wile
Never so fine spun, should yourself beguile
Of what in her was yours.

Gallipot.   Yet Prue 'tis well;
Play out your game at Irish, sir: who wins?
Mistress Openwork. The trial is when she comes to bearing.   315
Laxton. I scorned one woman, thus, should brave all men,
And – which more vexed me – a she-citizen;
Therefore I laid siege to her: out she held,
Gave many a brave repulse, and me compelled
With shame to sound retreat to my hot lust;   320
Then seeing all base desires raked up in dust,
And that to tempt her modest ears I swore
Ne'er to presume again, she said her eye

310. heart,] *Reed;* heart; *Q.*

308–9. *only . . . slanders*] The sense is clear if *but* is read as 'if not': 'the stains on women's characters are just only if not the result of men's slanders'. Cf. III.i.81ff.

314. *Irish*] a board game similar to backgammon played with dice and counters. Cotton, *Compleat Gamester* (1674), p. 154, noted that it took longer to play than backgammon.

315. *bearing*] a term in the games of Irish and backgammon for the removal of a piece at the end of the game; with a play on 'child-bearing'. Cf. Cotton, *Compleat Gamester*, p. 155, 'make what convenient hast you can to fill up your own Tables, and beware of blotting; that done, bear as fast as you can' (cited by Hoy). Cf. Dekker and Webster, *N.H.*, IV.i.267–8, 'did not I tell you old man, that sheed win any game when she came to bearing?' (cited by Dyce). Cf. also H. Porter, *Two Angry Women of Abingdon*, I.i (ed. H. Ellis, *Nero and Other Plays* (1888), p. 102).

321. *base . . . dust*] i.e. as a fire covered with ashes in order to keep it in without active burning (*O.E.D.*, 'rake', v.1, 5a); cf. V.ii.36–7. *Dust* may also signify 'a condition of humiliation' (*O.E.D.*, sb.1, 3c). Several breaks in the pattern of rhyming couplets occur in the speech but the sense is not impaired and there is no reason to suppose with G. R. Price that lines have been omitted ('The Manuscript and the Quarto of *The Roaring Girl*', *The Library*, 5th ser., XI (1956), p. 181, n. 1). Such breaks are not, in any case, uncommon in Middleton or Dekker.

Would ever give me welcome honestly;
And – since I was a gentleman – if it run low,   325
She would my state relieve, not to o'erthrow
Your own and hers; did so; then seeing I wrought
Upon her meekness, me she set at nought;
And yet to try if I could turn that tide,
You see what stream I strove with. But sir, I swear   330
By heaven and by those hopes men lay up there,
I neither have nor had a base intent
To wrong your bed. What's done is merriment;
Your gold I pay back with this interest:
When I had most power to do't, I wronged you least.   335

Gallipot. If this no gullery be, sir –
All.   No, no, on my life!
Gallipot. Then, sir, I am beholden – not to you, wife –
But Master Laxton, to your want of doing ill,
Which it seems you have not. – Gentlemen,
Tarry and dine here all.
Openwork.   Brother, we have a jest   340
As good as yours to furnish out a feast.
Gallipot. We'll crown our table with it. – Wife, brag no more
Of holding out: who most brags is most whore.   *Exeunt.*

---

330. with.] *This ed.;* with, *Q.*   333. bed.] *M. Thesis;* bed, *Q.*   336. sir –]
Reed subst.; sir, *Q.*   *All*] *This ed.; Omnes Q; Open./Gos., &c. Dyce.*   339.
not. –] *Dyce;* not *Q.*   343. s.d.] *Exeunt omnes. Q.*

---

327. *did so*] i.e. she did so (ellipsis); see Abbott, § 244.

328. *meekness*] compassion.

329. *to try if I could*] i.e. in my attempt to.

330. *stream*] current.

335.] Cf. II.i.142–5.

336. *All*] Perhaps this speech should be given to Laxton. The *my* suggests a single speaker rather than a group, and Gallipot's reply, l. 337, sounds like a response to Laxton.

340. *jest*] possibly in the sense 'narrative of exploits'.

341. *furnish out*] complete, fill out; perhaps also with the sense 'decorate, embellish' (*O.E.D.*, 5b).

343. *who ... whore*] Cf. Dekker and Webster, *W.H.*, IV.ii.49–50, 'be not precize, / Who writes of *Vertue* best, are slaues to vize'. The thought is close to *Ham.*, III.ii.224–5, 'The lady doth protest too much, methinks.'

Act V

[V.i]

Enter JACK DAPPER, MOLL [*dressed as a man*], SIR BEAUTEOUS
GANYMEDE, *and* SIR THOMAS LONG.

Jack Dapper. But prithee, Master Captain Jack, be plain and
    perspicuous with me: was it your Meg of Westminster's
    courage that rescued me from the Poultry puttocks,
    indeed?

Moll. The valour of my wit, I ensure you, sir, fetched you off   5
    bravely when you were i' the forlorn hope among those
    desperates. Sir Beauteous Ganymede here and Sir
    Thomas Long heard that cuckoo – my man Trapdoor –
    sing the note of your ransom from captivity.

Sir Beauteous. Uds-so, Moll, where's that Trapdoor?   10

Moll. Hanged, I think, by this time; a justice in this town, that
    speaks nothing but 'Make a mittimus, away with him to

V.i] *Dyce; not in Q.*   7. desperates.] *Reed;* desperates, *Q.*   10. *Sir Beauteous*] *Sir Bewt. Q passim.*

---

    1. *Jack*] A generic name for a man, *Jack* is apparently used as familiar name
for Moll when she wears male attire.

    3. *Poultry puttocks*] i.e. officers of the Poultry Counter: cf. III.iii.110 and n.

    5. *ensure*] assure.

    fetched . . . off] delivered, brought out of difficulty (*O.E.D.*, 16, cites 1648
as the earliest recorded usage).

    6. *forlorn hope*] 'In early use, a picked body of men, detached to the front to
begin the attack; a body of skirmishers'; used figuratively 'of persons in a
desperate condition' (*O.E.D.*). Hoy cites several instances in Dekker.

    7. *desperates*] i.e. catchpoles: men habituated to daring or desperate tasks
(*O.E.D.*, 2).

    8. *cuckoo*] fool.

    10. *Uds-so*] corrupted form of 'God save my soul': see III.ii.157n.

    12–13. *Make . . . Newgate*] apparently an almost proverbial expression for a
severe and unsympathetic magistrate; cf. the anonymous, *How a Man May
Choose a Good Wife from a Bad* (*c.* 1601–2), ed. A. E. H. Swaen (Louvain,

Newgate', used that rogue like a firework to run upon a
line betwixt him and me.

All. How, how?   15

Moll. Marry, to lay trains of villainy to blow up my life; I smelt
the powder, spied what linstock gave fire to shoot against
the poor captain of the galley-foist, and away slid I my
man like a shovel-board shilling. He struts up and down
the suburbs, I think, and eats up whores, feeds upon a   20
bawd's garbage.

19. shilling.] *Collier;* shilling, *Q.*

1912), ll. 797–8, where Justice Reason pronounces, 'And is this all? make me a
Mittimus, / And send the offender straitwaies to the gaile'; also Middleton?,
Wit at Several Weapons, IV.i (Beaumont and Fletcher, *Works,* IX, ed. A. R.
Waller (Cambridge, 1910), 108), 'He was ev'n brought to Justice *Aurums*
threshold, / There had flew'n forth a *Mittimus* straight for *Newgate.*' Hoy
cites *W. of E.,* IV.i.213–14. A *mittimus* is a warrant to commit to jail (from the
Latin first word of such a writ). *Newgate* was one of the gates of Old London
built in the reign of Henry I, and incorporating the city's chief prison, used
mainly for felons and debtors.

13–14. *firework ... line*] a common image in Dekker: cf. *2 H.W.,* II.i.212,
N.H., IV.iii.90–1, *W.B.,* III.i.89–90. Actual fireworks on lines are called for
in *I.T.B.N.,* II.i.192 s.d. Such pyrotechnics are described by John Bate, *The
Mysteries of Nature and Art* (1634), sigs. L2–3.

16. *trains*] lines of gunpowder laid as a fuse to an explosive charge (*O.E.D.,*
sb.1, 13a).

17. *linstock*] a staff pointed at one end for thrusting in the ground, and with a
forked head at the other for holding the gunner's match. Cf. Middleton,
B.M.C., II.ii.288–90, 'O Cupid, grant that my blushing prove not a linstock,
and give fire too suddenly to the Roaring Meg of my desires!'; also Dekker,
Lust's Dominion, III.ii.193, *Match Me in London,* V.ii.20, *W.H.* (a character is
named Linstock), *N.S.S.,* IV.ii.153, *W.B.,* V.v.o.2.

18. *captain of the galley-foist*] a 'term of contempt', in support of which Hoy
cites Beaumont and Fletcher, *Scornful Lady,* I.ii.45–8, and Thomas Kil-
ligrew, *Parson's Wedding,* I.i. A *galley-foist* was a state barge, especially that
used by the Lord Mayor of London on state occasions. Dekker seems to have
been fond of using the term for large women; cf. *2 H.W.,* IV.iii.35–6, and
W.H., V.iii.5–6.

19. *shovel-board shilling*] 'The popular amusement of Shovel-board or
Shuffle-board consisted in driving a coin or disk by a blow with the hand
along a highly polished board into compartments marked out at one end of it.
... The coin most commonly used was a shilling', *Shakespeare's English,* II,
467. Cf. *Wiv.,* I.i.138–40.

20. *eats up*] (1) takes over, annexes (i.e. as a pimp) (*O.E.D.,* 18b); (2) has
sexual intercourse with (cf. Partridge, p. 98)?

21. *garbage*] (1) refuse, with a play on 'Ralph': see Dramatis Personae, l.
18n.; (2) takings from theft: see l. 327n. below (*lifters*).

Sir Thomas. Sirrah Jack Dapper –

Jack Dapper. What sayst, Tom Long?

Sir Thomas. Thou hadst a sweet-faced boy, hail-fellow with
    thee to your little Gull: how is he spent?   25

Jack Dapper. Troth, I whistled the poor little buzzard off o' my
    fist because when he waited upon me at the ordinaries, the
    gallants hit me i' the teeth still and said I looked like a
    painted alderman's tomb, and the boy at my elbow, like a
    death's head. – Sirrah Jack, Moll.   30

Moll. What says my little Dapper?

Sir Beauteous. Come, come, walk and talk, walk and talk.

Jack Dapper. Moll and I'll be i' the midst.

Moll. These knights shall have squires' places, belike then. –
    Well Dapper, what say you?   35

Jack Dapper. Sirrah Captain Mad Mary, the gull, my own
    father – Dapper, Sir Davy – laid these London boot-
    halers, the catchpoles, in ambush to set upon me.

All. Your father? Away Jack!

---

22. *Sir Thomas*] *T. Long. Q passim.*   37. Dapper, Sir Davy] *Q subst.;* Sir
Dauy Dapper Bowers.

---

24. *hail-fellow*] on most intimate terms; cf. Dekker, *S.H.*, vii.69–71 (Revels
ed.).

25. *to*] in the character of, as.

spent] (1) used up; cf. *2H4*, III.ii.117–18; (2) employed.

26. *whistled ... off*] released from, sent off (a falconry term).

buzzard] 'inferior kind of hawk, useless for falconry' (*O.E.D.*, sb.1, 1a).

28. *hit ... teeth*] proverbial: Tilley, T429.

29. *painted alderman's tomb*] in reference to the coloured effigies on the
sumptuous tombs of aldermen.

29–30. *boy ... head*] alluding to the placement of a representation of a skull
as a *memento mori* on tombs: cf. Dekker, *Match Me in London*, V.ii.98–102:
'*Gaz.* .... thy wife for the hoope ring thou marriedst her withall, hath sworne
to send thee a Deathes head.   *Cordo.* Sworne!   *Gaz.* Sworne, were thy case
my case; I would set a Diuell at her elbow in the very Church.'

34. *knights ... places*] i.e. a reversal of their ceremonial positions: cf. Middleton, *Civitatis Amor* (Bullen, VII), p. 285, 'each knight between his two
esquires well apparelled, his footman attending, and his page riding before
him'.

37. *Dapper, Sir Davy*] Q's presentation is in keeping with Moll's addressing of Jack as 'Dapper'; Bowers alters to *Sir Dauy Dapper* without comment.

37–8. *boot-halers*] marauding or foraging soldiers, highwaymen.

38. *set upon*] attack.

Jack Dapper. By the tassels of this handkercher, 'tis true; and   40
     what was his warlike stratagem, think you? He thought,
     because a wicker cage tames a nightingale, a lousy prison
     could make an ass of me.

All. A nasty plot!

Jack Dapper. Ay: as though a counter, which is a park in which   45
     all the wild beasts of the city run head by head, could tame
     me!

               Enter the LORD NOLAND.

Moll. Yonder comes my Lord Noland.

All. Save you, my lord.

Lord Noland. Well met, gentlemen all: good Sir Beauteous   50
     Ganymede, Sir Thomas Long – and how does Master
     Dapper?

Jack Dapper. Thanks, my lord.

Moll. No tobacco, my lord?

Lord Noland. No, faith, Jack.   55

50. *Lord Noland*] *L. Nol. Q passim.*

---

40. *tassels*] 'Small handkerchiefs of about four inches square, with a button
or tassel at each corner or edged with gold lace, were folded and worn in hats
as favours', *Shakespeare's England*, II, 109. Cf. Middleton, *C.M. in C.*,
III.ii.50–5 (Revels ed.), where the gossips use their tasselled handkerchiefs
for 'pocketing' sweetmeats.

42. *wicker ... prison*] Cf. Middleton, *T.C.O.O.*, IV.iii.50–2, 'O, 'tis a secret
delight we have amongst us! we that are used to keep birds in cages, have the
heart to keep men in prison, I warrant you.'

43. *make an ass of me*] cited by *O.D.E.P.*; cf. 'as dull as an ass' (Tilley,
A348).

46. *wild beasts*] Cf. William Fennor, *Compters Common-wealth* (1617), pp.
54–5, 'There [i.e. in the Counter] lies your right-worshipfull poore Knight,
your worshipfull beggerly Esquire, your distressed Gentleman, your
Mechanicke Tradsman, your prating Pettifogger, and iuggling (lyers I would
say) Lawyers, all these like so many beasts in a Wildernesse desire to prey one
vpon the other.'

54.] Cf. James I, *Counterblaste to Tobacco* (*Workes* (1616)), p. 222: 'And is it
not a great vanitie, that a man cannot heartily welcome his friend now, but
straight they must be in hand with *Tobacco*: No it is become in place of a cure,
a point of good fellowship, and hee that will refuse to take a pipe of *Tobacco*
among his fellowes, (though by his owne election hee would rather feele the
sauour of a Sinke) is accounted peeuish and no good company, euen as they
doe with tipling in the colde Easterne countreys. Yea the Mistresse cannot in a
more manerly kind, entertaine her seruant, then by giuing him out of her faire
hand a pipe of *Tobacco*.' See Intro., p. 38.

Jack Dapper. My Lord Noland, will you go to Pimlico with us?
    We are making a boon voyage to that nappy land of spice
    cakes.
Lord Noland. Here's such a merry ging, I could find in my
    heart to sail to the World's End with such company. Come   60
    gentlemen, let's on.
Jack Dapper. Here's most amorous weather, my lord.
All. Amorous weather?   *They walk.*
Jack Dapper. Is not amorous a good word?

Enter TRAPDOOR *like a poor soldier with a patch o'er one eye, and*
            TEARCAT *with him, all tatters.*

Trapdoor. Shall we set upon the infantry, these troops of foot?   65
    – Zounds, yonder comes Moll, my whorish master and
    mistress; would I had her kidneys between my teeth!
Tearcat. I had rather have a cow-heel.
Trapdoor. Zounds, I am so patched up, she cannot discover
    me. – We'll on.   70

---

68. *Tearcat*] *T. Cat. Q passim*.

---

56. *Pimlico*] the Pimlico Inn at Hogsden (Hoxton): see IV.ii.13–15n. The
pleasures of Pimlico are set forth in a pamphlet, *Pimlyco. Or, Runne Red-Cap.
Tis a mad world at Hogsdon* (1609).

57. *boon voyage*] prosperous, fortunate journey: an anglicisation of *bon
voyage*.

nappy] heady, strong: probably in reference to the ale for which Pimlico was
famous.

59. *ging*] company, gang.

60. *World's End*] Taverns so named were located in Spring Gardens,
Knightsbridge, and in King's Rd., Chelsea, west of Battersea Bridge. 'In both
cases the name indicated the distance of the tavern from London' (Sugden, p.
571); the sense may also be merely figurative; cf. 'It is a great journey to the
world's end' (Tilley, J78).

62. *amorous*] lovely; the response suggests that Jack's use is pedantic or
eccentric (possibly a malapropism for 'amiable'?).

64.2. all tatters] wearing ragged clothes.

68. *cow-heel*] the foot of a cow stewed to form a jelly; the earliest *O.E.D.*
citation (1665), from Moufet and Bennet, *Health's Improvement*, refers to it as
a restorative. Cf. Dekker and Webster, *N.H.*, II.i.222–4, and the anonymous,
How a Man May Choose a Good Wife from a Bad, ed. A. E. H. Swaen
(Louvain, 1912), ll. 1604. An association with the cloven foot of the devil may
also be intended: cf. Middleton, *B.B.* (Bullen, VIII), p. 28, 'whilst I thumped
downstairs with my cowheel'.

Tearcat. *Alla corago* then.

Trapdoor. Good your honours and worships, enlarge the ears
    of commiseration, and let the sound of a hoarse military
    organ-pipe penetrate your pitiful bowels to extract out of
    them so many small drops of silver as may give a hard   75
    straw-bed lodging to a couple of maimed soldiers.

Jack Dapper. Where are you maimed?

Tearcat. In both our nether limbs.

Moll. Come, come, Dapper, let's give 'em something; 'las,
    poor men, what money have you? By my troth, I love a   80
    soldier with my soul.

Sir Beauteous. Stay, stay, where have you served?

Sir Thomas. In any part of the Low Countries?

Trapdoor. Not in the Low Countries, if it please your man-
    hood, but in Hungary against the Turk at the siege of   85
    Belgrade.

Lord Noland. Who served there with you, sirrah?

Trapdoor. Many Hungarians, Moldavians, Valachians, and

---

71. Alla corago] popular slang. Tearcat's version of the Italian, *coraggio*:
courage (an exhortation); Herford and Simpson note in reference to Jonson,
Case is Altered, I.v.6, 'The prefix *Alla* is merely Balthasar's blundering'; cf.
All's W., II.v.90, *Temp.*, V.i.258.

74. *bowels*] '(considered as the seat of the tender and sympathetic emotions,
hence): Pity, compassion, feeling, "heart"' (*O.E.D.*, sb.1, 3a).

76. *straw-bed*] a bed or mattress filled with straw: see W. Harrison, *Description of England*, ed. G. Edelen (Ithaca, N.Y., 1968), p. 201.

78.] possibly with a bawdy quibble, picked up in the reference to the Low
Countries, l. 83.

85–6. *Hungary ... Belgrade*] *Belgrade*, 'the capital of Serbia ... was held by
the Hungarians from 1086 to 1522, when it was taken by the Turkish Sultan
Solyman' (Sugden, p. 55). Trapdoor's claim is impossible. *The Turk*: i.e.
Solyman the Magnificent.

88–96.] I have retained Q's spellings of place-names, as they are probably
phonetic, and any inaccuracies are very likely deliberate.

88–9. *Moldavians ... Sclavonians*] i.e. soldiers from the general regions
under Hungarian rule. Moldavia is 'one of the Danubian provinces lying
north of Walachia and east of Transylvania ... and during the 16th century
was under the control of the Turks' (Sugden, p. 349). Walachia is 'the southern of the 2 provinces of Roumania, lying on the north bank of the Danube,
between Hungary and Bulgaria. The name Vlachs, or Wallacks ... was originally applied to all the Slavonic peoples of the Balkan district. Walachia, lying
between the Turkish and the Hungarian Kingdoms, was constantly involved
in their wars' (Sugden, p. 551). Transylvania or Siebenburgen constituted
'the east portion of Austro-Hungary, lying between Hungary proper,

Transylvanians, with some Sclavonians; and retiring
home, sir, the Venetian galleys took us prisoners, yet freed   90
us, and suffered us to beg up and down the country.

Jack Dapper. You have ambled all over Italy then?

Trapdoor. O sir, from Venice to Roma, Vecchio, Bononia,
Romania, Bolonia, Modena, Piacenza, and Tuscana with
all her cities, as Pistoia, Valteria, Mountepulchena,   95
Arrezzo, with the Siennois and diverse others.

Moll. Mere rogues, put spurs to 'em once more.

Jack Dapper. Thou lookest like a strange creature – a fat
butter-box – yet speakest English. What art thou?

Tearcat. Ick, mine here? Ick bin den ruffling Tearcat, den brave   100

100–4.] *as in Scott; black letter in Q.*

Moldavia and Walachia. It became subject to Hungary in A.D. 1004, but
gained its independence under John Zapolya in 1538, and was supported by
the Turks against the Hungarians during the 16th century' (Sugden, p. 522).
Sclavonians (Slavonians) was used generally in reference to the Slav races; but
cf. Dekker, *Belman*, sigs. C1v–2r, 'forthwith did the wicked Elder
[c]ommaund the young *Slauonians* that stood about him, to disfurnish him
that was so vnskilfull in the *Rudiments* of *Rogerie* of his best garment, and to
carry it presently to the *Bowsing Ken*', where the term is used loosely of the
company of young rogues.

90. *Venetian ... prisoners*] Thomas Coryat describes the pitiful case of an
Englishman made a galley-slave by the Venetians for accepting money as a
mercenary and afterwards fleeing (*Crudities* (ed. Edinburgh, 1905), I, 414).

93. *Vecchio*] Civitavecchia, the port of Rome.

93–4. *Bononia ... Bolonia*] 'One and the same place' (Dyce): Bologna.

94. *Romania*] Romagna.

Tuscana] Tuscany.

95. *Valteria*] Volterra.

Mountepulchena] Montepulchiano.

96. *Arrezzo*] Arezzo: Q's doubled *r* possibly signifies a heavy burr.

Siennois] i.e. Sienese, inhabitants of Siena; cf. 'Senoys', *All's W.*, I.ii.1.

99. *butter-box*] contemptuous term for a Dutchman.

100–4.] Cf. Dekker, *G.H.* (ed. Pendry), p. 107, '... if you read a *mittimus* in
the Constable's look, counterfeit to be a Frenchman, a Dutchman or any other
nation whose country is in peace with your own, and you may pass the pikes;
for being not able to understand you, they cannot by the customs of the City
take your examination and so by consequence they have nothing to say to
you.' The speech is presented essentially as it appears in Q since it seems to be
a more or less phonetic rendering, and is not strictly meant to be understood
in any case. Like the 'Dutch' speeches of Hans van Belch in Dekker and
Webster's *N.H.*, the passage is printed in Q in black letter. According to J. B.
Berns of the Instituut voor Dialectologie, Amsterdam, the forms are mainly

soldado. Ick bin dorick all Dutchlant gueresen. Der shellum
das meere ine beasa, ine woert gaeb; Ick slaag um stroakes on
tom cop, dastick den hundred touzun divel halle; frollick,
mine here.

Sir Beauteous. Here, here – [*About to give money*] let's be rid of   105
their jobbering.

Moll. Not a cross, Sir Beauteous. – You base rogues, I have
taken measure of you better than a tailor can, and I'll fit
you as you – monster with one eye – have fitted me.

Trapdoor. Your worship will not abuse a soldier!   110

Moll. Soldier? – Thou deservest to be hanged up by that
tongue which dishonours so noble a profession. – Soldier,
you skeldering varlet? – Hold, stand, there should be a
trap-door hereabouts.   *Pull*[*s*] *off his patch.*

Trapdoor. The balls of these glaziers of mine – mine eyes – shall   115

---

101. *Dutchlant*] Dyce; *Dutchlant. Q.*   105. s.d.] *Dyce subst. (after l. 106).*

Low-German with some High-German elements ('Dutch' and 'Dutchland' –
derived from 'Deutsch' – were often used in the 17th century in reference to
Germany). The grammar and sense are somewhat confused, but the meaning
is roughly as follows, 'I, my lord? I am the ruffling Tearcat, the brave soldier. I
have travelled through all Dutchland. [He is] the greater scoundrel who gives
an angry word. I beat him directly on the head, that you take out a hundred
thousand devils. [Be] merry, sir.' Among the remoter phonetic approxim-
ations are *meere*, the comparative of *viel*: much; *beasa (böse)*: angry; *ine (ihn)*:
him; *dastick (dass dich)*: that you; *stroakes (stracks)*: directly. In Dekker, *A
Strange Horse-Race*, sig. D4r, '*Schellum* in Dutch, a Theife' appears in the
margin. *Ruffling* is presumably in refernce to his rogue status: see l. 154n.
below. *Hundred touzun divel*] cf. Dekker, *W.B.*, V.ii.12–13, 'The little Captaine that's made all of fire, / Sweares (Flemming-like) by twenty thousand
Diuels'. *Frolic* = merry, joyous (*O.E.D.*); cf. *W. of E.*, II.ii.18.

106. *jobbering*] jabbering: 'Often applied, in contempt or derision, to the
speaking of a language which is unintelligible to the hearer' (*O.E.D.*).

107. *cross*] a coin with a cross stamped on one side.

108–9. *I'll fit you*] See I.ii.142 and n.; playing here on the tailor image.

109. *monster with one eye*] Cf. Middleton, *W.B.W.*, V.i.7–9 (Revels ed.),
where the Ward remarks in reference to the stage trap-door, 'here rose up a
devil with one eye'; Moll possibiy makes joking reference to a related stage
convention.

113. *skeldering*] begging, sponging, swindling.

114. *trap-door*] punning on his name.

115–16.] with Trapdoor's characteristic bawdy innuendo.

115. *glaziers*] a cant term for 'eyes' (given in Dekker, 'The Canter's Dictionary', *L.C.* (ed. Pendry), p. 194, also *O.P.* (ed. Pendry), p. 303).

be shot up and down in any hot piece of service for my
invincible mistress.

Jack Dapper. I did not think there had been such knavery in
black patches as now I see.

Moll. O sir, he hath been brought up in the Isle of Dogs, and   120
can both fawn like a spaniel and bite like a mastiff, as he
finds occasion.

Lord Noland. [*To Tearcat*] What are you, sirrah? A bird of this
feather too?

Tearcat. A man beaten from the wars, sir.   125

Sir Thomas. I think so, for you never stood to fight.

Jack Dapper. What's thy name, fellow soldier?

Tearcat. I am called by those that have seen my valour,
Tearcat.

All. Tearcat?   130

Moll. A mere whip-jack, and that is, in the commonwealth of
rogues, a slave that can talk of sea-fight, name all your
chief pirates, discover more countries to you than either
the Dutch, Spanish, French, or English ever found out;
yet indeed all his service is by land, and that is to rob a fair, 135
or some such venturous exploit. Tearcat – foot, sirrah, I

---

116. *shot*] Cf. '*To shoot one's eyes*: to gaze eagerly' (*O.E.D.*, 'shoot', 17c).

119. *patches*] possibly playing on the sense, 'clowns' or 'fools'.

120. *Isle of Dogs*] 'The peninsula of the Thames between the Limehouse,
Greenwich, and Blackwall Reaches . . . The name is said to have been given to
it because the King's hounds were formerly kept there' (Sugden, p. 154).
Dyce remarks, 'It seems to have been a place where persons took refuge from
their creditors and the officers of justice.' Cf. Dekker, *Sat.*, IV.i.133–5.

121. *fawn . . . spaniel*] Cf. 'As flattering (fawning) as a spaniel' (Tilley,
S704).

123–4. *bird of this feather*] Cf. 'Birds of a feather will flock together' (Tilley,
B393).

131. *whip-jack*] Cf. Dekker, *Belman*, sig. D3v: 'Then there is another sort of
nimble fingred knaues, and they are called *Whipiacks*: who talke of nothing
but fights at Sea, Piracies, drownings and shipwracks, trauelling both in the
Shapes and names of Mariners, with a counterfeit Licence to beg from towne
to towne, which licence they call a *Gybe*, and the Seales to it *Iarkes*. Their
cullour of wandring from Shire to shire (especially along the Sea coastes) is to
harken after their Ship that was ouerthrowne, or for the marchandize stolen
out of her, but the end of their land voyages is to rob Booths at faires, which
they call *heauing of the Booth*. These *Whipiacks* will talke of the Indies, and of
all countries that lye vnder heauen, but are indeed no more but fresh-water
Souldiers.'

have your name, now I remember me, in my book of
horners: horns for the thumb, you know how.

Tearcat. No indeed, Captain Moll – for I know you by sight – I
am no such nipping Christian, but a maunderer upon the   140
pad I confess; and meeting with honest Trapdoor here,
whom you had cashiered from bearing arms, out at elbows
under your colours, I instructed him in the rudiments of
roguery, and by my map made him sail over any country
you can name, so that now he can maunder better than   145
myself.

Jack Dapper. So then, Trapdoor, thou art turned soldier now.

Trapdoor. Alas, sir, now there's no wars, 'tis the safest course
of life I could take.

Moll. I hope then you can cant, for by your cudgels, you,   150
sirrah, are an upright man.

---

138. *horns for the thumb*] a piece of horn fashioned like a thimble to protect
the thief's thumb from the knife-blade when cutting a purse. Cf. Thomas
Preston, *Cambises*, (ed. E. Creeth, *Tudor Plays* (Garden City, N.Y., 1966)), ll.
1004–5, 'Frequent your exercises – a horne on your thumb, / A quick eye, a
sharp knife, at hand a receiver.'

140. *nipping*] 'He that cuts the purse is called the *Nip*', Dekker, *Belman*, sig.
H2v.

140–1. *maunderer upon the pad*] professional beggar upon the way or road.

142. *out at elbows*] proverbial tag: Tilley, E102.

145. *maunder*] beg.

150. *cant*] speak in the slang of vagabonds and rogues; Dekker gives an
account of the development of the canting language in *L.C.* (ed. Pendry),
p. 190.

by your cudgels] A woodcut in Harman, *Caveat for Common Cursitors*
(1566), reproduced in *Shakespeare's England*, II, opposite p. 492, depicts an
upright man holding a staff.

151. *upright man*] Harman in *Caveat* gives the *upright man* second place in
the hierarchy of rogues, but Dekker ranks him first, *Belman*, sig. C4r–v: 'An
Vpright-man is a sturdie Big-bonde Knaue, that neuer walkes but (like a
comaunder) with a short truncheon in his hand, which he cals his *Filchman*.
At markets, Faires, & other meetings, his voyce among *Beggars* is of the same
sound that a Constables is of: it is not to be contrould, He is free of all the
shires in England, but neuer stayes in any place long, the reason is, his profession is to be idle, which being looked into, he knowes is punishable, and
therefore to auoid the whip he wanders. . . . this band of *Vpright-men* sildome
march without fiue or sixe in a company, so that country people rather giue
them mony for feare then out of any deuotion. . . . For these vpright men stand
so much vppon their reputation, that they scorne any *Mort* or *Doxie* should be
seene to walke with them; and indeede what need they care for them, when he

Trapdoor. As any walks the highway, I assure you.

Moll. And Tearcat, what are you? A wild rogue, an angler, or a
    ruffler?

Tearcat. Brother to this upright man, flesh and blood: ruffling   155
    Tearcat is my name, and a ruffler is my style, my title, my
    profession.

---

may commaund any *Doxie* to leaue another man and to lye with him; the other
not daring to murmure against it. An vpright man will seldome complaine of
want, for whatsoeuer any one of his profession doth steale, he may challenge a
share in it, yea and may commaund any inferiour *Rogue* to fetch in booty to
serue his turne. These carry the shapes of soldiers, and can talke of the *Low-
Countries*, though they neuer were beyond *Douer*.'

153. *wild rogue*] described by Dekker (following Harman closely), *Belman*,
sig. D2r: 'a *Wilde Rogue* ... is a spirit that cares not in what circle he rises, nor
into the company of what Diuels he falles: In his swadling clouts is he marked
to be a villaine, and in his breeding is instructed to bee so ... These *Wilde-
Rogues* (like Wilde geese) keepe in flockes, and all the day loyter in the fieldes,
(if the weather be warme) and at Brick-killes, or else disperse themselues in
colde weather, to Rich-mens doores, and at night haue their meetings in
barnes or other out-places, where (twentie or more in a company) they engen-
der male and Female, euerie one catching her whome he doth best fancy, the
stronger and more sturdie, keeping the weaker in subiection: their language is
bawdy talk, damned othes, and plots where to filtch the next morning, which
they perform betimes: rising as earely as the Sunne, and enioyning their
punckes to looke out for cheates, to make their meeting at night the merrier.'

angler] described by Dekker (following Harman closely), in *Belman*, sig.
D1r: 'An *Angler* is a limb of an *Vpright-man*, as being deriued from him: their
apparell in which they walke is commonly freize Ierkins and gally slops: in the
day time they Beg from house to house, not so much for releefe, as to spye
what lyes fit for their nets, which in the night following they fish for. The Rod
they angle with, is a staffe of fiue or sixe foote in length, in which within one
inch of the top is a little hole boared quite through, into which hole they put an
yron hooke, and with the same do they angle at windowes about midnight: the
draught they pluck vp, being apparel, sheets, couerlets, or whatsoeuer their
yron hookes can lay hould of.'

154. *ruffler*] given first place in the rogue hierarchy by Harman and ranked
second by Dekker, *Belman*, sig. D1r: 'The next in degree to him [the upright
man] is cal'd a *Ruffler*: the *Ruffler* and the *Vp-right-man* are so like in conditions, that you would sweare them Brothers: they walke with cudgels alike,
they professe armes alike, though they be both out at elbooves, and
will sweare they lost their limbes in their Countries quarrell, when either they are
lame by diseases, or haue bene mangled in some drunken quarrell: These
commonly are fellowes that haue stood aloofe in the warres, and whilst others
fought, they tooke their heeles and ran away from their Captaine, or else they
haue bene *Seruingmen*, whome for their behauiour, no man would trust with a
liuery: if they cannot spend their daies to their mindes by their own begging or
robbing of Countrie people that come late from Markets (for vppon those they

Moll. Sirrah, where's your doxy? – Halt not with me.

All. Doxy, Moll? What's that?

Moll. His wench. 160

Trapdoor. My doxy? I have, by the solomon, a doxy that carries
a kinchin mort in her slate at her back, besides my dell and
my dainty wild dell, with all whom I'll tumble this next
darkmans in the strommel, and drink ben booze, and eat a

---

161. doxy?] *Reed;* doxy Q.   162. kinchin] *Reed;* kitchin Q.   164. booze]
Bullen subst.; baufe Q.

---

most vsually excersise their trade) then do they compell the inferior subiects
of their common wealth (as *Rogues, Palliards, Morts, Doxies* &c) to pay tribute
vnto them. A *Ruffler* after a yeare or two takes state vpon him, and becomes an
Vpright-man (but no honest man.)'

158. *Halt*] (1) waver, vacillate; (2) play false; (3) playing on Trapdoor's
pretended lameness.

161–2. *doxy . . . dell*] Dekker describes the various degrees of women in the
commonwealth of rogues in *Belman*, sigs. D4v–E1r: '. . . the young ones and
the least are called *Kinchin-Morts*, and those are Girles of a yeare or two old,
which the *Morts* (their Mothers) carrie at their backes in their slates (which in
the *Canting* tongue are sheetes) . . . The second bird of this feather is a *Del*, and
that is a yong wench, ripe for the act of Generation, but as yet not spoyled of
her maiden-head: these *Dels* are reserued as dishes for the *Vpright-men*, for
none but they must haue ye first tast of them, & after the *Vpright-men* haue
defloored them, (which commonly is when they are verie yong) then are they
free for any of the brother-hood, & are called *Dels* no more, but *doxies*. Of
these *Dels* some are tearmed *Wilde-dels*, and those are such as are borne and
begotten vnder a hedge: the other are yong wenches that either by death of
parents, the villanie of Executors, or the crueltie of Maisters or Mistresses fall
into this infamous and damnable course of life. When they haue gotten the
title of *Doxies*, then are they common for any, and walke for the moste part
with their betters, (who are a degree aboue them) called *Morts*, but whensoeuer an *Vprightman* is in presence, the *Doxie* is onely at his commaund.
These *Doxies* will for good victualls or a small peece of money, prostitute their
bodies to seruingmen if they can get into any conuenient corner about their
Masters houses, & to ploughmen in Barnes, Haylofts or stables: they are
common pick-pockets, familiars with the baser sorts of cut-purses, and
oftentimes secret murtherers of those infants which are begotten of their
bodies. These *Doxies* haue one speciall badge to bee knowne by, for most of
them goe working of laces and shirt strings, or such like stuffe, onely to giue
colour to their idle wandring.'

161. *solomon*] given by Dekker in 'The Canter's Dictionary' (*L.C.*, ed.
Pendry, p. 195) as the equivalent of 'the mass'.

164. *darkmans*] night.

strommel] straw (variant of strummel).

ben booze] good drink.

fat gruntling-cheat, a cackling-cheat, and a quacking-   165
cheat.

Jack Dapper. Here's old cheating!

Trapdoor. My doxy stays for me in a boozing ken, brave
captain.

Moll. He says his wench stays for him in an ale-house. – [*To*   170
Trapdoor, Tearcat] You are no pure rogues.

Tearcat. Pure rogues? No, we scorn to be pure rogues; but if
you come to our libken, or our stalling-ken, you shall find
neither him nor me a queer cuffin.

Moll. So, sir, no churl of you.   175

Tearcat. No, but a ben cove, a brave cove, a gentry cuffin.

Lord Noland. Call you this canting?

Jack Dapper. Zounds, I'll give a schoolmaster half a crown a
week and teach me this pedlar's French.

Trapdoor. Do but stroll, sir, half a harvest with us, sir, and you   180
shall gabble your bellyful.

165–6. *gruntling-cheat ... quacking-cheat*] *Cheat* is cant for 'thing'; cf.
Dekker, *L.C.* (ed. Pendry), p. 191, '... a *grunting cheat* a "pig", a *cackling
cheat* a "cock" or a "capon", a *quacking cheat* a "duck".' 'To gruntle' means
'to make the noise of a swine'; cf. ll. 229–30 below.

167. *old*] great, abundant.

168. *boozing ken*] ale-house.

brave] worthy, excellent.

171. *pure rogues*] possibly 'ironical' as Bullen suggested, but Moll may be
asking if they are thorough rogues; they have confessed only to begging.

173. *libken*] place to sleep.

stalling-ken] house for receiving stolen goods.

174–6. *queer cuffin ... gentry cuffin*] Dekker in *L.C.* (ed. Pendry), p. 191,
enumerates the distinctions: 'The word *cove* or *cofe* or *cuffin* signifies a "man",
a "fellow", etc., but differs something in his property according as it meets
with other words, for a "gentleman" is called a *gentry cove* or *cofe*, a "good
fellow" is a *bene cofe*, a "churl" is called a *queer cuffin* (*queer* signifies "naught"
and *cuffin*, as I said before, a "man") and in canting they term a "Justice of
Peace" (because he punisheth them, belike) by no other name than by *queer
cuffin*, that's to say a "churl" or a "naughty man"; and so *ken* signifying a
"house", they call a "prison" a *queer ken*, that's so say an "ill house".'

175. *of*] in the person of.

179. *pedlar's French*] cant, underworld slang.

180. *half a harvest*] i.e. half their season of 'takings': cf. Dekker, *Belman*,
sig. H3v, speaking of termers, '... whereupon some of these *Boote-halers*, are
called *Termers*, and they plye Westminster Hal: Michaelmas Terme is their
haruest, and they sweat in it harder then reapers or hay-makers doe at their
works in the heat of summer'; also Middleton, *M.T.*, II.iii.210–13.

Moll. [*To Trapdoor*] Come you rogue, cant with me.

Sir Thomas. Well said, Moll. – [*To Trapdoor*] Cant with her,
    sirrah, and you shall have money – else not a penny.

Trapdoor. I'll have a bout if she please.   185

Moll. Come on, sirrah.

Trapdoor. Ben mort, shall you and I heave a booth, mill a ken,
    or nip a bung? And then we'll couch a hogshead under the
    ruffmans, and there you shall wap with me, and I'll niggle
    with you.   190

Moll. Out, you damned impudent rascal! [*Hits and kicks him.*]

Trapdoor. Cut benar whids, and hold your fambles and your
    stamps!

Lord Noland. Nay, nay, Moll, why art thou angry? What was
    his gibberish?   195

Moll. Marry, this, my lord, says he: 'Ben mort' – good wench –
    'shall you and I heave a booth, mill a ken, or nip a bung?' –
    shall you and I rob a house, or cut a purse?

All. Very good!

Moll. 'And then we'll couch a hogshead under the ruffmans,' –   200
    and then we'll lie under a hedge.

Trapdoor. That was my desire, captain, as 'tis fit a soldier
    should lie.

Moll. 'And there you shall wap with me, and I'll niggle with
    you,' – and that's all.   205

Sir Beauteous. Nay, nay, Moll, what's that wap?

Jack Dapper. Nay, teach me what niggling is; I'd fain be
    niggling.

Moll. Wapping and niggling is all one: the rogue my man can
    tell you.   210

Trapdoor. 'Tis fadoodling, if it please you.

Sir Beauteous. This is excellent; one fit more, good Moll.

---

187. *heave a booth*] rob a booth: see ll. 131n. In 'The Canter's Dictionary'
(*L.C.*, ed. Pendry, p. 194), Dekker gives, '*heave a bough*, rob a booth'; *bough*
and *booth* were apparently used indiscriminately.

    188. *couch a hogshead*] sleep: the phrase become proverbial (Tilley, H504).

    189. *wap . . . niggle*] cant terms for 'copulate'.

    192-3.] 'Speak better words and hold your hands and legs' (Dyce).

    202-3. *fit . . . lie*] i.e. presumably in bivouac.

    211. *fadoodling*] apparently a nonce word, a euphemism for 'copulation'.

    212. *fit*] (1) a part of a poem or song; (2) a strain of music.

Moll. [*To Tearcat*] Come, you rogue, sing with me.

               The Song.

	A gage of ben Rome-booze	
	In a boozing ken of Rome-ville	215
Tearcat.	*Is benar than a caster,*	
	Peck, pannam, lap, or popler	
	Which we mill in Deuce-a-ville.	
Moll, Tearcat.	*O, I would lib all the lightmans,*	
	O, I would lib all the darkmans,	220
	By the solomon, under the ruffmans,	
	By the solomon, in the harmans,	
Tearcat.	*And scour the queer cramp-ring,*	
	And couch till a palliard docked my dell,	

213.1. The Song] *Reed; to the right of l. 219 Q.*   217. pannam] *Bowers;* pennam *Q.* lap] *Bullen;* lay *Q.*   219, 226. Moll, Tearcat] *Bowers subst.; not in Q.*   222. harmans] *M. Thesis;* Hartmans *Q.*   223. Tearcat] *Q subst.;* Moll *Scott.* queer] *Dyce;* Quire *Q.*

214–27.] 'A quart pot of good wine in an ale-house of London is better than a cloak, meat, bread, butter-milk (or whey), or porridge, which we steal in the country. O I would lie all the day, O I would lie all the night, by the mass, under the woods (or bushes), by the mass, in the stocks, and wear bolts (or fetters), and lie till a palliard lay with my wench, so my drunken head might quaff wine well. Avast to the highway, let us hence, &c.' (Dyce). Cf. Dekker, *L.C.* (ed. Pendry), pp. 195–6. Q gives only the first two lines of the song to Moll, followed by two consecutive *T.Cat.* speech headings at ll. 216 and 223, so a heading or two is presumably missing. Various arrangements are possible, but the present one which follows Bowers brings Moll in for the refrains.

217. pannam] bread. Q's 'pennam' is probably a variant spelling.

lap] butter-milk or whey. Q's 'lay' is very likely a simple misprint for *lap*, as Reed proposed: cf. Dekker, *L.C.* (ed. Pendry), p. 195, 'If we maund pannam, lap or ruff peck'. Moll translates merely as 'drink' at l. 259 below.

223. queer cramp-ring] Dekker gives '*to scour the cramp ring*, to wear bolts' in 'The Canter's Dictionary' (*L.C.*, ed. Pendry, p. 195). *Queer* generally means bad or evil, as Dekker notes in *L.C.* (see ll. 174–6n. above).

224. palliard] described by Dekker (following Harman closely) in *Belman*, sig. D2v: '*A Palliard* ... likewise is cal'd a *Clapperdugeon*: his vpper Garment is an olde cloake made of as many peeces patchd together, as there bee villanies in him: this *Palliard* neuer goes without a *Mort* at his heeles whome he calles his wife. ... A *Palliard* caries about him (for feare of the worst) a Certificate (vnder a Ministers hand, with the Parishes name, which shall bee sure to stand farre enough) where this *Mort* and he were married, when all is but forged: many Irishmen are of this lowsie Regiment, & some *Welchmen*: And the better either to draw pittie from men, as also to giue cullor to their lame wandring,

> *So my boozy nab might skew Rome-booze*
> > *well.*   225

Moll, Tearcat.   *Avast to the pad, let us bing,*
> *Avast to the pad, let us bing.*

All. Fine knaves, i'faith.

Jack Dapper. The grating of ten new cart-wheels, and the
> gruntling of five hundred hogs coming from Romford   230
> market cannot make a worse noise than this canting lan-
> guage does in my ears. Pray, my Lord Noland, let's give
> these soldiers their pay.

Sir Beauteous. Agreed, and let them march.

Lord Noland. [*Gives money*.] Here, Moll.   235

Moll. [*To Trapdoor, Tearcat*] Now I see that you are stalled to
> the rogue and are not ashamed of your professions: look
> you, my Lord Noland here, and these gentlemen, bestows
> upon you two, two bords and a half: that's two shillings
> sixpence.   240

Trapdoor. Thanks to your lordship.

Tearcat. Thanks, heroical captain.

Moll. Away.

Trapdoor. We shall cut ben whids of your masters and
> mistress-ship wheresoever we come.   245

---

230. Romford] *Q* (*Rumford*).

---

with *Sperewort* or *Arsenick* will they in one night poyson their Leg, be it neuer
so sound, and raise a blister, which at their pleasure they can take off againe.'

225. So] so long as.

skew] an apparently unique usage as a verb, meaning 'drink'. *Skew*, 'a cup',
is common.

230–1. *Romford market*] Romford, a town in Essex twelve miles north-east
of London, held a famous hog market every Tuesday (possibly playing on
Rome-booze, Rome-ville). Cf. Middleton, *C.M. in C.*, IV.i.91 (Revels ed.).

236–7. *stalled to the rogue*] i.e. initiated or ordained as a rogue: cf. Dekker,
Belman, sig. C2r: 'This done, the *Grand Signior* called for a Gage of Bowse,
which belike signified a quart of drink, for presently a pot of Ale being put into
his hand, he made the young *Squier* kneele downe, and powring the full pot on
his pate, vttered these words. *I doe stall thee to the Rogue, by vertue of this
soueraigne English liquor, so that hence forth it shall be lawfull for thee to Cant
(that is to say) to be a Vagabond and beg, and to speake that pedlers French, or
that Canting language, which is to be found among none but beggers.*'

239. bords] shillings.

244. cut ben whids] speak good words.

Moll. [*To Trapdoor*] You'll maintain, sirrah, the old justice's
    plot to his face?
Trapdoor. Else trine me on the cheats: hang me!
Moll. Be sure you meet me there.
Trapdoor. Without any more maundering, I'll do't. – Follow,   250
    brave Tearcat.
Tearcat. I prae, sequor; let us go, mouse.

               Exeunt they two, manet the rest.

Lord Noland. Moll, what was in that canting song?
Moll. Troth, my lord, only a praise of good drink, the only milk
    which these wild beasts love to suck, and thus it was: 255

           A rich cup of wine,
           O it is juice divine!
           More wholesome for the head
           Than meat, drink, or bread;
           To fill my drunken pate   260
           With that, I'd sit up late;
           By the heels would I lie,
           Under a lousy hedge die,
           Let a slave have a pull
           At my whore, so I be full   265
           Of that precious liquor –

and a parcel of such stuff, my lord, not worth the opening.

Enter a Cutpurse *very gallant, with four or five* Men *after him,*
               one with a wand.

Lord Noland. What gallant comes yonder?
Sir Thomas. Mass, I think I know him: 'tis one of Cumberland.

---

250. do't –] *Dyce;* doo't, Q.   266. *liquor* –] *M. Thesis, Gomme;* liquor; Q.

248. *trine me on the cheats*] hang me on the gallows.
   250. *maundering*] 'muttering, talking' (Dyce); possibly playing on the cant
sense, 'begging'.
   252. *I prae, sequor*] 'Go first, I will follow' (Lat.: the present tense carries
the force of the future); the phrase occurs twice in Terence: *Andria*, I.171, and
Eunuchus, I.908.
   267.1. *gallant*] finely dressed, smart.
   267.2. *wand*] a light walking-stick (*O.E.D.*, 1c); or possibly a riding switch,
as Hoy suggests. Cf. Jonson, Chapman and Marston, *Eastward Ho*, II.ii.217
s.d., '*Enter Sir Petronell in Bootes, with a riding wan*', and Herford and
Simpson's note.
   269. *Cumberland*] a county in north-west England; the reference seems
chiefly for the sake of the name play which follows, l. 276.

1 Cutpurse. Shall we venture to shuffle in amongst yon heap of   270
    gallants, and strike?

2 Cutpurse. 'Tis a question whether there be any silver shells
    amongst them, for all their satin outsides.

All Cutpurses. Let's try!

Moll. Pox on him, a gallant? – Shadow me, I know him: 'tis one   275
    that cumbers the land indeed; if he swim near to the shore
    of any of your pockets, look to your purses!

All. Is't possible?

Moll. This brave fellow is no better than a foist.

All. Foist? What's that?   280

Moll. A diver with two fingers: a pickpocket. All his train study
    the figging-law, that's to say, cutting of purses and foist-
    ing. One of them is a nip: I took him once i' the twopenny
    gallery at the Fortune; then there's a cloyer, or snap, that
    dogs any new brother in that trade, and snaps will have   285

274, 294. *All Cutpurses.*] *Bowers subst.; Omnes Q.*   274. try!] *M. Thesis;* try?
Q.   278. *All*] *Omnes Q passim; L. Nol./S. Beau., &c. Dyce passim.*

---

271. *strike*] pick a pocket or cut a purse: see ll. 281–92n.

272. *shells*] money: see ll. 281–92n.

276. *cumbers*] harasses, distresses, troubles.

277. *purses*] 'Sixteenth-century purses were made of leather and silks, usually embroidered, and were drawn at the top by strings. Such strings were
often . . . adorned by tassels. They were carried in the sleeve, in hose, or hung
at the girdle' (Linthicum, p. 276).

279. *brave*] finely arrayed.

281–92.] Dekker describes the elements of the 'Figging Law' in *Belman*,
sigs. H2v–3r: 'This *Figging Law* (like the body of some monstrous and terrible
beast) stands vpon ten feete, or rather lifts vp proudly ten Dragon-like heads:
the names of which heads are these. *viz.* He that cuts the purse is called the
Nip. He that is halfe with him is the *Snap*, or the *Cloyer*. The knife is called a
Cuttle-bung. He that pickes the pocket is called a *Foist*. He that faceth the man
is the *Stale*. The taking of the purse is called *Drawing*. The spying of this
villanie is called *Smoking* or *Boyling*. The purse is the *Bung*. The money the
Shels. The act doing is called *Striking*.'

283–4. *twopenny gallery at the Fortune*] This gallery is described in the
builder's contract: see Chambers, *E.S.*, II, 436–7. Cf. Dekker, *Belman* (1st
ed.), sig. H3v, 'Others [i.e. thieves] haunt Play-houses onely and the Beare-
garden' (the 3rd ed. alters 'Play-houses' to 'Ale-houses'), and *Ravens
Almanacke*, sig. B2v, '. . . suffer mee to carrie vp your thoughts vpon nimbler
wings, where (as if you sat in the moste perspicuous place of the two penny
gallerie in a Play-house, you shall cleerelye, and with an open eye beholde all
the parts'. The *Fortune* was the theatre in which *R.G.* was first performed. See
I.ii.26n.

half in any booty. He with the wand is both a stale, whose
office is to face a man i' the streets whilst shells are drawn
by another, and then with his black conjuring rod in his
hand, he, by the nimbleness of his eye and juggling stick,
will in cheaping a piece of plate at a goldsmith's stall, make   290
four or five rings mount from the top of his caduceus and,
as if it were at leap-frog, they skip into his hand presently.

2 Cutpurse. Zounds, we are smoked!

All Cutpurses. Ha?

2 Cutpurse. We are boiled, pox on her; see Moll, the roaring   295
drab!

1 Cutpurse. All the diseases of sixteen hospitals boil her! –
Away!

Moll. Bless you, sir.

1 Cutpurse. And you, good sir.   300

Moll. Dost not ken me, man?

1 Cutpurse. No, trust me, sir.

Moll. Heart, there's a knight, to whom I'm bound for many
favours, lost his purse at the last new play i' the Swan –
seven angels in't: make it good, you're best; do you see? –   305
No more.

1 Cutpurse. A synagogue shall be called, Mistress Mary: dis-

304. Swan –] *This ed.;* Swanne, Q.

---

290. *cheaping*] bidding for, bargaining over.

291. *caduceus*] i.e. his wand; Mercury, the protector of thieves, carried a
caduceus and by association, 'mercury' came to mean 'a dexterous thief'; his
caduceus was often referred to as his 'wand' (*O.E.D.*, 7b).

293, 295. *smoked ... boiled*] See ll. 281–92n.

296. *drab*] whore.

304. *last new play i' the Swan*] See Intro., p. 12. The Swan Theatre was
situated on the south bank of the Thames in the north-east corner of Paris
Garden. The only surviving play known to have been performed there is
Middleton's *C.M. in C.* The so-called de Witt drawing depicts the interior of
this theatre.

305. *make it good*] See Intro., p. 14, for Moll Frith's involvement in the
recovery of a purse in 1621. In R. Brome's *Court Beggar* (1639–40), II.i, Cit-
wit is to go to 'honest Moll' in search of his purse after having had his pocket
picked. He later professes that she conducts a private trade for the retrieval of
such property. *The Life and Death of Mrs. Mary Frith* (1662) claims that she
acted as a receiver of stolen goods for much of her life.

307. *synagogue*] Dekker describes the meetings of the practitioners of the
Figging Law in *Belman*, sig. H4r–v: 'All the troopes of both sexes being sub-
iect to the discipline of the *Grand Nips* & *foists*, and from whome, the better to

grace me not; *pacus palabros*, I will conjure for you.
Farewell.

[*Exeunt* Cutpurses.]

Moll. Did not I tell you, my lord?   310

Lord Noland. I wonder how thou camest to the knowledge of
these nasty villains.

Sir Thomas. And why do the foul mouths of the world call thee
Moll Cutpurse? – A name, methinks, damned and odious.

Moll. Dare any step forth to my face and say,   315
'I have ta'en thee doing so, Moll'? I must confess,
In younger days, when I was apt to stray,
I have sat amongst such adders, seen their stings –
As any here might – and in full playhouses
Watched their quick-diving hands, to bring to shame   320
Such rogues, and in that stream met an ill name.
When next, my lord, you spy any one of those –
So he be in his art a scholar – question him,

---

321. name.] *Dyce;* name: *Q.*

---

receiue directions both what to doe, and what quarters to keepe (for they shift
their walkes according to the pleasure of the chiefe rangers, they haue a certaine house, sometimes at one end of the town, sometimes at another, which is
their hall; at this Hall the whole company doe meete verie orderly: by which
meanes whensoeuer any notable or workmanlike strok is stricken, though it
were as farre as the North-borders, yet can the rest of the *Fig-boies* heere
resident in London, tell by whome this worthy Act was plaide. At this solemn meeting in their Hall, they choose Wardens, and Steward: the Wardens
office is to establish wholesome Lawes to keepe life in their rotten common
wealth, and to assigne out to euerie man his Stations. The treasurers office is
verie truely (though he be an arrant theefe) to render an account of such
monies as are put into his hands vpon trust: for of euerie purse (that is cleanely
conueyed and hath good store of Shels in it) a ratable portion is deliuered (in
Banck as it were) to the Treasurer, to the intent that when any of them is taken
and cast into prison, a *Flag* of truce may presently be hung out, and composition offered to the wronged partie, thereby to saue a brother of the societie
from riding westward.' In *L.C.* (ed. Pendry), p. 200, he refers to an underworld gathering as a 'satanical synagogue', in allusion to Rev. ii.9.

308. pacus palabros] the Cutpurse's approximation of the Spanish *pocas
palabras*: 'few words' (cf. 'Few words show men wise' (Tilley, W799)). The
phrase was common: cf. Dekker, *Wonderful Year* (ed. Pendry), p. 57, Kyd,
Spanish Tragedy, III.xiv.118 (Revels ed.), *Shr.*, Ind. i.5, *Ado.*, III.v.15–16,
and the Latin form, *pauca verba*, which occurs in *Wiv.*, I.i.108, and *L.L.L.*,
IV.ii.155–6. See Herford and Simpson, IX, 380.

323. So] so long as.

Tempt him with gold to open the large book
Of his close villainies; and you yourself shall cant   325
Better than poor Moll can, and know more laws
Of cheaters, lifters, nips, foists, puggards, curbers,
With all the devil's blackguard, than it is fit

---

326. *laws*] Cf. 'figging-law': Dekker describes various similar 'laws' in *Belman*.

327. *cheaters*] described by Dekker in *Belman*, sigs. E3v–4r: 'Of all which *Lawes*, the *Highest* in place, and the *Highest* in perdition is the *Cheating* Law, or the art of winning mony by false dyce. Those that practise this study cal themselues *Cheaters*, the Dice *Cheaters*, and the money which they purchase *Cheates*: borrowing the tearme from our common Lawyers, with whom all such casuals as fal to the Lord at the holding of his *Leetes*, as *Waifes*, *Straies*, & such like, are said to be *Escheated to the Lords vse*, and are called *Cheates*.'

lifters] described by Dekker, *Belman*, sig. G4r: 'The *Lifting Law* . . . teacheth a kinde of lifting of goods cleane away. In such liftings are three sorts of Leauers vsed to get vp the baggage. *viz*. He that first stealeth the parcell is called *The Lift*. He that receiues it is the *Marker*. He that stands without and carries it away, is the *Santar*. The goods thus purchased, is called *Garbage*, which *Garbage* is sometime plate or Iewels, sometimes peeces of veluet, sometimes cloakes or Lawyers gownes, sometimes one thing sometimes another.'

puggards] probably 'thieves' of some description. This is the only recorded usage, although 'pugging' occurs in *Wint.*, IV.iii.7. As J. H. P. Pafford has noted in his new Arden edition (1963), *puggard* may have arisen from a misread manuscript 'pri' in 'priggard'; 'prigging' was a common cant term for thieving, especially of horses or 'prancers'.

curbers] explained by Dekker, *Belman*, sig. G2r: '. . . the *Curbing Law* teaches . . . how to hooke goods out of a window . . . This *Curbing Law* spreads it selfe into foure maine branches. He that hookes is calld the *Curber*. He that plays the spy is the *Warpe*. The *Hooke is the Curbe*. The goods are called *Snappings*. The *Gin* to open the window is a *Tricker*. The office of the *Curber* is for the most part betimes in the mornings (at the discharging of a watch) to be vp more earely then a noyse of shrugging fidlers; and the husbandrie which he followes, is in the day time to watch what shops or windowes stand fittest for his trade.'

328. *blackguard*] 'a guard of attendants, black in person, dress, or character; a following of "black" villains' (*O.E.D.*, 2); cf. Dekker, *L.C.* (ed. Pendry), p. 201, 'The great Lord of Limbo did therefore command all his black guard that stood about him to bestir them in their places and to defend the Court wherein they lived, threatening besides that his curse and all the plagues of stinking Hell should fall upon his officers, servants and subjects . . .'

328–9. *fit . . . wit*] a notion which occurs in Plato's *Republic*; cf. Sir Thomas Elyot, *The Governor* (ed. 1907, repr. 1962), pp. 293–300. See Intro., pp. 12–13. Thomas Coryat in his chapter on Venice in *Crudities* (1611), gave a detailed description of the famous Venetian courtesans, and included an engraving of himself with one (ed. Glasgow, 1905, I, opposite p. 408). Cf. Dekker, *P.W.* (ed. Pendry), p. 117–44.

Should be discovered to a noble wit.
I know they have their orders, offices,   330
Circuits, and circles, unto which they are bound,
To raise their own damnation in.
Jack Dapper.   How dost thou know it?
Moll. As you do: I show it you, they to me show it.
Suppose, my lord, you were in Venice.
Lord Noland.   Well.
Moll. If some Italian pander there would tell   335
All the close tricks of courtesans, would not you
Hearken to such a fellow?
Lord Noland.   Yes.
Moll.   And here,
Being come from Venice, to a friend most dear
That were to travel thither, you would proclaim
Your knowledge in those villainies, to save   340
Your friend from their quick danger: must you have
A black ill name because ill things you know?
Good troth, my lord, I am made Moll Cutpurse so.
How many are whores in small ruffs and still looks?
How many chaste whose names fill slander's books?   345
Were all men cuckolds, whom gallants in their scorns

---

333. do:] *M. Thesis;* do, *Q.*   342. know?] *Reed;* know, *Q.*

---

336. *close tricks*] secret customs or deceptions.
341–2. *must … know*] Cf. T. Coryat, *Crudities* (ed. 1905), I, 408: 'Neither can I be perswaded that it ought to be esteemed for a staine or blemish to the reputation of an honest and ingenuous man to see a Cortezan in her house, and note her manners and conversation, because according to the old maxime, Cognitio mali non est mala, the knowledge of evill is not evill, but the practice and execution thereof. For I thinke that a virtuous man will be the more confirmed and settled in virtue by the observation of some vices, then if he did not at all know what they were.' Cf. also Middleton, *T.C.O.O.*, V.ii.154, 'She that knows sin, knows best how to hate sin', and Dekker, *2 H.W.*, V.ii.210–12, 'I was in Bedlam once, but was I mad? / They made mee pledge Whores healths, but am I bad, / Because I'm with bad people?' See Intro., pp. 12–13.
344–5.] Cf. Dekker, *2 H.W.*, II.i.264–5, 'All are not Bawds (I see now) that keepe doores, / Nor all good wenches that are markt for Whores'.
344. *small ruffs*] Cf. Middleton, *F.H.T.* (Bullen, VIII), p. 69, 'diminutive as a puritan's ruff'; also Jonson, *Bartholomew Fair*, III.ii.112 (Revels ed.).
346–7.] a common proverbial construction; cf. 'If all fools wore white caps we should seem a flock of geese' (Tilley, F549).

Call so, we should not walk for goring horns.
Perhaps for my mad going, some reprove me;
I please myself, and care not else who loves me.
All. A brave mind, Moll, i'faith.   350
Sir Thomas. Come, my lord, shall's to the ordinary?
Lord Noland. Ay, 'tis noon sure.
Moll. Good my lord, let not my name condemn me to you or to
the world; a fencer, I hope, may be called a coward: is he so
for that? If all that have ill names in London were to be   355
whipped and to pay but twelvepence apiece to the beadle,
I would rather have his office than a constable's.
Jack Dapper. So would I, Captain Moll: 'twere a sweet tickling
office, i'faith.   *Exeunt.*

[V.ii]

Enter SIR ALEXANDER WENGRAVE, GOSHAWK *and* GREENWIT, *and
others.*

Sir Alexander. My son marry a thief! – That impudent girl
Whom all the world stick their worst eyes upon!
Greenwit. How will your care prevent it?
Goshawk.   'Tis impossible!
They marry close; they're gone, but none knows whither.
Sir Alexander. O gentlemen, when has a father's heart-strings   5

V.ii] *Dyce; not in Q.*   1. thief! –] *M. Thesis;* theefe, *Q.*

---

348. *mad*] wild, or eccentric: cf. Mad Moll.
353–4. *name ... world*] Cf. 'He that has an ill name is half hanged' (Tilley, N25).
356–7. *beadle ... constable's*] The constable's was apparently the more naturally desirable office by reason of wages, duties and possibly bribes. The beadle, an inferior parish officer, punished petty offenders, generally by whipping. The situation would be reversed in Moll's hypothetical instance. Cf. *Per.,* II.i.89–93.
358. *'twere*] it would be.
tickling] pleasing, diverting.

V.ii]
4. *close*] secretly.

Held out so long from breaking?

Enter a Servant.

                                    – Now what news, sir?
Servant. They were met upo'th' water an hour since, sir,
    Putting in towards the Sluice.
Sir Alexander.   The Sluice? – Come gentlemen,
    'Tis Lambeth works against us.

                                    [*Exit* Servant.]
Greenwit.   And that Lambeth
    Joins more mad matches than your six wet towns   10
    'Twixt that and Windsor Bridge, where fares lie soaking.
Sir Alexander. Delay no time, sweet gentlemen: to Blackfriars!
    We'll take a pair of oars and make after 'em.

---

6. breaking?] *Reed;* breaking: *Q.*   6.1.] *Gomme; on the right after l. 5*
Q.   12. Blackfriars!] *Collier;* Blacke Fryars, *Q.*

8–9. *the Sluice ... Lambeth*] 'The embankment along the Thames which
was built to protect the low-lying district of Lambeth Marsh from inunda-
tions. It was used as a landing-place for those who crossed the river to Lambeth' (Sugden, p. 471). *Lambeth* is 'a district on the south side of the Thames,
between Battersea and Southwark. Now densely populated, but in the 16th
and 17th centuries it was a low swampy tract of open country, and was known
as Lambeth Marsh. The only buildings of any importance were the palaces of
the Archbishop of Canterbury and the Bishop of Rochester. ... [Lambeth
Marsh] was a notorious haunt of thieves, prostitutes, and other bad characters' (Sugden, pp. 296–7).
    9.1.] No exit is marked in Q, and unless this is the same servant who enters
at l. 124.1 below, the s.d. is not required.
    9–11. *Lambeth ... soaking*] presumably in reference to the number of wed-
dings conducted by the Archbishop of Canterbury and the Bishop of Rochester, but possibly also glancing at the combination of holy and profane
within Lambeth itself (see ll. 8–9n.). John Nichol (Reed) surmised the *six wet
towns* to be 'Fulham, Richmond, Kingston, Hampton, Chertsey, Staines. –
The other intermediate towns are Chelsea, Battersea, Kew, Isleworth,
Twickenham, and Walton.' *Windsor Bridge* spans the Thames, connecting
Windsor with Eton opposite. Gomme notes that the phrase *where fares like
soaking* 'suggests the use of the riverside towns for sexual excursions'.
    12. *Blackfriars*] Blackfriars Stairs was a landing-stage on the north side of
the Thames, where Blackfriars Bridge now stands (Sugden, p. 64). This is
presumably the landing-stage closest to hand; from it Lambeth and the
Tower (l. 15) are in opposite directions – hence Sir Alexander's indecision.
    13. *pair of oars*] See IV.ii.165n.

Enter TRAPDOOR.

Trapdoor. Your son and that bold masculine ramp, my
 mistress,
 Are landed now at Tower.
Sir Alexander.   Heyday, at Tower?   15
Trapdoor. I heard it now reported.   [*Exit.*]
Sir Alexander.   Which way, gentlemen,
 Shall I bestow my care? I'm drawn in pieces
 Betwixt deceit and shame.

Enter SIR [GUY] FITZALLARD

Sir Guy.   Sir Alexander,
 You're well met, and most rightly served;
 My daughter was a scorn to you.
Sir Alexander.   Say not so, sir.   20
Sir Guy. A very abject she, poor gentlewoman! –
 Your house has been dishonoured! Give you joy, sir,
 Of your son's gaskin-bride; you'll be a grandfather shortly

15. Heyday] *M. Thesis;* Hoyda *Q.* 16. s.d.] *Gomme; Retires. M.
Thesis.* 18. *Sir Guy*] *Fitz-All. or Fitz-Alla. Q passim.* Alexander,] *Reed;*
Alexander. *Q.* 21. abject she,] *Dyce;* abiect, shee *Q.* gentlewoman! –]
Dyce subst.; Gentlewoman, *Q.* 22. has] *Gomme;* had *Q.* 23. gaskin-
bride] *Gomme;* Gaskoyne-Bride *Q.*

———————————————————————————————

 14. *ramp*] See III.iii.7n.
 15. *Tower*] in reference either to the Tower Wharf, situated along the river-
front of the Tower, or to the Tower Stairs, one of the Wharf's three landing-
stages (Sugden, p. 522).
 Heyday] See II.i.168n.
 16. s.d.] No exit is given for Trapdoor in Q before his re-entrance at l. 228.1
below – possibly an oversight, or an indication that he does not actually leave
the stage, but withdraws and comes forward at the appropriate moment later.
 20. *scorn*] object of contempt.
 22. *Your ... dishonoured*] i.e. in mocking contempt of Sebastian's supposed
marriage to Moll, and Sir Alexander's obstruction of the match with Mary.
Emendation to *has* is supported by l. 38 below.
 23. *gaskin-bride*] 'i.e. a bride who wears *gascoynes*, – gaskins, or galligaskins'
(Dyce). *Gaskins* were 'wide breeches made like shipmen's hose, except that
they reached to the knee only' (Linthicum, p. 208). William Harrison *Description of England* (ed. G. Edelen, p. 147), speaks of women wearing such
breeches: 'What should I say of their doublets with pendant codpieces on the
breast, full of jags and cuts, and sleeves of sundry colours? their galligaskins to
bear out their bums and make their attire to fit plum-round (as they term it)
about them?' (noted by Linthicum). *O.E.D.* cites also John Dryden, *The Kind
Keeper or, Mr. Limberham*, IV.i (*Dramatic Works*, IV, ed. Montague Summers
(1932)), 'one of my Daughters is big with Bastard, and she laid at her *Gascoins*
most unmercifully! every stripe she had, I felt it: the first fruit of Whoredom is
irrevocably lost!'

To a fine crew of roaring sons and daughters:
'Twill help to stock the suburbs passing well, sir.   25
Sir Alexander. O, play not with the miseries of my heart!
Wounds should be dressed and healed, not vexed, or left
Wide open to the anguish of the patient,
And scornful air let in; rather let pity
And advice charitably help to refresh 'em.   30
Sir Guy. Who'd place his charity so unworthily,
Like one that gives alms to a cursing beggar?
Had I but found one spark of goodness in you
Toward my deserving child, which then grew fond
Of your son's virtues, I had eased you now;   35
But I perceive both fire of youth and goodness
Are raked up in the ashes of your age,
Else no such shame should have come near your house,
Nor such ignoble sorrow touch your heart.
Sir Alexander. If not for worth, for pity's sake assist me!   40
Greenwit. You urge a thing past sense; how can he help you?
All his assistance is as frail as ours,
Full as uncertain where's the place that holds 'em.
One brings us water-news, then comes another
With a full-charged mouth like a culverin's voice,   45
And he reports the Tower: whose sounds are truest?
Goshawk. In vain you flatter him. – Sir Alexander –

---

24. daughters:] *M. Thesis;* daughters, *Q.*   26. heart!] *Collier;* heart, *Q.*   31. unworthily,] *Reed;* vnworthily. *Q; unworthily? Dyce.*   32. beggar?] *Reed;* beggar, *Q; beggar: Dyce.*   35. now;] *Dyce;* now. *Q;* now: *Reed.*   47. him. – Sir] *Reed subst.;* him sir *Q.*   Alexander –] *Reed; Alexander. Q.*

---

30. *refresh 'em*] restore, heal them (i.e. wounds).

35. *had*] i.e. would have.

37. *raked up in the ashes*] Cf. IV.ii.321 and n. The implication is apparently that age has stifled Sir Alexander's *fire of youth and goodness*.

44. *water-news*] i.e. of Sebastian and Moll *Putting in towards the Sluice* (l. 8 above).

45. *full-charged mouth*] punning on a cannon loaded with a charge. Stow, *Survey*, I, 166, describes the weekly artillery practice at the Tower. A *culverin* is a large cannon. Hoy cites Marston, *Scourge of Villanie*, iv.22, 'with whole culuering raging othes', and Dekker, *P.G.*, IV.iii.200; *N.S.S.*, II.i.79–81.

46. *reports*] punning on 'to fire (a gun)' (*O.E.D.*, 9c).

47.] Q's lack of punctuation after 'him' is confusing, particularly since Sir Guy replies. In the proposed reading, which follows Reed, Goshawk speaks

Sir Guy. I flatter him? Gentlemen, you wrong me grossly.

Greenwit. [*Aside to Goshawk*] He does it well, i'faith.

Sir Guy.   Both news are false,
 Of Tower or water: they took no such way yet.   50

Sir Alexander. O strange: hear you this, gentlemen? Yet more
 plunges!

Sir Guy. They're nearer than you think for, yet more close
 Than if they were further off.

Sir Alexander.   How am I lost
 In these distractions!

Sir Guy.   For your speeches, gentlemen,
 In taxing me for rashness, 'fore you all,   55
 I will engage my state to half his wealth,
 Nay, to his son's revenues, which are less,
 And yet nothing at all till they come from him,
 That I could, if my will stuck to my power,
 Prevent this marriage yet, nay, banish her   60
 For ever from his thoughts, much more his arms!

Sir Alexander. Slack not this goodness, though you heap upon
 me
 Mountains of malice and revenge hereafter!
 I'd willingly resign up half my state to him,
 So he would marry the meanest drudge I hire.   65

---

48. him?] *Dyce;* him, *Q.*   51. gentlemen?] *Collier;* Gentlemen, *Q.*   55.
rashness,] *Dyce;* rashnesse; *Q.*   58. him,] *Collier;* him; *Q.*   63. hereafter!]
Collier; hereafter: *Q.*

---

first to Sir Guy and is then interrupted when he begins to address Sir Alexander. *Flatter* in this context means 'to encourage or cheer (a person) with
hopeful or pleasing representations; to inspire with hope, usually on insuffi-
cient grounds' (*O.E.D.*, 9a), in reference to Sir Guy's claim that he can relieve
Sir Alexander's troubles (ll.33–5 above).

 49. *He does it well*] Greenwit, as at l. 92 below, remarks on the effectiveness
of Sir Guy's performance.

 51. *plunges*] See IV.i.154 and n.; playing here on *water*.

 52. *think for*] expect, suppose (*O.E.D.*, v.2, 12d).

 54. *distractions*] (1) disorders, confusions; (2) states of being drawn (physically or mentally) in different directions by conflicting forces (*O.E.D.*, 3a).

 55. *'fore*] Before.

 56. *engage . . . wealth*] i.e. pledge (or pawn) my estate to the value of half Sir
Alexander's wealth.

 59. *will*] (1) intent, purpose; (2) desire, wish.

 65. *So*] so long as, provided that.

Greenwit. [*To Sir Alexander*] He talks impossibilities, and you
    believe 'em!
Sir Guy. I talk no more than I know how to finish;
    My fortunes else are his that dares stake with me.
    The poor young gentleman I love and pity;
    And to keep shame from him – because the spring   70
    Of his affection was my daughter's first,
    Till his frown blasted all – do but estate him
    In those possessions which your love and care
    Once pointed out for him, that he may have room
    To entertain fortunes of noble birth,   75
    Where now his desperate wants casts him upon her;
    And if I do not, for his own sake chiefly,
    Rid him of this disease that now grows on him,
    I'll forfeit my whole state, before these gentlemen.
Greenwit. [*To Sir Alexander*] Troth, but you shall not under-
    take such matches;   80
    We'll persuade so much with you.
Sir Alexander. [*To Sir Guy*]   Here's my ring; [*Gives ring.*]
    He will believe this token. 'Fore these gentlemen
    I will confirm it fully: all those lands
    My first love 'lotted him, he shall straight possess
    In that refusal.
Sir Guy.   If I change it not,   85
    Change me into a beggar!
Greenwit.   Are you mad, sir?
Sir Guy. 'Tis done!
Goshawk.   Will you undo yourself by doing,

---

66. s.d.] *M. Thesis.*   68. me.] *Reed;* me, *Q.*   82. token.] *Collier;* token: *Q.*

---

71. *first*] possibly in allusion to the proverbial, 'The first love is the fastest'
(Tilley, L478); cf. Middleton, *M.D.B.W.*, V.ii.158–9, 'And she that makes a
fool of her first love, / Let her ne'er look to prosper.'
    77. *And if*] possibly 'an if': if indeed.
    80. *matches*] agreements, bargains.
    81. *persuade*] plead (*O.E.D.*, 9a).
    84. *My first love*] i.e. my love originally.
    'lotted] allotted.
    straight] straightway, immediately.

And show a prodigal trick in your old days?
Sir Alexander. 'Tis a match, gentlemen.
Sir Guy.   Ay, ay, sir, ay!
I ask no favour, trust to you for none;   90
My hope rests in the goodness of your son.   *Exit.*
Greenwit. [Aside to Goshawk] He holds it up well yet.
Goshawk. [Aside to Greenwit]   Of an old knight, i'faith.
Sir Alexander. Cursed be the time I laid his first love barren,
Wilfully barren, that before this hour
Had sprung forth fruits of comfort and of honour;   95
He loved a virtuous gentlewoman.

                    Enter MOLL [*dressed as a man*].

Goshawk. Life, here's Moll!
Greenwit. Jack!
Goshawk.   How dost thou, Jack?
Moll.   How dost thou, gallant?
Sir Alexander. Impudence, where's my son?
Moll.   Weakness, go look him!
Sir Alexander. Is this your wedding gown?
Moll.   The man talks monthly: 100
Hot broth and a dark chamber for the knight;
I see he'll be stark mad at our next meeting.   *Exit.*

---

90. favour, ... none;] *Dyce;* fauour; ... none, *Q.*   91. s.d.] *Exit Fitz-Allard.*
Q.   92, 93. s.dd.] *M. Thesis.*   96.1.] *to the right of l. 96 Q.*   102. s.d.] *Exit*
Moll. Q.

---

88. *show*] possibly in an elliptical sense, 'seem to do', as in *Sonn.*, xciv.2.
    prodigal] The term resonates with Sebastian's scheme; see Intro., pp. 17–18.
92.] As at l. 49 above, Greenwit and Goshawk comment on the persuasive-
ness of Sir Guy's performance. *Holds it up* = keeps it going; *of* = characteristic
of. See Intro., p. 34.
99. *look*] look for, seek (*O.E.D.*, 6a).
100. *monthly*] 'i.e. madly; as if under the influence of the *moon*' (Steevens);
cf. *lunatic*. This is the only occurrence recorded by *O.E.D.* Cf. Dekker, *L.C.*
(ed. Pendry), p. 228, 'A moon-man signifies in English a "madman" because
the moon hath greatest domination above any other planet over the bodies of
frantic persons.'
101. *hot broth ... dark chamber*] traditional treatments for the insane. The
3rd Madman in Webster, *Duchess of Malfi*, IV.ii.110–11 (Revels ed.), speaks
of 'three hundred milch-bats to make possets, to procure sleep', and the
'madly-used' Malvolio is 'kept in a dark house', *Tw.N.*, V.i.329; cf. also *Err.*,
V.i.243–8.

Goshawk. Why sir, take comfort now, there's no such matter;
    No priest will marry her, sir, for a woman
    Whiles that shape's on: an it was never known,   105
    Two men were married and conjoined in one!
    Your son hath made some shift to love another.
Sir Alexander. Whate'er she be, she has my blessing with her:
    May they be rich and fruitful, and receive
    Like comfort to their issue as I take   110
    In them. 'Has pleased me now, marrying not this,
    Through a whole world he could not choose amiss.
Greenwit. Glad you're so penitent for your former sin, sir.
Goshawk. Say he should take a wench with her smock-dowry:
    No portion with her but her lips and arms?   115
Sir Alexander. Why, who thrive better, sir? They have most
      blessing,
    Though other have more wealth, and least repent:
    Many that want most know the most content.
Greenwit. Say he should marry a kind youthful sinner?
Sir Alexander. Age will quench that; any offence but theft   120
    And drunkenness, nothing but death can wipe away;
    Their sins are green even when their heads are grey.

105. an] *M. Thesis;* and *Q.*   106. one!] *M. Thesis;* one: *Q.*   111. them.]
Collier; them, *Q.*   'Has] *Reed subst.;* Ha's *Q.*   116. Why,] *Reed;* Why?
Q.   117. repent:] *Collier;* repent, *Q.*   120. that;] *Reed;* that, *Q.*
122. Their ... their] *Reed;* There ... there *Q.*

---

    103. *no such matter*] referring to the projected marriage of Sebastian and
Moll.

    104–6.] Cf. Middleton, *Widow,* V.i.402–5.

    110. *to their issue*] in respect of their children.

    113. *sin*] presumably in allusion to the threatened disinheritance of his son.

    114. *smock-dowry*] i.e. a dowry of her smock only (cited by *O.E.D.*).

    116–17. *They ... repent*] Cf. Luke vi.20, 'Blessed be ye poore: for yours is
the kingdome of God' (Geneva).

    118.] Cf. 'Who can sing so merry a note as he that cannot change a groat'
(Tilley, N249).

    119. *sinner*] prostitute, unchaste woman (marriage would make her honest).

    120–1.] The apparent incoherence reflects Sir Alexander's confused state
of mind; see Intro., pp. 34–5.

    121. *drunkenness*] Nashe lists *drunkenness* among the seven deadly sins in
Pierce Penilesse (*Works,* ed. R. B. McKerrow, rev. F. P. Wilson (Oxford,
1958), I, 204–8). The association occurs also in *Revenger's Tragedy,*
IV.ii.183–4 (Revels ed.), 'The worst of all the deadly sins is in him, / That
beggarly damnation, drunkenness'; also V.i.54–5.

    122.] Sir Alexander refers to the sins of a prostitute, and implies a contrast
with Greenwit's statement, l. 113. The sense is clarified by a corresponding

Nay, I despair not now, my heart's cheered, gentlemen:
No face can come unfortunately to me. –

Enter a Servant.

Now sir, your news?
Servant.   Your son with his fair bride   125
    Is near at hand.
Sir Alexander.   Fair may their fortunes be!
Greenwit. Now you're resolved, sir, it was never she?
Sir Alexander. I find it in the music of my heart.

Enter MOLL [*in female dress,*] *masked, in* SEBASTIAN's *hand, and*
            [SIR GUY] FITZALLARD.

See where they come.
Goshawk.   A proper lusty presence, sir.
Sir Alexander. Now has he pleased me right. I always
    counselled him   130
    To choose a goodly personable creature:
    Just of her pitch was my first wife, his mother.
Sebastian. Before I dare discover my offence,   [*Kneels.*]
    I kneel for pardon.

---

124. me. –] *Dyce;* me, *Q.*   124.1.] *to the right of* newes? *l. 125 Q.*   131.
creature:] *Dyce;* creature, *Q.*

---

passage in *Revenger's Tragedy*, II.iii.126–32 (Revels ed.): 'I may forgive a
disobedient error, / That expect pardon for adultery, / And in my old days am
a youth in lust! / Many a beauty have I turn'd to poison / In the denial,
covetous of all: / Age hot is like a monster to be seen; / My hairs are white, and
yet my sins are green.' (noted by R. A. Foakes). Cf. 'Like a leek, he has a white
head and a green tail' (Tilley, L177). Hoy notes Dekker, *2 H.W.*, I.ii.42–3,
'tho my head be like a Leeke, white: may not my heart be like the blade,
greene?', and cites, in reference to these lines, Chaucer, *Canterbury Tales* (ed.
F. N. Robinson (1957)), ll. 3877–80, and passages in Dekker, *Lanthorne*, sigs.
L1v–2r (ed. Pendry, p. 250), and *N.H.*, IV.i.133.
    124.1.] As at l. 9.1 above, no exit is marked for this servant; but this may be
the one that Sir Alexander addresses at l. 187 below.
    127. *resolved*] convinced, satisfied.
    129. *lusty*] (1) beautiful, gaily dressed; (2) joyful, merry; (3) sexually lustful.
presence] person.
    132. *pitch*] height, stature.
    my first wife, his mother] The play gives no suggestion that Sir Alexander
has remarried; the reference may have some lost significance.
    133. *discover my offence*] with a play on unmasking Moll as his bride.

Sir Alexander.   My heart gave it thee
    Before thy tongue could ask it –   135
    Rise; thou hast raised my joy to greater height
    Than to that seat where grief dejected it.
    Both welcome to my love and care for ever!
    Hide not my happiness too long: all's pardoned;
    Here are our friends. – Salute her, gentlemen.   140

                              They unmask her.

All. Heart, who? This' Moll!
Sir Alexander. O my reviving shame! Is't I must live
    To be struck blind? Be it the work of sorrow
    Before age take't in hand!
Sir Guy.   Darkness and death!
    Have you deceived me thus? Did I engage   145
    My whole estate for this?
Sir Alexander.   You asked no favour,
    And you shall find as little: since my comforts
    Play false with me, I'll be as cruel to thee
    As grief to fathers' hearts.
Moll.   Why, what's the matter with you,
    'Less too much joy should make your age forgetful?   150
    Are you too well, too happy?
Sir Alexander.   With a vengeance!
Moll. Methinks you should be proud of such a daughter –
    As good a man as your son!

---

135. it –] *M. Thesis;* it, *Q.*   136. height] *Reed subst.;* height. *Q.*   137. it.]
Reed; it, *Q.*   138. for ever!] *Dyce subst.;* for euer, *Q.*   139. long:] *This ed.;*
long, *Q.*   140. friends. –] *Dyce;* friends, *Q.*   140.1.] *to the right of l. 140*
Q.   141. who? This' Moll!] *M. Thesis;* who this *Mol? Q;* who this? Moll?
Reed; who's this? Moll! *Dyce;* who is this *Mol? Bowers.*   142. shame!] *Reed;*
shame, *Q.*   147. little:] *Reed;* little, *Q.*   149–50. you, . . . forgetful?] *Dyce;*
you? . . . forgetfull, *Q.*   152. daughter –] *M. Thesis;* daughter, *Q.*

---

137. *dejected it*] cast it down.

141.] The sense of the Q reading, 'Heart, who this *Mol*?', is unclear. Dyce,
followed by recent editors, emended 'who' to 'who's'. But *this* occasionally is a
contraction of 'this is' (Abbott, § 461); see Middleton, *W.B.W.*, III.ii.30 and
n. (Revels ed.). Several other instances occur in Middleton: see W. W. Greg,
'Some Notes on Crane's Manuscript of *The Witch*', *The Library*, 4th ser.,
XXII (1942), 217, *Game at Chess*, V.ii.86, and *S.M.T.*, III.7 (Revels ed.); also
Shakespeare, *Shr.*, I.ii.44, and *Meas.*, V.i.131. The apostrophe has been
added for clarity, not to alter the word. F. D. Hoeniger conjectures that *Heart*
picks up l. 134 above, and proposes 'Heart? To this Moll?'.

150. *'Less*] unless.

Sir Alexander.   O monstrous impudence!

Moll. You had no note before: an unmarked knight;
    Now all the town will take regard on you,   155
    And all your enemies fear you for my sake:
    You may pass where you list, through crowds most thick,
    And come off bravely with your purse unpicked!
    You do not know the benefits I bring with me:
    No cheat dares work upon you with thumb or knife,   160
    While you've a roaring girl to your son's wife!

Sir Alexander. A devil rampant!

Sir Guy. [*To Sir Alexander*]   Have you so much charity
    Yet to release me of my last rash bargain,
    An I'll give in your pledge?

Sir Alexander.   No, sir, I stand to't:
    I'll work upon advantage as all mischiefs   165
    Do upon me.

Sir Guy.   Content: bear witness all then,
    His are the lands, and so contention ends.
    Here comes your son's bride 'twixt two noble friends.

Enter the LORD NOLAND *and* SIR BEAUTEOUS GANYMEDE, *with*
MARY FITZALLARD *between them, the* Citizens *and their* Wives
with them.

Moll. [*To Sir Alexander*] Now are you gulled as you would
    be: thank me for't,
    I'd a forefinger in't.

Sebastian.   Forgive me, father;   170

164. An] *M. Thesis;* And *Q.*

---

153. *monstrous*] recalling I.ii.127–35.

154. *note*] (1) distinction; (2) reputation, fame.

157. *list*] please, choose.

158. *come off*] (1) escape, get clear; (2) leave the field of combat.

160. *cheat*] The meaning required by the context is 'thief' or 'swindler',
though not recorded in *O.E.D.* in this sense until 1664; cf. IV.ii.275 and n.
  thumb or knife] see V.i.138 and n.

161. *to*] as, for.

162. *devil rampant*] a mock-heraldic construction. *Rampant* means 'rearing
on the hind legs and showing fierceness'; a play on *ramp* (see III.iii.7n.) may
be intended.

164. *An ... pledge*] possibly proferring Sir Alexander's ring.

169. *would be*] desire, wish to be.

170. *forefinger in't*] Cf. 'To have a finger in the pie' (Tilley, F228).

Though there before your eyes my sorrow feigned,
This still was she for whom true love complained.

Sir Alexander. Blessings eternal and the joys of angels
Begin your peace here to be signed in heaven!
How short my sleep of sorrow seems now to me,   175
To this eternity of boundless comforts
That finds no want but utterance and expression.
– [*To Lord Noland*] My lord, your office here appears so
     honourably,
So full of ancient goodness, grace, and worthiness,
I never took more joy in sight of man   180
Than in your comfortable presence now.

Lord Noland. Nor I more delight in doing grace to virtue
Than in this worthy gentlewoman, your son's bride,
Noble Fitzallard's daughter, to whose honour
And modest fame I am a servant vowed;   185
So is this knight.

Sir Alexander.   Your loves make my joys proud.
– [*To Servant*] Bring forth those deeds of land my care laid
     ready –   [*Servant fetches deeds.*]
And which, old knight, thy nobleness may challenge,
Joined with thy daughter's virtues, whom I prize now
As dearly as that flesh I call mine own.   190
– [*To Mary*] Forgive me, worthy gentlewoman, 'twas my
     blindness:
When I rejected thee, I saw thee not;
Sorrow and wilful rashness grew like films
Over the eyes of judgement, now so clear
I see the brightness of thy worth appear.   195

Mary. Duty and love may I deserve in those,
And all my wishes have a perfect close.

---

174. heaven!] *Reed;* heauen, *Q.*   191. blindness:] *Dyce;* blindnesse *Q.*

174. *signed in heaven*] Cf. I.i.73ff.
179. *ancient*] venerable, old-fashioned.
181. *comfortable*] strengthening, supporting, cheering (*O.E.D.*, 1).
188. *challenge*] lay claim to, claim as due (in reference to Sir Guy's position as negotiator of the marriage portion and partner in the pledge) (*O.E.D.*, 5a).
193. *films*] morbid growths upon the eyes (*O.E.D.*, 4).
196. *those*] i.e. the eyes of judgement.

Sir Alexander. That tongue can never err, the sound's so
    sweet.
    Here, honest son, receive into thy hands
    The keys of wealth, possession of those lands   200
    Which my first care provided; they're thine own;
    Heaven give thee a blessing with 'em! The best joys
    That can in worldly shapes to man betide
    Are fertile lands and a fair fruitful bride,
    Of which I hope thou'rt sped.
Sebastian.   I hope so too, sir.   205
Moll. Father and son, I ha' done you simple service here.
Sebastian. For which thou shalt not part, Moll, unrequited.
Sir Alexander. Thou art a mad girl, and yet I cannot now
    Condemn thee.
Moll.   Condemn me? Troth an you should, sir,
    I'd make you seek out one to hang in my room: 210
    I'd give you the slip at gallows and cozen the people.
    – [*To Lord Noland*] Heard you this jest, my lord?
Lord Noland.   What is it, Jack?
Moll. He was in fear his son would marry me,
    But never dreamt that I would ne'er agree!
Lord Noland. Why? Thou hadst a suitor once, Jack; when wilt
    marry?   215
Moll. Who, I, my lord? I'll tell you when, i'faith:

198. sweet.] *Collier;* sweete, *Q.*   202. 'em!] *Reed;* 'em, *Q.*

---

201. *my first care*] Cf. l. 84 and n., above.

205. *sped*] provided, furnished.

206. *I . . . simple service*] The phrase appears to have been common: it occurs
also in Massinger, *Believe As You List*, III.ii.21 (*Dramatic Works*, III, ed. P.
Edwards and C. Gibson (Oxford, 1976), where the editors gloss, 'I have
served you well', and cite also Chapman, *An Humorous Day's Mirth*,
xiv.157–8, 'I have done simple service amongst you'. The following instance
in G. Pettie (tr.), *The Civile Conuersation of M. Steeuen Guazzo* (1581), sig.
j1v, suggests that an element of modesty attends Moll's use of the phrase:
'*Alas you wyll be but vngentle Gentlemen, yf you be no Schollers: you wyll doo
your Prince but simple seruice, you wyll stande your Countrey but in slender
steade, you wyll bryng your selues but to small preferment, yf you be no Schollers.*'
The phrase occurs also in *Deceytes of Women* (n.d.), sig. 13r.

208–9. *Thou . . . thee*] Sir Alexander modulates to the more familiar forms in
addressing Moll.

211. *the slip*] The play by which Follywit and his associates make their
escape in Middleton *M.W.M.M.*, V.ii, is called 'The Slip'.

When you shall hear
Gallants void from sergeants' fear,
Honesty and truth unslandered,
Woman manned but never pandered,   220
Cheaters booted but not coached,
Vessels older ere they're broached;
If my mind be then not varied,
Next day following, I'll be married.
Lord Noland. This sounds like doomsday.
Moll.   Then were marriage best,   225
For if I should repent, I were soon at rest.
Sir Alexander. In troth, thou'rt a good wench; I'm sorry now
The opinion was so hard I conceived of thee:

Enter TRAPDOOR.

Some wrongs I've done thee.

---

221. Cheaters] *Dyce query;* Cheates *Q.*   228.1.] *to the right of* thee. *l. 229 Q.*

217–24.] Cf. Dekker, *W.B.*, I.ii.231–51.

220. *manned*] (1) provided with a husband; (2) possessed sexually by a man (Partridge, p. 145). Cf. Beaumont and Fletcher, *Valentinian*, II.iv.57–9 (*Dramatic Works*, IV, ed. F. Bowers (Cambridge, 1979)).

221.] Cf. Dekker, *Belman*, sig. E4r, 'But now, there are so many profest *Cheaters*, and so many that giue countenance to their occupacion, that they might make an armie sufficient to giue the Turke a battaile: now are they not hungry thread bare knaues, but gallants that ruffle in silkes, and are whorried through the streetes in Coaches, their purses being full of Crownes, and their fingers being held vp able to commaund the proudest Curtizan.' *Booted* commonly signifies in the s.dd. of contemporary plays that a character has come from riding (e.g. Dekker and Webster, *N.H.*, IV.i.207.1 and IV.iii.0.2). See Alan Dessen, *Elizabethan Stage Conventions and Modern Interpreters* (Cambridge, 1984), pp. 39–40. Moll apparently awaits the time when *cheaters* are allowed the expense of a horse (or simply footwear), but not the extravagance of a coach. Justice Overdo savours the 'special enormity' of 'A cutpurse of the sword! the boot, and the feather!' in Jonson's *Bartholomew Fair*, II.iii.11–12 (Revels ed.). *O.E.D.* gives 1612 as the earliest recorded usage of *coached*.

222. *Vessels*] Cf. Middleton, *B.M.C.*, I.ii.16–21: '*Laz.* . . . so it pleaseth the Destinies that I should thirst to drink out of a most sweet Italian vessel, being a Spaniard. *Pilch.* What vessel is that, signior?   *Laz.* A woman, Pilcher, the moist-handed Madonna Imperia, a most rare and divine creature.' Partridge (p. 212) cites *Oth.*, IV.ii.83–5. *Broached* is used in a sexual sense related to 'to pierce, stab, thrust through' (*O.E.D.*, v.1, 1).

225–6.] *Then . . . rest*] possibly glancing at the proverbial sayings, 'Marry today and repent tomorrow' (Tilley, M694), and 'Marry in haste and repent at leisure' (Tilley, H196).

228.1.] See l. 16 and n., above. As his name suggests, Trapdoor possibly makes one or more entrances from the stage trapdoor with comic effect; this may be the case here.

Trapdoor.   Is the wind there now?
　　　'Tis time for me to kneel and confess first,   230
　　　For fear it come too late and my brains feel it.
　　　– [*To Moll*] Upon my paws I ask you pardon, mistress.
Moll. Pardon? For what, sir? What has your rogueship done
　　　now?
Trapdoor. I have been from time to time hired to confound you
　　　By this old gentleman.
Moll.   How?
Trapdoor.   Pray forgive him;   235
　　　But may I counsel you, you should never do't.
　　　Many a snare to entrap your worship's life
　　　Have I laid privily – chains, watches, jewels –
　　　And when he saw nothing could mount you up,
　　　Four hollow-hearted angels he then gave you,   240
　　　By which he meant to trap you, I to save you.
Sir Alexander. To all which, shame and grief in me cry guilty.
　　　– [*To Moll*] Forgive me; now I cast the world's eyes from
　　　me,
　　　And look upon thee freely with mine own:
　　　I see the most of many wrongs before thee   245
　　　Cast from the jaws of Envy and her people,

---

243. me; now] *Dyce subst.;* mee now, *Q.*   245. thee] *Reed;* hee *Q;* me *Dyce.*

---

229. *Is the wind there*] referring to the altered state of affairs; cf. 'Is the wind in that door' (Tilley, W419).

239. *mount you up*] i.e. on the gallows: cf. I.ii.233, IV.i.8, 34.

245. *before thee*] *Before* means 'displayed to, or brought to the attention of' (*O.E.D.*, 5a). Reed's emendation of Q's 'hee' to *thee* gives wider reference to the injuries done to Moll than does Dyce's to 'me', and is preferred on this account.

246. *jaws of Envy and her people*] Cf. Dekker, *Troia-Nova Triumphans,* ll. 276–82: 'there appeare aboue (on the battlements) *Enuy,* as chiefe Commandresse of that infernall *Place,* and euery part of it guarded with persons representing all those that are fellowes and followers of *Enuy*: As *Ignorance, Sloth, Oppression, Disdaine,* &c. *Enuy* her selfe being attired like a *Fury,* her haire full of Snakes, her countenance pallid, meagre and leane, her body naked, in her hand a knot of Snakes, crawling and writhen about her arme.'; and ll. 337–9, '*Vertue* hauing by helpe of her followers, conducted the Lord Maior safely, euen, as it were, through the iawes of *Enuy* and all her Monsters'. *Envy* (malice, ill-will) carried a much stronger meaning at this time than at present.

And nothing foul but that. I'll never more
Condemn by common voice, for that's the whore
That deceives man's opinion, mocks his trust,
Cozens his love, and makes his heart unjust.   250
Moll. Here be the angels, gentlemen: they were given me
As a musician; I pursue no pity –
Follow the law, an you can cuck me, spare not;
Hang up my viol by me, and I care not!
Sir Alexander. So far I'm sorry, I'll thrice double 'em   255
To make thy wrongs amends. –
Come, worthy friends, my honourable lord,
Sir Beauteous Ganymede, and noble Fitzallard,
And you, kind gentlewomen, whose sparkling presence
Are glories set in marriage, beams of society,   260
For all your loves give lustre to my joys:
The happiness of this day shall be remembered
At the return of every smiling spring;
In my time now 'tis born, and may no sadness
Sit on the brows of men upon that day,   265
But as I am, so all go pleased away!   [*Exeunt.*]

---

247. that.] *Dyce;* that, *Q.*   253. an] *Ellis;* and *Q.*   not;] *Dyce;* not
Q.   259. gentlewomen] *Dyce;* Gentlewoman *Q.*   264. my] *Q;* May
Bowers.

---

248. *voice*] (1) opinion (*O.E.D.*, 3a); (2) rumour, report (*O.E.D.*, 4a).

253. *cuck me*] i.e. set me in a cucking-stool. An amusing, detailed account of
this punishment (generally reserved for scolds and shrews) is given in the
ballad, 'The Cucking of a Scold', H. E. Rollins (ed.), *A Pepysian Garland*
(Cambridge, 1922), pp. 72ff.

259. *gentlewomen*] i.e. the citizen's wives.

260. *beams of society*] Cf. Dekker, *Shoemaker's Holiday*, xxi.100–2 (Revels
ed.), 'shines not Lacy's name / As bright in the world's eye as the gay beams /
Of any citizen?'

264. *my*] Bowers's emendation to 'May', apparently on the suggestion of
smiling spring, is unnecessary.

Epilogue

A painter, having drawn with curious art
The picture of a woman – every part
Limned to the life – hung out the piece to sell.
People who passed along, viewing it well,
Gave several verdicts on it: some dispraised   5
The hair, some said the brows too high were raised,
Some hit her o'er the lips, misliked their colour,
Some wished her nose were shorter, some the eyes fuller;
Others said roses on her cheeks should grow,
Swearing they looked too pale, others cried no.   10
The workman, still as fault was found, did mend it,
In hope to please all; but, this work being ended,
And hung open at stall, it was so vile,
So monstrous, and so ugly, all men did smile
At the poor painter's folly. – Such we doubt   15
Is this our comedy: some perhaps do flout
The plot, saying, 'tis too thin, too weak, too mean;
Some for the person will revile the scene,
And wonder that a creature of her being
Should be the subject of a poet, seeing,   20
In the world's eye, none weighs so light; others look
For all those base tricks published in a book –

Epilogue] *Scott; Epilogus Q.*   10. no.] *Collier;* no, *Q.*   18. scene,] *Reed;* Scœne. *Q.*

Epilogue] probably spoken by Moll.

1–15.] No source for this anecdote has been traced; the opening lines of Horace's *Ars Poetica* are vaguely similar and may have been an influence.

1. *curious*] skilfully, elaborately, or beautifully wrought.

6. *brows*] eyebrows.

15. *doubt*] suspect, or fear.

18. *person*] dramatic character.

22–6. *base ... unfit*] apparently a snipe at Samuel Rid, the author of the 'Martin Markall' pamphlets; see F. W. Aydelotte, *Elizabethan Rogues and Vagabonds* (1913, repr. 1967), and this editor's 'The Date of *The Roaring Girl*', *R.E.S.*, new ser., XXVIII (1977), 19–20.

Foul as his brains they flowed from – of cutpurses,
Of nips and foists, nasty, obscene discourses,
As full of lies, as empty of worth or wit,   25
For any honest ear or eye unfit.
And thus,
If we to every brain that's humorous
Should fashion scenes, we, with the painter, shall,
In striving to please all, please none at all.   30
Yet for such faults, as either the writers' wit
Or negligence of the actors do commit,
Both crave your pardons: if what both have done
Cannot full pay your expectation,
The Roaring Girl herself, some few days hence,   35
Shall on this stage give larger recompense;
Which mirth that you may share in, herself does woo you,
And craves this sign: your hands to beckon her to you.

FINIS.

23. cutpurses] *Reed;* Cut-purse *Q.*

---

23. *cutpurses*] The rhyme with 'discourses' and the plural forms of 'nips' and 'foists' support Reed's emendation to the plural. The verse line in which this occurs occupies the full width of the printer's measure in Q, so lack of space may have given rise to the omission.

24. *obscene*] disgusting, repulsive.

28–30.] proverbial; cf. 'He that would please all and himself too undertakes what he cannot do' (Tilley, A193), 'He that all men will please shall never find ease' (M526), and 'It is hard to please all parties' (P88).

28. *humorous*] fanciful, capricious, whimsical.

29. *with*] like; see Abbott, § 195.

35–6.] See 'The Date of *The Roaring Girl*', pp. 21–2.

APPENDIX A

Lineation

All departures from Q are recorded in the following list. Significant arrangements by other editors are cited, whether adopted by the present text or not.

[I.i]
35–6. The ... me!] *Collier; one line in Q.*

[I.ii]
43–4. You ... asleep.] *This ed.; one line in Q.*
56–7. With ... stool.] *Dyce; one line in Q.*
91.] *Bowers; lines divided* proceed, / end? *Q.*

[II.i]
52–3.] *Bullen; verse divided* french. / smoake. *Q.*
70–1.] *Dyce; verse divided* manners, / 'em. *Q.*
163–5. I ... mouse?] *Dyce; prose in Q.*
173–4.] *This ed.; verse divided* Tobacco / vpon't. *Q.*
209–10.] *Ellis; verse divided* man/woman. *Q.*
344.] *Collier;* Masse here she is. *a separate line Q.*
383–4.] *Collier; verse divided* Mistreship, / kindnesse. *Q.*
392–3.] *Bullen; verse divided* Gentlemen. / munch. *Q.*
395–8.] *Dyce; verse divided* boord, / thither, / way, / well. *Q.*

[II.ii]
46–52. The most ... faithfully.] *Dyce; prose in Q.*
52–3. A pox ... now;] *This ed.; one line in Q.*
126–7.] *Reed; one line in Q; verse divided* poysoned. / quickly, *Bowers.*
133–4.] *Dyce; prose in Q.*

[III.i]
62–4. Yes ... tongue!] *Dyce; prose in Q.*
64–8. There's ... 'em!] *Collier; lines divided* pace, / it, / em, *Q.*
79–80. That ... lifetime.] *Dyce; verse divided* sight/lifetime; *Q.*
113–14. Would ... thine,] *Collier; one line in Q.*
167–8. Your ... too!] *Dyce; prose in Q.*

186–7. Well ... entertainment.] *Dyce; prose in Q.*

194–5. I'll ... do.] *Dyce; one line in Q.*

[III.ii]

51–2. Laxton ... praise.] *Collier subst.; prose in Q.*

55.] *Scott; on the same line as l. 54 in Q.*

81. Steal – steal –] *Bowers; prose in Q.*

81–2. What ... see't.] *Bowers; one line in Q.*

82–4. O ... undone.] *Bowers; prose in Q; verse divided* downfal / ever, / undone! *Dyce.*

84–5. What ... tear'st?] *Dyce; one line in Q.*

91–4.] *Collier; prose in Q.*

108–9. Sweet ... bosom?] *Collier; one line (turned over) in Q.*

136–7. Or ... thee.] *Dyce; prose in Q.*

147–50. Forty ... Prue?] *Collier; prose in Q.*

169–70. Has ... stomach?] *Dyce; one verse line in Q.*

217–18. He ... you.] *Reed; one line in Q.*

231–3. Umh ... sending.] *Dyce; prose in Q.*

240–2. I'll ... diseased –] *Dyce; verse divided* common/diseased. — *Q.*

259–60. Yes ... part,] *Collier; one line (turned over) in Q.*

[III.iii]

102–3. When ... prisoner?] *Dyce; one line in Q.*

110–11. I ... you.] *Dyce; one line in Q.*

114–15. This ... sir.] *Dyce; verse divided* he/sir. *Q.*

[IV.i]

18–19. She ... myself.] *Dyce; prose in Q.*

82–7.] *Q; verse divided* one / 'em / sir, / ne'er / chamber, / walls. *Dyce; ll. 82–3 divided as verse* sir/taught. *Bowers.*

110–11.] *Q; verse divided* Ay, ay, ay, / choosing. *Dyce.*

135.] *Dyce; prose in Q.*

135–42.] *Q; prose in Collier.*

143–6.] *Q; verse divided* ballads, / brokers / them; / then. *Dyce.*

148–9.] *Collier; prose in Q.*

149–50. Peace ... be.] *Dyce; prose in Q.*

151–2. My ... wary.] *Dyce; one line in Q.*

189–97.] *Q; verse divided* whoremasters. / sir. / son, / him. / that. / sir. *Dyce.*

[IV.ii]

106. 'Sfoot ... husband!] *M. Thesis; a separate line in Q.*

132–3. Ha ... eyes] *Dyce; one line in Q.*

139–40. Is't ... yet?] *Dyce; prose in Q.*

141–6.] *Q; verse divided* staies / credit —— / Baboone? / blancket. *Bowers.*

157.] *Reed; prose in Q.*

161–3.] *Dyce; prose in Q.*

165–73. With ... speak.] *Dyce; prose in Q.*

177–9.] *Dyce; prose in Q.*

183–90.] *Dyce; prose in Q.*

195–6. Who ... wife's.] *Dyce; one line (turned over) in Q.*

231–2. No ... that!] *Dyce; one line in Q.*

258–61.] *Collier; prose in Q.*

272–3. I'll ... spitting.] *Dyce; prose in Q.*

277–84.] *Dyce; prose in Q.*

288–9. A very ... On.] *Dyce; prose in Q.*

297–9.] *Dyce; prose in Q.*

301–2. I ... will.] *This ed.; one line in Q.*

313–14. Yet ... wins?] *Dyce; prose in Q.*

[V.i]

99. What art thou?] *Reed; a separate line in Q.*

100–4.] *Dyce; lines divided* Tear-Cat, / Dutchlant. / Beasa / gaeb. / Cop: / halle, / Here. *Q.*

256–66.] *Collier; lines divided* Diuine, / bread, / late, / die, / full / Lord / opening. *Q.*

353–7.] *Reed; lines divided* world: / that? / whipt, / rather / Constables. *Q.*

[V.ii]

9–11. And ... soaking.] *Dyce; prose in Q.*

14–15. Your ... Tower.] *Reed; two lines divided* rampe / Tower. *Q.*

16–18. Which ... shame.] *Dyce; two lines divided* care? / shame. *Q.*

53–4. How ... distractions!] *Dyce; one line in Q.*

85–6. If ... beggar!] *Dyce; one line in Q.*

110–11. Like ... them.] *Dyce; one line in Q.*

120–1. Age ... drunkenness,] *Dyce; one line (turned under) in Q.*

125–6. Your ... hand.] *Dyce; one line in Q.*

133–4. Before ... pardon.] *Dyce; one line in Q.*

134–5. My ... it –] *Dyce; one line in Q.*

164–6. No ... me.] *Dyce; two lines divided* aduantage, / mee. *Q.*

208–9. Thou ... thee.] *Collier; prose in Q.*

233–5. Pardon ... gentleman.] *Dyce; prose in Q.*

[Epilogue]
26–7.] *Reed; one line in Q.*

APPENDIX B

Press Variants

A list of the copies collated and the abbreviations used will be found in the Intro., pp. 1–2.

In the case of Sheet D the first stage of correction precedes the original setting, and the second stage of correction precedes the first stage; in the case of Sheet I the first state resetting precedes the original setting, and the second state resetting precedes the first state resetting. Elsewhere the reading before the bracket is that of the corrected state of the forme.

SHEET A (outer forme)
Corrected: BL 2, Bod, CCC, NLS, V & A, Folg, Hunt, Pforz, Taylor.
Uncorrected: BL 1, Bost.
Sig. A3r
  Epistle
    16 Sta-/tute] Sta-/ute
          cod-peece] cod-peice
          book] booke
Sig. A4v
  Dramatis Personae
        Dramatis] Drammatis

SHEET B (inner forme)
Corrected: BL 1, BL 2, Bod, CCC, NLS, V & A, Bost, Hunt, Pforz, Taylor, Yale.
Uncorrected: Folg.
Sig. B1v
    I.i.25 in truth ſir] intruthſir
        36 ſlakes] ſlackes
        37 ſaiſt] ſaith
        38 *viva*] *vive*
        40 What] Wthat
        41 brought $\Big]$ brough*t* $\Big\}$ (consecutive lines in Q)
        42 *Neatfoote* *Neatfoo te*

Sig. B2r

    I.i.60 Ha!] Ha:

      61 ſhape?] ſhape:

      64 prey] pray

         eyes] eyes,

      66 a loathed] aloathed

      83 gold] gold,

      87 heire?] heire,

Sig. B4r

    I.ii.63 met] met,

      85 fray] fray,

      86 mad,] mad

      87 question] question,

SHEET C (inner forme)

Corrected: BL 2, Bod, CCC, NLS, V & A, Folg, Hunt, Pforz, Taylor, Yale.

Uncorrected: BL 1, Bost.

Sig. C2r

  running-title Girle] Girel

    I.ii.182 I'me] Ime

      184 I'me] Ime

      203 *Simon*] ▋*imon*

      206 Ile] ile

      208 burnt?] burnt.

SHEET D (inner forme)

First stage corrected: BL 1, NLS, Bost.

Uncorrected: BM 2, Bod, CCC, V & A, Folg, Hunt, Pforz, Yale.

Sig. D4r

    II.i.356 Hogſ-/den] Hogſ-/dcn

Second stage corrected: Taylor.

    IIi.401 *Open.*] *Gal.*

      402 *Gal.*] *Tilt.*

      404 *Tilt.*] *Gal.*

      407 *Tilt.*] *Gal.*

      408 *Tilt.*]*Gal.*

  catch word M.*Gal.*Come] Come

SHEET H (outer forme)

Corrected: BL 1, BL 2, Bod, CCC, V & A, Bost, Folg, Hunt, Pforz, Taylor, Yale.

Uncorrected: NLS.
Sig. H1r
  III.iii.188 child] child,
     189 debts,] debts
     210 Serieant] Seriant
       flie Maiſter] flieᛁMaiſter
     216 Serieants] Seriants
Sig. H2v
  IV.i.66 *Moll*] *Moll,*
     68 nine] mine
     72 pitty] pitty,
     78 viall,] viall
     85 putᛁvs] put vs
       as wel as] as well
       can:it] can: it
Sig. H3r
  IV.i.112 againe?] againe.
Sig. H4v
  IV.i.204 them] them.
     207 houſe,] houſe
     211 three] there

SHEET H (inner forme)
Corrected: BL 1, BL 2, Bod, CCC, V & A, Bost, Folg, Hunt, Pforz,
Taylor, Yale.
Uncorrected: NLS.
Sig. H3v
  IV.i.141 execution] excution
     162 quarter] qnarter

SHEET I (inner forme)
(As in Bowers, an asterisk signals a variant occurring in reset type.)
Reset (first state): BL 1, Hunt.
Original: BL 2, CCC, NLS, V & A, Bost, Folg, Pforz, Taylor, Yale.
Sig. I1v
 *running-title GirIe] Girle
  *IV.ii.58 *omitted*] the
     *62 they deale] deale they
     *65 donc] done
     *68 wil] will
     74 whʌ] why
     76 do] doe

        81 duck mee] duckmee
      *94 Poticariſhip] Potticariſhip
Sig. I2r
    IV.ii.96 *Lax.* ⎤ *Lax.*
         98 *Lax* ⎦ *Lax.* (consecutive lines in Q)
      126 ſomebeldame] ſome beldame
Sig. I3v
    IV.ii.195 m akes] makes
            peticot e] peticote
      196 beſide] beſides
      198 moon] moone
Sig. I4r
   *IV.ii.224 try] try,
     *225 you] you,
     *226 'twas] t'was
     *227 beate] beat
     *231 *Miſt. Opeu,*] *Miſt, Open.*
           No: – – – –] No: ——
     *233 *Mai.*] Maiſt.
   *234.1 aud] *and*
          Somner] *Sommer*
     *236 *Gall.*] *Gal.*
     *237 *Greene.*] *Green.*
          ſnaffling] ſnafling
     *239 *Gall.*] *Gal.*
     *240 – – – – I] —— I
          head ſir] headſir
     *243 ſir.] ſir,
     *244 *Greene.*] *Greene.*
   *244–5 and/you] and you/
     *246 doe] do
          Craſtino] *Craſtina*
     *248 *Gall.*] *Gal.*
     *249 *Greene.*] *Green.*
Reset (second state): Bod.
Sig. I1v
    IV.ii.74 why] whʌ

SHEET K (outer forme)
Corrected: BL 1, BL 2, Bod, CCC, NLS, Bost, Folg, Pforz, Taylor,
Yale.

Uncorrected: V & A, Hunt.
Sig. K1r
  IV.ii.305 being] beng

SHEET M (outer forme)
Corrected: Bod, CCC, V & A, Folg, Yale.
Uncorrected: BL 1, BL 2, NLS, Bost, Hunt, Pforz, Taylor.
Sig. M1r
  V.ii.162 charity,] charity?
   163 bargaine?] bargaine,
   166 *Fitz-All.*] *Aitz-All.*

An apparent press variant on sig. H4v does not conform to the pattern of press correction seen elsewhere in sheet H:
  IV.i.207 heart .] heart.
The full stop follows 'heart' in the Bod, CCC, NLS, and Taylor copies, while the intervening gap appears in the BL 1, BL 2, V & A, Bost, Hunt, Pforz, and Yale copies; the Folg copy uniquely has the reading 'h eart .'

APPENDIX C

Dramatis Perſonæ.

Sir *Alexander Wengraue*, and *Neaſ-foot* his man.
Sir *Adam Appleton*.
Sir *Dauy Dapper*.
Sir *Beauteous Ganymed*.
Lord *Noland*.
Yong *Wentgraue*.
Iacke Dapper, and *Gull* his page.
Goſhawke.
Greenewit.
Laxton.

> *Tilt-yard.*
> *Openworke.* }Ciues & Vxores.
> *Gallipot.*

Mol the Roaring Girle.
Trapdoore.

> Sir *Guy Fitz-allard.*
> *Mary Fitz-allard* his daughter.

Curtilax a Sergiant, and
Hanger his Yeoman.

Miniſtr̃.

THE

APPENDIX D

Source Materials

<hr>

1. Anon., *The Life of Long Meg of Westminster* (ed. 1620), sigs.
B4r–C1v

The fourth Chapter.

Containing the merry skirmish that was betweene her and Sir Iames of
Castile a Spanish Knight, and what was the end of their Combat.

There was a great Suter to *Megs* Mistres called Sir *Iames* of *Castile*, to
winne her Loue, but her affection was set on Doctor *Skelton*: so that
sir *Iames* could get no graunt of any fauour: where vpon he swore, if
hee knew who were her Paramour, he would run him through with
his Rapier: The Mistresse (who had a great delight to be pleasant)
made a match betweene her and Long *Meg*, that she should goe drest
in Gentlemans apparell, and with her Sword and Buckler goe and
meete sir *Iames* in St. *Georges* field, if she beate him, she should for
her labour haue a new petticote: let me alone (quoth *Meg*) the deuill
take me, if I loose a petticote: and with that her Mistres deliuered her
a sute of white Satten, that was one of the Guardes that lay at her
house. *Meg* put it on, and tooke her whinyard by her side, and away
she went into Saint *Georges* fieldes to meete Sir *Iames*: presently after
came Sir *Iames*, and found his Mistres very melancholy, as women
haue faces that are fit for all fancies. What ayle you sweet heart, quoth
he, tell mee? hath any man wrongd you? If he hath, bee he the
proudest Champion in London, Ile haue him by the eares, and teach
him to know, Sir *Iames* of *Castile* can chastice whom he list: Now
(quoth she) shall I know if you loue me, a squaring long Knaue in a
white Satten doublet, hath this day monstrously misused me in
wordes, and I haue no body to reuenge it, and in a brauery, went out
of doores, and bad the proudest Champion I had come into St.
Georges fieldes and quit my wrong, if they durst. Now Sir *Iames*, if
euer you loued me, learne the knaue to know how he hath wrong'd
me, and I will grant whatsoeuer you shall request at my hands. Marry
that I will (quoth he) and for that you may see how I will vse the
knaue, goe with me, you and Master Doctor *Skelton*, and be eye
witnesses of my manhood.

To this they agreed, and all three went into St. *Georges* Fields, where Long *Meg* was walking by the Wind-milles. Yonder (quoth she) walkes the villain that abused me: follow me Hostesse quoth Sir *Iames*, Ile goe to him: Assoone as he drew nigh, *Meg* began to settle herselfe, and so did Sir *Iames*: but *Meg* past on, as thogh she would haue gone by: Nay sirha, stay quoth Sir *Iames*, you and I part not so, we must haue a-bout ere we passe, for I am this Gentlewomans Champion, and flatly for her sake will haue you by the eares: *Meg* replyed not a word, but out with her Sword, and to it they went, at the first boute *Meg* hitt him on the hand, and hurt him a little: but indangered him diuers times, and made him giue ground, following sow hotly, that she strooke Sir *Iames* weapon out of his hand, then when she saw him disarm'd, she stept within him, and drawing her Ponyard, swore all the world should not saue him: Oh saue me Sir (quoth he) I am a Knight and 'tis but for a womans matter, spill not my blood: wert thou twenty Knightes quoth *Meg*, and were the King himselfe heere, hee should not saue thy life vnlesse thou grant me one thing: whatsoeuer it be quoth Sir *Iames*. Marry quoth she, that is, that this night thou wayte on my trencher at Supper at this womans house, and when supper is done, then confesse me to be thy better at weapon in any ground in England. I will doe it sir (q*uo*d he) as I am a true Knight: with this they departed, and sir *Iames* went home with his Hostesse sorrowfull and ashamed, swearing his aduersary was the stoutest man in England.

Well Supper was prouided, and Sir *Thomas Moore* and diuers other Gentlemen bidden thither by *Skeltons* meanes, to make vp the Iest: which when sir *Iames* saw inuited, he put a good face on the matter, and thought to make a slight matter of it, and therefore before hand tolde Sir *Thomas Moore* what had befallen him, how entring in a quarrell for his Hostesse, he fought with a desperate Gentleman of the Court, who had foyld him, and had giuen him in charge to waite on his trencher that night: Sir *Thomas Moore* answered Sir *Iames* that it was no dishonour to be foylde by an Englishman, sith *Caesar* himselfe was beaten backe by their valour.

As thus they were discanting of the valour of Englishmen, in came *Meg* marching in her mans attyre: euen as she entred in at the doore, This, sir *Thomas Moore* (quoth sir *Iames*) is that English Gentleman, whose prowesse I so highly commend, and to whom in all valour I account my selfe so inferiour: and Sir quoth she, pulling off her Hat, and her hayre falling about her eares, hee that so hurt him to day, is none other but Long *Meg* of *Westminster*, and so you are all welcome.

At this all the company fell in a great laughing, and Sir *Iames* was
amazed, that a woman should so wap him in a whinyard: wel, he as
the rest, was faine to laugh at the matter, and all that supper time to
waite on her trencher, who had leaue of her Mistres, that she might
be maister of the feast: where with a good laughter they made good
cheere, Sir *Iames* playing the proper Page, and *Meg* sitting in her
Maiesty. Thus was Sir *Iames* disgracst for his loue, and *Meg* after
counted for a proper woman.

2. Robert Greene, *A Notable Discovery of Cosenage* (1591), sigs.
D2v–3r

Ah gentlemen, marchants, yeomen, and farmers, let this to you al,
and to euery degree els, be a caueat to warn you from lust, that your
inordinat desire be not a mean to impouerish your purses, discredit
your good names, condemn your soules, but also that your welth got
with the sweat of your browes, or left by your parents as a patrimony,
shalbe a pray to those cosening cros-biters, some fond men are so far
in with these detestable trugs, that they consume what they haue
vpon them, and find nothing but a *neapolitan* fauour for their labor.
Read the vii. of *Solomons prouerbs*, and there at large vew the description of a shameles and impudent curtizan: yet is there another kind of
cros-biting which is most pestilent, and thats this. Ther liues about
this town certain housholders, yet meere shifters and coseners, who
learning some insight in the ciuil lawe, walke abroad like parators,
sumners, and informers, being none at al either in office or credit, and
they go spieng about where any marchant, or marchants prentise,
citizen, welthy farmer, or other of good credit, ether accompanie
with any woman familiarly, or els hath gotten some mayd with child,
as mens natures be prone to sin, straight they come ouer his fallowes
thus, they sende for hym to a tauern, and there open the matter vnto
him, which they haue cunningly learned out, telling him he must be
presented to the Arches, and the scitation shalbe peremptorilie
serued in his parish church. The partie afraid to haue his credit crackt
with the worshipful of the citie, and the rest of his neighbors, and
grieuing highly his wife should heare of it, straight takes composition
with this cosener for some xx. marke, nay I heard ix. pound cros-
bitten at one time, and then the coosening informer or cros-biter
promiseth to wipe him out of the court, and discharge him from the
matter, when it was neither knowen nor presented: so go they to the
woman, and fetch her off if she be married, and though they haue this
grosse summe, yet oft times they cros-bite her for more: nay thus doe

they feare cittizens, prentices and farmers, that they finde but anie way suspicious of the like fault.

3. Robert Greene, *A Quip for an Upstart Courtier* (1592), sig. E2r–v

... for the Sumner it bootes me to say little more agaynst him, than *Chaucer* did in his Canturbury tales, who sayd he was a knaue, a bribar, and a bawd, but leauing that authority although it be authentical, yet thus much I can say of my selfe, that these drunken drowsie sons go a tooting abroad (as they themselues tearm it) which is to here if any man hath got his maid with child or plaies the goodfellow with his neighbors wife, if he find a hole in any mans coat that is of wealth, then hee hath his peremptorie scitation readie to scite him vnto the Archdeacons or officials court, there to appeare and abide the shame and penaltie of the lawe, the man perhaps in good credite with his neighbours, loath to bring his name in question, greseth the sumner in the fist, and then he wipes him out of the booke, & suffers him to get twenty with child so he keepe him warm in the hand: he hath a saieng to wanton wiues, & they are his good dames, and as long as they feede him with cheese bacon, capons, & such od reuersions they are honest, and be they neuer so bad, he swears to the officiall complaints are made vpon enuie and the women of good behauior: tush what bawdrie is it he will not suffer, so he may haue mony and good chere, & if he like the wench wel a snatch himselfe for they knowe all the whores in a country, & are as lecherous companions as may be, to be breefe, the sumner liues vpon sins of people, & out of harlotry gets he al his commodity.

APPENDIX E

Officium Domini Contra Mariam Frith

The following is taken from the transcript of folios 19–20 of the *Consistory of London Correction Book* given in Mulholland, 'The Date of *The Roaring Girl*', *R.E.S.*, new ser., XXVIII (1977), 31. Misdated by F. W. X. Fincham, its discoverer, and later, E. K. Chambers, the record's correct date is 27 January 1612. See Intro., p. 12. Those contractions which might puzzle readers have been expanded.

Officium Domini contra Mariam ffrithe
This day & place the sayd Mary appeared personally & then & there voluntarily confessed *that* she had long frequented all or most of the disorderly & licentious plac*es* in this Cittie as namely she hath vsually in the habite of a man resorted to alehowses Tavernes Tobacco shops & also to play howses there to see plaies & pryses & namely being at a playe about 3 quarters of a yeare since at *th*e ffortune in mans apparell & in her boot*es* & w*it*h a sword by her syde, she told the company there pr*e*sent *tha*t she thought many of them were of opinion *tha*t she was a man, but if any of them would come to her lodging they should finde that she is a woman & some other im*m*odest & lascivious speaches she also vsed at *tha*t time And also sat there vppon the stage in the publique viewe of all the people there pr*e*sent*e* in mans ap-parrell & playd vppon her lute & sange a songe. And she further confessed *tha*t she hath for this longe time past vsually blasphemed & dishonored the name of God by swearing & cursing & by tearing God out of his kingdome yf it were possible, & hath also vsually associated her selfe w*it*h Ruffinly swaggering & lewd company as namely w*it*h cut purses blasphemous drunkard*es* & others of bad note & of most dissolute behaviour w*it*h whom she hath to the great shame of her sexe often tymes (as she sayd) drunke hard & distempered her heade with drinke And further confesseth *tha*t since she was punished for the misdemeanors afore mentioned in Bridewell she was since vpon Christmas day at night taken in Powles Church w*it*h her peticoate tucked vp about her in the fashion of a man with a mans cloake on her

to the great scandall of diuers persons who vnderstood the same & to the disgrace of all womanhood And she sayeth & protesteth *that* she is heartely sory for her foresayd licentious & dissolute lyfe & giveth her earnest promise to carry & behave her selfe ever from hence forwarde honestly soberly & woma < n > ly & resteth ready to vndergo any censure or punishement for her misdemeanors afor < e > sayd in suche manner & forme as shalbe assigned her by the Lo: Bishop of London her Ordinary. And then she being pressed to declare whether she had not byn dishonest of her body & hath not also drawne other women to lewdnes by her perswasions & by carrying her self lyke a bawde, she absolutly denied *that* she was chargeable with eyther of these imputacions And therevppon his Lordship. thought fit to remand her to Bridewell from whence she nowe came vntill he might further examine the truth of the misdemeanors inforced against her without laying as yet any further censure vppon her.

Glossarial Index to the Commentary

An asterisk indicates that the annotation supplements information relating to sense, usage, or date provided by the *Oxford English Dictionary*. The form listed is usually that which appears in the text, but a basic form is sometimes given as the heading for a group of related forms. When a gloss is repeated in the annotations, only the initial occurrence is indexed.